She Was One of Us

She Was One of Us

Eleanor Roosevelt
and the American Worker

Brigid O'Farrell

ILR Press
an imprint of
Cornell University Press
Ithaca and London

First published 2010 by Cornell University Press
Printed in the United States of America

Library of Congress Cataloging-in-Publication Data

O'Farrell, Brigid.
  She was one of us : Eleanor Roosevelt and the American worker / Brigid O'Farrell.
    p. cm.
  Includes bibliographical references and index.
  ISBN 978-0-8014-4880-5 (cloth : alk. paper)
  1. Roosevelt, Eleanor, 1884–1962. 2. Working class—United States—History—20th century. 3. Labor movement—United States—History—20th century. 4. Women in the labor movement—United States—History—20th century. I. Title.

  E807.1.R48O34   2010
  973.917092—dc22   2010015487

Cornell University Press strives to use environmentally responsible suppliers and materials to the fullest extent possible in the publishing of its books. Such materials include vegetable-based, low-VOC inks and acid-free papers that are recycled, totally chlorine-free, or partly composed of nonwood fibers. For further information, visit our website at www.cornellpress.cornell.edu.

Cloth printing   10 9 8 7 6 5 4 3 2 1

Throughout the crowded years of her lifetime, Eleanor Roosevelt was the tireless champion of working men and women.... Wherever there were battles to be fought...for minimum wage or social security...on behalf of sharecroppers or migratory workers...against the unspeakable evils of discrimination, segregation or child labor...for the union shop or against spurious "right-to-work laws"...there you could find Eleanor Roosevelt.... She was an ardent advocate of the ideals of the United Nations...the architect of its Human Rights program...on our side...fighting for our right to organize...but more than that: *she was one of us.*

Eleanor Roosevelt Memorial Fund Pamphlet, AFL-CIO, 1963.

For Joyce L. Kornbluh

Contents

Photographs follow page 104

ABBREVIATIONS USED IN TEXT

ACWA	Amalgamated Clothing Workers of America
AF of L	American Federation of Labor
AFL-CIO	American Federation of Labor and Congress of Industrial Organizations
BSCP	Brotherhood of Sleeping Car Porters
CIO	Congress of Industrial Organizations
CIO-PAC	CIO Political Action Committee
ER	Eleanor Roosevelt
ERA	Equal Rights Amendment
Guild	American Newspaper Guild, The Newspaper Guild (TNG)
HUAC	House Un-American Activities Committee
IBEW	International Brotherhood of Electrical Workers
ICFTU	International Confederation of Free Trade Unions
ILGWU	International Ladies' Garment Workers' Union
ILO	International Labor Organization
IUE	International Union of Electrical, Radio and Machine Workers

NAACP	National Association for the Advancement of Colored People
NCF	National Civic Federation
NCPAC	National Citizens' Political Action Committee
NGO	nongovernmental organization
NIRA	National Industrial Recovery Act
NLRB	National Labor Relations Board
NRA	National Recovery Administration
NYWTUL	New York Women's Trade Union League
OPM	Office of Production Management
ORT	Organization for Rehabilitation through Training
SCHW	Southern Conference on Human Welfare
TWOC	Textile Workers Organizing Committee
TWUA	Textile Workers Union of America
UAW	United Automobile Workers
UE	United Electrical, Radio and Machine Workers
UMW	United Mine Workers
USWA	United Steelworkers of America
WPA	Works Progress Administration
WTUL	Women's Trade Union League

Prologue

She Was One of Us

Though she was born to a life of privilege and married to the president of the United States, the first lady was a working journalist and a union member. In late December 1936 Eleanor Roosevelt celebrated the first anniversary of her syndicated "My Day" column by joining the American Newspaper Guild. Carefully named to avoid alienating potential members with the word "union," the Guild had organized reporters, held its first convention, and signed its first contract just three years earlier, at the beginning of President Franklin D. Roosevelt's New Deal. ER, as she signed her letters to FDR, made clear at her January 5 press conference that she could not go on strike or walk a picket line, but, she explained, "I do believe in the things the guild is trying to do and I was told that I could join on that basis." The front page headline above her smiling picture in the *Guild Reporter* shouted "New Member."[1]

Eleanor Roosevelt was one of the most popular yet at the same time most vilified public figures of the twentieth century. She was consistently ranked as the most admired woman in the country during her lifetime, and a survey of historians rated her the most influential. Working people wrote to her directly about their problems, seeking empathy and action; she was their champion. In response to her support for labor, closely intertwined with her outspoken defense of civil rights and civil liberties, she was criticized by politicians, fellow journalists, and ordinary citizens. She had an extensive FBI file and was frequently accused of being a communist. Hate mail and death threats followed her across the country.

The exceptionally full and complex life of Eleanor Roosevelt has been described and interpreted by historians as well as psychologists, playwrights, family members, and friends. In this book we see her life through the eyes of American workers. Using their own words and hers as much as possible we trace her footsteps from the tenements of New York City to the White House, from local union halls to the convention floor of the AFL-CIO, from coal mines to political rallies to the chambers of the United Nations. Her compelling vision of labor rights as human rights was widely known during her lifetime but has been marginalized or forgotten since her death. By carefully examining ER's commitment to workers and her enduring partnership with the labor movement through the dramatic struggles of the first half of the twentieth century, we gain new insights into how her values were shaped and strengthened and how her commitments were translated into actions. Equally important, we return human rights to their central place in labor history.

The Roosevelts' ties to the labor movement were threaded through their lives together. Eleanor introduced Franklin to the tenements and sweatshops of the Lower East Side of Manhattan at the turn of the twentieth century. They learned about the world of skilled trade union men when Franklin was a state senator in Albany and then assistant secretary of the navy in Washington, DC. ER began advocating for workers' rights in the 1920s through her close friendship with Rose Schneiderman, a cap maker by trade and a fiery union organizer by vocation, who introduced the Roosevelts to the Women's Trade Union League.

As ER's reform ideas developed, her mutually beneficial relationship with labor deepened. Her dialogue with labor activists clarified issues that arose in the workplace and in politics. At the same time, organized labor provided a grass-roots platform for her broader reform agenda. During her twelve years as first lady, she built on her accomplishments and skills to expand her labor concerns beyond the problems of working women to include economic and social rights for all workers. After FDR's death she took her agenda to the United Nations, where she led an international team to craft the Universal Declaration of Human Rights, which included the right to join a union.

For Eleanor Roosevelt, helping people achieve better lives by taking individual responsibility and then acting collectively to remedy problems was a cornerstone of democracy, in good and bad economic times, during war and peace. She saw these convictions embodied in the labor movement. Labor leaders, including Walter Reuther, the visionary young president of the emerging United Automobile Workers, earned her praise and became her close friends. She criticized leaders who abused their power, but never wavered in her support for the rank and file. One of her adversaries, however, the influential journalist Westbrook Pegler, attacked ER as a dilettante and her labor allies as thugs.

ER's understanding of labor's role changed over time. As unions grew in membership and power, she expanded her concerns about organizing and strikes to include ending union corruption and discrimination. She applauded adding pension and health care benefits to bargaining for better wages and safer conditions. She challenged powerful unions to place their own workplace issues in a broader social context and assume the responsibilities of national and international leadership. She saw the movement develop as a key political force in advancing a liberal policy agenda such as full employment at home and economic aid abroad.

ER's core principles of workplace democracy, however, remained her model for democracy in the country and around the world. In 1961 ER told the AFL-CIO convention, "The labor movement—and perhaps I can say my movement, too, because I think sometimes I work as hard as any of you do—I feel that it is part of our job to keep alive the ideals that you started with, the ideals of really helping the people to better conditions, to a better way of life which is part of the basis of democracy." The story of how Eleanor Roosevelt became a union member, what it meant then, and why it matters now begins with a most unusual gathering on the shores of the Hudson River.[2]

1

Why Women Should Join Unions

> Mrs. Roosevelt asked many questions but she was particularly
> interested in why I thought women should join unions.
> Rose Schneiderman, *All for One*, 1967

Seamstresses and glove makers, laundry workers and printers mingled with fashionable society matrons, labor organizers, and politicians as they boarded a large rented boat and slowly lumbered up the Hudson River. On Saturday, 8 June 1929, the sun was shining and a warm breeze that rippled the water in the harbor would also stir the stifling hot air in the sweatshops and the laundries, the tenements and crowded streets of Manhattan's Lower East Side, all left behind for the day. As the jumble of buildings receded from view, the hillsides came into focus, lush with the deep green of the forests dominated by oak and maple trees among the evergreens. Flowers sparkled along the shoreline, redbud, dogwood, and mountain laurel, in stark contrast to the sheer rock formations. A train whistle screeched as railcars flashed by on the narrow tracks, speeding along the river's edge going north from the city to Yonkers, Greystone, and New Hamburg. As Rose Schneiderman later recalled, it was a beautiful day to celebrate the twenty-fifth anniversary of the Women's Trade Union League.[1]

On deck, distinguished New York citizens talked and laughed with recently arrived immigrants. Ladies wore lovely hats and sensible shoes, some of better quality than others. Men were dressed in dark suits and neckties, straw hats and bowlers, some more worn than others. Sounds of Yiddish, Italian, Polish, and Russian mixed musically with the English of high society and the Irish pub. The destination of these unusual traveling companions was Poughkeepsie, where buses waited to take them five miles north on the Old Post Road to Hyde Park and Springwood, the family home of Governor Franklin D. Roosevelt. Mrs. James Roosevelt, the governor's mother, had issued invitations for a gathering from two to six in the afternoon.

Rose Schneiderman was not on the boat. She and Maud Swartz, her friend and partner at the Women's Trade Union League (WTUL), had joined the Roosevelts at their home the night before to make final preparations and be on hand to greet the guests as they arrived. Eleanor Roosevelt reminded the governor about the event: his was the starring role, "the 'piece-de-resistance' tho they have a pageant at 3." The afternoon program overflowed with education, politics, song, and dance. Mary Dreier, one of the founders and wealthy activists known as "allies" in the WTUL, put the final touches on the pageant she had written for the occasion. Pantomime and songs told the story of working girls: the shirtwaist strikes of 1909, the devastating Triangle Company fire, employer resistance, and police brutality. The young women in the cast wore the working girls' shirtwaists and skirts and performed their show for over four hundred guests on the rolling lawn of the governor's mansion overlooking the Hudson River. Their voices rang out as they marched and sang, "Though to jail we had to hike, We won the strike, hurrah." Using drama, song, and stories, they told the history of the Women's Trade Union League and the struggle of working women to join unions. They educated as they sang and danced, a familiar technique for women's labor programs.[2]

Governor Franklin Roosevelt used the occasion to ask for labor's help and to show support for their cause. He announced his appointments to a new commission created by the legislature to make recommendations on an old age pension law for the state and called on organized labor to support the program, long a goal of the WTUL. While praising the League's work, he went on to note that "employers and employes [*sic*] alike have learned that in union there is strength.... There has also been a growing realization on the part of our people that the State itself is under obligation to those who labor, that the citizen who contributes by his toil to the wealth and prosperity of the commonwealth is entitled to certain benefits in return."[3]

Mrs. Thomas Lamont, chair of the League's finance committee, presented Schneiderman with a check for $30,000 to retire the mortgage on the League's clubhouse at 247 Lexington Avenue. As president of the League, Rose thanked her and acknowledged the contributions of the Roosevelts. She highlighted the improvements in wages and working conditions for women that the League had helped to accomplish in its twenty-five-year history. John Sullivan, president of the New York State Federation of Labor, and Mrs. Henry Goddard Leach, president of the state League of Women Voters, also spoke.

Supper was served on the terrace. Nell Swartz, a member of the State Industrial Board, had an opportunity to visit with Morris Feinstone, secretary of the United Hebrew Trades. Eleanor Roosevelt could talk with William Collins, an organizer for the American Federation of Labor. Pauline Newman, an organizer for the International Ladies' Garment Workers' Union (ILGWU), might catch the governor's ear for a moment. Young factory workers and members of the League enjoyed a very pleasant and unusual day before boarding the buses that took them back to the boat, sailing down the Hudson, and returning to the Lower East Side, praising the governor as they went. "Was not the Governor great," they enthused. "How democratic he is." The *New York Times* declared this "the first time that a labor organization had met in such a setting." It was not to be the last.[4]

This event marked a turning point for Eleanor Roosevelt. She had entered the 1920s with a basic understanding of work, politics, and unions. She first learned about dangerous working conditions, squalid tenements, and immigrant workers as a young girl volunteering with progressive reformers. Her aunt Bye, sister to Uncle Theodore Roosevelt, president of the United States, taught her about political power behind the scenes. Knowledge about the traditional world of male trade unions was gained through her husband's developing political career, but it was Rose Schneiderman and members of the Women's Trade Union League who transformed ER's basic awareness of labor issues into a core belief about unions and their ability to improve people's lives. These women conveyed the depth of the problems faced by working people and offered the union framework as a critical part of the solution on the factory floor, in the classroom, and at the statehouse. When ER asked why women should join unions, they explained to her that women, like men, should join unions to secure their rights on the job and in the community. She made sure that FDR heard their lessons as well.[5]

Some years later, speaking before a WTUL audience, ER said: "I truly believe that I understand what faces the great masses of people in the country today. I have no illusions that any one can change the world in a short time. . . . Yet, I do believe that even a few people, who want to understand, to help and to do the right thing for the great numbers of the people instead of for the few can help." The responsibility of individuals to work for the common good was one of her early core beliefs, and she credited her union friends with teaching her more than they realized. Accepted and valued by these working-class women, ER returned their friendship, incorporated their ideals and strategies into her own reform agenda, and joined forces with them to improve the lives of working women. She used her newly acquired knowledge and skills behind the scenes and in her public role as the governor's wife to support unions, orchestrating a mix of social, substantive, and political events that she carried with her to the White House.[6]

Starting on the Lower East Side

Her efforts to understand the world of work began in 1902, when eighteen-year-old Eleanor Roosevelt returned to New York City from Allenswood, a fashionable English finishing school. At Allenswood, under the fond guidance of headmistress Marie Souvestre, young Eleanor developed a lifelong love of theater, art, and music. Encouraged to be independent and to think for herself, she was exposed to new, liberal ideas. Mlle. Souvestre was an atheist, a feminist, and an English positivist. Led by Frederic Harrison, the positivists supported trade unions and legislation to help the working classes. Later she acknowledged that much of what she became in life "had its seeds in those three years of contact with a liberal mind and strong personality." She returned to New York to make her debut in society.[7]

A debutante's life was filled with theater and concerts, lovely lunches, elegant dinners, and elaborate balls, but ER could not make this social world her whole life. She soon joined a group of elite young women who formed the Junior League for the Promotion of Settlement Movements. Led by Mary Harriman and the daughters of several other wealthy New York families, they decided to do something useful for their city. They were part of a movement that swept through urban areas during the Progressive Era. By 1910 there were more than four hundred settlement houses across the country providing shelter, health care, and various forms of education and entertainment to the poor and to newly arrived immigrants. The movement was in full force on the Lower East Side of Manhattan at the turn of the century.[8]

Tall and willowy, with long golden hair swept back from her face and caught in a braid in back, ER dressed in the fashionable high-necked, long-sleeved blouse known as a shirtwaist and a slim ankle-length skirt. Family and friends noted her lovely blue eyes. She cut a stylish figure when taking the elevated train or the Fourth Avenue streetcar from cousin Susie Parish's house on the Upper East Side, then walking across the Bowery to the College Settlement on Rivington Street, two blocks south of Houston on the Lower East Side. She insisted on taking public transportation even at night and refused the rides offered in her friend Jean Reid's carriage. Passing drunken men on the street corners and in the saloons of the Bowery made her fearful, but she loved working with the children. At the settlement house, a stately six-story red brick building with a basketball court on the top floor, she taught calisthenics and dancing to children who had already put in long hours of work in the factories or doing piecework at home. They were the sons and daughters of Jewish and Italian immigrants who were flooding the wretched tenements to work in the rapidly expanding garment industry. Between 1881 and 1924, 2 million Jews emigrated from eastern Europe to the United States; the vast majority started their new lives in this neighborhood.[9]

ER valued her work and soon introduced her cousin Franklin D. Roosevelt, then a Harvard senior, to this new world. She remembered that a "glow of pride ran through her" when one of the little girls said that her father wanted ER to come to their home so he could give her something because the girl enjoyed her classes so much. "Needless to say, I did not go," she recalled, "but that invitation bolstered me up whenever I had any difficulty in disciplining my brood!" On another occasion a little girl was ill, and ER and Franklin went to visit the tenement where the child lived. "When we got out on the street afterward," she wrote, "he drew a long breath of air. Not fresh air, there in those crowded, smelly streets with pushcarts at the curb. But better than the air in that tenement. 'My God,' he said, aghast. 'I didn't know people lived like that!'" Eleanor and her "feller," as the children called Franklin, began an education that profoundly affected their views of the world.[10]

Learning about poverty, poor working conditions, and ways to confront these problems went well beyond giving dance lessons. Gathering the facts was a central tenet of the newly emerging field of social work and the basis on which to challenge existing laws and public policies, part of the Progressive Era "search for order." Firmly rooted in this tradition, ER believed that "nothing could be done, of course, until someone knew the facts: seeking for them, checking them, investigating to make sure of what was actually happening. All of this was necessary before anything could be done to better conditions." ER began the process of collecting data when she joined the Consumers League that winter. She went with an experienced older woman from the League to investigate garment factories and department stores. It had never occurred to her, she later recalled, that "the girls might get tired standing behind counters all day long, or that no seats were provided for them if they had time to sit down and rest. I did not know what the sanitary requirements should be in the dress factories, either for air or lavatory facilities. This was my first introduction to anything of this kind." When she investigated the sweatshops in which artificial feathers and flowers were made, ER was appalled. She later recalled:

> In those days, these people often worked at home, and I felt I had no right to invade their private dwellings, to ask questions, to investigate conditions. I was frightened to death. But this was what had been required of me and I wanted to be useful. I entered my first sweatshop and walked up the steps of my first tenement. It is hard to look back and remember the terrible world that, in actual years, is not really so long ago. . . . I saw little children of four and five sitting at tables until they dropped with fatigue, and earning tragically little a week. Conditions of employment were such that the workers were often in real physical danger and yet the average person was rarely aware of the situation.[11]

Through the Consumers League, ER was introduced to the "white list" and the potential power of the shopper. Members of the League evaluated retail stores and urged women to patronize only those stores on the list, which had been found to follow policies of equal pay for equal work, a ten-hour workday, and a minimum wage of $6 per week. She also learned about the need for legislation. One of the League's major goals was to enact child labor legislation to end the kind of sweating work for children that ER observed. Acknowledging companies that had good working conditions and lobbying for legislation to prohibit bad working conditions were strategies she would long remember.[12]

Other members of the Roosevelt family discouraged this volunteer work. They were concerned that ER might be hurt or that she might bring some disease home with her from the tenements filled with immigrants. But family members had gone to the Lower East Side before: ER accompanied her father there when she was only six years old to help serve Thanksgiving dinners to the newsboys and went with him to help at the Children's Aid Society. She accompanied other family members on charitable errands to Hell's Kitchen and the Bowery Mission, much in the tradition of her grandfather. The Junior League and the Consumers League, however, offered a new way to meet the charitable obligations of her class, one that was compatible with her father's work in the past but also offered a deeper understanding of the causes of social and economic problems. Eleanor wrote Franklin that she had spent the morning "at a most interesting class on practical Sociology!" adding, "Now, don't laugh, it was interesting and very practical and if we are going down to the Settlement we ought to know something." She took her work seriously, spoke up in meetings, and became a confidante of other debutantes.[13]

Yet ER's childhood experiences were quite different from life at Allenswood and volunteering in the tenements. The Roosevelts were one of the oldest and most distinguished families in New York. Anna Eleanor Roosevelt was the first of Anna and Elliott Roosevelt's three children. In 1892 her beautiful socialite mother died of diphtheria. In a few short years, however, Eleanor had learned insecurity and fear from her lovely but remote mother. Several months later her younger brother died of scarlet fever, and she and her youngest brother, Hall, were sent to live with their maternal grandmother, Mary Livingston Ludlow Hall, in her brownstone on West Thirty-seventh Street. Her father visited only occasionally. Elliot Roosevelt was lost to alcohol, drugs, and unsuccessful rehabilitation efforts, but he remained the primary source of love and encouragement for his young daughter until he died two years later, leaving ten-year-old Eleanor and her brother with the Halls in New York City. Summers were spent at the family estate in Tivoli on the Hudson River, with various aunts and uncles, often in states of distress. Alcoholism was one of several devastating and recurring problems that plagued this grand and wealthy family. While Grandmother Hall insisted on strict rules and cold baths, there were also tutors, French lessons, tennis, horses, and occasional raucous weekends with Uncle Theodore and the Oyster Bay Roosevelts. Eleanor later described a full but sad and lonely childhood despite the wealth and prominence of her family.[14]

ER's exposure to the world of work and social change soon came to an end when she assumed her adult place in the family social order. On 17 March 1905, she married Franklin Delano Roosevelt, her fifth cousin once removed. Uncle Theodore, former governor of New York and now president of the United States, gave his niece away at an elegant wedding ceremony in her cousin's home. Franklin completed his last year of law school at Columbia University, and their first child, Anna, was born on 3 May 1906. The next year he joined the firm of Carter, Ledyard and Milburn. His mother, Sara, and aunt Susie insisted that Eleanor could do more for the less fortunate by "serving on proper charitable boards and making modest donations, the appropriate activity for a young matron."[15]

ER was no longer teaching immigrant children or inspecting sweatshops, but she refined her organizational skills by managing her family and negotiating with her mother-in-law and the large Roosevelt clan. She moved the growing family several times a year from New York City to Hyde Park to their summer home on Campobello, a Canadian island off the coast of Maine. Later the itinerary would include Albany, Washington, DC, and Warm Springs, Georgia, with more children and an ever larger staff. During her first ten years of marriage, Eleanor gave birth to six children. These were years when women of the upper class were confined to home during much of their pregnancies. When she did go out, there were numerous social and family obligations that she was duty bound to fulfill, and fulfill them she did, while also supporting her husband's growing political ambitions.

Forming a Political Partnership

FDR's admiration for Theodore Roosevelt and his own political ambitions were no secret. In 1910 he decided to run for a state senate seat in New York, beginning his career as Uncle Theodore had in Albany. After conferring with his uncle, he decided to maintain some independence by running as a Democrat, his father's party, in the heavily Republican rural district encompassing Hyde Park. It was his first political victory. During this time Eleanor gave birth to their fourth child, Elliot. Anna and James were then four and three years old, respectively. Their third child, Franklin, had died in infancy, a heartbreaking experience for his mother.[16]

While ER professed to have no role in her husband's political life, she had also spent time in Washington, DC, with her aunt Bye during the formative years before she married. President Roosevelt was a frequent visitor to his sister's house, seeking her counsel in what became known as the "little white house." ER learned something of the passion and power of politics as well as how some women could participate even when they did not have the right to vote. She recalled, "In Washington, I gradually acquired a faint conception of the political world"; she loved being with her warm and welcoming aunt Bye. When the Roosevelts moved to Albany in 1911, their home soon became a place where people of influence and power congregated. The house on State Street was a meeting place for Franklin's constituents and for the liberal Democratic coalition that was opposed to the Tammany Hall machine of New York City. There, insurgents were sometimes joined by Tammany regulars. ER got to know many of the men, including the Tammany Twins: Robert Wagner, the thirty-three-year-old president pro tem of the state senate, and Alfred E. Smith, the assembly majority leader, both of whom became important to her and to the labor movement.[17]

In 1911 Wagner, Smith, and the Factory Investigating Commission began to develop reform legislation after the devastating Triangle Fire, which killed 146 garment factory workers, mostly young immigrant women. FDR was more involved in the agricultural issues of his rural district but seemed to learn and grow in that first year. By 1912 he favored a workmen's compensation bill, personally investigated work hazards in an Adirondack iron mine, and gave strong testimony at a legislative hearing supporting the thirty-two bills proposed by the commission. He expressed reservations about unions, especially the use of the boycott, but that did not stop him from reintroducing the workmen's compensation bill on behalf of the New York State Federation of Labor. He also moved from a neutral position to support for women's suffrage, a change attributed in part to the progressive debates at the time and to the active role of Teddy Roosevelt.[18]

In these early years ER learned much about the practical side of politics and a labor movement dominated by skilled tradesmen. She listened, observed, and went to the senate gallery to hear the debates and follow the issues, including labor issues that her husband was addressing. Social gatherings were a way to develop allies in the reform effort. FDR cited the Albany years as the beginning of ER's political involvement. She did not participate in the suffrage movement, however, nor did she publicly address the Triangle Fire or the work of the investigating commission.[19]

FDR came to admire Woodrow Wilson and supported his campaign for president on the Democratic ticket in 1912, despite Teddy Roosevelt's effort to recapture the White House with the new National Progressive Party. Eleanor apparently remained loyal to her uncle. FDR won reelection, and in early 1913 he was asked to join the new administration of President Wilson as an assistant secretary of the navy. This was a post he very much wanted, having long loved ships and the sea, but also because it was another position that Uncle Theodore once held. The family moved to Washington, DC. Their fourth son, also named Franklin, was born there in 1914, and their youngest child, John, in 1916.[20]

During these early years at the Navy Department, ER first showed her awareness of FDR's work with trade unions, which she attributed to loyal aide Louis Howe, as she described him, the gnome-like, frail, indefatigable Albany newspaperman. He went to Washington as Franklin's secretary and soon decided that they needed new experiences. Howe insisted that FDR find out about labor conditions in the navy yards, which were his special province in the department, and come in contact with the men. From ER's perspective "this was Franklin's first close contact with labor; and there is no doubt . . . that it was one of the turning points in his development. Certainly it proved of value to him later, both as governor and as president." With Howe at his side, Roosevelt invited the unions in and asked them to teach him. According to historian Frank Freidel, "hardly a day passed without a labor delegation visiting Roosevelt's office." This experience formed the base on which both FDR and ER would build labor support.[21]

As the buildup for World War I began, FDR represented the navy on several of the emergency labor boards and with Howe worked closely with labor leaders, especially the presidents of the International Machinists Union and the Metal Trades Council. ER's awareness of organized labor was reflected through her social role as she worked to connect people with her husband and with one another. When friends at the British embassy responsible for reporting on labor complained that they had to get information from the newspapers, she casually suggested to one of them "that the American Federation of Labor had a building filled with officials in the city of Washington." Knowing that the young Englishman would never call on people he did not know, she arranged for a luncheon with "a number of the heads of various unions, and from that time on [the British] were able to write more comprehensive reports, as they could verify newspaper stories by actual contact with the people involved."[22]

On 2 April 1917 a reluctant President Wilson led the United States to war. In addition to all of her family obligations, ER assumed more active volunteer roles, working at a Red Cross canteen, supervising a knitting room at the Navy Department to make sweaters and scarves for the sailors, and raising money to help care for the wounded. She began to regain her independence, sense of responsibility, and skills, but her life was shaken to the core in September 1918 when she discovered FDR's affair with her social secretary, Lucy Mercer. While this was clearly a watershed moment in the life of the Roosevelt family,

ER's independence, competence, and compassion were already formed, providing a foundation on which her life could be rebuilt: a life with Franklin, but also a life very much apart from him. Under pressure from FDR's mother, they agreed to stay together, but the relationship was forever changed.[23]

During these war years, government policies supported union organizing and management concessions in return for union pledges not to strike. Membership in the American Federation of Labor (AF of L) soared from around 2 million in 1916 to over 3.25 million when the war ended. FDR proudly claimed that there were no strikes or serious disagreements at navy installations or among navy contractors during his seven and a half years of leadership. The end of the war, however, was soon followed by the resumption of fierce hostility in labor-management relations. As the cost of living skyrocketed, with increases in food, rent, clothing, transportation, and taxes, the unions sought higher wages and new members, while employers tried to return to the prewar terms. In 1919 there were more than 2,600 strikes involving over 4 million workers.[24]

With the appointment of Mitchell Palmer as attorney general, the "Red Scare" began in earnest, and unions were a target. The Bolshevik Revolution in Russia and the founding of the Communist Party, USA, joined with concerns about anarchist violence to stimulate fear of a revolution in the United States. The Justice Department was soon infiltrating union meetings and rounding up anyone associated with socialists for deportation in the infamous Palmer Raids. A bomb exploded on the Palmers' doorstep in elegant Georgetown, where they were neighbors of the Roosevelts. Despite these events, ER was beginning to show more awareness and independent thinking about public issues, including labor, revolution, and race. In September 1919 she wrote to a friend, "Now everyone is concerned over strikes and labor questions and I realize more and more that we are entering on a new era where ideas and habits and customs are to be revolutionized if we are not to have another kind of revolution." In the midst of this labor strife, race riots erupted in Washington and ER replaced her entire white household staff with black workers.[25]

At the same time, other branches of the government were trying to bring various factions together, and ER provided firsthand reports. High priority was given to finding a way for labor and management to be more cooperative and end the wave of strikes. President Wilson called for an Industrial Conference beginning on 6 October, with fifty-eight members representing capital, labor, and the public. The meetings were chaired by Franklin Lane, secretary of the interior, who was seen as a neutral party. The Lanes were among the Roosevelts' closest friends in Washington; they met with several other couples on a regular basis for ER's scrambled egg dinners. Labor issues were FDR's responsibility at the Navy Department, but at the time he was in New Brunswick hunting with friends, which suggests that he did not see the meeting as critical. ER attended the conference and wrote to FDR about the collapse of the talks as the labor delegates walked out, the preparations for another labor meeting in the November, and the continuing threat of a coal strike.[26]

Just as the Industrial Conference ended with no resolution to the labor problems, three international meetings converged on Washington. The International Federation of Trade Unions and the Women's Trade Union League both called meetings in preparation for the month-long session of the International Labor Organization, convened as part of the new League of Nations. On 28 October, as trade unionists arrived from around the world, sixty thousand people gathered in downtown Washington and watched the labor parade honoring Samuel Gompers, president of the AF of L, and proclaiming the right of workers to organize in trade unions. The women's conference passed resolutions supporting child care for employed mothers and the eight-hour day, opposing child labor, and declaring that women should be represented at all future labor conferences.[27]

Because ER spoke French as well as German and Italian, she volunteered to attend one of the teas for the International Women's Conference, where she could be helpful as a translator. She remembered this conference as her first contact with the president, Margaret Dreier Robins, and other members of the Women's Trade Union League. She wrote to her mother-in-law, "I had an interesting amusing time at the tea for the delegates to the International Congress of Women Workers, 19 nations represented & of course a very advanced & radical gathering presided over by Mrs. Raymond Robins!" She also noted in her diary that she had talked with Mrs. Robins, Mlle. Bouillat, and many others.[28]

In 1920 ER first campaigned nationally as a candidate's wife. At the Democratic convention in San Francisco, FDR was nominated for vice president of the United States, with James M. Cox, governor of Ohio, at the top of the national ticket. ER joined the campaign train. Although Louis Howe had been part of their lives since their days in Albany, it was on this campaign trip that he began to engage ER in the issues and to encourage her public speaking. She acquired valuable new skills that enabled her to play a more independent political role. Cox, Roosevelt, and Al Smith all lost in the Republican landslide that saw the election of Warren G. Harding and Calvin Coolidge as president and vice president of the United States. Nathan Miller became governor of New York.[29]

The Roosevelts found themselves back in New York. FDR and those around him saw the defeat of the national ticket as a temporary setback. He formed a law partnership and became vice president of the Fidelity and Deposit Company, a bonding business that insured government contracts. One of his clients was the American Construction Council, which included unions involved in low-cost housing projects; here he learned about wages and practices in the building trades. He observed the powerful construction union leaders, such as Big Bill Hutcheson, president of the Brotherhood of Carpenters. They had tested each other during the war, and Roosevelt found Hutcheson "tough as armor plate." While caring for their five children and managing schools, staff, and various houses, ER attended classes in typing, shorthand, and cooking. She joined the board of the nonpartisan League of Women Voters and directed its national legislation committee, learning to read the *Congressional Record* and to discuss and summarize bills relevant to the League's progressive agenda. A competent, skilled hard worker, she helped negotiate internal disputes and was soon elected vice chair.[30]

In the summer of 1921, when the Roosevelt family congregated at Campobello, they faced a devastating crisis. After an outing with the children, FDR returned to the house chilled and wet and promptly went to bed. He would never walk unassisted again. Felled by what was ultimately diagnosed as polio, Franklin began the arduous schedule of therapy to regain the use of his paralyzed legs which would continue for the rest of his life. The strain on this robust family was overwhelming, but at the same time the illness helped to strengthen the frayed relations between husband and wife. ER undertook full-time nursing responsibilities, and Franklin learned to rely on her in new ways. Warm Springs, Georgia, where FDR established a treatment center for polio, was added to the list of homes they regularly visited. Friends thought that he became more serious during this period and more "conscious of other people ... of weak people, of human frailty."[31]

Once the medical routine was in place, ER was ready to expand her public career to include helping to rehabilitate FDR's public role. With encouragement from Howe, she made an effort to keep Franklin's name before the public, while continuing to develop into a political force in her own right. Her work began in earnest with the New York State Democratic Party. After women won the vote in New York State in 1917, followed by the Nineteenth Amendment to the U.S. Constitution in 1920, they were of new interest to the political parties. In 1922 Nancy Cook, then assistant to the first director of the newly formed Women's Division of the New York State Democratic Party, invited ER, as the wife of the former vice presidential candidate, to give a speech to a large fund-raising event. Building on her apprenticeship with the League of Women Voters, and working with Cook and her partner, Marion Dickerman, ER soon became an integral part of the New York reform network.[32]

Described by historians as social feminists, the women in this network had fought for the right to vote, but they saw suffrage as only one of many reforms necessary to help women achieve economic, social, and political equality. Engaged in a wide range of issues, and opposed to the narrow focus of an equal rights amendment, they played a critical role in New York policies and politics. Legislation was a necessary strategy to protect women workers and to improve the wages and working conditions of men as well. The women belonged to the City Club, the League of Women Voters, the Joint Legislative Conference, and the Women's Trade Union League, which was where ER met Rose Schneiderman.[33]

A Labor Education Begins

In 1903 several trade unionists and social reformers met in Boston at the same time that the American Federation of Labor was gathering there. Among the settlement house leaders and union activists who wanted to form an organization modeled after the British Women's Trade Union League were Jane Addams of Hull House; Leonora O'Reilly, a shirtmaker; Vida Scudder, a professor; Mary Kenny O'Sullivan, a union organizer; and William Walling, a social worker. They invited unions that included women in their trades to talk with them about forming a new organization. Representatives came from the Retail Clerks, the Amalgamated Meat Cutters and Butcher Workmen, the Boot and Shoe Workers, and the United Garment Workers.[34]

Membership in the Women's Trade Union League was open to all men and women, union and nonunion, who were, as Schneiderman reported, "in sympathy with the aims and aspirations of the trade union movement." A constitution was adopted and objectives were established, including aiding women workers to organize, assisting the organized to improve their working conditions, starting clubs and lunchrooms for women working in factories, and helping arrange entertainment for workers. Samuel Gompers of the AF of L voiced restrained support for the WTUL, though he insisted on approving all the organizing activities, which were the lifeblood of the unions. Branches soon opened in Chicago and New York City. The organization gave the unions a way to show they were doing something for women. Financial assistance was very limited, however, and tensions between union men, union women, and middle-class reformers ran high. Nevertheless, the WTUL generated a new community for women in the factories, and they were joined by workers making gloves and artificial flowers and women's and men's clothing, as well as printers, cigar makers, and teachers.[35]

The national and local Leagues were always an uneasy alliance between wealthy women "allies" and "working girls." There were also tensions between the American-born working women, often employed in more skilled jobs, and the immigrant workers, many of whom were Jewish socialists. Over the years they succeeded in forging working relationships. Allies helped organize women workers, housed strikers, joined picket lines, got picketers released from jail, defended them in court, and assisted with contract negotiations. The allies were particularly effective at getting prominent women to volunteer to march in picket lines, improving press coverage of the strikes, and raising money to support these efforts. Under the direction of founder Margaret Dreier Robins, they established a year-long residential school in Chicago to train women organizers and raised scholarship money to enable working women to attend. As struggles with the male-dominated unions continued, attention increasingly focused on education programs and legislative efforts to protect all working women. Gradually the factory women assumed leadership of the organization.[36]

When Eleanor Roosevelt and Rose Schneiderman met in 1922, the New York League was run by union women. Schneiderman was president and Maud Swartz was secretary. Eleven of the twelve board members were union members, with Mary Dreier, sister of the founder, the only remaining "ally" in a policy-making position. The goals of the New York WTUL continued to shift from union organizing toward legislative solutions and educational activities. Unemployment was high. The labor movement, which had previously included many socialists of various political persuasions, was rent by a fierce struggle between adherents of communism and anticommunists. Schneiderman proposed buying a house where the women could meet and hold classes and parties. A cafeteria would help offset the costs. She saw the house as "a haven of peace when there was strife in the labor movement caused by the Communists, for the League was absolutely non-partisan and non-political." Mrs. Willard Straight, one of the wealthiest women in the city, agreed to chair a fund-raising committee to pay for the house and began with a tea for her friends. She invited Eleanor Roosevelt. Schneiderman reported: "From the moment we were introduced I was impressed by her simplicity of manner and her lovely eyes. As we shook hands, she told me how nice it would be for the League to have its own house and how glad she would be to help us."[37]

Rose Schneiderman was small, she said, like her "mother and...grandfather...four-and-a-half feet tall," with fiery red hair and a powerful voice honed on the street corner soapbox circuit of the Lower East Side. Born in 1882 in the small village of Savin, then part of Russian Poland, she immigrated to the United States with her family in 1890 and settled in the tenements, where her father took up his tailoring trade. Like ER, Rose lost her father quite suddenly when she was only ten years old. Her widowed mother had no money and spoke no English. Rose and two young brothers were placed in orphanages until they were old enough to help support the family. She went out to work at the age of thirteen and became a cap maker by trade. A few years later, when the family went to live with an aunt in Canada, Schneiderman learned a great deal about socialism and trade unions, as well as a love of music and theater. When she returned to New York City, she began organizing the Jewish and Italian immigrants in the sweatshops and factories at about the same time ER was volunteering at the Rivington Street Settlement House.

She was organizing the mothers of the children ER taught and the women who worked in the factories ER inspected. Pauline Newman, a friend and colleague in the International Ladies' Garment Workers' Union, described the factories as places that were cold in winter, hot and smelly in summer, without drinking water, where "the dirt, smells and vermin were as much a part of the surroundings as were the machines and workers."[38]

Schneiderman soon became a union leader: she organized her local of the United Cloth Hat and Cap Makers Union, was elected secretary, and at the age of twenty-two became the first woman elected to a General Executive Board. She joined the new Women's Trade Union League and threw herself into the "Uprising of Twenty Thousand" in 1909, when young women marched from their factory sewing machines into the streets of New York City. After the Triangle Fire of 25 March 1911, she challenged the leading progressives and social reformers. Speaking fierce words but in a voice barely above a whisper, she told the crowd assembled in the Metropolitan Opera House: "I would be a traitor to these poor burned bodies if I came here to talk good fellowship. We have tried you good people of the public and we have found you wanting." She lobbied for the recommendations of the State Factory Investigating Commission which followed the tragedy, organized for the newly formed International Ladies' Garment Workers' Union, and campaigned for women's suffrage.[39]

Schneiderman met Maud Swartz, another working-class suffrage speaker, in 1912, when she heard her talking to a group of workers in fluent Italian. Maud O'Farrell Swartz, daughter of a flour miller in County Kildare, emigrated from Ireland at the turn of the century when she was eighteen. One of fourteen children, she had spent a painful childhood in German and French convents. Like ER, she spoke several languages, including French and Italian. She easily found work as a proofreader in a foreign language printing plant in New York. After a brief and unhappy marriage to Lee Swartz, whom she never officially divorced, she was on her own. She joined the WTUL at Rose Schneiderman's invitation and then joined the powerful Typographical Union, Local 6. The two women formed a deep and lasting friendship that included interests in theater and music, as well as socialist politics and trade unionism.[40]

As a testament to her leadership role in the labor movement, Schneiderman was a candidate for the U.S. Senate on the ticket of the newly formed American Labor Party of New York State in 1920. She ran on a broad platform of economic reform and made a bold call for racial equality, but amid serious divisions within the labor movement, she had made enemies as well as friends. She had been active in socialist politics, and her agenda for working women often challenged the male leadership. Some called her "Red Rose" and dubbed the WTUL a "tail to the Socialist kite." Red-baiting was central to the campaign against her, and Schneiderman lost, along with Cox, Roosevelt, and Smith.[41]

Despite the red-baiting, after the tea at Mrs. Straight's house, ER invited Schneiderman to the Roosevelt home on Sixty-fifth Street for a Sunday night scrambled egg supper. The key question ER asked her was, why should women join unions? Schneiderman recalled:

> She was very genial in a hail-fellow-well-met sort of way.... There was a chafing dish on the dining table, and Mrs. Roosevelt made the eggs herself while a coffee urn bubbled away. Naturally we talked about the work I was doing. Mrs. Roosevelt asked many questions but she was particularly interested in why I thought women should join unions. I remember so well telling her that that was the only way working people could help themselves. I pointed to the unions of skilled men and told her how well they were doing. By contrast, women were much worse off because they were less skilled or had no skills and could be easily replaced if they complained. They were working for $3.00 a week for nine or ten hours a day, often longer. It all seemed understandable to her. There was no doubt about that.[42]

The Women's Trade Union League and the garment unions, where many of the women leaders received their training and maintained their active membership, introduced ER to "social unionism," in contrast to the more narrowly job-focused unionism of the skilled trades. They not only sought better jobs and working conditions but also negotiated for better housing and health care and provided apartments and banking services. Members were offered educational opportunities as well as performances of music, dance, and theater. The leaders saw a positive role for government and political action and had strong international ties rooted in their immigrant and often socialist backgrounds.[43]

The social gatherings soon expanded beyond the house on Sixty-fifth Street to Hyde Park and Campobello. Rose Schneiderman first mentioned going to Campobello in August 1923, with Nancy Cook and Marion Dickerman. She and Maud were invited to Hyde Park in 1926, when, she recalled:

> F.D.R. and Louis Howe picked us up at the League and we had a gay ride up. Something happened to the motor along the way so while the mechanic fixed the car, we ate hot dogs, that staple of the Roosevelt cook-outs and picnics.... We had a wonderful visit and went home Sunday feeling exhilarated and very happy over the broadening of our friendship with the Roosevelts. It was on this trip that I first met Mrs. James Roosevelt.... After that, both of us were invited many times and usually stayed at Val-kill.... There was a swimming pool which meant so much to F.D.R., and in front of the cottage was the Val-kill River on which I once had the temerity to take F.D.R. rowing.[44]

The union women were aware that they were not fully welcomed by ER's mother-in-law, but they seemed to admire her willingness to participate in their fun. In 1928 Schneiderman recalled a two-week vacation at Hyde Park, "one with Nancy and Marion at Val-kill and the second with the F.D.R.'s at the big house. It was the election year and Eleanor spent a lot of time campaigning.... Mrs. James, as we called F.D.R.'s mother, was always very charming. I am sure she did not really approve of some of F.D.R.'s friends, but she made the best of it and always entered into the gaiety." A skit they developed while Eleanor and Franklin were at the Vanderbilts' for lunch included "Mrs. James" covered with jewelry and playing Mrs. Al Smith, the governor's wife. Nancy Cook was Smith's aide, Belle Moskowitz, and Maud was the pope. "Marion and I were members of the Democratic Party," she concluded.[45]

The educational value of these social gatherings was reinforced over the next several years by ER's work with the WTUL. Eleanor Roosevelt's membership was approved in January 1923, according to the minutes of the executive board meeting of the New York chapter. She immediately focused on the finance committee, arranging luncheons and introducing Schneiderman to a wide range of potential patrons, including the very wealthy Mrs. Astor and Mrs. Vanderbilt. ER kept detailed accounts of her fund-raising efforts. The WTUL soon became a family activity as well. One of the early teas for the finance committee was sponsored by ER and Mrs. James Roosevelt; Eleanor's daughter, Anna, joined in 1925. The Roosevelts offered to host a Christmas party for the children of unemployed workers, complete with a decorated tree, refreshments, and gifts such as books and games, clothes, and toys, as well as a magic show and singing, and ice cream and cake for each child. The two youngest boys, Franklin Jr. and Johnny, became "deputies of Santa Claus," and FDR joined in the festivities the first year by reading aloud from the classic *A Christmas Carol.*[46]

ER quickly moved to help on the education committee. The New York League offered courses in English, literature, current history, economic history, and the economics of industry, as well as pottery and interior design. She helped find volunteer instructors at Columbia University's Teachers College, and once a week she read to the group and brought books, hot chocolate, and cookies to the clubhouse. The committee was active in support and in recruiting students for the Bryn Mawr Summer School for Women in Industry. ER met Hilda Smith, the Bryn Mawr dean who directed the summer program for factory women on the women's college campus, and learned firsthand about the value of labor education for strengthening workers as trade unionists and as citizens.[47]

One of the most successful efforts of the New York WTUL was the Women's Compensation Service headed by Maud Swartz. Beginning in 1922, she acted as an advocate for women workers under the Workmen's Compensation

Law, educating them about their rights and helping them file claims and access services. Swartz reported that from 1924 to 1926, 1,313 cases were handled and 906 were closed. ER served on this compensation committee during that period, furthering her knowledge of working conditions and the problems of individual working women and their families.[48]

ER also advocated that women receive government appointments. In 1924 Schneiderman was asked by Governor Al Smith to be his representative at a national conference on child labor in Washington, DC. She wrote to ER: "I am sure it must be by your doing, dear Eleanor. I was really astounded when the appointment came. Frankly, I do not know whether it was a wise political move. However, I shall be very quiet about it and not let him in for anything that might embarrass him." Just a few years before, Belle Moskowitz, one of Governor Smith's top aides, had taken Schneiderman's name off a list of people invited to discuss postwar labor policy. Moskowitz claimed she was not "practical," but Schneiderman had been targeted by the anticommunist Lusk Committee, and others interpreted it as an attempt to protect Smith from people considered subversive.[49]

During these years ER also mastered the art of grass-roots party building, persuading women to use their newly won right to vote. Traveling up and down the state organizing women for the Democrats, she became well known in political circles nationwide. While 1924 was a disaster for the Democrats, it was a new start for both Roosevelts. With the encouragement of Louis Howe, ER accepted an offer from the chair of the Democratic National Committee to put together a platform of women's issues. Under her direction a prestigious advisory committee, which included Maud Swartz, met for two days in Madison Square Garden. Delegates from around the country spoke in support of their proposed resolutions. The executive committee finalized the recommendations for the platform committee, including a wide range of subjects from conservation and child welfare to prison reform. The recommendations on women and industry, presented by Rose Schneiderman, called for support of the eight-hour day, minimum wage boards, equal pay, and a federal employment service. They boldly declared, "We believe in the workers' right to organize and bargain collectively." ER, as chair of this committee, was now on record in support of the right to join a union.[50]

This platform also marked ER's alignment in a defining split within the suffrage movement. In 1920 Alice Paul formed the National Woman's Party, and by 1923 it had managed to have the Equal Rights Amendment introduced in Congress. The ERA banned all discrimination based on sex. Schneiderman and the WTUL led the campaign opposing what they called "blanket legislation" because they believed it would destroy the protection they had worked so hard to achieve for women struggling in the poorest-paying jobs. They saw the law as an attack on labor legislation in general by a group of conservative, professional, upper-class women. While they believed in equality, they saw this amendment as an abstraction that would do nothing to help the factory women working day after day on the shop floor. WTUL members who opposed protective legislation had already left the organization, so the lines were drawn for a bitter fight that would drain the resources of much of the women's movement for several decades. The National Woman's Party presented its case for the ERA at the advisory committee meeting, but it was rejected. Combining her experiences as a volunteer on the Lower East Side and her new role with the WTUL, and drawing on the experiences of her friends in the labor movement, ER agreed. She opposed the Equal Rights Amendment until the 1940s and never directly challenged the union women's position.[51]

While ER and the committee received notice from the *New York Times,* they were ignored by the Democratic National Convention when it was called to order in New York City just a few weeks later. She waited in the sweltering 100 degree heat during the day and into the early morning hours, but the all-male resolutions committee rejected the women's planks. For the first time ER learned that women stood "outside the door of all important meetings and waited." She wrote, "I did get my resolutions in, but how much consideration they got was veiled in mystery behind closed doors." The convention was a triumph for FDR, however. He made his return to the national political scene with a rousing nomination speech for Al Smith, "the Happy Warrior of the political battlefield." After the convention became deadlocked, Smith lost the nomination to John W. Davis, a Wall Street lawyer.[52]

Schneiderman worked closely with ER but maintained her political independence. Thanking Eleanor for her efforts on behalf of women at the convention, Rose nevertheless acknowledged that she would not be voting for the Democratic ticket; she stuck with Robert La Follette, presidential candidate of the Progressive Farmer-Labor Party. In the fall ER attended the New York State Democratic convention, where she represented the WTUL on behalf of the eight-hour day and minimum wage legislation. She seconded Al Smith's renomination for governor in a highly acclaimed speech and campaigned actively against Smith's opponent, her cousin Theodore Roosevelt Jr. Smith lost the presidential nomination but kept the governor's mansion, while Davis and La Follette lost the presidency to Calvin Coolidge.[53]

Now a national leader among Democratic women, ER began to write articles and columns. She contributed two pieces to the *Women's Democratic Campaign Manual* that year, issued by the Democratic National Committee: "Why I Am a Democrat" and "How to Interest Women in Voting." Expressing her moderate support of labor in a conciliatory manner, she wrote: "I am not unmindful of the necessity that business must prosper and that capital should have its just reward, but the balance must be kept proportionate among the various activities of our people; those who manufacture, those who till the soil, those who work for science, art, and education all alike must prosper for the better development of the race and the country." In 1925 she helped found and became editor of the *Women's Democratic News.*[54]

By the mid-1920s women's unemployment was rising and wages were falling, but the League continued some organizing efforts, exposing ER to another side of union life. In December 1925 Sadie Reisch was hired as an organizer from Local 22 of the ILGWU, where she was a business agent. Her first focus was on organizing bag makers, aiding the International Union of Paper, Pulp & Sulphite Workers, as well as organizing hotel and steam laundry workers. ER joined the organizing efforts. On 9 December 1926, the *New York Times* headline read "Notables in Strike March. Mrs. F. D. Roosevelt among Them." She and eight other prominent women participated in a mass picket demonstration by three hundred women in support of striking paper box makers. Eight of the strikers were arrested for ignoring a police order to move on and charged with "disorderly conduct."[55]

With her new union friends, ER expanded the education program she and FDR had begun at the Rivington Street Settlement House. They had a good time, but the union women were aware of their educational role as well. ER always gave them full credit for her union education. Pauline Newman described visiting the Roosevelt home and talking with Franklin: "We'd go up there sometimes and had fun. At other times, we'd just sit and talk and he would come out and join us. . . . [B]ut whenever we came we talked about labor conditions and legislation." According to their friend and colleague Frances Perkins, Schneiderman and Swartz "were among the people who could bring F.D.R. new and stimulating ideas after his illness. . . . [Eleanor] began to bring in everybody, old friends and new acquaintance, who could share their experiences and their ideas with him." Schneiderman later recalled:

> One of FDR's great talents was getting people to talk about the things they knew. Of course, Maud and I were delighted to tell him all we knew about the theory and history of the trade union movement. . . . We told him about the sweat shops and the tuberculosis rate in the printing industry before the unions were organized and regulated hours and wages. We told him about the prevailing thirteen-hour day, with a longer day on Saturday because Sunday was a day off. We told him about wages for four and five dollars a week, of how the trade unions were the first to get children under ten out of the factories, and of the improvement in the textile industries where the unions had been organized for years. We told him everything we had learned in our years in the labor movement.[56]

Frances Perkins, who would become FDR's secretary of labor, argued that these discussions with union women between 1925 and 1928 were critical to

FDR's deeper understanding of the labor movement. The same can be said for ER. Perkins later wrote:

> These intelligent trade unionists made a great many things clear to Franklin Roosevelt that he would have hardly known any other way.... He was soon learning from these girls a great deal about the trade union movement. He saw it in a new light. While he was well disposed toward it, he never had understood with real detail the purpose of the movement. He had neither seen the background of exploitation in industries from which the movement had grown in England and in this country, nor had he been a technical academic student of the movement itself.[57]

While Perkins downplayed FDR's earlier work with men in the skilled trades unions in Albany and Washington, her basic point was that he gained a new level of understanding of unions that had not been provided by the men he knew and perhaps he could not have heard from them. In later years, when he talked to union leaders he would rely on what he had learned from these women, showing a depth of understanding that surprised them. One labor leader said to Perkins: "You'd almost think he had participated in some strike or organizing campaign the way he knew and felt about it." He also learned about the broader view that some unions had of social change beyond the workplace concerns of the skilled trades. From these experiences Franklin and Eleanor Roosevelt received a fine labor education that helped prepare them for their next political task.[58]

Moving to the Governor's Mansion

Eleanor Roosevelt and Rose Schneiderman joined forces at a crucial moment for the labor movement. New technologies fueled dramatic increases in productivity, requiring new skills while also increasing unemployment. For example, the automatic switchboard, dial telephone, and teletype accelerated communication, offering new jobs for women while throwing messengers out of work. The workforce was changing rapidly. Restrictive immigration laws dramatically reduced the number of foreign workers, and large numbers of farm workers, both white and black, moved to the cities. The number of women entering the workforce increased by over 25 percent during the decade, as many women worked to supplement their husband's inadequate wages or to support the family when their husband was unemployed. The gap between rich and poor widened. Workers in the South earned less than those in other regions; the unskilled were paid poorly and worked irregularly. Women earned only about half of what men did, and most toiled in jobs assigned predominantly to women. Black men and women, who were excluded from many workplaces and discriminated against in others, earned much less than whites. Few workers had benefits or ways to resolve grievances on the job. Unemployment rates between 1920 and 1928 ranged from 5 to 13 percent, a troubling sign of economic instability.[59]

The labor movement was unable to cope with these conditions, particularly because employers mounted an antiunion offensive after the war. Union membership dropped from a peak of over 5 million in 1920 to 3.4 million in 1929. At the end of the decade unions represented only 10 percent of the nation's 30 million workers, a decline of almost 20 percent in ten years. Modest union growth was limited to skilled workers, largely white and male, in a handful of industries such as construction. The few industrial unions declined rapidly, while expanding industries such as automobiles and steel were largely unorganized. In 1920, with more than half a million members, the United Mine Workers (UMW) was the largest and most powerful union in the country, but it collapsed along with much of the mining industry as the market contracted, prices fell, and competition from alternative energy sources grew.[60]

Internal stress from the left was intense during this period. Infighting between liberals, socialists, and communists almost destroyed the International Ladies' Garment Workers' Union, to which Rose Schneiderman, Pauline Newman, and many other women labor leaders belonged. The ILGWU's membership dropped from over 105,000 to 32,000 during the decade. ER came directly under anticommunist attack for her work on the Bok Peace Prize in 1924 and vociferously disagreed with those who fed red-baiting inside and outside the labor movement. J. Edgar Hoover began her FBI file that same year.[61]

ER soon challenged the National Civic Federation (NCF). The Roosevelts belonged to this alliance of labor, capital, and government representatives formed to address the problems of industrialization. Samuel Gompers and Theodore Roosevelt were among the early participants, but the group became increasingly conservative. In 1927, when founder Ralph Easley sent out one of his frequent warnings about the dangers of radicalism, ER replied by arguing against "the fool organizations which are constantly sending out propaganda and letters of warning as to the Bolshevik who is to be found around the corner and under every bed," adding, "I think we are in much more danger in this country of hysteria on this subject than we are of lack of information."[62]

In 1928 Mathew Woll, vice president of the AF of L and president of the International Photo-Engravers Union, was the most visible labor leader in the NCF. He asked members to sign postcards that would go to members of Congress and the press that read, "I approve of the NCF endeavor to bringing an end to Communist propaganda in the United States." ER sent her card back strongly disagreeing and charging that the NCF's propaganda and fear were having a negative effect. Easley then set up a meeting with ER and Woll, where she told them both that the "AFL was using the Communists scare to gain sympathy." Easley left the meeting in an outburst for which he later apologized, but continued to lecture her about the number of Communist Party cells in American factories, the fact that no one in Washington was monitoring the dangerous situation, and ER's lack of time to "make a comprehensive study of the extent and menace of Communism in this country." ER was unmoved.[63]

As another presidential campaign loomed, ER did not attend the Democratic National Convention, ambiguously citing family reasons, but FDR was there and again nominated Al Smith for president. She did co-chair the National Women's Committee of the Democratic Party and worked tirelessly for Smith's election. Smith could not seek reelection as governor and wanted FDR to succeed him. Howe thought it was too soon. At the New York State Convention, when no one else could reach FDR to discuss putting his name in nomination, Smith asked ER to call him. Once connected with her husband, she assured him that she knew he would do what he felt was expected of him; she then turned the phone over to Smith and left to catch a train. The next day, FDR was on the ticket for governor of New York State. ER did not campaign with him but instead focused her efforts on Smith.[64]

ER's union friends helped, sometimes in undercover ways. In a handwritten letter Maud Swartz wrote, "Dear Eleanor...I have a little information which I think will be of use to you if you go to see Mr. Smith," and went on to refer cryptically to a great friend who "told me that said lady contributed $6,500 to Smith's presidential campaign.... If all she says is true then of course Smith would protect her at any costs." Publicly, Frances Perkins, then chair of the Industrial Board of New York State, asked Schneiderman to help persuade the trade unions to support FDR. Union members knew Smith and had voted for him, but Roosevelt and Perkins feared that labor would not turn out to vote, which would hurt FDR and Smith. Perkins thought "Schneiderman was awfully good. She could be sent into almost anything in New York City...whether they were men's or women's organizations.... She was a very effective person."[65]

In the end FDR became governor of New York, but Smith lost the presidency to Herbert Hoover. As ER prepared to move to Albany, the Women's City Club held a luncheon to honor three women: Ruth Baker Pratt, a Republican and the first woman from New York State elected to Congress; Edith Lehman, wife of the newly elected lieutenant governor, Herbert Lehman; and Eleanor Roosevelt, wife of the newly elected governor. Over seven hundred people attended. An informal dinner for ER followed. Eleanor Roosevelt had become a political force in New York State, and now she would have to adjust to being the governor's wife. Her union friends were thrilled. They would put the Roosevelts' labor education to work in the governor's mansion.[66]

Women reformers moved from the edges of power to become active play-ers in FDR's Albany administration. On the public side, one of the governor's first actions was to promote Frances Perkins to industrial commissioner of New York State, the first woman to hold such a position. This was a major advance for women, particularly for those in the WTUL. Schneiderman and Pauline Newman had worked with Perkins since the days of the Factory Inves-tigating Commission after the Triangle Fire. For much of the 1920s she had administered the Workman's Compensation Act, hearing cases and deciding their merits. Before this board Maud Swartz tirelessly represented women workers who had been injured or whose husbands had been hurt at work. Perkins attended League functions and was invited to speak at their events. They shared a history of working for social justice.[67]

Perkins's appointment also highlighted the behind-the-scenes work of the governor's wife. While professing not to give her husband political advice, ER wrote to FDR: "I hope you will consider making Frances Perkins Labor Commissioner. She'd do well and you could fill her place as Chairman of the Industrial Commission by one of the men now on [the] Commission and put Nell(e) Swartz (now Bureau of Women in Industry) on the Commission so there would be one woman on it." She assured him, "These are suggestions which I'm passing on, not my opinions for I don't mean to butt in." ER or-chestrated a visit to Warm Springs by Molly Dewson, then president of the New York Consumers League, not only to talk with the governor about mini-mum wage legislation but also to recommend Perkins for the labor position, an idea originally suggested by ER. As Dewson put it, "Having through Mrs. Roosevelt a direct line to the Governor, to Louis [Howe], and to Jim [Farley], and having such a sympathetic operator, was an incalculable time saver."[68]

ER kept up a grueling pace. Committed to retaining her independence, she left Albany on Sunday nights and spent three days each week in New York City. She taught at Todhunter, a small private school for young women, and checked on the Val-Kill furniture factory at Hyde Park, both of which she co-owned with her friends Marion Dickerman and Nancy Cook. Her ongoing work with the Democratic Women's Committee went on behind the scenes. Publicly she continued to support the League's legislative agenda and helped with membership and fund raising. The March 1929 issue of the national WTUL's *Life and Labor,* for example, announced that the New York Member-ship Campaign would include five Monday luncheons with Mrs. Franklin D. Roosevelt as chairman. At the first luncheon, when ER introduced Robert W. Bruere of *Survey Magazine* to discuss the state of industry, she highlighted the educational role of the League, saying that "education was needed to train workers to lead the labor movement intelligently and unselfishly to a worth-while goal." Subsequent luncheon topics included the causes and remedies of unemployment, the practicality of the five-day week, and labor-management cooperation. The intent was to attract members, educate them, and in turn have them interest other friends, creating an "ever widening circle of support and influence" for the Women's Trade Union League.[69]

In the debate over the five-day workweek ER articulated her understanding of work. Paul Brissenden, professor of economics at Columbia University, argued that the five-day week was feasible only through cooperation among employers brought about by legislation. Merwin K. Hart, chairman of the New York State-Wide Economic Congress, argued that it should be entirely an employer option, for it could ruin some industries and would limit individual rights. When he suggested that ER would not want to be told that she could work only five days a week, she at first agreed, but then added that it depended on the type of work. Repeating a single motion all day long in a factory was not the same as doing work you enjoyed. "Work is living for me," she said. "The point is whether we live in our work."[70]

ER lived in her work, and the union women shared her passionate commitment to working for social justice. Her lifelong friendship with Rose Schneiderman, enduring ties between an upper-class matron and a working-class organizer, developed at least in part because they found shared experiences in their very different pasts. Both women had been young when they lost beloved fathers who had encouraged them. They both had younger brothers to care for. ER's aloof mother had died; Mrs. Schneiderman, while warm and loving, was forced to place her children in orphanages. Maud Swartz spent much of her youth alone in French convent schools. When these women met, their painful youths were behind them. Maud was forty-three years old and separated from her husband, Rose was forty and never married, and Eleanor was thirty-eight and had been betrayed by her husband. Each woman knew profound feelings of loss and loneliness. Eleanor and Rose both related their cautious and controlled emotions in adulthood to their childhood experiences. Schneiderman wrote to her lifelong friend Pauline Newman in 1917: "I know just how alone one can feel. . . . whatever I have done, could not be done any other way because of the kind of personality that I am. . . . I am used to going without the things most wanted." Some years later ER told her confidante Lorena Hickok that her inability to let herself be free emotionally was rooted in her childhood: "I think it was when I was a child & is now a habit."[71]

These women had much more to share: learning about socialism, music and theater, the tenements and sweatshops, the Triangle Fire, the Albany years, stories about Europe, conversations in French or Italian. Stories were exchanged. Frances Perkins described a visit when the governor's mansion was full of guests, so she and ER shared a third-floor room. After Perkins admired a necklace given to ER by her father, ER spoke of how important he had been to her and how she had been passed from one relative to another after his death, never really having a home of her own even after her marriage.

While Perkins did not reciprocate with stories of her life, Schneiderman and Swartz may have been more forthcoming, in part to convey the realities of their working lives. One summer, for example, when they were visiting ER at Campobello, her union friends told the two youngest Roosevelt sons about life in the tenements, the conditions workers faced, and the world of trade unionists. ER wrote to a friend: "It was a world they had never known and they were enthralled. Later, when someone asked one of my sons, 'Who's been staying with you?' he replied, 'Oh, some of Mummie's strange friends. But they are darned interesting, too.'"[72]

Although they came from entirely different worlds, these women shared the kind of early personal experiences on which the emotional bonds of friendship could be built. The Roosevelts' basic understanding of unions for skilled tradesmen provided a substantive base on which to develop their working relationships as they learned about more progressive unions and their broader social agendas. During the 1920s ER and these women shared their early experiences, built on their related skills, and developed their vision of the future. As they and the labor movement were challenged by the Great Depression, the WTUL's twenty-fifth anniversary party at Springwood became a distant memory.

2

HERE COMES MRS. ROOSEVELT

The President's wife today discussed wages and working
conditions, safety precautions and mining methods, with miners
black with coal dust.
United Mine Workers Journal, 1 June 1935

Thousands of citizens lined the streets, flags flying overhead, as official
cars wended their way along the river toward the Willow Grove Mine number 10, near the small community of Neffs, Ohio. The mine was twelve miles
west of Wheeling, West Virginia, tucked in a valley by a small stream. On
this day, 21 May 1935, company officials and union officers awaited their
visitor at the entrance to the mineshaft. Smiling and eager, First Lady Eleanor Roosevelt arrived at noon and accepted a large bouquet of roses and
spring flowers presented by the United Mine Workers of America. The men
held her in such high esteem that they defied an age-old superstition that it
brought bad luck for a woman to go down into a coal mine. Just two years earlier a *New Yorker* cartoon had poked fun at the idea that the first lady might
venture into a mine on one of her inspection trips. Wherever controversial
issues arose, she was known for going to see the situation for herself. Her
penchant for listening to the concerns of ordinary people endeared her to
many, although others were shocked. ER herself had described the cartoon
miners "as looking up in surprise and saying with undisguised horror, 'Here
comes Mrs. Roosevelt!'"[1]

Lorena Hickok, the former newspaperwoman and close friend who accompanied ER on this journey, first described the deplorable conditions of
the mine workers and their families in her reports to Harry Hopkins, head
of the Federal Emergency Relief Administration, in 1933. In preparation for
the trip, ER told her it would be two hours long "and we will get dirty. So

wear suitable clothes, if you know what is suitable. I confess I am stumped." ER declined the pair of new overalls provided for her but accepted a gray coat, donned a miner's cap, and took a seat in the first car of a six-car train heading two miles down into the mine. Adolphus Pacifico, vice president of the UMW local, explained the mine operations. For over an hour and a half they watched four hundred miners at work in what was thought to be a model mine, one of the safest in the nation. Willow Grove had been purchased by the Hanna Company, based in Cleveland, in 1931. The owners had installed new machinery and were running three shifts. The United Mine Workers *Journal*, a union paper read by miners across the county, reported:

> Standing with one foot on a pile of coal, under a mountain two and a half miles from daylight, the President's wife today discussed wages and working conditions, safety precautions and mining methods, with miners black with coal dust.... Farther into the mountain the cars came at last to the "regular workings," where Mrs. Roosevelt got off and walked along a low, narrow passage to see how they do it.... Mrs. Roosevelt wanted to know how much the miners make here, how steady their work is, how the machines work.[2]

ER emerged from the mine late in the afternoon and spoke briefly with three hundred miners who were ending their shift. Happy to have the opportunity see how they worked, she wished them success. Then the party stopped at a local church for dinner with the miners' families and went on to Bellaire, Ohio, where they attended a celebration for the People's University. Founded just six months earlier, the school enrolled about two hundred adult students and offered forty courses, from English and economics to knitting and bridge, taught by instructors from the local community. Teachers volunteered their time, and there were no fees for the students. In the hall filled with almost 2,500 people, ER declared that she was proud of "the struggle we are making, striving not to get back to old financial conditions but to new and better things. You cannot understand the problems we are up against today unless you understand the economic background." An orchestra played and a girls' choir sang. Then she traveled on to Steubenville, Ohio, where a crowd of two thousand watched her board a train for Washington, DC.[3]

The unions, the country, and Eleanor Roosevelt had traveled a great distance over the years, from the WTUL's twenty-fifth anniversary party on the shores of the Hudson River to the depths of the Willow Grove mine and the People's University. Unemployment was the overwhelming issue. Union membership continued its steady decline after the onset of the Great Depression. ER worked tirelessly with the WTUL as new solutions to the growing problems were tested in Albany. Economic equality and stability became central to her thinking about the democratic process, and she entered the White

House firmly committed to labor unions as an important way to improve the lives of working women.[4]

The advent of President Franklin D. Roosevelt's New Deal did not end the depression, but the policies and programs that emerged enabled a dramatic resurgence of unionization. Legislation established the right to join a union and bargain collectively, starting with the National Industrial Recovery Act of 1933 and culminating in the National Labor Relations Act of 1935. Union membership grew quickly, but peaceful labor-management relations and economic recovery were elusive. Employer resistance strengthened, the number and duration of strikes increased, and violence escalated. A far more outspoken advocate of labor than her husband, yet closely tied to FDR's policies and politics, ER refined her own "principles on labor" as she worked more closely with the reemerging unions and they grappled with the new federal programs. With her friends from the WTUL at her side, ER helped shape, implement, and publicly support a New Deal for all workers. Her familiar world of women workers expanded to include men from the garment factories of New York City to the copper mines of Arizona. Adding press conferences and books to her public relations tools, she supported the right to join a union, challenged company control of entire communities, and championed workers' education.[5]

The failure of the AF of L to seize the opportunities created by the legislation, combined with the militant response of workers across the country, led John L. Lewis and the mine workers to spearhead the formation of the Committee for Industrial Organization, which would become the Congress of Industrial Organizations (CIO). ER negotiated between the various unions as they realigned over time and, for the next twenty years, consistently called on the labor movement to reunite. In August 1935 the New Yorker cartoon "For gosh sakes, here comes Mrs. Roosevelt" and the picture of her trip to the Willow Grove Mine were used to frame ER's article "In Defense of Curiosity" in the *Saturday Evening Post.* She quietly defended her activities and called on all women to be curious, to recognize and to act on the many connections between their interests at home and the rest of the world.[6]

Economic Problems and Politics in Albany

After the 29 October 1929, stock market crash, followed by widespread and deepening economic uncertainty, political leaders fiercely debated the seriousness of the situation and what policymakers should do about it. On 22 January 1930 President Hoover announced that the unemployment trend was turning around and the country was on the way to recovery. Frances Perkins, state industrial commissioner in Albany, studied the numbers and issued a blistering denunciation. In New York State the January figures were worse than for any previous month in the last sixteen years. While she encouraged an increase in public works programs and improvements in state personnel agencies, she primarily focused on helping the governor create a program of unemployment insurance. FDR was the first major politician to support such a program, announcing his commitment when he and ER traveled to the Governors' Conference in Salt Lake City. The British system of unemployment insurance impressed Rose Schneiderman the most, though she was unable to persuade the WTUL's national executive board to support such a program. She nevertheless wrote to ER remarking that FDR's statements at the conference had been warmly received by the public and praising ER's own speech.[7]

As the Great Depression deepened, ER recognized that "unemployment is paramount to all other ordinary considerations." She passed beggars and breadlines on the streets of New York City and received thousands of letters asking for assistance. She forwarded requests to state and local officials for response and, when all avenues of aid failed, she did her best to find jobs for individuals who asked for her help. Constantly she urged her husband to move faster. They argued about the need for a state unemployment compensation program, and at one point he turned on her sharply and exclaimed, "I agree with Uncle Teddie that you can't get too far ahead of the people." When asked by a colleague to push him harder on old age pensions, she threw her hands up into the air and replied, "We have argued so long that we are no longer on speaking terms on that subject."[8]

Addressing unemployment became more urgent as joblessness afflicted people in all sectors of the economy, across class and region. It would eventually affect almost a third of the workforce. There was no national policy of unemployment relief. Hoover viewed the problem as a state responsibility. FDR disagreed, but early in his second term as governor he took up the challenge. Convinced that the relief efforts of local governments and charitable organizations were inadequate, he called the Republican-controlled legislature into special session. It passed the Wicks Bill, creating the Temporary Emergency Relief Administration, which quickly became a model for other states and the federal government.[9]

Schneiderman added the right to unemployment relief to her long-standing advocacy of unionization for women workers. In 1930, when she and ER spoke to a conference on housing for women, she appealed "for the organization of working women as the only means of increasing present wages and obtaining the improvements needed at this time." By 1931 she was demanding a more equitable distribution of the relief money to women factory workers. Estimating that fifty thousand women were out of work and desperate, she argued that women, who often supported themselves and other family members, were "as much entitled to assistance as any other class of worker." In

January 1932 Schneiderman led a delegation of women unionists to Albany to lobby the governor for supplemental relief for unemployed women.[10]

As the needs of working women increased, the Women's Trade Union League was less and less able to help, despite ER's fund raising and the group's strong ties to the Roosevelt administration. In 1932–33 ER donated the proceeds from her radio shows to the New York Women's Trade Union League (NYWTUL) to keep the doors open. Union support declined with union membership. Training programs were dropped and classes canceled because women could not pay even the token fees required. The small loan program for unemployed women was curtailed. Schneiderman and the WTUL also lost their savings when their labor-sponsored bank failed. Schneiderman cut her own salary and lent the League organizer Sadie Reisch to the ILGWU. Other WTUL branches suffered a similar fate, and in February 1932 the *Life and Labor Bulletin* suspended publication.[11]

During this same time period, ER and the WTUL addressed other problems as well as unemployment. Now active players in FDR's Albany administration, the women discussed prison contract labor and the need to improve conditions for domestic workers. FDR appointed Schneiderman to represent New York State at an international convention of pubic employment services, and she served on child labor and prison labor commissions at his request. ER wrote articles and chaired sessions on these topics for the WTUL. In the face of mounting pressure to lay off married women and reserve the available jobs for men, who were presumed to be breadwinners with families, she defended the right of married women to work. ER not only recognized that many working-class women were breadwinners but also rejected the notion that middle-class women should be confined to domesticity and volunteer work. In a time of emergency, she argued, "it may be necessary to voluntarily relinquish your work if the other partner is earning enough for the family to live on, but as a permanent concession to the needs of society I rebel."[12]

The Roosevelts helped with strikes despite the harassment meted out to strikers by management and their condemnation in the press. FDR worked to resolve a strike by ILGWU Local 22, led by Sadie Reisch. ER supported Local 38 when Mary Hillyer led the women out of Fifth Avenue dressmaking shops. After two weeks, 450 striking workers settled with the firm of Hattie Carnegie, but "seven girl strikers" were arrested for disorderly conduct at another firm. David Dubinsky, then secretary-treasurer of the union, was arrested and appeared in West Side Court. In a letter to Hillyer, the governor's wife praised "the movement which has as its object improvement of conditions for those women workers in the dressmaking establishments where, up to this time, the women workers have not been organized." Covering the strike and including the letter, the *New York Times* described ER as "noted for her sympathies toward organized labor, and especially toward women in industry."[13]

FDR's campaign for reelection raised the stakes for his policy decisions in 1930. He spent much of his first term addressing the problems of farmers, strengthening public utilities systems, and reforming prison labor. The Republican-dominated legislature balked at labor initiatives, especially the eight-hour day and forty-eight-hour week for women and children. FDR told Rose Schneiderman that it would be a "long, hard, up-hill fight" and the best he could do was to build a party record to "get the support of the real liberals and progressives." Yet FDR also received the support of William Green, president of the AF of L, who praised his personal inspiration and leadership on economic, industrial, and social legislation supported by labor. The governor addressed the state labor convention and led with unemployment insurance, remarking that "some might call him a Bolshevik" for supporting the proposal. He highlighted his efforts to secure legislation to limit the hours of work for women and children and establish a minimum wage. Focusing on the committee he created to oppose dumping prison-made goods, he noted that the members included John Sullivan, president of the New York State Federation of Labor, and Rose Schneiderman of the WTUL. In October the nonpartisan campaign committee of the state federation advocated the governor's reelection. This was an unprecedented level of endorsement from labor, helping create Roosevelt's landslide victory.[14]

Early in his second term FDR appointed Maud Swartz secretary of labor for New York State, the first trade unionist to hold this office. ER backed her appointment. She wrote to Schneiderman, "Franklin has already spoken to me about Maud and Sara McPike [the incumbent secretary] and he has written Miss Perkins that he is quite willing to [have] Miss McPike removed, so I think the way is clear for Maud," She signed off, "Affectionately." In December, Maud wrote "My Dear Eleanor" to express gratitude for "all the good words and kind acts you have put in to make this appointment possible.... I understand there is a lot of work awaiting me." Over the next six years Swartz represented organized labor in Albany, establishing a precedent for future secretaries.[15]

As conditions worsened across the county, Franklin Roosevelt took his programs onto the national stage. He fought for the Democratic presidential nomination against his old friend Al Smith. In an unprecedented move FDR flew to Chicago to accept the nomination in person and famously pledged "a new deal for the American people." Just a week later ER spoke to an audience of two thousand in Chautauqua, New York. Her call to "reconstruct the economic system" so that one group did not prosper while the rest starved was broadcast nationwide. She concluded that the "financial structure of our country is man made and must be man controlled" and she told her audience that "labor must receive its just reward." As a national campaign team was assembled, ER's friend Molly Dewson agreed to lead the Women's Division of the Democratic Party. Working together, they proposed that a vice chair-woman be appointed in every state and a committeewoman in every county. The women would be in direct touch with Dewson for campaign literature and expense money. Draft work plans for each state would be sent to ER. The women rejected a twelve-page campaign document drafted by the men and developed their own single-issue "Rainbow Fliers" written by and for women. A determined group of women "grass trampers" went door-to-door in key areas. ER did not campaign directly for her husband, but she sometimes joined the campaign train, worked tirelessly for the New York ticket headed by Herbert Lehman, and spoke out strongly in defense of her husband's record, despite misgivings about what his victory would mean for her own future.[16]

As a matter of policy, the WTUL and AF of L did not endorse presidential candidates. William Green, a Democrat, maintained an official silence as the executive council reaffirmed its nonpartisan policy. John L. Lewis of the United Mine Workers endorsed Hoover, and Big Bill Hutcheson of the Carpenters Union was made chairman of the Republican labor committee. For the most part the needle trades unions backed Socialist Norman Thomas. Only Dan Tobin of the Teamsters and George L. Berry of the Printing Pressmen worked for Roosevelt. Breaking with tradition, on 8 October the National Progressive League announced that Rose Schneiderman, president of the WTUL, supported Roosevelt because of his "labor record and his unequivocal stand upon the question of public utilities and water power control." She joined Sidney Hillman of the Amalgamated Clothing Workers (ACWA), who had become an adviser to FDR's Brain Trust. His union was excluded from the AF of L because of jurisdictional differences. But it had little influence on the campaign. There was no collective bargaining plank in the Democratic platform, and Roosevelt spent far more time seeking votes from farmers and progressive Republicans than from labor.[17]

Roosevelt won 56 percent of the popular vote and carried all but six states in the electoral college. The Democratic Party also won control of both houses of Congress, enabling FDR to move quickly to change federal policy. Workers, especially urban workers and coal miners, deserted the Republicans and cast their protest vote for Roosevelt rather than Norman Thomas or the Communist Party candidate William Z. Foster. Historian Irving Bernstein concluded that "seldom, if ever, in American history had there been so dramatic a reversal in so short a time." Rose Schneiderman immediately wrote to the president-elect assuring him that his lopsided victory "shows clearly that we are ready as a nation to take forward steps in the reconstruction of our social order."[18]

Although ER was a "reluctant First Lady," fearing the loss of her independent political voice, her friends in the WTUL were jubilant. Schneiderman wrote to her: "We know of no other woman who has the social vision and the understanding of the needs of work-a-day folk which you have.... We are more proud than we can say to have a member of the League in the White House." In February 1933 the WTUL gave a farewell dinner in ER's honor. She thanked her friends and acknowledged their role in educating her about the problems working people faced and the solutions that were possible through government policies and labor union actions. She took that education with her to the White House, and her friends in the New York WTUL stood ready to help.[19]

A New Deal for Labor

Even before Franklin D. Roosevelt was inaugurated as president of the United States on 4 March 1933, Eleanor Roosevelt continued speaking out on behalf of workers, both publicly and personally. *Scribner's Magazine* introduced the first lady to its readers as one "who has given of her energy and great ability for years to efforts to secure improved working conditions for labor." In "Protect the Worker, the State's Responsibility for Fair Working Conditions, by Mrs. Franklin D. Roosevelt," which appeared in the March issue, ER decried the lowering of labor standards, declaring, "It is necessary to stress the regulation by law of these unhealthy conditions in industry." She singled out women who "are not unionized" but also noted that "even unions have temporarily lowered their standards in order to keep their people at work." She concluded, "It is a matter of self-preservation to treat the industrial worker with consideration and fairness at the present time."[20]

On a personal level ER practiced what she preached, effectively putting pressure on stores where she shopped and creating new employment opportunities for women. She threatened to boycott Milgrim's, a clothing boutique in New York City where the seamstresses were on strike. David Dubinsky from the ILGWU came to discuss the situation with her. Herman Milgrim, the shop owner, sent her a telegram to assure her that the strike had been settled satisfactorily to both sides. He was quite upset and, he told ER, "very anxious to explain the facts to you when you come in for your fitting which will be ready Thursday, October 12." As first lady she added the press conference to her ways of communicating with the people, and she entertained only women reporters, increasing the number of women with newspaper jobs. These women understood ER's commitment to labor. Ruby Black, assigned by the United Press to cover the press conferences, devoted a portion of her biography of Eleanor Roosevelt to union activities. In a chapter titled "Union Member and Union Supporter" she wrote:

> Mrs. Roosevelt's principles on labor were well defined early in her life, and were invariable: collective bargaining is the reasonable and just basis

for labor relations; "company towns"—even those governed by the "best" paternalism—do not provide a good basis for independent living; for the benefit of the unorganized, minimum wages and maximum hours should be established by law; "apprenticeship systems" should not be used to maintain a steady supply of cheap labor; every means of workers' education ought to be employed, with government help if necessary.[21]

FDR appears to have given little thought to organized labor in his first hundred days, which focused on economic recovery. Indeed his first official act on labor issues before he arrived in Washington was to ignore the wishes of the AF of L and appoint Frances Perkins secretary of labor. William Green and his executive board considered this cabinet post to belong to them. They had several candidates, and Frances Perkins was definitely not one of them. She was deeply concerned that her appointment would cause great difficulty, but the president-elect persuaded her to accept. She was eminently qualified, as well as being a loyal and trusted colleague, and FDR wanted to be the first president to appoint a woman to the cabinet. Green denounced the appointment immediately, but other labor leaders were more open-minded. Sidney Hillman had worked hard for FDR and was eager to meet with the new secretary. David Dubinsky said it was not his place to advise the new president; he seemed to prefer Perkins to an AF of L union president who did not share his progressive views.[22]

Both Frances Perkins and Eleanor Roosevelt denied that ER had anything to do with FDR's cabinet choice, but Molly Dewson organized a public campaign on Perkins's behalf, and ER was delighted with her selection. The first lady and the secretary had a strong but complicated relationship. They approached workplace issues with distinct yet overlapping ties to the labor movement and very different approaches to the media. ER became a journalist, skillfully used the media, and was able to work selectively with and advocate for progressive unions, along with many other issues and groups she supported. Perkins disliked the press, was singularly focused on employment issues, and had to address the entire labor movement in the process of developing, passing, and administering labor legislation that not all labor leaders supported. Their new roles were soon recognized by union leaders such as Dubinsky and Hillman.[23]

As one of her first acts, Secretary Perkins held a conference with labor leaders to underline the administration's concern for labor issues and solicit their ideas on relief for the unemployed. Along with William Green and representatives of the AF of L, she invited Sidney Hillman and Rose Schneiderman. The labor advisory group discussed a proposal to shorten the workweek to thirty hours, which had already been introduced in Congress by Senator Hugo Black, a Democrat from Alabama. The AF of L eventually agreed to the legislation as a way to put more workers back on the job. The legislation also contained language guaranteeing a worker's right to join a union. According to Perkins, FDR thought that the legislation was unconstitutional and worried that it lacked employer support. He agreed to have Secretary Perkins testify at congressional hearings and try to amend the bill, but he also started the process of developing a more comprehensive alternative.[24]

Rose Schneiderman made sure ER knew about the discussions, writing:

> Together with other members of a Labor Advisory Committee we considered the 30-hour week bill and made suggestions for amending the bill so as to give employers some lee-way. We all felt that it is necessary that the bill also carry a provision for industry boards which shall have power to fix minimum wage rates for the specific industry. We also discussed public works programs which could be launched right away providing, of course, the appropriation is there. We later went to see the President on both these measures and were much heartened by his understanding and willingness to help.[25]

ER welcomed the information but regretted that her friend had not come to see her while she was in the capital. Several days later Eleanor Roosevelt attended the House Labor Committee hearing on the Black bill when Frances Perkins testified. She was accompanied by Ishbel MacDonald, daughter of the British prime minister Ramsay MacDonald, who was visiting the White House. FDR called Perkins first, and she agreed that they could come, acknowledging that "the attendance of Miss MacDonald and Mrs. Roosevelt made it a matter of considerable publicity." Having the first lady attend a congressional hearing was so unprecedented that four hundred people crowded into the hearing room. According to Perkins, FDR was publicly committed to the idea of using legislation to regulate working conditions and to mitigate the hardships of unemployment. She saw no evidence that amendments would be added to the bill, and work was well under way on an alternative that would include the right to join a union. FDR's commitment was expressed not only by the secretary of labor's testimony but also by the appearance of his wife at the hearing.[26]

Economic recovery was a critical topic of policy debate within the administration. One group of advisers favored employer self-regulation and wanted to weaken the antitrust laws. Others, including Perkins, supported massive public works projects to put people to work and increase consumption. With both approaches in mind, a comprehensive bill, the National Industrial Recovery Act (NIRA), was sent to Congress less than a month after defeat of the Black bill. Title I encouraged voluntary cooperation to stabilize prices, prevent unfair competition and overproduction, raise wages, limit hours of work, end child labor, and improve working conditions. Section 7A gave unions the right to organize and bargain collectively. Title II established a public works construction project. The president had become "convinced" that the recovery bill must include a guarantee of collective bargaining and win the backing of both industry and labor. Perkins later suggested that the section on unions was added almost as an afterthought when she had Green review the language. Others attributed the inclusion of Section 7A to Lewis, whose economic adviser W. Jett Lauck had been advocating a similar economic plan for the coal industry since the mid-1920s. FDR was committed to a bill that had something for everyone; the inclusion of organized labor was no doubt reinforced by his wife and Rose Schneiderman.[27]

The National Recovery Administration (NRA) under the direction of General Hugh Johnson was established to administer the act. Working with Secretary Perkins, three advisory boards representing industry, labor, and consumers were set up to determine the codes for each industry. FDR appointed Rose Schneiderman to the Labor Advisory Board to set the codes affecting working women. For many years the WTUL's efforts to organize women had met with resistance and hostility from the male union leaders. Now Schneiderman joined these leaders on an equal footing, sharing an office and a secretary with Sidney Hillman and meeting regularly with William Green, David Dubinsky, and John L. Lewis. Mary Anderson, director of the Women's Bureau at the Department of Labor, noted the change in the relationships: "It threw consternation into the Executive Council of the AFL when the League was heartily endorsed by the White House. The boys like to get on the bandwagon. It also got across . . . that women really do amount to something."[28]

On 15 June, the day before the president signed the NIRA, ER held a press conference and introduced Schneiderman. The two women talked about the codes and the importance of hearing workers' opinions. As ER explained, "only where they are organized do women get equal pay for equal work." Rose Schneiderman considered her work on the NRA Labor Advisory Board the high point of her career; looking back she wrote: "It still thrills me that I had a part in bringing about monumental changes in the lives of working men and women. . . . The greatest of these came when Section 7A was included in every code. It gave workers the right to collective bargaining through representatives chosen by themselves, not by their employers[,] and it legalized the worker's right to join a union."[29]

The ILGWU and the Blue Eagle

How labor unions and the government could effectively address rising unemployment and falling wages was the key question these leaders faced in 1933. Experts estimated that one out of every four workers could not find

a job, and the annual earnings of full-time employees in all industries fell by
25 percent from 1929 to 1933. Women, African Americans, farm laborers,
and children earned as little as a nickel an hour, not even enough to buy
a loaf of bread. Unions were in a much weaker position than ten years before. The International Ladies' Garment Workers' Union had declined from
105,000 members in 1920 to only 40,000 in early 1933. The union was in
debt, could not pay the electric bill, and had to suspend publication of its
newspaper, *Justice.* In June 1932, when David Dubinsky became president
of the union, he acknowledged: "Our union is at a low ebb, its very life may
be uncertain.... If it is destined that I be its undertaker,... I shall not try to
duck my fate."[30]

David Dubinsky, Sidney Hillman, and John L. Lewis all watched the
development of the NIRA very carefully and moved swiftly once it became
law. While William Green and the AF of L craft unions hailed the bill as
the "magna carta" of labor, they did not embark on new organizing campaigns. For Dubinsky, however, the passage of the NIRA precipitated "two
months that shook the Ladies' Garment Industry" as a wave of strikes ended
in substantial victories. Although Eleanor Roosevelt and Dubinsky had
crossed paths in New York during the 1920s, their strong working relationship began with the New Deal. Their mutual concern for working women,
collective bargaining, labor legislation, and consumer activism provided a
strong basis for their alliance, as well as for a personal friendship that endured until ER's death.[31]

Standing just five feet, five inches tall, his speech rich with the heavy accent
of his native Poland, David Dubinsky was an avowed socialist. The youngest
of eight children born to a Jewish family in the tsarist Russian Empire, he fled
to the Lower East Side of Manhattan in 1910 at the age of eighteen. A skilled
cutter by trade, he emerged from the internal struggles of his union in the
1920s as a staunch anticommunist. Although he became president of a union
in disarray, the ILGWU was deeply committed to the idea of "social unionism," in stark contrast to most of the AF of L unions. The core union function
was to negotiate stable work, reasonable hours, and fair pay for women and
men of many ethnic and racial backgrounds. Critical to the union's appeal
to its diverse and seasonally employed membership were a health care system that workers could use directly; a retreat in the Pocono Mountains where
union members could bring their families for a vacation or to attend educational programs; decent housing at affordable prices; musical productions
and cultural activities to support the soul as well as the body; and a vision of
what was important to working people that included an active international
perspective. ILGWU leaders believed that government had a positive role to
play in guaranteeing the rights of labor. Dubinsky soon shifted his political
activities from the Socialist Party to the Democrats. These core union values

guided him over the next four decades as he helped shape the American labor movement from his base in the New York City garment district.[32]

Dubinsky and the ILGWU, however, were not always egalitarian in practice. The organization was controlled by men, although the vast majority of members were women. Most leaders were Jewish and Italian immigrants, a balance that never reflected the increasing proportion of African American and Puerto Rican members. While some locals were quite democratic, the leadership did not always represent what was best for the rank and file. Women in particular found it difficult to make their way up the union hierarchy. Yet Maida Springer, a young African American woman who became a union activist and later worked with ER, often said that even "with all of its bumps and warts," the union was still the best way to improve the lives of workers. Much the same was said of "DD," as Dubinsky was affectionately known. He jumped into the New Deal with his enormous energy, sparkling wit, and famous temper. While most at home riding his bicycle around the streets of Lower Manhattan early in the morning, he became comfortable visiting the White House with his wife Emma and daughter Jean.[33]

Dubinsky was a master strategist, orchestrating cooperation with management, mass strikes, and the NRA code hearing process to advance unionization and improve wages and working conditions. He was in contact with Rose Schneiderman and aware of her access to ER and the White House. He immediately set to work with the New York employer associations to standardize conditions in the coat and suit industry through an NRA code that prohibited child labor, established a thirty-five-hour week, set up unemployment insurance, and granted a substantial increase in wages. In the all-important dress industry, which was much less stable, he organized the nonunion employers and stalled the NRA hearings until after the coat and suit code was approved. Two weeks later, on 16 August 1933, he called a general strike in the dress industry. Sixty thousand workers, mostly women, walked out in New York City and in shops from New Haven to Camden. Praising the strike as one of the largest work stoppages in New York history, a reporter for *Justice* wrote, "All came out of the factories with song on their lips and with victory glowing in their eyes."[34]

A settlement reached four days later contained terms similar to the coat and suit code, which were then written into an NRA code for the dress industry. The timing had been crucial. While Irving Bernstein gave credit to Hillman for helping Dubinsky in Washington, Dubinsky was grateful for Rose Schneiderman's help. He acknowledged her importance, noting to his executive board that "Rose has a lot to say in Washington. If anybody does not do the right thing Rose Schneiderman knows the address of the White House. If it is not the President, it is the First Lady to whom she makes her complaints."[35]

Maida Springer captured the excitement of the early days of the New Deal. Born Maida Stewart in Panama to parents of African descent, she arrived at Ellis Island with her parents in 1917, when she was just seven years old. She attended a private but segregated high school and tried several jobs, including work in a garment factory. After graduation she married Owen Springer, an immigrant from Barbados, and was able to stay home with their son until the Great Depression hit. Owen took a large cut in salary, and Maida went back to the dress shops. At a time when striking workers joined the union en masse the Italian American dressmakers' Local 89 became the largest local in the nation, with 40,000 members; Dress Local 22 grew to 28,000. Maida Springer was one of 4,000 African Americans to join the ILGWU. She vividly described the beginning of her union activism:

> When the strike was settled, industry-wide, then we had to begin to build the union. Just hundreds and thousands of workers were enrolled into the garment workers' union, and this was a great excitement.... Everyone who was not Italian belonged to Local 22, the dressmakers. We had 32 nationalities. We prided ourselves on this.... When we had our celebration in Madison Square Garden after we won the general strike, everybody from the Met was there to sing for the workers. "Pan y Rosa, Bread and Roses." That's why I say that, for me, the trade union movement was always a great love affair and a great excitement.[36]

As workers struggled to organize unions in major industries across the country, they came up against recalcitrant employers who refused to recognize them. The NRA did not usher in the era of labor-management peace that the Roosevelts had hoped for. Employers fought Section 7A at every turn. Enforcing the NRA codes proved difficult; many employers, known to the workers as chiselers, broke the rules. Unions established monitoring bureaus and developed procedures to help with implementation, but the last weapon of self-defense was the strike. In the late summer of 1933, the number of days lost to strikes quadrupled. A board to mediate labor disputes was quickly put into place, and the Roosevelts' old friend Senator Robert Wagner of New York agreed to serve as chair.[37]

Some NRA codes incorporated the discrimination against women that had long existed in industry. As early as August, Schneiderman was concerned about unequal wages and called on the first lady to intervene. ER returned from Hyde Park to meet with Johnson and Perkins, and the principle of equal pay for equal work was soon announced as the basis for all the codes. Sixty codes were revised, and eventually 75 percent of the 493 codes provided for equal pay. Yet wage differences by sex remained embedded in the others. In the end, wages increased and working conditions on the shop floor improved for many women, contributing to what historian Alice Kessler-Harris has termed "incremental change." On this issue, too, Eleanor Roosevelt had a positive influence on government policy.[38]

The ILGWU and ER also engaged in consumer activism. For years both unions and employers in the clothing industry had talked about putting a label in garments to certify that the employer paid decent wages and offered reasonable working conditions. On 11 April 1933, representatives of women workers and manufacturers met in New York City and agreed to develop a label that would "assure the public that certain fixed standards have been followed by the manufacturers," especially that the garment had been made by workers who received a fair wage. ER was the principal speaker. Maintaining her independence, she addressed the conference as an individual citizen, not as first lady. She endorsed the proposal and "urged that the women newspaper writers and advertising experts be called in to formulate a publicity campaign that would stress the humanitarian appeal of the movement." ER argued that the label idea had to be combined with an education program for consumers.[39]

David Dubinsky shared the podium with ER. He told the group that "the average earnings of workers in the needle trades was below the minimum of subsistence and that unless this movement was checked there would be a return to the insanitary sweatshop of twenty-five years ago." Soon Schneiderman asked ER to be honorary chair of the National Committee for the Abolition of Sweatshops and for the Promotion of an Identification Label on Women's Clothes—if it would not get her into "hot water." ER's role in Washington was not yet clear. She declined to be chair but continued her strong support for the label idea.[40]

The NRA offered another opportunity for collaboration when its Blue Eagle logo with the slogan "We Do Our Part" became national symbols. The agency had no power to enforce the codes it negotiated with employers, however, and the legal staff thought that the entire act would be found unconstitutional. General Johnson turned to the idea of awarding a Blue Eagle symbol to publicly acknowledge companies for their voluntary compliance with the codes. Some historians overlook this effort altogether, while others deem it mere "ballyhoo." For Dubinsky and ER, however, the logo reflected a serious strategy to mobilize workers and housewives, the wealthy and the poor. While organizing and collective bargaining were the bedrock of the union strategy, education and consumer support were also important. Placing labor representatives in top government positions and passing better laws were not enough. Mobilizing the general public was essential in order to make labor legislation effective and to legitimate the role of unions in the economy.[41]

Eleanor Roosevelt firmly believed that a new social order was developing and consumers had an important role in economic reconstruction. Her first book, *It's Up to the Women,* appeared in November 1933. Addressing women across class lines, she wrote, "We are going through a great crisis in this country and . . . women have a big part to play if we are coming through it successfully." She called on working women to demand equal pay for equal work and to join existing unions or form new ones. Wealthy women should live more frugally, she urged, and treat the people who worked for them with respect, offering decent wages and working conditions. She advocated for the right of all women to work, including married women. She offered menu suggestions and money-saving tips to housewives and called on all women to "create a will to peace." ER devoted an entire chapter to the NRA and women's responsibility to use their buying power to establish a permanent basis for fair pay. The Blue Eagle initiative, which sought to involve citizens in the New Deal, went back to the "white list," a strategy that was popular when ER had worked with the Consumers' League at the turn of the century. Consumer power now offered a way to change the world, and members of the ILGWU were powerful grass-roots partners. On 13 October 1933, ER and her daughter, Anna, sewed the first Blue Eagle labels onto garments made under the coat and suit code. Union workers handed ER a beautiful fur coat, and Dubinsky proudly stood at her side as she sewed in the label. Their work together during 1933 marked the beginning of a long partnership between ER, Dubinsky, and the ILGWU.[42]

Implementing the NRA codes proved very difficult, and Rose Schneiderman made sure that ER was aware of the problems. In 1935 ER visited Puerto Rico, where Schneiderman was working on behalf of the NRA in the island's garment industry. This visit was ER's first official tour on behalf of the president, and it demonstrates the many different ways she supported workers and combined friendship with work, publicity with writing, and advocacy with government policy. With reporters, photographers, and government officials in tow, she traveled to Puerto Rico by way of brief stops in the Virgin Islands, Cuba, Haiti, and the Dominican Republic. Residents of Puerto Rico had been granted U.S. citizenship in 1917, but the island was very much a colonial territory. Officials kept ER away from any sign of labor strikes, the independence movement that was gaining strength, and the political upheavals that were taking place across the Caribbean and Central America. Neither ER nor Schneiderman mentioned these disturbing issues, but the labor conditions they observed were disquieting indeed.[43]

Schneiderman saw her job as protecting the women working in the garment industry at the code hearings. She reported on her observations and helped ER respond to questions from factory owners. The poverty in Puerto Rico was overwhelming, and she hoped that ER's presence would help her efforts to improve a dire situation. Schneiderman was discouraged because of the indescribably low wages, the high cost of living even for basics such as rice and beans, and the lack of decent housing and clean water. While some garments were made in factories, other tasks were done by women and children working at home. Schneiderman showed ER ten-year-old girls and their mothers and grandmothers sewing under "cruel conditions." At Schneiderman's request, ER wrote a letter to the needlework code hearings to support the use of higher-quality materials to help Puerto Rico compete with France and Belgium rather than China. ER suggested that FDR should see the "vile slums" for himself and send labor and industrial people to assess the situation, which he did.[44]

Schneiderman agreed to an NRA code for factory and home workers in Puerto Rico but in private called the process and its results "a farce, a travesty." The code was impossible to enforce; work was simply shifted from factory to home, and women factory workers lost their jobs. "The only hopeful note in this picture," she observed, "is the fact that the workers are organizing very rapidly. Mr. Dubinsky of the ILGW is going to send them $100 a month for organizing purposes." Puerto Rico was a growing source of cheap labor and workers had asked the ILGWU for help. Rose Pesotta went to the island on her first assignment as union vice president and issued a critical report: "The NRA officials have not the slightest idea of how to correct glaring injustices nor do they appear to be interested in labor problems."[45]

Despite the difficulties in the most disadvantaged regions, unions hailed the New Deal's labor policy. Shortly after ER and Schneiderman returned from Puerto Rico, the Italian American dressmakers were invited to the White House to celebrate their successes in New York. On behalf of the local, Sister Margaret Di Maggio presented the Roosevelts with plaques "intended to commemorate the first anniversary of the New Deal and to express publicly the faith of the Italian dressmakers in the ultimate success of the labor policy of the NRA." ER's plaque was inscribed from her "fellow workers." With Dubinsky and Schneiderman at her side, ER "conversed amiably with others about trade union activities among the women, relating several interesting episodes revealing her own steadfast allegiance to the cause of labor and political liberty." A year later ER made a cameo appearance in *Marching On,* a movie about the struggles of garment workers and the history of the ILGWU. Her support for a union representing thousands of immigrants—eastern European Jews, Italians, and Puerto Ricans, many of them socialists—gave the workers a level of respect and visibility that was radical for the times.[46]

ER, like Rose Pesotta, never forgot Puerto Rico and kept trying to help working people there long after her visit. Ruby Black suggests that for a time ER spent almost as much effort on projects for Puerto Rico as she did on Arthurdale, the model community of miners in West Virginia in which she took a special interest. During these years ER's labor concerns were expanding beyond the garment and textile workers. Coal and copper miners, John L. Lewis, and the United Mine Workers Union were especially important resources as she learned about the danger and exploitation faced by these workers and the lack of democracy in their isolated communities.[47]

Miners and Company Stores

The Roosevelts had a much more volatile relationship with John Llewellyn Lewis and the UMW than with Dubinsky and the ILGWU. Lewis was born in 1880 in Lucas, Iowa, the son of an immigrant Welsh mining family, with unionism in his blood. His father was blacklisted for fifteen years because of his efforts on behalf of the Knights of Labor. The eldest of eight children, John entered the mines when he was fifteen, working a ten- to eleven-hour day for $1.60. On his relentless rise through the union hierarchy, he became a formidable public figure. He towered over others, literally and figuratively, at six feet and 230 pounds. His massive head with thick brown hair parted down the middle, intense blue eyes, mustache-like eyebrows, and legendary scowl were known far beyond the coalfields he sought to tame. His thunderous voice and rhetorical style were heard on the radio and in speeches across the country. A caring family man with a wife and three children, he didn't drink, gamble, or womanize.[48]

A brilliant negotiator and pragmatist, Lewis was also a ruthless leader who spared no one to gain and maintain his power. Although the UMW belonged to the AF of L, it organized everyone in the industry rather than workers in a specific trade. By the late 1920s Lewis was eager for government intervention to stabilize the coal industry and support union organizing. Thoroughly rooted in the community and culture of mine workers, he was willing to compromise, but he was also militant and unafraid to resort to violence. The mine workers' interests came first. He said knowingly of himself:

> Think of me as a coal miner, and you won't make any mistakes.... I have laid down in a mine tunnel with my face in a half inch of water, and pulled my shirt up over my head, expecting to die the next minute in an explosion.... I have never faltered or failed to present the cause or plead the case of the mine workers... not in the quavering tones of a feeble mendicant asking alms, but in the thundering voice of the captain of a mighty host, demanding the rights to which free men are entitled.[49]

John L. Lewis joined forces with Franklin Roosevelt. In the summer of 1933 Lewis threw every penny his union had into organizing the miners. Under the slogan "The President wants you to join the union," organizers saw a new strain of labor militancy, and the United Mine Workers soared to 400,000 members. Lewis joined the Labor Advisory Board established by Secretary Perkins. With Roosevelt's backing, the first NRA code for the coal industry was signed on 21 September 1933. The miners had a good contract. In exchange for government-insured stability in an industry on the brink of economic disaster, the companies agreed to "check-off union dues from the miners' weekly pay; to provide a huge raise and a basic industry-wide scale for a 40 hour week; to no longer pay miners in scrip or force them to live in company houses and buy in company stores; to send no lad under 17 into the pits; and, not least, to set up procedures for handling grievances." For the next few years, Lewis and FDR were on the same powerful team.[50]

ER had little exposure to the male-dominated world of mining, but her concern for workers' lives in the community as well as on the job drew her attention to this vital industry. In June 1933 the Associated Press reported that ER had met with a committee of hard rock miners in Tucson at the home of her good friend Isabella Greenway, a mine owner and future congresswoman from Arizona. Twenty miners presented a petition declaring that 100,000 men were out of work as the result of copper mines closing in fourteen states. They wanted a tariff on foreign copper and asked the first lady to bring "the matter to the attention of the national administration." A debate ensued, with Greenway arguing for a higher tariff because African miners worked for pennies a day, while ER advocated helping other nations increase their standard of living. Then, in a press conference, ER used the copper miners' situation as an example of the need for a broader worldview. "Their problem is much more than a mining problem," she told reporters; "it concerns the standards of living not only for themselves but in other parts of the world.... We should educate public opinion not to profit by labor anywhere unless it was done under decent living conditions.... We are creating a new social conscience. Social living and social conscience has to extend to the whole world in order that we may keep what we consider most precious in our own civilization."[51]

ER's concern for miners and their families soon became inextricably linked to the emerging program for homestead communities. Early in the administration her close friend Lorena Hickok left her newspaper job and moved to the family quarters at the White House. Presidential adviser Harry Hopkins hired her to travel around the country and report back on what she saw happening to people on relief. In long reports to Hopkins and detailed letters to ER, she described the life struggles of unemployed men and women. From West Virginia she wrote: "Scott's Run, a coal-mining community, not far from Morgantown, was the worst place I'd ever seen.... On either side of the street were ramshackle houses, black with coal dust, which most Americans would not have considered fit for pigs. And in those houses every night children went to sleep hungry, on pile[s] of bug-infested rags, spread out on the floor." The WTUL was helping miners blacklisted after a strike whose destitute families, evicted from company housing, were living in ragged tents. After ER made her first trip to Scott's Run, Hickok reported that FDR told his wife, "Get those families out of those tents before Christmas," and "with the help of the Quakers and Harry Hopkins, it was done." Then the administration began to develop the homestead community called Arthurdale.[52]

Subsistence homestead communities were established with federal aid in rural areas where the primary industry had collapsed and was unlikely to be revived, leaving residents stranded as well as impoverished. In a small-scale social experiment, miners in Appalachia, displaced farmers in the drought-stricken Midwest, and residents of declining communities in other regions were given sturdy prefabricated houses, small plots of land, animals, and seeds for a garden so they could become more self-reliant. Planners hoped that new industries would be attracted to these areas. The government funded schools, clinics, and community centers. The program had a great appeal for the president and became one of ER's major policy efforts, even though it met a good deal of resistance in Congress and its idealism was ridiculed by the press. Through her many trips to Arthurdale, Eleanor Roosevelt got to know the miners and their families.[53]

ER wrote about her visit to Scott's Run and the hard lives of miners and their families in magazine articles. She described the miners' wives making the best of bad conditions yet continuing to dream of better lives, concluding, "No business can be fundamentally sound where the human beings connected with it and who actually are the basis of whatever that business does, do not receive in return for their labor, at least, a minimum of security and happiness in life." She was particularly critical of the "company store," which overcharged miners' families for essential goods, deducted the bill from the men's wages, and kept them perpetually in debt. Employers used these and other abusive practices to control community life, preventing union organization or any other form of local democracy.[54]

ER raised these issues privately with company executives, union leaders, and administration officials. When J. S. Dudley of Hygrade Food Products in West Virginia wrote to her defending the "industrial store" and assuring her that the UMW was satisfied with the system, she immediately sent the letter to Lewis and asked for his point of view. He quickly responded, condemning the "reprehensible methods" practiced by company stores and expressing his support for the safeguards being developed through the NRA for workers not protected by collective bargaining agreements. ER stood with Lewis on this contentious matter. Lewis was skeptical about subsistence homesteads, however, and dismissed many of the community activities that ER and other labor leaders such as Dubinsky endorsed. Gardner "Pat" Jackson, one of his assistants, reported that Lewis was "disdainful of serious efforts to encourage and invite public opinion in back of his efforts. . . . [H]e felt that his individual leadership was sufficient actually to carry the day." While ER never lost sight of the miners and their families, she would eventually find herself unable to work with Lewis, who remained committed to militancy and confrontation. In the meantime, she followed the miners into the Willow Grove Mine and spoke at People's University.[55]

Teaching Citizenship

The growing workers' education movement found a natural ally in Eleanor
Roosevelt. The programs drew on her experiences as a teacher at the Todhunter School, where she had come to appreciate education as a means of
fostering the public good. Leading this effort was Hilda Worthington Smith,
known to her friends as Jane. Her family had an estate on the Hudson across
the river from the Roosevelts in Hyde Park, and she was part of ER's circle
of reform-minded peers. As part of the Women's Trade Union League network, she helped educate ER about the needs of workers and the weaknesses
in the economic and social system. At the Bryn Mawr Summer School for
Women in Industry, she was an able administrator, as well as a teacher and
poet. Genteel and gracious, she encouraged laundry workers and trolley driv-
ers to express themselves through poems, and trained them in union organizing. Caroline F. Ware, historian, social scientist, and friend, described Smith
as "a unique combination of the visionary, the realistic activist, the pioneer,
guided always by an unshakable common sense which never permits her to
substitute ideology, conventional wisdom or lofty principle for the direct approach to meeting a clearly perceived human need." A Bryn Mawr graduate,
Smith helped found the Affiliated School for Workers in 1926 and donated
her own home to become the year-round residential Hudson Shore Labor
School after the Bryn Mawr program closed.[56]

Workers' education was integral to achieving a more just society, for training individuals to take responsibility and act collectively. Both ER and Smith
believed that if all of the parties to industrial disputes were educated and had
access to information, critical thinking skills, and a historical perspective,
unions and corporations could cooperate and resolve their differences without resorting to strikes and violence. While workers' education programs included union and nonunion workers, collective action was always one of their
goals. They taught practical skills, including public speaking, organizing, and
negotiating, and prepared women for leadership positions in their unions.
New Deal labor laws were soon included in the curriculum.[57]

Early in the New Deal, ER requested that Smith send her a draft radio
address for the annual dinner of the Affiliated Schools for Workers, an organization established to expand workers' education for women and men while
reducing the competition among programs for increasingly limited funds.
The association included, in addition to Bryn Mawr, the Southern School for
Women Workers, the Barnard School, and the Wisconsin School for Workers. In her talk ER recalled having visited the Bryn Mawr Summer School
during the 1920s when her friend Marian Dickerman was teaching. "Many of
us felt the importance at that time of educating the workers of the nation," she
told her audience. Articulating one of her core principles, ER declared that

workers' education programs offered an "opportunity to teach the obligations of citizenship in this new social order which depends so largely for its success on the responsibility accepted by each individual worker as a citizen."[58]

Workers' education soon became part of the New Deal. The Federal Emergency Relief Administration (FERA) was quickly put in place to address the problems of the unemployed, under the direction of former New York relief administrator Harry Hopkins. Smith secured a meeting with Hopkins in an attempt to raise money for the Affiliated Schools. Soon she agreed to join the administration as a specialist in workers' education. Within FERA, the Emergency Education Program immediately set to work. Quickly the number of teachers, administrators, and clerical employees reached almost 200,000. They taught a wide range of courses in settings as varied as public schools, workplaces, churches, union halls, and homes. Within the program, the Workers' Education Project offered classes at times and places convenient to the workers and involved laborers and unions in advisory committees to develop the curriculum. The federal government coordinated the program with states and local communities. By the spring of 1935, almost 45,000 men and women were attending 1,800 classes taught by 480 instructors in 570 communities. Workers' education was the smallest and the most controversial of the programs offered by FERA and, later, the Works Progress Administration. Never before had the federal government supported a nationwide program to make educational resources available to factory workers and the unemployed.[59]

Like Schneiderman, Smith maintained her access to the White House through memos to and meetings with Eleanor Roosevelt. She solicited the first lady's support both for the broad program of workers' education and for specific projects such as educational camps for unemployed women. ER was especially helpful with these camps because so little had been done to address the problems of unemployed women. Smith used conferences and press conferences, letters, memos, and ER's inspection visits to build support for her program in good times and keep it from collapse in bad times.[60]

ER's support was put to the test when the House Un-American Activities Committee, chaired by Congressman Martin Dies, targeted workers' education in one of its first hearings. HUAC charged that workers' education was controlled by communists; headlines blared, "Reds Rule FERA Schools." News stories from New York to Washington State kept up a steady critique of the educational and teacher training programs. The student body and staff were criticized not only for being communist but also for being racially integrated. Smith defended the policy of presenting every point of view in economics, history, and politics, and ER argued for unions: "Of course, if you do not approve of unions nor of allowing workers to become educated you might disapprove. They do discuss communism, but I have always believed ignorance was a sure way to fall a victim to propaganda." Workers' education programs continued to expand, despite the criticism, in no small part because of ER's support. Workers' education and union membership grew in tandem, but industrial peace and economic recovery did not follow.[61]

Progress but Not Peace

In May 1934 ER took her message of labor peace to 2,700 delegates at a YWCA convention on peace and progress. She emphasized that there should be progress for everybody, not just a few, and that required including cooperation between industry and labor. She asked whether those who called labor "a menace" considered what work was like before labor unions and "what happens today in those industries in which labor unions are weak." But there was little cooperation between industry and labor. That summer the city of San Francisco was shut down by a general strike that originated with the International Longshoremen's Union, and by September, textile strikes, too, stretched from New England to the Carolinas.[62]

ER issued a call for higher ethics from leaders of labor and industry. She chose the New York Herald Tribune Institute as a forum to challenge employers who bribed labor leaders to manipulate workers and alleged that some labor leaders had ties to racketeering. "If labor as a group is going to be an important factor in the running of this country," she argued, "the integrity and loyalty of all labor leaders to their own people and in their dealings with their employers must be unquestioned." She warned that local organizers must fairly represent the workers or they would have no lasting effect. In February 1935 ER again called for cooperation between industry and labor. When asked at a press conference about her objectives for promoting economic recovery in the next two years, she said that, first and foremost, labor and industry had to act responsibly toward each other and the public; they were interdependent, and would prosper only if they prospered together. Of employers she said, "I would like to see a willingness to realize that labor must share to a greater extent and receive a fairer return for its part in the world's work, and that capital shall accept the fact of a more limited and reasonable return." From organized labor she wanted to see more recognition of their responsibilities to the public and problems addressed "not only as problems of organized labor, but as problems of the country as a whole."[63]

Union membership skyrocketed, but economic recovery remained a distant goal. The NRA codes were far less successful than hoped, as employers found ways of getting around them, sometimes with the administration's assistance. On 27 May 1935, ruling on a suit brought by the Schechter Brothers' kosher poultry business, the U.S. Supreme Court declared the NIRA unconstitutional, determining that Congress could not delegate its lawmaking authority to an administrative agency such as the NRA. In addition, the federal government was restricted to regulating interstate commerce, while this firm did business only in the state of New York. FDR took up the challenge, claiming that the Court wanted to return to the "horse and buggy definition of interstate commerce" and comparing the impact of the decision to that of the *Dred Scott* case, which upheld the property rights of slave owners throughout the United States. He turned to Robert F. Wagner, his Senate colleague from New York, and belatedly threw his support behind the National Labor Relations Act, known as the Wagner Act.[64]

Wagner had seen the need for stronger legislation to establish a balance of power between industry and labor, but FDR had paid little attention. Schneiderman and the WTUL, however, worked with Wagner on the National Labor Relations Act, a bill guaranteeing the right to form or join a union, to bargain collectively, and to strike. Employers were prohibited from interfering, using coercion against union activity, dominating existing unions, or refusing to bargain in good faith. The National Labor Relations Board was created to supervise union elections and resolve disputes. The bill was limited to workers in the private sector and left many unprotected, including domestic and farm workers, yet it was hailed as a major step forward for the labor movement. FDR had been lukewarm at best because the legislation offered little to employers, but just weeks after ER's visit to the Willow Grove coal mine, FDR signed the Wagner Act, breathing new life into union organizing.[65]

The New Deal expanded that year to include the Works Progress Administration, which employed millions of people on projects across the country. As most were in male-dominated industries such as construction, however, relatively few served women workers. The National Youth Administration was created by executive order, with strong support from ER, to help students stay in school and to develop training for young people who had finished school only to join the ranks of the unemployed. On 14 August 1935 FDR signed the Social Security Act. Despite its limitations and exclusions, it was a first step toward creating a social safety net. ER's trade union women friends had lobbied lawmakers to include clauses prohibiting discrimination against women. As the NRA closed and the National Labor Relations Board took shape, Schneiderman returned to New York and the WTUL. After spending part of her vacation with ER and several others at Campobello, she took up her last big battle, "fighting to organize the laundry workers and the hotel workers."[66]

Labor support for New Deal programs was far from unanimous. Some AF of L unions resisted government interference in organizing, deemed unemployment compensation a communist idea, and objected that minimum wage legislation would lead to maximum wages and the end of unions. Jim Carey, the young leader of the new electrical workers union, remarked that Senator Wagner and the New Deal were so far ahead of much of the existing labor movement that they looked more pro-labor than many of the unions. The federal government had succeeded in passing a national labor law giving unions a legal structure under which to organize the unorganized and to harness the newly militant workers into a formidable industrial and political force. Most of the AF of L resisted this effort.[67]

John L. Lewis pleaded for organizing in mass production industries with large workforces such as the growing automobile industry, but the AF of L continued to resist, staying with its model of craft unionism and relying on its stronghold among skilled, largely native-born, white, and predominantly male workers. On 19 October 1935, at the AF of L convention in Atlantic City, this difference in strategy culminated in a dramatic confrontation. "Big Bill" Hutcheson, head of the Carpenters Union, epitomized the federation's contempt for some of the new unions it had chartered and for the young dissident workers who attended the convention, while Lewis was the leading advocate for industrial unionism. When Hutcheson tried to silence several young rubber workers, Lewis exploded. Insults flew across the room, and suddenly, according to historian Robert Zieger, "the fifty-five-year-old Lewis vaulted a row of chairs, drew back his fist, and decked the sixty-one-year-old Hutcheson." Lewis relit his cigar and proceeded to the rostrum while the bloodied Hutcheson was helped from the hall.[68]

Lewis immediately called a meeting of like-minded labor leaders and established the first CIO, the Committee for Industrial Organization, within the AF of L. The three largest unions behind the CIO—Lewis's UMW, Dubinsky's ILGWU, and Hillman's ACWA—saw the opportunity opened by the New Deal and threw the full weight of their unions, both money and people, into organizing the unorganized regardless of the jurisdictional complaints of the AF of L. Several leaders, including Dubinsky, saw this move as a way to save the AF of L and to direct militant workers away from communist organizations. Others, including Lewis and Hillman, increasingly saw the fight as with the AF of L itself, not with the left wing of the labor movement.[69]

ER, building on her base in New York, worked with all three of these unions. She ceremonially sewed a Blue Eagle label into a union-made coat; she donned a hard hat and went deep into a coal mine to learn about wages, working conditions, and safety issues. Drawing on her experiences and her women friends, undeterred by criticism, she expanded her union base, supported legislative efforts, developed new initiatives such as the homestead projects, and helped build the workers' education program. Soon steelworkers, autoworkers, and electrical workers in the country's heartland would look up to say, not with horror, but with pride, "Here comes Mrs. Roosevelt."

3

PRACTICING WHAT YOU PREACH

First Lady Votes in Guild Minority
New York Times headline, 26 September 1940

On 25 September 1940, after enjoying dinner in her apartment in New York City, Eleanor Roosevelt went uptown to attend her first meeting of the American Newspaper Guild, CIO. Arriving at the Hotel Capitol on Eighth Avenue and Fifty-first Street, she showed her Guild card at the door and received a slip entitling her to vote. She quietly took a seat in the fourth row next to Lewis Gannett, book critic for the *New York Tribune*. With almost 350 members in the room, many eyes turned toward her, but no one on the speakers' platform acknowledged her presence. As the meeting got under way, she sat silently, writing in a small notebook.[1]

The most controversial issue was the question of endorsing FDR's bid for a third term. John F. Ryan, Guild organizer, reported on the contentious CIO state convention in Rochester. He criticized Sidney Hillman for his maneuvers to ensure that the convention threw its official support behind FDR in direct conflict with Lewis, an isolationist bitterly opposed to being drawn into the European war, who was then in an unlikely alliance with the communists. Some Guild members had been refused admission, and two were ejected from the hall. Ryan then launched into a critique of Roosevelt's policies, receiving mixed reactions from the audience. When he declared, "I have no doubt that President Roosevelt would drag us into this war by the heels if he could," someone yelled, "That's the Communist opinion," others called Ryan out of order, and the fight was on. A heated debate about the domestic and foreign policies of FDR and his opponents ensued, punctuated by boos and cheers, charges and countercharges. When the vote was finally called to "file" rather than "accept" the report, the first lady raised a steady hand, holding a folded ballot to indicate that she was a member in good standing, and voted aye. The motion was defeated 140 to 85: ER's union local had approved a report very critical of FDR. She had voted with the minority but remained committed to the union.

After one of the officers finished denouncing FDR from the dais, he handed Gannett a note asking if ER would meet with the officers after they adjourned. Gannett passed the request along to ER, and she agreed to join them. The Guild's national president, Donal Sullivan, finally rose to address the gathering after midnight. They adjourned when he finished speaking, but an informal meeting followed, lasting until after one in the morning, in which ER aired her disagreements with many of the members. She began by stating that she "did not come to this meeting to debate issues," then noted: "I didn't speak at it, but now since you ask me the question, I will reply. No, I don't agree with you." Two decades later Lewis Gannett recalled the incident as "a great tribute to a great personality, Eleanor Roosevelt, and also, on the whole, the Guild and the word and idea of democracy."[2]

FDR's second term had been marked by fierce struggles for democracy in the workplace and in the union hall. With the help of a new political alliance with labor, he was reelected by a landslide in 1936. But the New Deal faced mounting resistance at home and the imminent threat of war abroad. ER's syndicated newspaper column, "My Day," proved to be a powerful platform for explaining and defending unions to the public and for connecting with workers on a personal level. Joining the union had great symbolic value, but she also gained firsthand experience with democracy in the local union hall. As she celebrated the WTUL's national convention and cultural successes like the union play *Pins and Needles,* she began to articulate more clearly how she saw the connection between unions and democracy on the national stage.

ER's vision of peaceful negotiations by reasonable representatives of contending groups, however, was severely tested by sit-down strikes, recession, industrial and racial violence, shifting political alignments on the left, and sharp divisions within the labor movement. As the battles for union recognition raged across the country, ER stood with the auto and steelworkers in the North and textile workers in the South and took her defense of California's migrant workers to Capitol Hill. She entered her third term as first lady firmly committed to democracy as she saw it demonstrated in the labor movement. She practiced what she preached—even when, as in the 1940 vote of her union local, she was in the minority.

Joining the Guild

On 31 December 1935 Eleanor Roosevelt published her first "My Day" column for the United Feature Syndicate. She described a quiet evening by the fireplace and lunch the next day with sixteen guests at the White House, most of them young friends of her children. Publicly she presented herself as "more a painter of pictures and reporter of unimportant events!" than one of those "who interpret events and influence the public through their own expressions of opinion." The column appeared six days a week and was being distributed to sixty-two papers with a circulation of over 4 million. By 1940, syndicate manager George Carlin wrote to ER, "*My Day* goes on and on, not because it is written by the wife of the President of the United States, but because it is an honest projection of one of the great personalities of our own time."[3]

Despite ER's modesty, her column was influential, offering a vision of stability and hope to workers and the unemployed as the Great Depression dragged on and war began to overtake Europe. In diary format she noted who came to tea, reviewed books she was reading, and discussed the children's activities and her husband's health. Amid these homey details she interspersed social and political commentary on the world in general and the New Deal in particular. From the very beginning ER used the column as a way to educate the public about the labor movement. While she frequently wrote about issues that were important to working women and the unemployed, at least once or twice a month she focused specifically on unions. Sometimes she was critical, but she always adopted a constructive viewpoint.

Union members read "My Day" faithfully. Evy Dubrow, legendary lobbyist for the ILGWU, remembered being influenced by the column: "She had a great effect on all of us young people. And even the older women like my sister and my mother.... [S]he loved Mrs. Roosevelt." Eula McGill, who organized southern textile workers, affirmed that she always read "My Day": "Oh yes, oh yes!" Douglas Fraser, former president of the United Auto Workers (UAW), recalled his days on the assembly line when the workers would read ER's column, and not just because they knew she was on their side but because it was interesting. Rose Schneiderman expressed a sentiment shared by many, writing to her dear friend, "I follow your whereabouts through your column and that makes me feel as though I were in close touch with all you are doing." The president of the Arkansas State Federation of Labor confirmed these feelings when he closed a letter asking for help with tenant farmers: "May I add that My Day has an appeal to the 'rank and file.'... I hear many expressions of appreciation of these daily 'talks' from you."[4]

ER discussed unions as a positive and increasingly important part of American life at a time when they were being vilified by other columnists, business leaders, and politicians. Right from the start she gave the labor movement, and especially union women, a place at her White House table. She elaborated on the need for workers to be educated to participate in the democratic process as unionists and as citizens. On 21 January 1936, for example, ER reported that at a White House luncheon with women from across the country, "Miss Rose Schneiderman and Mrs. Maud Swartz represented the point of view of labor." A week later, after she met with a group of thirty-three supervisors of workers' education, she declared that "workers of our country should have an opportunity to study the labor movement and the economic problem of the day." Another column noted a strike on Fourteenth Street, where for days ER had seen "pickets walking up and down . . . striking because of unfair conditions or poor wages." She wondered why the parties did not sit down with a board of arbitration and work out their difficulties. She argued that unions for domestic servants could develop minimum standards so maids could work an eight-hour day and receive decent wages rather than toiling endlessly for very little pay. As the year drew to a close, she wrote about the annual Christmas party for children at the WTUL, which had started with her two youngest sons in 1925. Thirty-five children enjoyed entertainment, presents, cake, and ice cream.[5]

As unions came under increasingly violent attack, Eleanor Roosevelt made a very personal statement in support of the labor movement: on the first anniversary of her column she joined the newly formed American Newspaper Guild. The already meager wages for newsroom employees had fallen by 12 percent between 1930 and 1934, while their hours had grown longer. As a group the reporters were generally sympathetic to the New Deal. All they needed was leadership, which Heywood Broun provided. An unlikely labor leader, he was raised in Manhattan, educated at Harvard, and married to a feminist. He had a successful literary career; indeed he was credited with writing the first newspaper column. His long-standing left-wing sympathies prompted him to take action when he realized how many of his journalist colleagues were struggling to survive. On 7 August 1933 Broun called for the organization of a newspaper writers' union. In December he was elected president of the new union and vigorously pursued a forty-hour, five-day week, minimum wages, and paid vacations for the newsroom.[6]

Broun had addressed Eleanor Roosevelt directly in his column. Just before she entered the White House, he had encouraged her not to conform to the traditional role of a president's wife. "I would hold it against her rather than in her favor" he wrote, "if she quit certain causes with which she has been associated simply on account of the fortuitous circumstances that [her husband] happens to have been chosen as President." He argued that she was a human being and had a right to her own career. In 1937 he reported that pecan workers in San Antonio wanted ER to run for president, and while he knew she wouldn't, he considered it a reasonable idea: "It seems to me, at the moment Eleanor Roosevelt has a deeper and closer understanding of the needs and aspirations of millions of American than any other person in public life."[7]

Heywood Broun and the American Newspaper Guild welcomed Eleanor Roosevelt with open arms. Here, as in other aspects of her public life, ER proceeded despite the complexities of her family's position. Not only was FDR receiving complaints about the Guild, but also Anna Roosevelt and her husband, John Boettiger, had been hired by the Hearst Corporation to run the *Seattle Post-Intelligencer.* Hearst had recently settled a bitter strike with the Guild, the AFL-affiliated Teamsters were challenging the new CIO union, and Hearst was demanding financial cuts that led to layoffs, which the Guild was resisting. Anna wrote to her mother at length about stupid, insensitive executives and inexperienced and ideological union leaders. She sought firsthand reports from her mother's meetings with Broun at social gatherings. When talking with ER at the Guild picnic, Broun counseled patience with the new young union leaders, but Anna concluded that his leadership was endangering the union movement for writers. She boldly reminded her mother of her influence, remarking that it would be a major blow to the union if ER resigned. Facilitating communication between contending parties but holding her ground, as she did in so many other circumstances in which her family's personal or political interests were involved, ER passed Anna's concerns on to Broun but did not resign.[8]

That same year FDR held an off-the-record press conference with newspaper publishers and editors who were angry with the president about the Wagner Act and feared that their papers would be unionized by the Guild. FDR assured them that the new union leaders were young and inexperienced and in time would be able to "see the whole picture instead of just the passionate picture of a new movement." The nation, he told them, had to adjust to collective bargaining. Publishers must have taken small comfort from this meeting, given that the president's wife was a member of the very union they were complaining about and his arguments echoed those of ER and Broun.[9]

Two years later, in 1939, Heywood Broun died of pneumonia at the age of fifty-one. ER expressed her deep respect and genuine affection for him. She acknowledged that while not everyone approved of the Guild, he had "done a great service for many newspaper people." Three thousand mourners crowded into St. Patrick's Cathedral for his funeral, with newspaper people joined by politicians and the cultural elite of the city. Just ten days later Dick Henry, president of the Denver chapter of the Guild, announced that the executive board had nominated Eleanor Roosevelt to succeed Broun as president. Harry Wohl, president of the Chicago chapter, telegraphed her, "You are only figure in America able to take [the] place of Heywood Broun." ER quickly declined the offer on the grounds that she couldn't possibly take a full-time job. Some speculated that the communist faction within the Guild was trying to use her. The executive board decided to leave the position vacant until the next convention.[10]

ER thought carefully about the support she gave to different groups, and on two occasions she withdrew from organizations when she disagreed with their policies. She resigned from the Daughters of the American Revolution in 1939 when they barred the world-renowned contralto Marian Anderson from singing at Constitution Hall because she was African American. In a powerful gesture of support for racial equality, ER helped arrange a concert on Easter morning at the Lincoln Memorial, where Anderson sang before a huge crowd and a nationwide radio audience. ER was willing to take a stand and demand that organizations act on the basis of clear principles. She vigorously defended the American Youth Congress against charges of communism, inviting its leaders to stay at the White House and attending their hearing at a time when the left-wing group was under attack by members of Congress, but she withdrew her support when she concluded that they were no longer being honest with her and acting constructively. ER was careful not to allow herself to be used by others for their own purposes. Although she found opposition to new ideas within the Democratic Party discouraging, she rejected the idea of turning to a third party as some of her progressive friends did when Henry Wallace challenged Harry Truman in 1948. When confronted with personal attacks and charges of communism in her own union, she chose to stay and make changes within the organization.[11]

The CIO unions were directly affected by the international crises. When the German-Soviet Non-Aggression Pact was signed in 1939, leaders of the Communist Party USA immediately reversed position and strenuously opposed aid for Western allies. They were joined by the leaders of several unions, including the American Newspaper Guild, but strongly opposed by others led by Hillman who was committed to FDR's policies in Europe. Westbrook Pegler, one of the most influential New York columnists, began a crusade against communism, which he suspected had infiltrated the press and influenced the New Deal. He used his considerable investigative skills and vitriolic writing style to attack the labor movement in particular. He uncovered the criminal past of two prominent union officials, both of whom went to jail, and he won a Pulitzer Prize for exposing labor racketeering. His relentless campaign against organized labor helped shape a key element in the conservative efforts to roll back the New Deal and the Wagner Act. The American Newspaper Guild and Eleanor Roosevelt were two of his prime targets.[12]

Pegler was one of the most popular and controversial columnists of the 1930s and 1940s. The son of a well-known reporter, he wrote a syndicated column, "Fair Enough," for the *New York World-Telegram*. In 1940 the *Saturday Evening Post* described him as one of the leading editorial forces in the country. His column appeared six days a week and was syndicated in 174 newspapers, reaching an estimated 10 million readers. Even his critics described him as an artist and a man of great courage, but they also charged him with giving aid and comfort to domestic fascists. Originally a supporter of the Roosevelts and the New Deal, Pegler became increasingly critical of the entire family. ER confided to her daughter that she disliked Pegler and his attacks, though she refused to acknowledge that she read what he wrote.[13]

The clash entered the public eye in August 1940. Delegates to the Guild convention in July told ER that a small group from New York City, with Communist Party connections, had dominated the meeting, forced through resolutions, and blocked proposals to condemn communism. Some members publicly resigned, but May Craig, a friend of ER's who was a Washington correspondent for several Maine newspapers, counseled her not to quit, for "that would ruin us and do no good. It would please the publishers who don't want a Guild anyway." Soon a "My Day" column acknowledged problems within the union, but because ER felt that the Guild was having a positive effect, she announced that she would become more active. She wrote: "Until you have done your very best to make an organization useful, you have no right to leave it. For these reasons, I am *not* resigning." She began to attend meetings, write about the issues, and generate more press from her colleagues.[14]

Pegler boldly asserted that the Guild was controlled by communists and that ER was ineligible for membership because she wasn't a real newspaperwoman. When asked to comment on the piece, she said that she did not usually answer statements by Mr. Pegler, but her new five-year contract for her column made her a bona fide journalist. Because of her opposition to communism, however, she told her readers that she would start going to Guild meetings to fight communism, and if she were not a useful member, then she would resign. Pegler, calling her "a diarist and a dilettante," declared that the first step toward rehabilitating the Guild would be "to get rid of the ineligibles, starting with her." The issue would be used as campaign material against Roosevelt in the 1940 election.[15]

FDR advised her to ignore the column, and ER agreed. George Carlin, who syndicated both Pegler and ER, assured her that her column stood on its merits and that she was indeed a newspaper columnist of the first order. Her stand sparked an immediate reaction from the New York Guild. Nat Einhorn, executive secretary, wrote to assure her the Guild was pleased that she planned to become more active. She offered to come to meetings as an ordinary member so she could get to know people and understand the union's problems, if he would give her more advance notice. In a handwritten note ER asked, "Since Mr. Pegler says I am not eligible would you like a chance to decide?" Einhorn quickly confirmed her eligibility for membership, notified her of the next meeting, provided a copy of the Guild constitution, and noted that since her place of employment was New York but her assignment was Washington, she could have membership in both locals. Her dues were $2.50; she promptly sent a check.[16]

ER's increased involvement with the Guild began with the Burke-Wadsworth conscription bill in 1940, the first peacetime draft in U.S. history. This selective service legislation was a bipartisan bill that required just one year of service and limited deployment to the Western Hemisphere. FDR and his Republican challenger, Wendell Willkie, both supported it, but there was union opposition from left and right. ER approved of the bill but saw conscription more broadly as a form of government service in a democracy. When the Guild sent out a circular criticizing the legislation, she responded with a letter "to register immediately my violent opposition to many of your statements," she told the officials. In language that was unusually harsh, she charged that "to make sweeping statements seems to me stupid beyond words," and she dismissed as "claptrap" the contention that the measure was a run-up to war. While agreeing that corporations as well as workers needed to sacrifice to protect the nation, she argued that "more unselfish willingness to serve for the good of the people is what we really need—not a group of democratic citizens who are always asking and never giving."[17]

In October the Los Angeles chapter of the Guild issued a leaflet and resolutions in line with the Communist Party positions of the day, refusing to criticize the execution of Russian dissidents, Stalin's peace pact with Hitler, and the USSR's takeover of Finland. ER went on record opposing what she called this "foolish bit of pussy-footing." In mid-December she announced her support for a slate of officers to oppose the board of the New York Guild. The new slate's platform opposed the present leadership "on the ground that— regardless of whether the individuals concerned are enrolled members of the Communist Party or not—their actions over a period of years have paralleled the Communist party line."[18]

The left-wing incumbents won, largely because the election was conducted by referendum, and the New York City local, at the center of the publishing industry, had far more members than other locals. That same month Eleanor Roosevelt attended her first meeting of the Washington Guild. With her "ivory knitting needles clicking away" she listened to speeches and voted with the majority, passing Mary Craig's resolution "to denounce communism, fascism, and Nazism." The Guild, however, was affiliated with the CIO and therefore involved in a much larger political challenge within the labor movement led by Lewis and the UMW.[19]

Politics and the CIO

By 1936 the success of the new CIO was tightly linked to the policies of Franklin Roosevelt and the New Deal. John L. Lewis, along with Sidney Hillman, David Dubinsky, and others, created Labor's Non-Partisan League. The United Mine Workers backed it with half a million dollars, which (as historian Robert Zieger reminds us) was a staggering sum in the 1930s. Much of the money went directly to FDR's campaign. In New York, Dubinsky and Hillman took the lead in forming the American Labor Party to back New Deal Democrats running for office and to show that labor was a political force to be reckoned with. Lewis met with Roosevelt, campaigned for him, and made nationwide radio addresses on his behalf. The CIO unions mobilized members in an entirely new effort to get out the vote, while the AF of L had little involvement.[20]

ER's role in the national campaign was controversial, especially in the South, where party leaders worried about many things, including her outspoken views on labor and race. At the convention she declined to attend a breakfast for women delegates organized by Molly Dewson because she didn't want to cause trouble, but she was otherwise active. In the spring an article by ER appeared in the UMW *Journal.* The formal photograph, showing her in an evening dress with a long beaded necklace, was in sharp contrast to the picture of her in a hard hat at the mine just months earlier, but both stories reflected her support for the mine workers who were campaigning for FDR. Continuing her labor argument for community-level democracy, she called on the miners' wives to "do all within their power to do away with what is ordinarily known as the company town and the company stores.... [T]he ultimate result is bad when people are not free to develop themselves."[21]

As she had for so long, Schneiderman sent ER political information that she knew would also interest the president. On 16 April, for example, she wrote praising Dubinsky's "courageous" resignation from the Socialist Party to support FDR and relaying that Max Zaritsky, president of her own cap makers' union, would soon follow suit. ER had her secretary forward the letter to the president, highlighting the paragraph having to do with politics. That same day FDR's secretary forwarded the letter to Jim Farley, Democratic Party national chairman, with a memorandum from the president instructing Farley to decide when an announcement should be made.[22]

After the convention ER received a long letter from Farley indicating, among other things, that he would cooperate with the new Labor Party that Hillman was organizing in New York and thought they would garner 150,000 votes. Dubinsky was a Roosevelt elector at the convention for the American Labor Party. Despite his firm anticommunist commitment, forged in the union during the 1920s, in the last days of the campaign he was attacked by the Republicans as a communist. They called on Roosevelt to repudiate Dubinsky and the entire American Labor Party. FDR did not distance himself. In fact on 27 October the first lady spoke to 150 cheering women standing by their sewing machines at the Hudson Waist & Dress Company on Staten Island. She accepted a big bouquet of chrysanthemums from Mrs. Louis S. Gregorio, ILGWU, and told the women, "The President, I think, has shown himself to be a friend of labor and to women who work." Franklin Roosevelt won the 1936 election in an overwhelming landslide, in no small part thanks to the new CIO alliance closely connected to his wife.[23]

FDR's reelection fortified union organizing efforts, but New Deal labor reforms met with violence at the workplace. Wisconsin's Progressive senator Robert M. La Follette held congressional hearings on industrial violence, which conservatives often linked to alleged communist activities. According to the report of his congressional Committee on Civil Liberties, between 1934 and 1936 employers spent over $80 million to spy on unions and block their efforts to organize. Republic Steel stockpiled an arsenal of weapons, and Ford employed a paramilitary force of three thousand armed men. Union members and sympathizers were routinely harassed, beaten, and fired. The committee found that union rights protected by the Wagner Act were being denied through terror, intimidation, and armed brutality. Bart Logan, a white Alabama organizer for the left-wing International Union of Mine, Mill and Smelter Workers, an interracial union affiliated with the CIO, was one of only two southern witnesses to appear before the committee. Arrested three times for labor activity, he had been denied a lawyer and a jury trial and sentenced to work on a chain gang. He testified that when he was questioned about his communist activities, he was asked about his contacts with Heywood Broun and Eleanor Roosevelt.[24]

Facing brutal repression, workers were denied any semblance of democracy. As union organizing and strikes spread, ER expanded her concerns from clothing factories and mines to include steel and auto plants. In Flint, Michigan, where the Reuther brothers were leading an organizing campaign at General Motors, the UAW adopted a new form of action, the sit-down strike, inspired by workers in France. As the men occupied the plants, stopping production and keeping the company from employing strikebreakers, the strikers' wives surged into the streets, marching and singing and blocking the police. Despite the frantic efforts of pro–New Deal governor Frank Murphy, GM president Alfred P. Sloan refused the offer of government mediation from Secretary of Labor Frances Perkins. An injunction was issued, and the militia, the cavalry, and the National Guard were called out.[25]

John L. Lewis flew to Detroit to negotiate. When GM turned off the heat in the plants, workers opened the windows, and the entire complex was at risk of being destroyed. As car production declined dramatically, and under increasing pressure from the government, General Motors finally came to the table and on February 11 signed an agreement recognizing the UAW as the sole bargaining agent in the plants. Chrysler soon followed suit. UAW membership surged from 88,000 at the time of the strike to over 200,000 at the end of the year.[26]

After ER's 26 January 1937, press conference, a reporter noted that although she did not mention the sit-down strikes, the reporters "naturally" referred to them in connection with her statement that "if we are going to settle things peaceably, we have to have a spirit of good will. The fear and distrust we have are at the base of the impossibility of getting people together to talk things over rationally and reach reasonable conclusions." In response to a visit from several young women in New York who were unemployed because of their union's demands for a decent wage, a forty-hour week, and better conditions, she wrote: "Many people do not believe in unions. Unquestionably unions and their leaders are not always wise and fair any more than any other human beings. There are only two ways to bring about protection of the workers, however, legislation and unionization."[27]

On the same day the UAW reached the settlement with General Motors, ER offered a direct defense of the sit-down strikers themselves, using a human rights argument. In response to one of her readers who advocated using tear gas and armed force to evict the strikers, she concluded that for this woman property rights were all-important and "human rights meant so little that she is willing to cause blood-shed before every effort has been made to accomplish a peaceful settlement."[28]

The UAW victory in Flint accelerated the pace of organizing in other industries. In 1936 Lewis and the CIO took the initiative to establish the Steel Workers Organizing Committee. Steelmakers watched the action in Flint closely, and on 2 March, U.S. Steel agreed to recognize the steelworkers' union. More than 300,000 members signed up with the committee within two months after U.S. Steel's capitulation. By August the CIO as a whole claimed over 3.4 million members, making it larger than the AF of L. The labor movement received an unexpected boost from the U.S. Supreme Court in a set of rulings that represented a reversal of its previous tendency to overturn labor legislation. Between 29 March and 24 May, the Court upheld the Washington State minimum wage law for women, the Social Security Act, and, most important for labor, the National Labor Relations Act, securing the right to organize and join a union. Tensions mounted. As ER traveled the country giving speeches and inspecting programs, she was welcomed by thousands, was insulted by others, and received death threats from the KKK. In Shreveport, Louisiana, the police were so concerned that they stayed with her in her hotel sitting room for five hours.[29]

The growing strength of organized labor only made Henry Ford more determined to resist the UAW. On 26 May 1937 the "Battle of the Overpass" left Walter Reuther and the UAW organizers beaten and bloody as they handed out leaflets at Ford's sprawling River Rouge complex. Four days later, on Memorial Day in South Chicago at the Republic Steel plant, police attacked workers and their families who had gathered for a picnic while the pickets marched peacefully. Ten men were left dead, seven shot in the back. Thirty others, including women and children, suffered gunshot wounds. The newsreels were sent to La Follette's Committee on Civil Liberties. That evening Eleanor Roosevelt went with friends to the Rock Creek Cemetery in Washington, where the statue *Grief* had become her place for contemplation.[30]

Republic Steel led the group that came to be known as "Little Steel" (in contrast to the corporate giant, U.S. Steel) in a violent and vicious campaign to stop the union, including a public relations campaign painting the CIO as a communist-led organization. Lewis pressured Roosevelt to support the workers, but many people were uneasy about the sit-down strikes and blamed unions as well as management for the rise in militancy, wildcat strikes, and violent conflicts. The president was confident that voters were tired of the extreme positions on both sides; drawing from Shakespeare's *Romeo and Juliet* he declared, "A plague on both your houses." ER worried at this show of impartiality and offered her support for the CIO by attending a gathering of the Newspaper Guild. In July more workers were killed in Youngstown, Cleveland, and Warren, Ohio, and the Little Steel strike ended in defeat for the workers.[31]

The wave of strikes was the subject of long discussions after FDR got to Hyde Park in August. ER, whose faith had been restored in her husband's good intentions toward labor, wrote to Hickok that FDR believed "in the democratic process and [feels] everyone has been getting educated lately and perhaps he's right." On Labor Day, Lewis responded to what he perceived as FDR's betrayal, thundering, "It ill behooves one who has supped at labor's table and who has been sheltered in labor's house to curse with equal fervor and fine impartiality both labor and its adversaries when they become locked in deadly embrace." Schneiderman immediately wrote to ER that she thought Lewis was out of line and did not represent the labor movement or working people.[32]

By fall, what opponents called a "Roosevelt Recession" got under way as industrial production slowed and unemployment soared. Industries the CIO was organizing were hardest hit. Neither Ford nor Little Steel yielded, and the AF of L, less affected by the economic downturn, offered charters to workers of all skill levels and began to grow in numbers and influence. The deepening divide within the labor movement troubled the WTUL, which was trying to stay neutral. In a letter Schneiderman asked ER to address a mass meeting of women department store workers but explained that the union had voted to join the CIO. The NYWTUL had decided to work with the CIO, though Schneiderman expressed concern that doing so might result in "being thrown out on our ear here from [the] central body and the state federation." At the same time, she acknowledged that if the League voted to stay with the AF of L, it would lose its New York constituency. She attached a confidential copy of the executive board resolution but cautioned that ER might "not want to mix into this brawl." ER thought the matter over and decided "perhaps it is best for me not to attend any meeting until the labor situation clarifies itself and there ceases to be internal conflict."[33]

The conflict was not resolved and resulted in an open rupture. On 14 November 1938, the renamed Congress of Industrial Organizations convened its first national convention in Pittsburgh. Lewis was elected president, Murray and Hillman vice presidents, and James B. Carey, the twenty-seven-year-old president of the United Electrical, Radio and Machine Workers (UE), secretary-treasurer. Even though ER belonged to the Newspaper Guild, a CIO union, Carey recalled that she would do whatever she could to help labor as a whole. The tightrope she walked was stretched tighter, however, because when the new organization was formed, Dubinsky withdrew. The ILGWU remained independent for two years, attempting to bring the factions together, but in 1940 the garment workers returned to the AF of L. When asked by the press about the dissent within organized labor, ER understatedly replied that she would be very happy if the labor movement reunited, for "a divided house is always less able to look after its own interests."[34]

Regretful, but undaunted by these internal struggles, ER continued to advocate for labor. Early in 1939, when many balls were held in honor of the president's birthday and to benefit the victims of polio, she declined to attend the one at the George Mason Hotel in Alexandria, Virginia. The waitresses there were on strike for wages of more than fifty cents a day, and ER refused to cross the picket line. Waiters and waitresses should not be required to depend on tips, she said; "you should know what you are going to earn when you go to work." She explained that the reliance on tips was unfair to both the consumer and the worker while letting the employer off the hook. As long as tips were necessary, however, she was generous; that year she was voted the best tipper among women patrons by the union of railway dining car employees.[35]

ER worried publicly that labor was losing some of its strength because of the split. She kept in touch with what was happening across the country. For example in Texas she toured unionized needlework companies and met with an employer and union organizer in the pecan industry. She took up the issue of teaching young people about the labor movement and gave a radio address for the fifteenth anniversary of the Pioneer Youth Organization, which she described as a union summer program for workers' children. Stories about union-based community service projects, such as the nursery school being supported by the plasterers' union and the music program sponsored by the musicians' union in St. Louis, appeared in her column.[36]

The proposed changes to the Works Progress Administration (WPA) education programs that limited their availability to unions and excluded courses in topics such as labor education were of great concern. ER attended the Hudson Shore Labor School and worked with Hilda Smith to develop a worker service program within the limitations of the cuts that the program had experienced in the previous eighteen months. Directors of workers' education programs from twenty-eight states and cities met at Hyde Park. When the Workers' Alliance met in Washington, DC, to lobby for a CIO-backed bill to support 3 million WPA jobs, "Mrs. FDR," as the CIO *News* called her, argued that "far greater than any financial debt is the cost to the nation of underfed, under-privileged workers and their children." Many wrote to ER attacking the group as communist, but she argued that even though she disagreed with the Alliance about many things, it was critical for people to get together and talk. By speaking to the members, she felt that she offered an alternative to communism and demonstrated that "someone at least near to the seat of government is willing to listen to their troubles." ER offered a sympathetic ear and a supportive voice to workers in the Deep South as well.[37]

Organizing in the South

FDR's second term was overshadowed by the war in Europe and the recession at home. Hitler, Mussolini, and Franco were on a relentless path of destruction. While some Americans wished to insulate the United States from foreign conflict, others espoused homegrown varieties of fascism and anti-Semitism. The economy lost two-thirds of the gains made since March 1933, and by 1938 an estimated 12 to 14 million people were unemployed. Yet New Deal programs were being reduced through federal budget cuts. While the president's attention was increasingly focused on the international scene, the first lady continued to champion domestic issues.[38]

Miss Lucy Randolph Mason, who found a staunch ally in ER, was an unlikely person to become the public face of the CIO in the South. The daughter of an Episcopal minister, she was born in northern Virginia in 1882, the same year as Rose Schneiderman. In a region of the country where ancestry mattered, Mason was a member of both the United Daughters of the Confederacy and the Daughters of the American Revolution. Growing up in a deeply religious family grounded in the social gospel, she began to work on consumer issues and women's suffrage in her youth. She learned about union struggles and the rich history of labor protest in the South through her work with the YWCA in Richmond and the Southern Summer School for Women Workers.[39]

Mason, small with prematurely gray hair, combined ladylike charm with a forceful voice. After she moved north as general secretary of the National Consumers League, she became an expert on the NRA codes. In Washington she met labor leaders such as Lewis and Hillman and became friendly with ER. When Mason wanted to return to the South, Lewis hired her as the southern spokesperson for the Textile Workers Organizing Committee in Atlanta. Unlike many of her northern colleagues, she showed no hesitation in casting her lot with the CIO in a part of the country where the threads of race, labor, and communism wound into battles of epic proportions.[40]

Miss Lucy, as she was known locally, spent the next sixteen years, until her retirement at the age of seventy-one, traveling around the South presenting labor's case to a southern establishment that few union organizers could ever reach. Meeting with conservative newspaper editors and joining picket lines, she used her reputation and dignified demeanor to help protect workers facing violent opposition and crowds of vigilantes. A strong advocate for workers' education, she championed the Southern Summer School for Women Workers and brought ER to the defense of the Highlander Folk School, a controversial interracial labor program accused of being communist, a charge leveled at most interracial activities. Like Schneiderman, she communicated her political and labor news and views directly to the first lady and the president. ER also shared her own letters from Mason with FDR.[41]

Every day she felt the "sinister suppression of democracy by civil authorities" and did not hesitate to inform the White House about the reactionary businessmen and manufacturers who opposed all efforts to organize textile workers. In 1938 FDR, grown weary of the southern conservative Democrats who fought his programs, sought primary challengers for nine Democrats up for reelection who had attacked the New Deal. He agreed to a study proposed by southern liberals: their "Report on Economic Conditions of the South" found that the region was the country's biggest economic problem. Although it led the world in the production of cotton, tobacco, and other products, per capita income was half the national average, voting rights were limited to 12 percent of the population, and the schools were inadequate. Roosevelt embraced the report, and Lucy Mason personally thanked him for his support.[42]

At the time the report was released, Mason and ER had lunch together in Atlanta to discuss a proposed conference on economic and civil rights. Mason and other liberal southerners, both white and black, were forming a new organization to challenge the power structure by reducing poverty, ending discrimination, enfranchising voters, restoring economic viability, and establishing a fair system of justice, which included the right of workers to organize. The first Southern Conference on Human Welfare (SCHW) was planned for November in Birmingham, Alabama, and ER agreed to be a keynote speaker.[43]

The founding SCHW conference is often remembered for ER's quiet but visible opposition to Jim Crow: she refused to sit in segregated seating after police commissioner "Bull" Connor ordered the participants, one-fourth of whom were black, to segregate themselves to conform to city ordinances. Mason provides another notable example from that conference of how she and others in the labor movement relied on ER for assistance. After years of struggle in the cotton mills, the Textile Workers Organizing Committee (TWOC) finally negotiated an agreement with the Merrimack Mill in Huntsville, Alabama, but then management refused to sign the contract. A year-long strike followed, and mill managers began evicting workers from their company-owned homes. A Women's Emergency Committee on Evictions and Welfare assessed the situation and found "destitution, overcrowding, and undernourishment." Mason persuaded several newspaper editorial boards to support arbitration, but the impasse continued as the cold winter months set in. The Merrimack local sent a delegation to the SCHW conference with the specific intention of telling ER about their situation. They contacted Mason, and she arranged a meeting after ER's speech. As the crowd gathered, the police formed a circle around ER so the men could tell their story. Mason recalled:

> I'll never forget that sight. Mrs. Roosevelt, tall, lovely, gracious, shaking each work-hardened hand and bending her head to catch what each man said. They made their requests—for army tents for shelter to keep their families from sleeping outdoors, investigation of their plight, and aid from federal agencies. To all, Mrs. Roosevelt said, "I don't know what the President can do. I will tell him all you have told me. I know he will do what he can, but remember there are many limits to his power to help."[44]

As she and Mason left for her train, arm in arm, ER expressed cautious hope that her husband would be able to do something once she told him about the workers' plight. The next morning the union men were elated over ER's promise to take their story to the president. FDR requested the National Labor Relations Board to send investigators to Huntsville immediately and inform him of the situation. According to Mason, the personal appeal to ER and her intervention with the president were crucial: "The evictions stopped, relief was given, and it became possible for the National TWOC to rent an empty hotel for the evicted families. In the end a contract was secured."[45]

At the SCHW conference, union members included mine workers, steelworkers, and tenant farmers. They passed resolutions to improve housing, education, farm credit, and labor conditions. Race issues were addressed directly, with resolutions calling for an end to segregated meetings, discrimination in education, the poll tax, and lynching. SCHW established an ongoing organization, the Southern Conference Education Fund, directed by Frank Graham, president of the prestigious University of North Carolina. Organized labor became a major source of financial support, and Mason took a leading role on the executive council. While the SCHW was quickly overwhelmed by anticommunist attacks, ER and Mason maintained their connection. For the next two decades they continued to cooperate with the Southern Conference Education Fund.[46]

Hostilities continued at home and abroad. On 26 November 1940 ER lunched with Mason to discuss the desperate situation for CIO organizing efforts in Memphis. George Bass from the United Rubberworkers had arrived that summer to lead an organizing campaign at the Firestone plant. Identified in the press as a foreign labor agitator despite having been born in Tennessee, Bass was harassed at every turn. After acknowledging that black workers would be admitted to the union, he was severely beaten and narrowly escaped death when his car was overturned, hit with lead pipes, and doused with gasoline. The match failed to ignite, and the police arrived, but neither the district attorney nor the Justice Department took any action.[47]

Mason hoped that the White House could put pressure on "Boss" Crump, the local Democratic national committeeman, who was flouting the party platform with his antiunion stance. ER asked Mason for a report to "put in the President's private letter box by his bed" and promised she would then talk with him about the problem. Soon a special representative from the attorney general's office appeared in Memphis to investigate charges that the city administration was denying civil rights to union organizers. The district attorney and city commissioner claimed they had no knowledge of such activities and insisted that, regardless of the past, "there would be no such violations in the future." According to Mason, this sudden interest in protecting civil rights "had a most salutary effect. There was no repetition of the incidents and...CIO people could come and go unmolested."[48]

Joining Mason and ER at lunch that day was James Dombrowski, director of the Highlander Folk School in Monteagle, Tennessee, an innovative education program for workers aimed at developing union leaders in the South. ER agreed to visit the school in the spring if possible. Founded in 1932, Highlander eventually turned its focus from the labor movement to civil rights, but Mason and ER were unwavering in their support. The school was one of the programs in which ER's concerns for labor and civil rights overlapped. Like all of the labor education programs ER backed, Highlander was the target of red-baiting, from Grundy County, Tennessee, where Highlander endorsed the reelection of a union-backed sheriff, to the Dies committee in Washington,

DC. In an attempt to show that ER supported subversive activities, a local bank released to the press a copy of her $100 check to Highlander. Bank officials justified releasing confidential records by accusing the school of being antigovernment—that is, communist—claiming that its funding was therefore a matter of public interest.[49]

On *Pins and Needles*

Union democracy met with somewhat more success in New York. As FDR began his second term, ER celebrated with her core union supporters in the WTUL and the ILGWU and more clearly articulated the connection between unions and democracy. In 1936, when the WTUL held its first convention of the decade, several delegates and WTUL officers stayed at the White House. "A waitress, a stenographer and a dressmaker from New York and a textile worker from Alabama have unpacked their bags in the Lincoln room of the White House," reported the *New York Times*. The president greeted them upon their arrival, and ER joined them for breakfast each morning. Pauline Newman noted in *Justice* that they had a chance to talk informally with the president. One of the southern delegates said she was impressed by ER's "great sense of humanity" and because "she knows the facts." Speaking to the convention, ER emphasized the important role of the WTUL to educate not only union members but also nonunion members to take action "where just the unions themselves cannot do it." William Green, Labor Secretary Perkins, and Senator Wagner also spoke.[50]

Eula McGill, a textile worker from Alabama, was one of the women who stayed at the White House. Just twenty-five years old, tall, with dark curly hair and a soft smile, she had quit school and started to work as a spinner in the Dwight Textile Mill near her home in Resaca, Georgia, when she was just fourteen. She worked the night shift, 6 pm to 6 am, with no rest breaks or time to eat, leaving her young son with her parents. She had been a delegate to the Birmingham Central Labor Union, where a small group was starting the first Women's Trade Union League chapter in the South, and was invited to attend the convention in Washington on a scholarship. McGill's picture appeared in reports on the convention in the *New York Times* and the *Birmingham Herald*. "I had gone and asked my boss if I could be off," she later recounted. "I never told him why. He never asked me. But when all this came out in the paper about us being guests of the White House, when I got back I didn't have a job because of my union activity."[51]

Though McGill was fired, she "never regretted it." She stayed with friends and family that year and helped to organize bakery workers, iron ore miners, and steelworkers. Eventually, she had a long career with the Amalgamated

Clothing Workers. Whenever ER was coming to the South, her secretary would contact McGill, and she would go to see her if possible. McGill was at the 1938 Southern Conference for Human Welfare and was part of the escort committee when ER addressed the ACWA convention in 1944. She did not tell ER when she was fired because "She would have tried to help. I didn't want to bother her."[52]

Not long after the convention the WTUL suffered a sad loss with the unexpected death of Maud Swartz. Just a few days after she and Rose Schneiderman had attended FDR's second inauguration dinner, Swartz had a heart attack. ER praised her friend in "My Day" and attended the funeral, which meant a great deal to Rose. Maud, she told ER, "would have been terribly pleased at the honor of having you there. I shall miss Maud terribly. We had been pals for twenty-three years." This was a time of great transition for Schneiderman. She had cousins still in Poland under Nazi threat, her mother had recently died, and for the first time in her adult life she moved to an apartment on her own. In typical fashion she threw herself into her work.[53]

Schneiderman was quickly appointed to succeed Swartz as New York's secretary of labor while continuing as head of the WTUL. ER sent congratulations, but some League members resented her absorption in her government responsibilities, which left the organization with little leadership or new initiatives. After the Supreme Court upheld Washington State's minimum wage law, Schneiderman proposed a minimum wage law for New York that finally passed. After what she called "our own Thirty Years War," the women met with some organizing success. ER and Schneiderman recorded a radio program together that focused on a woman's right to work outside the home and on the need for women to receive a salary for the work they did at home. They also discussed the proposed Fair Labor Standards Act, the last major piece of New Deal legislation providing minimum wages and maximum hours for women and men. ER forwarded her comments to the president.[54]

As always, the Equal Rights Amendment was on the agenda. The two women met at Hyde Park in August to discuss the Business and Professional Women's convention's endorsement of the amendment. ER reaffirmed her long-held belief that "for industrial workers the situation is entirely different" from that of professionals. "If the public really understood the situation, they would treat this question from the point of view of the realities rather than accept a theory, which is a fine theory, but has no relation whatsoever to the realities of the situation for the industrial woman worker."[55]

The ILGWU continued to make progress in its organizing drives and union label campaigns. Less than a week after the election ER was in Minneapolis and St. Paul to deliver a talk on world peace. Representatives of the ILGWU wanted her to sew the first label in a coat as she had done in New York City. She was not available, but in *Justice* the front-page story was headlined "First

Lady Urges ILGWU Label on All Women's Wear," followed by ER's letter encouraging every woman to look for the label when she shopped. In the
middle of a major organizing drive, the union had signed a label agreement
with some of the leading dress factories. The article reported that throughout
labor union circles in the Northwest "the endorsement given to the ILGWU
Label by the First Lady of the Land will serve as a mighty stimulant towards
its spread and acceptability by retailing interests everywhere."[56]

Perhaps the most unusual collaboration between ER, Rose Schneiderman,
and David Dubinsky centered on the ILGWU's theatrical production *Pins
and Needles.* In 1935 the ILGWU formed its own Labor Stage Company and
the ILGWU Players. Theater and music were part of social unionism and a
potent way to reach out to the thousands of new young members. This performance turned out to be a very different kind of musical revue. The music
was light, the dances were fast, and the lyrics both funny and full of "social
significance," as sung by union members from the shop floor. They sang and
danced about labor conditions, politics, and international relations. *Pins and
Needles* was an overwhelming success, playing for three years on Broadway
and making two national tours from New York to Los Angeles. It became
the longest-running musical of the 1930s and earned about $1.5 million for
the ILGWU.[57]

One of the show's biggest fans was Eleanor Roosevelt. A few months after
it opened, Schneiderman wrote to ER noting that she had seen Dubinsky.
"He wondered when you were going to see *Pins and Needles* and if you
would please let him know ahead of time so that he can save seats for you."
ER attended the next month seated between the two of them and went back-
stage to congratulate the union performers. ER devoted her "My Day" column to the performance, concluding, "No one could be disappointed by this
entertainment."[58]

After Dubinsky sent pictures of the production and the sheet music to ER,
she asked if he would come to the White House and perform a few sketches
for the president—especially "Four Little Angels of Peace," a song critical of
Hitler, Mussolini, British foreign secretary Anthony Eden, and Emperor Hi-
rohito of Japan. On 3 March the cast went to Washington to put on a short-
ened version of the show for the twenty-fifth anniversary of the Department of
Labor. On the way there, they were whisked into the White House to perform
for FDR. They were taken completely by surprise. "One of the biggest thrills
of my life," enthused one cast member. "He was aware that we rehearsed after
working in the shops," said another. ER "seemed to be aware of every person
in the room, making certain that everyone met the President and was well
looked after." Another cast member remarked, "The President roared; but
the person who liked it best was Mrs. Roosevelt." According to Dubinsky,
ER made sure that he sat next to the president, and FDR took everything,

"including the domestic political digs, with great good humor." The show was edited for political reasons as well as time limitations, but it was perhaps the first theatrical performance to take place in the White House.[59]

The national media coverage including magazines such as *Look, Life,* and *Vogue* gave momentum to the idea of a road show. When the show returned to Washington in December, the opening night was sponsored by the national WTUL, and ER gladly served as honorary chair. The show evoked praise as well as controversy everywhere. The Daughters of the American Revolution warned members that it was "so profane, so Communistic and so broad in its implications as to make it unfit for any child to see and to make an adult ashamed to be in its audience." In Des Moines people lined up to get their money back. The National Broadcasting Company banned the songs from its radio network. *Pins and Needles* was also criticized by the left for underplaying class conflict. On the road the performers were beset by racism as they defended their black cast members and by anti-Semitism as they stood up for their Jewish members. Sometimes they found themselves with no place to sleep or eat because they refused to patronize places that would not admit everyone.[60]

The labor movement's international concerns were expressed in songs such as "Four Little Angels of Peace." Many union members were distraught over the war in Spain, Japan's aggression on the Asian mainland, and especially the advances made by Hitler and Mussolini. The garment unions were leading efforts to help the Jews in Europe, many of them family members and friends. "Sick with anguish," Schneiderman asked ER and Frances Perkins for help for her cousins in Poland, and joined a labor consortium to help Jewish refugees flee Germany, Austria, and Poland and resettle in Palestine. Support for the Léon Blum refugee colony in Palestine was chaired by William Green, and Schneiderman organized the women's committee. At a fund-raising dinner for 1,500 people at the Astor Hotel, ER was a featured speaker.[61]

In her column ER was quite critical of the other speakers at the head table. While union leaders were doing more than most other Americans to address the atrocities that were occurring overseas, they were wrapped in a cloak of smugness, she said, patting themselves on the back for being lucky enough to live in the land of the free. Green could be proud of the AF of L's achievements, but, she asked her readers: "Are you free when you can't earn enough, no matter how hard you work, to feed and clothe and house your children properly? Are you free when your employer can turn you out of a company house and deny you work because you belong to a union?" ER saw no room for complacency about the problems at home as Americans addressed the problems abroad.[62]

ER's close ties with the garment unions reached a high point in 1940, as she came to see democracy in action in the union. On Sunday, 2 June,

Eleanor Roosevelt assumed a new role as keynote speaker at the ILGWU international convention held at the World's Fair in New York. Over 120,000 people crowded into the Court of Peace to celebrate the union's fortieth anniversary. Musicians from the Metropolitan Opera Company performed, as did the Eva Jessye Choir, hailed as the nation's foremost African American choir, and the union symphony orchestra and chorus. Dubinsky introduced ER as a "staunch believer in the rights of labor" and a genuine advocate of equality for women in every walk of life.[63]

In her address ER outlined what she saw as the fundamental similarities between unions and democracy: "In a trade union, each member, while he may have his own preferences and the freedom to say and do as he likes, must in the interest of the union, discipline himself to achieve results for all of the members. That is so in the labor movement as a whole.... That is so in a democracy. You have to learn respect for the individual but you have to learn also that each individual must have self-discipline and unselfishness in the interest of the whole group." She warned that the nation was facing a serious crisis and must respond with reason and not fear. She placed her trust in the members and hoped "that this nation will prove that we can carry forward the banner of Democracy."[64]

Although she was a well-known member of the CIO-affiliated Newspaper Guild, ER addressed the ILGWU at the convention where the union voted to return to the AF of L. Calling on labor "to come together and be unified again in order to attain its maximum strength," she set an example for all of the union members. In "My Day" she shared the profound impression the gathering had made on her with millions of readers:

> As I looked out over those faces and listened to them sing "The Star Spangled Banner," it seemed to me that my faith in the reality of our democracy was deepened. When you feel something deeply, it is doubly hard to be articulate. Here stood a cross section of our people from many lands, bringing us an infinite variety of backgrounds and cultures. However, in all of them one felt, a confirmation of our determination to remain free and cooperatively to work out our destiny in the world. . . . I get such a sense of power and solidarity from a meeting like yesterday's, that I can face the uncertainty of the future with far more strength and courage.[65]

Labor and the Third Term

The Democrats were resoundingly defeated in the 1938 midterm elections, despite FDR's efforts on behalf of liberal candidates, and soon the warring labor factions realigned politically. In addition to the split between the AF of L and the CIO, friction emerged within the CIO itself. John L. Lewis was strongly opposed to any intervention in the war in Europe and increasingly opposed to the possibility of a third term for FDR. Sidney Hillman, by contrast, had strong ties to Europe, was increasingly concerned about the threat of fascism, and joined the administration's National Defense Advisory Commission, bringing the CIO closer to Roosevelt. At the same time, Dubinsky brought the ILGWU back into the AF of L. Ever the political activist, Dubinsky was committed to helping in Europe and saw Lewis's position as closer to that of the communists. The two leaders of the CIO and AF of L united behind a third term for FDR in opposition to Lewis.[66]

ER played a prominent role in this campaign. In January 1940 the UMW held its golden anniversary convention. Lewis used the occasion to continue his criticism of Roosevelt and to warn against the looming threat of war. He thundered: "Let no politician believe or dream that he is going to solve the unemployment question . . . by dragging America into war. . . . The formula of taking our young men and making cannon fodder out of them and covering the rest of the nation with grief and lamentations . . . that day is gone if my voice and strength can make any contribution to prevent it." ER was concerned about a break between Lewis and the president and aware of how difficult both men could be. Lewis's assistant Pat Jackson and his wife joined a family dinner at the White House. As Jackson recalled, after dinner "Mrs. Roosevelt asked me to sit alone with her. . . . She told me that she and I had a very special responsibility to try and prevent a break between John L. Lewis and her husband. She said, with charming candor, 'you and I, Mr. Jackson, are both working for the same kind of people. They are both prima donnas. We've got to try to control this prima donna quality in both of them.' "[67]

The Democratic convention was threatening to fall apart over FDR's choice of the liberal Henry Wallace to replace John Nance Garner as his running mate. In a hurriedly arranged trip, ER flew to Chicago and rallied thousands of delegates behind the ticket with her cry that this was "no ordinary time." She did not convince Lewis, however. On 25 October he endorsed Republican Wendell Willkie. In a powerful, hate-filled speech broadcast across the nation, Lewis condemned FDR and vowed to resign as president of the CIO if Roosevelt were reelected. ER wrote to her friend Jim Carey, "This is a serious threat and a dangerous way to function in a democracy." Lucy Mason proffered her resignation from the CIO to protest the speech. Lewis, however, had misread working men and women. They voted overwhelmingly to reelect Roosevelt. At the CIO convention following the election, Hillman saw to it that the resignation of John L. Lewis was offered and accepted, and the beloved Phil Murray, soon to lead the United Steelworkers of America (USWA), was elected president of the CIO.[68]

ER began to criticize Lewis more strenuously, but she never wavered in her support for the mine workers. Just after the election, for example, the UMW wrote to her about the Neely-Keller Mine Inspection Bill. She urged her readers to talk to their representatives about safeguarding workers in dangerous industries. While the bill was pending in Congress, she wrote, "1,598 workers have died in accidents, some of which are believed to be due to faulty inspection. I know only too well that no legislation can completely correct any situation, but it seems to me that the people of this country would not want to neglect any steps which might make a little safer the lives of the men in this industry, which is basic in our economy."[69]

Going to Congress on Behalf of Migrant Workers

As FDR prepared the United States for war, ER remained attuned to the problems of ordinary people. Despite eight years of innovative policies and programs, unemployment and poverty remained high. While unions grew in numbers and power, farmers lost their land, and millions of men, women, and children moved from south to north and east to west in search of a livelihood. Drought and dust storms, as well as the invention of the tractor, forced untold numbers of families off the farm and drove them west. In one year alone, an estimated 5 million people made interstate moves, 1 million of them connected with farming. Nowhere was the impact of this problem greater than in California. On 22 April 1940, John H. Tolan, a member of the House of Representatives from California, became chair of the newly created Select Committee to Investigate the Interstate Migration of Destitute Citizens.[70]

In defense of the migrants, ER testified before a congressional committee. Camps for the migrant workers were part of the New Deal programs for emergency relief. She reported on the people and the conditions in these camps just as she did on other New Deal programs. On one tour she visited several migrant camps in the San Joaquin Valley before addressing a packed house of students at Stanford University. The *Stanford Daily* reported that ER "expressed dismay with sanitary conditions in the majority of private camps, but praised the government camps for their attempts to rehabilitate the Dust Bowl refugees."[71]

Frances Perkins and CIO representatives testified before Tolan's committee, arguing that workers on large farms and in agricultural industries such as canning, packing, and processing should be brought under the federal wage and hour laws. Several days later the first lady told the committee that people living in the camps had no idea what it meant to be a citizen, so oppressive were the conditions under which they labored. ER's testimony followed that of Mrs. David Thomas, there with five of her children to tell the committee about their travels in search of work and about union membership fees that were too high. When asked about the fees, ER strongly opposed this or any other form of union racketeering and suggested that Congress "get the head of the local up here and have it out with him, and do something about it."[72]

While the newspaper headlines highlighted the first lady's focus on planning for peace and ending racketeering, it was the Thomas children who won ER's attention. "A finer family you could not ask to see," she reported. Her readers, however, focused on Mr. Thomas. Some found his electrician union's membership fee of $300 objectionable—one CIO member wrote that the entry fee for his union was $1.50 and could be paid in installments by those who had been out of work—while others defended it as justified by the benefits received and the maintenance of high work standards. After reading her avalanche of mail, ER called for "real out in the open discussion of the whole situation."[73]

As FDR began his third term, ER remained a staunch union member, increasingly concerned with the nation's defense but unwilling to abandon economic and social programs at home. In her own union local she defended the communists' right to speak but also defended her right to disagree with them. In order to remain a member of the American Newspaper Guild, she switched from the New York City local to the one in Washington, DC. She gained an understanding of democracy in the labor movement from experience in her own local, as well as from the successes and failures of the unions across the country. The labor movement became an integral part of her political work, and she drew strength from its meetings. As a union member in good standing, she was able to inspire other union members with her words and deeds and helped to define their goals to the general public as the nation prepared for war.

4

In Her Own Way

Just a word in these days of crisis and of storm and stress to express
my deep appreciation for the great service you are rendering in
your own way.

A. Philip Randolph to Eleanor Roosevelt, 5 August 1943

By 1940 A. Philip Randolph, president of the Brotherhood of Sleeping
Car Porters, could say that he knew Mrs. Roosevelt very well, as "they had
met and talked about various questions." The September 1940 issue of *The
Black Worker,* the official union paper, announced that the first lady would
address the biennial convention in New York. Eleanor Roosevelt's presence
symbolized her growing commitment to labor and civil rights issues despite
the increasing pressure to curtail these rights as war approached. Just two
months before the election, her appearance before the largest black union
in the United States was shocking to those in both parties who were determined to keep African Americans on the political margins. On Monday evening, 16 September, ER entered the grand Mecca Temple on West Fifty-fifth
Street. The hall was filled with men and women who worked as porters and
maids on the trains that carried her and thousands of others across the county.
On stage she joined her friends and colleagues Dr. Mary McCleod Bethune,
director of Negro Affairs for the National Youth Administration, and Walter
White, secretary of the NAACP. From the podium ER praised the union's
achievements and assured the delegates of her continued support.[1]

The paper conveyed the symbolism of the occasion for union members
and the public: "The vision of democracy in action passes in review before
the audience, and also the future greatness of an America which recognizes
and grants to all its citizens a full share of their rights under the Constitution:
as the First Lady of the Land, Mrs. Eleanor Roosevelt moves gracefully out of

the Mecca Temple escorted by one who has long served well the public of her native land—a Pullman porter—while the audience sings with verve and éclat, 'God bless America.'" ER's name led the roll call when Randolph wanted to highlight the Brotherhood's prestige and power.[2]

But this was not an occasion for speeches alone. ER learned from African American citizens how they had been denied the opportunity to serve their country in the armed forces: doctors and dentists turned away, high school teachers beaten by white soldiers at recruiting stations. The U.S. Army upheld segregation, assigning black soldiers to separate units commanded by white officers which performed laborious support roles rather than being trained for combat, and blacks were entirely excluded from the air corps. After the speech ER met with Randolph and his colleagues. Then, by going directly to FDR with her information, she helped arrange a meeting for them with the president. He gave thought to the resistance of the military to integration, as well as the public outcry in the black community against segregation in the armed forces. Just weeks before the presidential election, his staff weighed southern white votes against the increasing number of northern black votes. While segregation remained the policy, African Americans' status within the armed forces was advanced when FDR made two key appointments: Colonel Benjamin Davis, the grandson of slaves, was promoted to brigadier general in the U.S. Army, and William Hastie, dean of Howard University Law School, was named a civilian aide to Secretary of War Henry Stimson. Both appointments were welcomed by the black community and opposed by the military and civilian defense leaders. Stimson blamed the situation on "Mrs. Roosevelt's intrusive and impulsive folly."[3]

Historians mark this period as the beginning of an important shift in ER's thinking about racial issues, from the need to provide equal opportunities to the importance of ending all discrimination. While unwavering in her commitment to democracy in the workplace, ER also reconsidered her depression-era labor positions in response to the booming war economy, emerging leaders, and growing hostility and violence toward her domestic reform agenda. She came to believe that the right to strike should be given up voluntarily and that arbitration was a viable alternative to work stoppages. She felt that with some government help, women could turn to unions to address their workplace issues, so her opposition to the Equal Rights Amendment lessened. For African American workers, however, she was convinced that stronger government intervention was needed to prohibit discrimination in defense industries.[4]

ER increasingly put her message of citizenship in an international perspective and took that message to union meetings large and small, calling for workers' involvement in the political process as well as in the workplace. Behind the scenes and in the public eye she fought those who wanted to rescind labor's rights and formed alliances with younger labor leaders whose social agenda she shared. With her picture on the cover of *Time* magazine, ER's status as the "world's foremost female political force," was attributed in part to her husband's power, but also to her influence on public opinion. Ranked by the popular *Reader's Digest* as one of the ten most powerful people in Washington, ER worked to strengthen the labor movement for all workers, men and women, black and white, during wartime and in the peace to follow. A. Philip Randolph expressed what many progressive labor leaders and rank-and-file workers felt when he wrote to "My Dear Mrs. Roosevelt" to say "just a word in these days of crisis and of storm and stress to express my deep appreciation for the great service you are rendering in your way to the cause of democracy in general, and justice for the Negro people in particular."[5]

The Right to Strike in Wartime

In his fireside chat with the American people on 29 December 1940 President Roosevelt declared: "We must have more ships, more guns, more planes— more of everything. . . . We must be the great arsenal of democracy." Three months later FDR signed the Lend-Lease Bill giving aid to Great Britain but stopping short of entering the war raging in Europe. The military buildup accelerated as the army and navy requested billions of dollars for defense, nearly 1 million young men were drafted, and unemployment dropped below 10 percent for the first time in over a decade. Union membership surged, but 1941 saw the largest number of strikes since 1919.[6]

Writing from Florida, ER spelled out clearly her most basic principles regarding labor and democracy. She told her readers that union organization was "the only protection that the worker has" to improve and protect wages and working conditions, and that fair contracts would benefit employers as well. Union leaders were no more infallible than employers, politicians, or government officials. They should be held to the same standards as other leaders, she believed, but abuses did not justify an attack on the "fundamental right of organization for mutual support." No one should be forced to join a union, but the right to explain the principles behind labor unions should be safeguarded, workers should be free to listen to advocates of organizing without fear of retaliation, and, she concluded, they should have the right to join a union.[7]

ER's expressions of solidarity with labor were carried across the nation. On 5 February 1941 she met with striking workers from the International Brotherhood of Electrical Workers (IBEW) at the Leviton Manufacturing Company in Brooklyn, telling them that she had "always felt it was important that everyone who was a worker join a labor organization." She praised the high ideals of the labor movement, which stood for the interests of the group rather than for the selfish interests of individuals. Sounding the familiar theme of personal responsibility and group action, she said, "Only if we cooperate in the battle to make this country a real democracy where the interests of all people are considered, only when each one of us does this will genuine democracy be achieved." The IBEW *News* reported that her address was distributed by wire to more than two thousand newspapers and was broadcast over the radio networks. A front-page story appeared in the *New York Times,* and the speech was printed in the *American Federationist,* the AF of L paper. Jim Carey later expressed the importance of her role, writing to her: "The strikes to which millions of workers are subjected are very great. They frequently feel almost desperately misunderstood by their fellow Americans. It is more reassuring than even you can ever know to have it made plain to them that one in your position understands that so simply and so deeply."[8]

As labor unrest grew, strikes threatened production goals. Almost 2.5 million men and women went out on strike in 1941. Many workers with union contracts had not received pay increases since 1937. CIO unions led almost 70 percent of the striking workers in defense-related industries such as steel, shipbuilding, and aircraft. FDR created the Office of Production Management (OPM) and named Sidney Hillman, president of the Amalgamated Clothing Workers, and William Knudsen, president of General Motors, as co-directors to set the standards for the war economy. Unlike most union leaders, Hillman had supported FDR from the beginning of the New Deal, and they now had a close working relationship.[9]

This federal office was an unlikely role for the Russian-born rabbi's son who had arrived in New York City with his younger brother Harry in 1907. Having given up his religious studies, he became well versed in Darwin, Marx, political activism, and trade union organizing. He moved to Chicago and worked as an apprentice cutter, where he met and married Bessie Abramowitz, button sewer and labor agitator. They had two daughters, but Bessie remained active in the union. With thousands of skilled and unskilled workers and the support of Chicago's progressive reformers, they formed the Amalgamated Clothing Workers of America. In suit and tie, with wire-rimmed glasses, Hillman looked more the Talmudic scholar than labor leader. Although he never lost his Yiddish accent, he was able to hone the skills that would earn him the title of "labor statesman."[10]

Hillman developed a vision of industrial unionism that included not only negotiations with employers over wages, working conditions, and grievance procedures but also the provision of unemployment insurance, low-cost housing cooperatives, and a system of labor banks. He remained independent of the AF of L and joined the Socialist Party but also learned to negotiate with employers, politicians, academics, and lawyers. After joining the New Deal he sought Eleanor Roosevelt's support for his political activities, and ER turned to him for advice about labor issues, asking his help to resolve disputes on projects such as at a factory in Arthurdale, West Virginia, where she insisted on a union workforce.[11]

A staunch supporter of FDR's foreign policy, Hillman took a leave of absence from the ACWA to assume his new job as co-director of OPM with Knudsen. Their roles were never equal, however, and Hillman lacked the authority necessary to prevent business as usual. His attempts to use government military contracts to enforce labor laws met with limited success. As massive walkouts loomed at critical defense plants, he urged FDR to establish the National Defense Mediation Board. This tripartite board, with representatives from industry, government, and labor, successfully established industrywide wage patterns for the first time and erected a system of "industrial jurisprudence" on the shop floor. ER praised the board at her press conference, stating, "We must, as far as possible, find...ways of meeting the objections of both sides."[12]

Numerous proposals for antilabor legislation were introduced in the House of Representatives. One bill called for strikes on defense work to be prosecuted as "treason." FDR let it be known that he was going to rely on the new mediation system, and ER called the treason penalties "perfect nonsense." At her press conference she explained that as usual whenever two groups justify what they are doing, there were bound to be differences of opinion, but the patriotism of either side was never in question. As mediation proved unable to prevent strikes, legislation to curtail union activity moved ahead. FDR soon sent 2,500 armed National Guard troops to break a strike in the aviation industry, with CIO leaders blaming the Communist Party for the walkout.[13]

When Germany invaded the Soviet Union on 22 June 1941, the U.S. Communist Party immediately shifted its position again, this time to support FDR and prepare for war. Unions began pledging not to strike but to settle grievances through arbitration. John L. Lewis and the United Mine Workers, however, retained staunch isolationist views and opposed the emerging industrial relations system. In the fall Lewis took the miners out on strike after the National Defense Mediation Board ruled against them as they sought a union shop for the "captive mines" owned by the large steel companies. As the blast furnaces came close to shutting down, FDR sent the case to a special arbitration panel; ER expressed relief. The panel ruled in favor of the miners, but the news arrived on 7 December 1941, the day Japan attacked Pearl Harbor.[14]

Labor leaders quickly took no-strike pledges for the duration of the war. Even Lewis joined the call for unity, and employers agreed to refrain from lockouts. FDR established a new War Production Board and a more powerful War Labor Board to settle disputes. Hillman, who had alienated both the left and the right while at the OPM, returned to his union. In exchange for pledges not to strike during the war, to accept limited wage increases, and to cooperate with efforts to improve production, the government approved a "maintenance of membership" formula whereby newly hired workers in organized plants automatically joined the unions and paid dues. Under this system union membership increased by almost 50 percent during the war, from over 9 million to almost 15 million.[15]

Conservatives took advantage of the war to wage a campaign against the labor movement, and ER rose to its defense. Westbrook Pegler and other influential journalists charged that unions were not merely unpatriotic but corrupt. When newsreels were shown in the theaters, audiences began to boo pictures of striking workers. A series of Gallup surveys in 1941 found that the majority of people opposed the right of defense workers to strike, and most believed that union leaders possessed too much power. Once again ER was one of Pegler's prime targets. During the first six months after Pearl Harbor he criticized her for refusing to cross a picket line at a theater, calling her support for the strikers an "unmistakably Hitlerian attitude." *Time* magazine described her friend Joseph Lash as a "pinko." Pegler characterized ER as an aggressive politician who ran with "bands of thugs and extortioners with union charters." ER requested more information from the unions and continued to write positive labor stories. After her review of the 1942 film *Native Land*, a documentary about labor struggles and Ku Klux Klan activities narrated by the left-wing singer Paul Robeson, Pegler called the film communist propaganda and the leaders of the AF of L "terrible liars." Addressing ER he asked, "Would you be willing to listen to proof, or is that asking too much of your time?" ER proposed a meeting, but both the CIO and the AF of L advised her against taking the bait.[16]

The vast majority of unions kept their no-strike pledges, and the unauthorized wildcat strikes that did occur had only minor impacts on production. Other problems seemed more intractable. Unions were increasingly critical of the wartime freeze on wages. The Textile Workers' convention condemned FDR's formula limiting pay raises but leaving profits and prices unchecked as "unjustified, unnecessary, unrealistic and undemocratic." Shortly after the resolution passed, ER strode onto the stage at Carnegie Hall to address the 1,100 delegates and a national radio audience. Speaking about labor's role in the postwar world, she urged the union to adopt a more statesmanlike and worldwide approach. But, recognizing workers' grievances with administration policies, she requested time to speak after the broadcast, when she could offer honest and constructive criticism. First, she urged labor to reunite; then she acknowledged the hardships workers had faced and admitted that wages and prices were not always fair. The fault, however, lay not only with Congress and the administration but also with people who did not speak out. She called on citizens in a democracy to be eternally vigilant, articulate their positions, and vote to make the government responsive to the will of the people.[17]

Just as ER was advocating that workers engage in political action, the mine workers were threatening a strike of disastrous proportions. In May 1943, after a long visit from British prime minister Winston Churchill to plan the Allied invasion of Europe, FDR was met with a strike in the coal mines. After arguing for months with the War Labor Board over a pay increase of two dollars a day, Lewis led 500,000 miners out on strike, closing more than three thousand mines. Steel mills shut down, railroads cut back, and production of guns and tanks slowed. Public opinion polls showed Lewis to be the most unpopular man in the country, and public anger over the strike turned against the entire labor movement.[18]

While continuing to bring the plight of workers to the attention of the public, ER criticized Lewis as irresponsible. The *New York Times* reported, "Mrs. Eleanor Roosevelt urged the United Mine Workers today to halt their strike action and resort to governmental agencies to gain their rights." In three short paragraphs she argued again that workers had an inalienable right to strike, but they should give it up voluntarily and work with government mediators. At the same time, in her "My Day" column ER reiterated her long-standing concern that company-dominated mining towns were undemocratic and recognized the need to protect workers from the rising cost of living, especially when they had no choice but to buy goods at inflated prices from company-owned stores. She did not condone the work stoppages but felt that the miners deserved some concessions. She concluded, "The whole principle of company stores and company houses is a bad one, and I hope some day we will get rid of them."[19]

ER was not above appeals to patriotism in her efforts to persuade both sides to settle the conflict. The strike had interrupted the flow of coal, which was vital for the production of weapons carried by the sons of the miners who were fighting in far-off places. "When everything else is said and done," she wrote, "this is the question that the parents of these boys will ask themselves as they sit idly day by day—'Are we making it harder for our boys?' They trust you, Mr. John L. Lewis, are you letting them down? Coal Operators, how will your sons feel?" Using the president's emergency war powers, FDR took over the mines and ordered the miners back to work, reminding them that they worked for the government, "and it is their duty no less than that of their sons and brothers in the Armed Forces to fulfill their war duties." Lewis complied and the men returned, but they staged two subsequent walkouts, and an agreement wasn't reached until 1944.[20]

Both the Roosevelts feared, with good reason, that the coal strike would lead to bitter antilabor feelings and antilabor legislation. The Smith-Connally War Labor Disputes Act was working its way through Congress. ER publicly criticized the bill and encouraged FDR to veto it, but in private she blamed Lewis. She wrote to Lash: "I'm upset about all the things happening to labor & yet I think they have to a large extent brought it on themselves. The split in their own ranks, the slowness to clean up in the unions that needed to be cleaned from within, John L. Lewis & poor public relations always spell disaster." FDR did veto the Smith-Connally Act, but Congress overrode him. While limited to wartime, this was the first successful legislative attack on New Deal labor policy, and included expanded presidential authority to curtail strikes, threatened strike leaders with criminal penalties, and prohibited political campaign contributions by unions. David Kennedy concludes that it was "a transparent effort to slap at Roosevelt and stem the growth in labor's political influence that the New Deal had fostered."[21]

That summer the first lady sought respite in the hills and streams of Nevada, taking long walks at sunrise and in the evening under the moon and stars. She told her readers, "We cannot settle strikes by refusing to understand their causes, we cannot prepare for a peaceful world unless we give proof of self-restraint, of open mindedness, of courage to do right at home, even if it means changing our traditional thinking and, for some of us, a sacrifice of our material interests." When one reader accused unions of undermining the war effort, she called on others to praise workers for their "magnificent achievement in production." In the fall, while visiting an estimated 400,000 servicemen in camps and hospitals in the Pacific, she heard soldiers from mining families in Pennsylvania and West Virginia bitterly criticize the strikes and John L. Lewis. ER concluded that the situation was not entirely Lewis's fault but rather "the fault of all of us, who should have paid attention long ago to the conditions under which the miners worked."[22]

ER drew on the letters that ordinary people sent her to present opposing points of view to her readers. When the wife of a strip miner enclosed pay statements to show how little her husband earned, ER not only shared the information in her column but also presented the mine owners' response, as well as her skepticism about their defense. More important, she encouraged working people to tell their own stories and chastised her newspaper colleagues for emphasizing labor unions' shortcomings over their accomplishments. At the sixth CIO convention in late 1943 she told the delegates that the unions "should tell the story of injustices, of inequalities, of bad conditions, so that the people as a whole in this country really face the problems." The problems of women and African Americans in the labor force were of special concern to her, but the strategies she advocated to advance their rights took different directions during the war.[23]

Equal Pay and the ERA

As women entered the workforce during the war, they replaced men who went off to war and they responded to the opportunities created by the booming economy. Some took the high-paying skilled jobs typified by "Rosie the Riveter," but most found work as clerks and seamstresses and in the other low-paying jobs in which women were already employed. ER focused on government and employer support for child care to help working mothers and equal pay to protect those taking skilled jobs in war plants, but she saw unionization as the best way for working women, as full citizens, to protect themselves. As the number of union women increased, ER's opposition to the Equal Rights Amendment lessened. The WTUL remained staunchly opposed to the ERA and moved closer to the AF of L, but this time she did not follow the League's lead.[24]

In 1942 ER declared that if she were young again, she would go into a factory and learn a skill. She advised women not to marry too young but to expand their horizons and contribute to their country. In September she joined FDR on a cross-country tour of factories and military bases. ER paid special attention to the women who were involved in war production. In the new Ford aircraft plant at Willow Run in Michigan, the first lady saw hundreds of union women working side by side with men as riveters, welders, blueprint readers, and inspectors. She wrote to Joseph Lash that FDR was amazed by the increase in women workers: "At last he is interested in nursery schools, family restaurants, etc." The president approved the first government-sponsored child care centers under the Lanham Act, although child care remained controversial for those who thought that the mothers of young children should stay at home.[25]

All across the country, managers spoke to ER about the need for more women workers, and she advocated a wide range of community services to help them. By 1944 more than half of employed women were married and over thirty-five years old; one-third of them had young children. Child care and cafeterias in the workplace were no longer optional but necessary. When ER toured the Cadillac and Packard plants in Detroit, where over half the workers were women, she praised their child care programs but concluded that the needs of most working mothers were not being adequately met. As the war progressed, she noted how much more the British government was doing. In the United States, she wrote, "when there is a cafeteria where the workers get hot meals, it is always shown with great pride as though it were a tremendous achievement, when actually it is essential. . . . [W]omen workers in the textile mills in some parts of our country are expected to work a full eight hours with no time off for lunch. . . . [T]he basic reason must be that many of us have not yet learned that human beings are not machines."[26]

Equal pay for equal work was important policy for women during the war. ER and her colleagues at the WTUL were as committed to this issue under the War Labor Board as they had been under the National Recovery Administration. The UAW and the UE had filed an equal pay complaint against

General Motors, and the War Labor Board ruled that when women and men performed the same quantity and quality of work, wage differences because of sex were discriminatory. This ruling was quickly followed by General Order 16, which allowed companies to adjust the wages for women and men on a voluntary basis and permitted equal pay clauses to be added to collective bargaining agreements.[27]

The WTUL had lobbied for this policy and was quick to follow up on enforcement. Republican governor Thomas E. Dewey asked Rose Schneiderman to stay on as secretary of the New York Department of Labor, but she declined and returned to full-time work as WTUL president. On a cold January morning she joined ER for breakfast in New York. They had much to talk about. Both women were to appear at a joint rally for the women's auxiliaries of the AF of L, the CIO, and the Railroad Brotherhoods in February. They knew that the gains women were making in the wartime labor force were temporary, so they were concerned about postwar planning. Perhaps the most important issue on their agenda, however, was equal pay. A survey by the New York State Department of Labor found that more than 150 plants reported differences in their wage scales for men and women, despite the rulings of the War Manpower Commission. The WTUL was preparing an equal pay bill to be introduced in the New York legislature in March. Toward the end of February the women met again at the Cosmopolitan Club, this time with a number of New York State union leaders "anxious to talk over the problems of the League and its opportunities for usefulness in the future." In June ER lunched with William Green, Phil Murray, and other national union leaders to discuss the WTUL.[28]

The WTUL, however, was losing strength and focus. The split between the AF of L and the CIO had had a damaging effect. The AF of L had pushed Schneiderman not to admit women who were affiliated with CIO unions as WTUL members by threatening to withdraw its financial support, meager as it was. Meanwhile, some young union women supported the Equal Rights Amendment and were deciding not to join because of the group's unbending opposition to the ERA. As unions increasingly offered their own labor education programs, the League's programs were seen as less necessary.[29]

Recognizing the growing strength of union women, ER began to moderate her stand on the ERA. She was still opposed but took her lead from the broader base of women in both the AF of L and the CIO. As early as 1939 she told a news conference that the stand taken by the National Woman's Party was ideal but not yet practical. In early 1944 she warned Schneiderman that the opponents of the ERA needed to adopt new tactics. She proposed a Department of Labor survey of sex-based legislation to determine what protective legislation was still necessary. ER argued, "Women are more highly organized, they are becoming more active as citizens, and better able to protect themselves, and they should in all but certain very specific cases which are justified by their physical and functional difference, have the same rights as men." She shared the letter with Secretary Perkins, who informed her that a study was underway. The Democratic Party endorsed the ERA in the party platform, but union women remained opposed, and ER declined to make a statement.[30]

Working women flooded into unions during the war. The number of female union members rose from 800,000 in 1940 to 3 million by 1944. They went on strike, attended labor education programs, and gradually assumed leadership roles in their locals. A 1944 UAW survey reported that three-quarters of the locals responding had at least one female shop steward and 60 percent had women on their executive boards. The number of women delegates to the national convention increased from eight in 1940 to seventy-three six years later. Formal barriers to women's membership came down, although some locals challenged the new policy. By 1945 women were no longer barred from unions in the AF of L or CIO, and separate women's locals were a thing of the past, with the exception of the bookbinders.[31]

ER had high expectations for women's participation in the democratic process of the unions. Her message on the importance of women's active engagement is visible in two events she attended with her friend Dorothy Bellanca, vice president of the ACWA-CIO. In November 1941 ER joined Bellanca at a meeting of clothing workers in Troy, New York. The *Advance* reported, "With the simplicity and friendliness which have made her famous, Mrs. Roosevelt climbed the old wooden stairs of the Troy headquarters to talk over workers' problems in a real down-to-earth fashion." She began by telling them: "It is your duty as leaders to see that everyone works together to do his share of the work and not leave the responsibilities to a few. Some people look only for the flaws in a union. If all members become active and work together, they can remedy such flaws." She encouraged them to work together to make a better life, starting in their communities and spreading to the world.[32]

In May 1944 ER addressed the national convention of the Amalgamated Clothing Workers of America in Chicago. Sidney Hillman introduced her. In a speech on citizenship she told the delegates that helping nations around the world and meeting the needs of the poor at home required that people register and vote, exercising their responsibilities as citizens in a democracy. At the luncheon honoring Dorothy Bellanca's thirty years of service to the union, ER praised her friend in similar terms: Bellanca, she said, "has drawn other women into the active work of the union, she has represented them on the board, and she has probably been more effective than anyone else in making them feel their responsibilities."[33]

ER did not publicly challenge the ACWA or the ILGWU about having so few women in their leadership, as she did the Democratic Party. She did, however, rebuke the CIO unions, both privately and publicly. When ER was told that Phil Murray had agreed to the principle of full employment in the postwar period but felt that women whose husbands made enough to support them should be barred, she told her friend Jim Carey that she was surprised that Murray "should agree to anything that sounds like Hitler." Carey quickly assured her that this report was not accurate and that the debate had focused on the need to "provide work opportunity for all those able and willing to work at their highest skills." ER was clearly not satisfied and reiterated that she refused to accept the implication that "any group of women, because they are women, are banned as such!" Emphasizing her displeasure, ER's signature slipped from "very cordially yours" in their first exchange to "sincerely" in the last letter.[34]

The next year ER publicly chastised the CIO for the lack of women at its convention. In a speech before the assembled delegates she observed, "There doesn't seem to be a great many women here and yet I want to say a special word to women because the gentlemen have had the running of the world a very long while and women have only just begun to take a more active part in citizenship." She went on to talk about the growing political importance of women, the many women who would be considered for appointments in the administration, and most important to her, the need to engage women members as active participants in the union even though it added to their existing list of responsibilities.[35]

ER acknowledged the problems encountered by minority women on a personal level. In the war economy black women were no longer limited to jobs in domestic service, and the resulting shortage of servants was blamed on Eleanor Roosevelt. White women accustomed to having black servants at their beck and call circulated rumors about "Eleanor Clubs" set up by servants to demand higher wages and shorter hours. At ER's request the FBI conducted a special investigation and found that no such clubs existed. ER wrote in her "If You Ask Me" column that instead of forming clubs maids should "enter a union and make their household work a profession." Concerned as always about putting her principles into practice, ER wrote to Jim Carey asking about working conditions at the Lerch Dry Cleaners, where the White House had its laundry done. She had heard that the workers were underpaid, black women especially, and she did not want to patronize the establishment if that was the case. Carey responded that the firm was notoriously antilabor and recommended the smaller Aladdin Cleaners on Columbia Road, which had one of the best CIO contracts.[36]

On the national level, black women had moved into new job openings during the war, but racial discrimination was rampant in the factories and shipyards, and they faced hostility and violence from white women as well as men. They were caught in the middle of struggles between gender and race, but still their working lives improved under policies and programs that ER advocated for women, as well those won by the black labor movement led by A. Philip Randolph.

Sleeping Car Porters and Fair Employment

"Charismatic," "exquisite in bearing," "master of rhetoric and oratory," "handsome," "commanding," "courtly": otherwise dispassionate historians use these words to describe Asa Philip Randolph. An African American labor leader adored by his followers, he was considered haughty and aloof by others. Some of his colleagues in the black community distrusted him, and he was a perpetual thorn in the side of many white labor leaders. All agreed, however, on his stature as a leader of the labor movement and the civil rights movement, which he saw as inseparable. Born in Crescent City, Florida, in 1898, Randolph was the son of the Reverend James William Randolph, a tailor and ordained minister, and Elizabeth Robinson Randolph, a skilled seamstress. He graduated valedictorian of the class of 1907 from the only academic high school for African Americans in the state. He gravitated to New York, became active in the Socialist Party, and took up the struggle for social justice on the street corners of Harlem. Lucille Green, a graduate of Howard College, a widow, and an entrepreneur, became his wife. She shared his socialist politics and earned enough to support them both. He joined forces with Columbia student Chandler Owen to found and edit *The Messenger*. Under their leadership it became an influential journal that gave voice to claims of discrimination and injustice, and opposition to World War I.[37]

Randolph became a union leader when he was recruited by the black men who worked as porters on Pullman cars. By 1925 George Pullman's company manufactured and operated sleeping cars on most of the nation's major railroads. Over twelve thousand porters and maids, almost all African American, provided service on the cars. Even though they were steadily employed, the porters earned more from tips than from their wages; they had to pay for their own food, lodging, and uniforms, were not allowed to ride as passengers on Pullman coaches, and could not be promoted to the whites-only job of conductor. White passengers condescendingly called them all "George." The porters had tried several times to organize a union, but the company hired spies, fired union activists, and set up a "company union," which the workers could not control. In June 1925, five hundred porters formed the Brotherhood of Sleeping Car Porters (BSCP) and asked Randolph to be their leader. He was a well-known speaker and writer, he had a reputation for honesty, and he was not a porter, so he was employed by the union and the Pullman Company could not fire him.[38]

The organizing drive was long and slow, given the vulnerability of black workers in general and the strict surveillance exercised by the Pullman Company. Like other labor leaders, Randolph saw the opportunity presented by the New Deal. Membership surged when the NRA protected the right of workers to organize. When an election was held in 1935, the BSCP was certified as the legitimate representative of porters and maids. The group was the first black union to be granted a charter by the AF of L. Despite Randolph's philosophical ties to Lewis and the CIO, he felt that he needed the AF of L's backing in negotiations with the Pullman Company. Two years later he signed a contract with Pullman, which he announced as "the first victory of Negro workers over a great industrial corporation."[39]

A. Philip Randolph and Eleanor Roosevelt shared fundamental commitments to democratic justice and to the active participation of all citizens in public life, regardless of color and class. They both thought that public opinion and racial alliances were important, and both were committed to the labor movement as the best way for workers to improve their lives. The fact that they also differed over key issues and strategies makes their relationship all the more remarkable. Randolph, a lifelong socialist, never joined ER in the struggles of the Democratic Party, which she saw as central to social and economic progress. He saw economic exclusion and political marginalization as inextricably intertwined and not capable of being resolved through traditional politics. In 1941, when meetings with the president failed to produce significant results, Randolph expanded his goals to include ending discrimination in the defense industries and changed his strategy from holding meetings and conferences to the radical display of power through marches and demonstrations. He began to mobilize African Americans across the country to converge on Washington, DC, for a massive march to demand defense industry jobs, a threat to disrupt the capital which ER and other liberals found alarming.[40]

Randolph was determined to seize the possibilities offered by the defense industry buildup. Large corporations receiving government contracts not only flouted the labor laws but also openly discriminated against African Americans, either excluding them from employment outright or consigning them to the most menial jobs. While ER and others succeeded in getting black youth trained in National Youth Administration programs, they were turned away by potential employers. Others were denied entry to trades because the unions refused membership to all but white workers. Randolph proposed that ten thousand African Americans march down Pennsylvania Avenue to protest job discrimination. With union leader Milton Webster, he embarked on a tour of the southern divisions of the BSCP to try out the idea. In town after town, black people set aside their fears and were galvanized to take action. Randolph formed a national March on Washington Committee, and the sleeping car porters took the message to their communities. The call was amplified in the black press, money was raised, field offices were established, trains were hired. Organizers expected that 25,000 black citizens would march on Washington demanding that FDR issue an executive order ending discrimination in national defense.[41]

The first lady was also traveling the country that spring, visiting black housing projects and homes, colleges, and churches, and returned with stories for FDR that expressed African Americans' growing determination to become full participants in civic life. Worker solidarity, however, required racial equality within the unions. Some African American workers were militant trade unionists, such as Chicago's black packinghouse workers and the 35,000 black members of the UMW. In the steel and auto industries, however, many black workers had decent jobs and were wary of union racial policies, a stance reinforced by fierce antiunion campaigns on the part of employers. Earlier that spring, during a strike at Ford, Mary McCleod Bethune had sent a confidential memo to ER explaining how company managers had used black workers in their antiunion campaign. She predicted a bloody race riot if black employees were used as strikebreakers in Ford's back-to-work effort. ER quickly passed the memo to the president, who supported efforts to bring the black workers out of the plant to stand with the labor movement.[42]

Black workers, often in dangerous but critical jobs, were crucial to the industrial organizing effort; even many prejudiced whites realized that they could not be successful without enlisting blacks. The 1941 CIO convention condemned discrimination for weakening the country in the fight against Hitler. Still, racial tensions broke out on the shop floor. When black workers launched protests and strikes demanding fair treatment not only in hiring but also in transfers and upgrades, white workers who opposed these policies staged walkouts. Conflicts over equal access to housing and recreational facilities were common.[43]

Sidney Hillman was well aware of the racial problems in the defense industries and attempted to address them, bringing in leading black New Dealers to help. Will Alexander was his consultant in charge of minority employment, and Robert Weaver was chief of the Negro Employment and Training Branch. As complaints about discrimination in defense industries came in, Hillman sent a letter to defense contractors reminding them of their obligation to hire all qualified applicants, but his co-director, William Knudsen, did not sign it. Neither industry nor unions cooperated. Hillman was no more successful at using the defense contracting mechanism to enforce antidiscrimination policies than he had been in enforcing the labor laws.[44]

Walter White and Aubrey Williams went to see ER about the problem. She used one of the many letters she had received as impetus to push Hillman. The Washington Youth Council had complained that black workers were being discriminated against in defense program activities. The first lady asked

Hillman to investigate, but he was slow to respond. On 25 May the president sent a note to Knudsen and Hillman suggesting that a certain percentage of black workers be hired for factory work on the basis of their qualifications. Knudsen, responding for Hillman as well, rejected this idea and assured the president that quiet pressure on contractors and unions would be enough to increase hiring of African Americans. ER took the initiative to invite a group of black leaders and government officials to lunch at the White House to discuss training, defense production, and contracting. As he did with black leaders around the country, Hillman claimed that progress was being made, but Weaver and others countered with the facts of rising black unemployment and discrimination by employers. Alexander wanted nondiscrimination clauses written into government contracts and contractors held responsible for compliance. ER was convinced that more needed to be done, but exactly what remedy might work remained unclear.[45]

As ER was pressuring Hillman, Randolph set 1 July as the date for the March on Washington. FDR wanted the march called off, fearing chaos, injuries, and the negative effect on Capitol Hill. He turned to his wife for help. ER was worried about this new tactic and tried to change Randolph's mind. When that failed, she helped negotiate a compromise. First, ER assured Randolph that she had discussed with the president his invitation to address the gathering, but she feared that the march was a serious mistake and would set back progress toward integration, particularly in the army. She cautioned in a letter, "One must face situations as they are and not as one wishes them to be." Randolph respectfully disagreed but had her letter published in the *Pittsburgh Courier,* a black newspaper with national circulation, to present her point of view as that of an influential person who was "a strong and definite friend of the Negro."[46]

Finally, with the help of New York City's mayor Fiorello La Guardia, other New Dealers, and ER, a meeting was arranged with the civil rights leaders and FDR, Secretary of War Stimson, Secretary of the Navy Frank Knox, and OPM heads Knudsen and Hillman. ER had left Washington for the Student Leadership Institute at Campobello, but in addition to her behind-the-scenes work, she wrote a column on the problem clearly stating that African Americans were unable "to participate in national defense, or to obtain employment in defense industries." She then provided an example of a successful ILGWU training program that assisted young black women to move out of domestic service and into union factory jobs without racial discrimination. She called on employers and unions to solve this problem.[47]

In the White House meeting Randolph uncharacteristically cut short the president's storytelling and asked FDR "to issue an Executive Order making it mandatory that Negroes be permitted to work in these [defense] plants." When the president replied that he couldn't do it, Randolph said, "I'm sorry

Mr. President, the march cannot be called off." When asked how many people he planned to bring, Randolph answered, "One hundred thousand, Mr. President." No one knew whether it was a bluff; even Randolph had been surprised by how eager ordinary African Americans were to participate in this demonstration.[48]

A committee was formed, the executive order was drafted, and Randolph reviewed and strengthened several versions. From Campobello, ER helped get Randolph's agreement on a final draft and then urged FDR to sign it. On 25 June the president signed Executive Order 8802. For the first time the federal government acknowledged employment discrimination and called on employers and labor unions "to provide for the full and equitable participation of all workers in defense industries, without discrimination because of race, creed, color or national origin." The Fair Employment Practices Committee was established to investigate grievances, monitor compliance, and publicize findings. Randolph telegraphed ER that the executive order had been signed and the march had been called off. He offered his sincere gratitude for her help; she returned his respect and affection, expressing her hope that this was only a starting point and that there would be more progress to come. Benjamin McLaurin, a vice president of the BSCP, reaffirmed the importance of ER's understanding of justice and her ability to persuade the president to address the problems. Executive Order 8802 and the Fair Employment Practices Committee were a turning point in the fight for black rights and a major victory for Randolph and his union.[49]

ER continued to work with Randolph and Hillman. When the Brotherhood of Locomotive Firemen and Enginemen, which excluded black locomotive firemen from membership, negotiated a contract that would bar blacks with decades of experience from working on new engines and routes, Randolph declared the union was forcing African Americans "off the trains upon the human scrap-heap of unemployment." The BSCP organizing committee announced a new National Citizens' Committee to inform the public about this outrageous situation, and ER agreed to act as honorary chair. Hillman attempted to provide integrated housing for workers in the rapidly expanding defense industries. Aware of ER's commitment, he wrote to both ER and FDR seeking support for Defense City, an integrated housing project for UAW workers in Ypsilanti, Michigan. Although FDR asked the Federal Housing Administration to look into the proposal, it was eventually rejected by Ford.[50]

Once the United States entered the war, African Americans were determined to secure democracy and racial equality at home as well as victory over fascism abroad. Racial tensions escalated as whites fiercely resisted blacks' integration into industrial workplaces and urban neighborhoods. Both blacks and whites migrated to northern and western cities in unprecedented numbers as the demand for workers multiplied. As historian David Kennedy describes it, "by the summer of 1943 Detroit thundered with war production and throbbed with racial tensions." "Hate strikes," in which whites refused to work with blacks, reached a peak, and racial tensions mounted over inadequate and segregated housing, transportation, and recreation. That summer, in the sweltering heat on Belle Isle, an amusement park on an island in the Detroit River, tensions boiled over. On a Sunday afternoon 100,000 people, mostly black, gathered to cool off. The bridge to the mainland was packed, fights broke out between black and white teenagers, rumors flew, and soon riots raged through the streets with gangs of whites and blacks attacking each other and anyone else in their way. It took 3,800 federal troops to restore order. At the end of the riot, twenty-five blacks and nine whites were dead and nearly a thousand people were injured.[51]

ER lamented this conflict, admitting that she would prefer not to think about it because it "gives one a feeling that, as a whole, we are not really prepared for democracy." She was sick at heart, she wrote, "over race riots which put us on par with Nazism which we fight"; the violence "makes one tremble for what human beings may do when they no longer think but let themselves be dominated by their worst emotions." For some the cause of the bloodshed was clear. The *Jackson Daily News* declared: "It is blood on you, Mrs. Roosevelt. You have been personally proclaiming and practicing social equality at the White House and where ever you go." ER was undeterred. She hosted the opening of the CIO's integrated canteen in Washington, DC, a racially segregated city, where white hostesses mixed with black soldiers and sailors. For this embrace of the most feared form of "social equality," she was vilified in papers across the country. Lucy Mason wrote to her about a racial strike at the Alabama Dry Dock and Shipbuilding Company in Mobile, in which management blamed the violence on the new executive order.[52]

Early in 1945 ER noted in "My Day" that she had met with a group of union women who were going to Great Britain on an exchange visit. Although her column said nothing about the delegation's makeup, one of the four women was Maida Springer, the young garment worker who had become very active in the ILGWU. Dubinsky recommended her for the program, and she became the first African American woman to represent labor internationally. In New York she was honored by a luncheon of over one hundred labor and civil rights leaders. But racial issues quickly surfaced when Springer arrived in Washington. Segregation policies in the capital meant that she could not stay at the same hotel with the other three women, take a taxi to the meetings, or get a cup of coffee in the nearby diner. While honored to stay in the home of the esteemed black leader Mary McLeod Bethune, Springer felt that she was being used by the government as a symbol of racial progress that didn't exist. She was ready to quit. Bethune put the events in perspective for her and also called Eleanor Roosevelt, who made a car and driver available, enabling all four women to travel around the city in safety. Tea at the White House was part of the preparation for the trip, and Springer was excited. In retrospect, what impressed her most was how ER put them at ease: "She tried to give us a sense of the importance of our mission and the problems that we faced because we were going directly to England." The trip was the beginning of a long and distinguished international career for Maida Springer.[53]

A Secret Weapon

On 28 August 1942 the first lady wrote to "My dear Mr. Reuther" to say, "I shall be delighted to have you dine with me at the White House on September 3rd, at 6:45 Pm." Walter Reuther, the thirty-five-year-old tool and die maker from Wheeling, West Virginia, just the same age as the Roosevelts' eldest son, was head of the General Motors Department of the UAW, and he had caught the attention of ER as well as the president. In her autobiography ER recognized 1942 as the year she came to know "some of the younger men, like James Carey and Walter Reuther, who were coming rapidly to the fore in the labor movement." As Reuther put it, "Mrs. Roosevelt and I became really very, very close and warm friends." Initially he talked to her about his ideas because she had the president's ear; he declared that she was his "secret weapon" during the war years. After the war, as ER and Reuther worked together to advance the cause of justice in the labor movement, the Democratic Party, and the nation, he became an adviser and confidant. Eleanor Roosevelt connected with the new labor visionary, and they quickly developed a deep and lasting friendship that centered on their shared vision of a democracy in which workers are full citizens.[54]

Walter and two of his brothers, Victor and Roy, were emerging labor leaders. Their parents, Valentine and Anna, were German immigrants firmly grounded in the Socialist Party, and their father, a beer wagon driver, was active in the local labor movement. The parents instilled in their five children a strong commitment to social justice, trade unionism, and political action. Walter Reuther left high school before graduating and took up the skilled trade of tool and die making. In 1927 he was lured to Detroit, toolbox in hand, where he earned more money, had more responsibilities, and honed his skills at Ford's River Rouge plant. He switched to the night shift and finished high school.[55]

Reuther never lost a day's work at the beginning of the Great Depression, but he was painfully aware of the deteriorating conditions around him. He became more politically active but left Ford in 1932 for an interesting experiment going on in Russia. The Soviets had purchased from Ford all the equipment necessary to manufacture the Model A and were recruiting skilled workers to help establish a huge factory in Gorky. In January 1933 Walter and Victor Reuther set off on a three-year adventure. Speaking German and then Russian, they rode bikes around Europe, visited relatives in Germany, saw firsthand Hitler's rise to power, and finally took up work at the Gorky plant in the early days of industrial planning and worker participation. They were impressed with Soviet planning but aware of the increasingly repressive tactics of the regime. The brothers traveled home by way of China and Japan, returning to a very different Detroit in 1936. Reuther's biographer Nelson Lichtenstein described that year as a turning point for Walter: "He got married, won election to the United Automobile Workers executive board, ran a successful strike, and established a powerful union base among the thousands of autoworkers on Detroit's West Side."[56]

By 1940 Reuther had become a leader of the anticommunist left, both in the labor movement and on the national stage. He supported FDR's bid for a third term and delivered the UAW's thirteen-city radio reply to John L. Lewis when the UMW leader endorsed Willkie. Hillman appointed him to the national manpower training committee. Reuther took seriously the president's call for the United States to become the arsenal of democracy and believed that some of the best ideas for managing war production could come from the workers. He proposed to transform the entire unused capacity of the auto industry into one huge aircraft production unit through his "500 Planes a Day" plan. After Pearl Harbor he proposed a "Victory through Equality of Sacrifice Program" to balance proposed changes in labor standards with a ceiling on profits, a cap on executive salaries, rationing, and price controls. Although his plans were rejected by industry and Congress, ER was impressed that "someone is doing some thinking."[57]

ER's thinking on full employment and postwar reconversion was invigorated in the summer of 1943 by a long conversation with Reuther, then a vice president of the million-member UAW. Walter and May Reuther spent a warm Sunday at Val-Kill. They sat in the sun and talked for several hours, then enjoyed supper on the porch and watched a brilliant sunset. ER's young guests had hopes and dreams for their lifetime. "Prosaic things like new industries, expanded peacetime production, better relations and cooperation between management and labor," she told her readers, "translated themselves into new and wonderful living for people whose lives have been drab in the past." To her daughter, Anna, she wrote: "He is much the most interesting labor leader I've met & I hope you meet him. . . . Now he is dreaming dreams of the Postwar World & you would find him interesting." To her friend Joseph Lash she remarked: "That young man has imagination. He wants the President to include some 2d line leaders like himself with the big boys." She put him in touch directly with Bernard Baruch, who was already working on wartime and postwar adjustment policies with Congress.[58]

Reuther expanded on some of his ideas in a thank you note. He saw workers as an integral part of the leadership needed to achieve national goals. He wanted American labor to change its "narrow pressure group thinking and become a dynamic, positive movement in the mobilization of broad, democratic forces in America." He attributed the slump in war production to the failure to include the human factor in the equation as well as the machines. In his words, management and high-powered advertising executives in charge of war production agencies were "under the illusion that American labor can be mobilized by the same promotional techniques used to sell cigarettes and toothpaste." He proposed as a test case the Willow Run plant, which he was confident could "get a minimum of thirty percent increase in bomber production without any additional manpower." ER was both "interested and horrified" by his letter.[59]

In his 1944 State of the Union message President Roosevelt took up the challenge of postwar planning. He ended his speech with a call for economic security in peacetime through an economic bill of rights ensuring decent jobs, housing, education, and medical care for workers and families, farmers and businessmen, of all races and religions. FDR wove all the threads implicit in the New Deal into a stronger fabric for postwar society. After listening to the speech over the radio, ER told her readers that this "second bill of rights" stated in specific terms what had been the goals of the New Deal since 1933. She cautioned, however, that to achieve these aims, the burdens of war had to be shared equally.[60]

FDR didn't mention unions in his call for national service, but the next day ER brought them into the discussion. The sacrifices had to be shared, she wrote, pointing out that while unions had agreed not to strike during the war, there were still problems in the workplace that needed to be fixed. Challenging the press to report on labor's accomplishments as well as its shortcomings, she concluded, "It would be helpful if the newspapers would begin to chronicle the gestures of self-sacrifice that have been made by every group." When asked in a press conference about steps to prevent postwar unemployment, ER emphasized again the importance of cooperation "in the world" as well as in the country, urging that industry, labor, and government work together, echoing the themes of her union convention speeches. But Congress was in the control of conservatives, and FDR's proposals met strong resistance and were soon blocked.[61]

How to achieve reconversion from a wartime to a peacetime economy was fiercely debated within the White House in 1944. James Byrnes, director of the War Mobilization Board, led the argument for the military, insisting on continued restriction of civilian production and arguing that any sign of complacency could give strength to the enemy. Large businesses agreed, fearing that they would lose civilian production opportunities to the small companies. Donald Nelson, director of the War Production Board, thought it was time to begin an orderly process of transition. Lifting restrictions on materials such as aluminum that were no longer needed for the war effort would enable small companies to begin building schools, hospitals, and appliances. As defense plants wound down, government programs would be needed to help workers transfer to other jobs. ER unequivocally joined Nelson in this debate, arguing for plans to keep current workers employed and ensure jobs for the returning soldiers. Reuther led the labor supporters, finding that neither Byrnes nor Nelson had realistic plans. Baruch, then heading the postwar adjustment effort under Byrnes, shared information with ER, and she asked Reuther for more information on his proposals as well.[62]

In addition to their conversations, Reuther sent ER long letters and supporting documents about his ideas, including one for a "Peace Production Board" or "Office of Peace Mobilization" to "present a practical plan that will capture the imagination and arouse the interest of millions of our people." He did not see military requirements and civilian conversion as a conflict of interests. He realized the need for legislation in the long run, but he saw short-term programs and executive action as necessary to meet immediate needs and counter criticism in the coming presidential campaign. ER sent his ideas on to Baruch, who responded with a serious and detailed critique. Like Jim Carey, Lucy Mason, and others, Reuther also asked the first lady for help with individual cases. Cancellation of a navy contract, he told her, was threatening the jobs of thirteen thousand workers at the Brewster Aeronautical Corporation, and ER promised to bring it to the president's attention. She in turn asked Reuther for advice on issues such as a veterans' employment preference that might pit veterans against workers. Some of these ideas and requests found their way into ER's notes for the president, but in the end FDR agreed with Byrnes and the military leaders. The government remained focused on all-out war production with increased unemployment.[63]

Standing together on the other side, ER and Reuther continued to collaborate and to face criticism from conservatives. To ER's secretary Reuther commented that the first lady had "the rare combination of courage, integrity, intelligence and charm blended into human kindness and understanding that entitles her to a place in history as the greatest woman in modern times." He continued: "Having felt the warmth of Mrs. Roosevelt's kindness, it is inconceivable how the apostles of reaction, ignorance and hate can continue to carry on their insidious propaganda. When I hear them, I am tempted to actually do some of the things that Pegler has wrongfully accused me."[64]

A Fourth Term Ends

In the spring and summer of 1944, as an Allied victory seemed more assured, attention turned again to presidential politics. By most accounts both

FDR and ER were ambivalent about a fourth term, but the president announced that he would accept the nomination. ER reported that she was making only "non-political" speeches about registering and voting. Under the banner of a new organization, however, labor played a key role in this campaign. Sidney Hillman, who had returned to the ACWA, put together the foundations of a permanent political organization that would stop the left from moving toward an independent labor party and ensure a Roosevelt victory with a more liberal platform. This strategy required bringing communists and anticommunists together under one banner, closely linked to the Democratic Party.[65]

CIO-PAC was the nation's first political action committee. In the summer of 1944 Hillman established the National Citizens Political Action Committee (NCPAC) to showcase middle-class support for labor's agenda. Many CIO officials were assigned to political work in the election campaign. Lucy Mason was so effective in the South that Hillman appointed her to the executive committee of NCPAC. The groups achieved some successes in the primaries. Martin Dies, conservative chairman of the House Un-American Activities Committee, withdrew from his race. A report issued by that committee in July accused the CIO-PAC of being the political arm of the New Deal administration, a violation of the Hatch Act, which prohibited political action by civil servants. In a list of seventy-two telephone calls from CIO-PAC officials to the White House and other federal agencies, chief among those involved was Eleanor Roosevelt. The targets of CIO-Pac and NCPAC activity suspected ER of exercising influence illegitimately.[66]

When the first lady urged unity for the labor movement at the Textile Workers' convention that year, she was talking about the CIO and the AF of L. Yet she was also aware of the disagreement within the more progressive wing of the labor movement about working with persons and groups affiliated with the Communist Party. The anticommunists, or the right, included Reuther and Carey of the CIO, as well as Dubinsky from the AF of L. The left faction, led by Hillman, had renewed ties to the communists, who were fully behind FDR and the war effort. A firestorm between the left and right wings of the more progressive unions erupted in New York State's party elections. No one watched New York politics more closely than the Roosevelts, especially in an election year.

The American Labor Party, established by Hillman and Dubinsky in 1936, had come largely under the control of Dubinsky by 1942. Hillman offered his new political action committee as a way to restructure the party, but Dubinsky saw the move as a way for the communists to gain control. The president met with both Dubinsky and Hillman. According to Hillman biographer Steven Fraser, ER supported Dubinsky and was said to fear "the impact of the 'red' issue on working-class ethnics, Irish, Polish, and Italian voters especially."

La Guardia intervened with a peace plan, and FDR received a guarantee from Hillman that no communists would serve in the leadership of the state Democratic Party. The left-wing forces won the election. Although Hillman kept his pledge, Dubinsky and his followers withdrew and established the Liberal Party, which became a political force in its own right.[67]

After the primary ER questioned Hillman, who defended his attempts to unite the party and presented the defeat of the right-wing clique as "essential to the building of full progressive support for the policies of the administration, foreign and domestic, and for the President himself." Dubinsky, after talking with Schneiderman, wrote to ER to state his case. He never characterized Hillman or the ACWA as communists, but he felt that Hillman had "succeeded in pulling political chestnuts out of the fire for the Communists who had lost their place on the ticket." In the end, FDR's name appeared as the nominee of all three: the American Labor Party, the Liberal Party, and the Democratic Party.[68]

At his wife's urging FDR engaged in the campaign and gave his first major speech to the Teamsters Union in September. ER wrote a column for the ACWA's special edition of the *Advance* for women voters, titled "Women Must Use Their Power," and spoke to ILGWU Local 142, but was unable to accept Dubinsky's invitation to a major ILGWU campaign event. Roosevelt won reelection, but his margin of victory had slipped. He carried the labor vote, but the CIO-PAC efforts had not increased support for FDR even in labor strongholds. The unions, which had supported incumbent Henry Wallace for vice president, were frustrated when the nomination went to Harry Truman, despite the rumor that Roosevelt had instructed party leaders to "clear it with Sidney." Nonetheless, the CIO-PAC became permanent, and NCPAC took on a life of its own, reaching well beyond the labor movement to garner support for a liberal agenda. As ER prepared to address the CIO convention after the election, there was no more serious talk about a third party.[69]

Addressing the seventh CIO convention in Chicago, ER first thanked the delegates for their efforts in educating their members and turning out the vote. She turned immediately to the demands of peace and the need to educate citizens to watch over their representatives, propose legislation, and be active in their communities. She warned of the difficult challenges that lay ahead and emphasized the need to put as much effort into creating the peace as had been put into winning the war. She talked about the situation of returning veterans, education, and urban and rural problems and placed them in an international context, for she saw them all as interconnected. How the United States solved domestic problems would affect the world as a whole, she declared. ER then returned to the theme of personal responsibility in a democracy, where citizens do not merely act for the good of the nation but "want the good of the whole world" and "are willing even to pay the price of peace just as they paid the price of war." Murray thanked her effusively for providing the inspiration to go forward.[70]

As FDR began an unprecedented fourth term as president of the United States, he journeyed to Yalta to meet with Churchill and Stalin to plan for peace, accompanied by his daughter, Anna. Her request to accompany her husband having been denied, ER turned to her many activities and obligations. She praised the unions' refugee relief efforts, spoke out on the needs of women in the postwar world, and championed migrant workers. When Jim Carey sent her a full report on the founding convention of the World Federation of Trade Unions in London, she asked Secretary Perkins for her thoughts on the recommendations. In response to a telegram from Walter Reuther reading, "would like very much to chat with you," she arranged to meet him on 12 April. FDR had gone to Warm Springs, Georgia, for a much-needed rest. On that afternoon ER was urgently called back to the White House. Steve Early, the president's press secretary, and Dr. Ross McIntire, his physician, came to her sitting room and told her "the President had slipped away."[71]

Walter Reuther was in a taxi on his way to the White House that afternoon for his meeting with ER. When word of the president's death was announced over the radio, he told his daughter, "the news shattered my concentration. I had been listing different proposals to present to [ER]. But destiny had its own plans." Eleanor Roosevelt immediately went to Warm Springs and accompanied the president's body on the funeral train to Washington and then to Hyde Park. Thousands of people lined the tracks at stations and crossroads in an overwhelming display of sadness and respect for the man who had led them out of the Great Depression and through World War II. For many he was the only president they had ever known. In the months after the funeral, Eleanor said that she was most touched by the thousands of people who wrote to tell her their stories about how the policies and programs that her husband started had improved their lives: "In many cases he had saved them from complete despair." She would carry on his legacy, but very much in her own way.[72]

A young Eleanor Roosevelt, 1898. ER, just fourteen years old, before she left for the Allenswood School in England. Franklin D. Roosevelt Presidential Library and Museum.

A young Rose Schneiderman, ca. 1908.
Rose Schneiderman, in her twenties,
sewing cap linings at the time she is
emerging as a new leader of the United
Cloth Hat and Cap Makers Union.
UNITE HERE Archives, Kheel Center,
Cornell University.

Women's Trade Union League party,
1929. Rose Schneiderman and Governor
Franklin D. Roosevelt visit during the
twenty-fifth anniversary party for the
New York Women's Trade Union
League, Hyde Park. Rose Schneiderman
Photographs Collection, Robert F. Wagner
Labor Archives, Tamiment Library, New
York University.

The Roosevelt family, 1919. Eleanor and Franklin Roosevelt with their children Anna, James, Elliott, Franklin Jr., and John are joined by FDR's mother, Sara, in Washington, DC. Franklin D. Roosevelt Presidential Library and Museum.

Hearings at the U.S. Capitol, 1933. First Lady Eleanor Roosevelt, Ishbel MacDonald, daughter of the British prime minister, and Secretary of Labor Frances Perkins leaving the U.S. Capitol after Secretary Perkins testified on the Black bill. UPI/ACME, © Bettmann/Corbis.

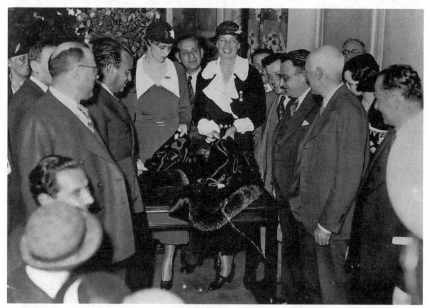

Sewing a Blue Eagle label, 1933. ER sews in the first NRA Blue Eagle label with daughter Anna on her right and David Dubinsky, president of the ILGWU, on her left. UNITE HERE Archives, Kheel Center, Cornell University.

Coal miners, 1935. ER travels into the Willow Grove No. 10 coal mine led by members of the United Mine Workers Union, Bellaire, Ohio. UPI/ACME, © Bettmann/Corbis.

Mrs. Roosevelt Writes for Miners' Wives

Written by Mrs. Franklin Delano Roosevelt especially for publication in the United Mine Workers Journal

By ELEANOR ROOSEVELT

I am very glad of the opportunity to contribute this short article to the United Mine Workers Journal because I have long had it in my mind to write of something which has come to my attention in my contacts with certain parts of the coal fields in this country.

After the Napoleonic wars, it was found that Europe was over-run with itinerant peddlers because soldiers who were discharged had spent so many years in the army under direction that they really could not organize themselves into any kind of existence where initiative and management were necessary.

Much the same thing, it seems to me, occurs when human beings live for too long a time in company towns, whether they be mining towns or mill towns. The mere fact that they have no choice as to where and how they will live, that they have no real choice as to where they will buy, destroys initiative.

If the employer is a good one and thoughtful they may get their wages on time and have a little extra cash, but if the mine is poor their wages are always behind hand and the amount of extra cash that ever filters into anybody's hand is apt to be pretty small, so budget making and the management of money is really not a part of the workers' lives.

Again, if the employer is interested he may provide a certain amount of recreation, some extra educational facilities, but the mere fact that these

ELEANOR ROOSEVELT

are given and not planned for and arranged by the workers themselves does in the long run a harmful thing, until gradually this type of life saps the people's initiative.

The men may not suffer quite as much because in their daily work they have to meet emergencies and make certain decisions, but the women find it harder and harder to plan a life or to make any changes, no matter how much they long for them, in a life which depends so entirely on what other people plan for them and give them.

It seems to me that the wives of the working men should do all within their power to do away with what is ordinarily known as the company town and the company store. They should come together in a group and consult as to what they can do to help the community as a whole by realizing that their value as human beings is to develop their own personalities and make their own special contribution to society, and that children and grown people should be allowed to plan their own lives and do the things which give them satisfaction. They should try to get the school to help in doing this, not only for the children but for themselves. They should try to make the pattern of their own lives rather than to let it be made for them. No matter how good the employers' intentions may be, the ultimate result is bad when people are not free to develop themselves.

"Miners' Wives," 1936. ER writes an article for the wives of union miners. *United Mine Workers Journal*: courtesy of Historical Collections and Labor Archives, Special Collections Library, The Pennsylvania State University.

Pins and Needles, 1938. President Franklin D. Roosevelt and David Dubinsky, president of the ILGWU, visit with the cast of the ILGWU Broadway musical *Pins and Needles*, performed at the White House. Photograph by H. Rubenstein and K. Joseph: UNITE HERE Archives, Kheel Center, Cornell University.

REC'D AUG 14 1940

August 10, 1940

My dear Mr. Einhorn:

I did not mean in writing my column of
August 3 that I had not been asked to speak at
meetings of the Guild. That means nothing. I
could speak and still know nothing about Guild
members or their activities.

If I attended meetings as an ordinary member
month in and month out, I would get to know people
and understand problems. I have not received the
notices of the meetings, probably because everyone *in my office*
knew I could not go at five day's notice.

You doubtless have a regular date and if
you will let me know what it is, I shall plan
to come, and I hope I'll wait until I know something before I presume to speak.

Very sincerely yours,

Eleanor Roosevelt

*Since Mr. Pegler says I am not
eligible would you like a chance
to decide? I am of course willing
to leave the decision with the Guild.*

Newspaper Guild letter, 1940. This is one of several exchanges between ER and Nat Einhorn of the New York Newspaper Guild regarding the status of her union membership in response to columnist Westbrook Pegler's charges that ER was not qualified to be a member. The handwritten portions read "in my office" (in the margin) and "Since Mr. Pegler says I am not eligible would you like a chance to decide? I am of course willing to leave the decision with the Guild." New York Newspaper Guild Records, Robert F. Wagner Labor Archives, Tamiment Library, New York University.

ILGWU convention, 1940. ER listens to the musical performance as a speaker at the ILGWU convention, New York World's Fair, with Senator Robert F. Wagner and David Dubinsky, president of the ILGWU. Photograph by John Albok: Albok Collection, box 11, f. 83, Collection of The New-York Historical Society. Scan courtesy of the Franklin D. Roosevelt Presidential Library and Museum.

Tolan hearings, 1940. ER testifying before Congressman Tolan's committee on the conditions of migratory farm workers. This was the first year a president's wife testified before Congress. Earlier that year she testified on housing. UPI/ACME, © Bettmann/Corbis.

Leviton strike, 1941. ER speaking to the striking workers of the IBEW at the Leviton Company, Brooklyn. UPI/ACME, © Bettmann/Corbis.

CIO Canteen opening, 1944. Folksinger Pete Seeger performing at the new CIO Canteen, Washington, DC, with ER in the audience. This was a controversial social meeting place because it was racially integrated. Photograph by Joseph A. Horne: Library of Congress.

CIO convention, 1944. ER with James B. Carey, CIO secretary-treasurer, and Lucy Randolph Mason, southern representative, at the seventh CIO convention in Philadelphia. Alexander Archer, Union Photography: IUE Records, Special Collections and University Archives, Rutgers University.

CIO convention, 1944. ER addressing the CIO's seventh constitutional convention, Phil Murray, president, to her left. IUE Records, Special Collections and University Archives, Rutgers University.

ACWA convention, 1944. ER with Dorothy Bellanca, vice president, and Sidney Hillman, president, at the fourteenth ACWA convention lunch to honor Bellanca in Chicago. UNITE HERE Archives, Kheel Center, Cornell University.

International labor exchange, 1945. Maida Springer (far right), ILGWU-AFL, with (left to right) Grace Blackett (UAW-CIO), Anne Murcovich (American Federation of Hosiery Workers–CIO), and Julia O'Conner Parker (IBEW-AFL), represent the American labor movement on a U.S. Office of War Information exchange. They meet with ER at the White House before leaving for eight weeks in England. The George Meany Memorial Archives/RG 96-001, 21/155.

Hudson Shore Labor School dinner, 1948. ER with Bessie Hillman, vice president of ACWA, and Hilda Worthington Smith, director of the Hudson Shore Labor School, attending a fund-raising dinner for the school. Photograph by Alexander Archer: Franklin D. Roosevelt Presidential Library and Museum.

ORT program, Paris, 1948. ER finds time during the final negotiations for the Universal Declaration of Human Rights to visit the ORT training program in Paris, supported by the ILGWU and other U.S. unions. International News Photos, 37 Rue Caumartin, Paris: UNITE HERE Archives, Kheel Center, Cornell University.

The Universal Declaration of Human Rights, 1949. ER displays a full copy of the declaration. United Nations: Franklin D. Roosevelt Presidential Library and Museum.

CIO wives, 1954. ER with (left to right) May Reuther (UAW), Bessie Hillman (ACWA), and Marge Carey (IUE), the wives of CIO union presidents, at the last CIO convention before the merger with the AF of L. UNITE HERE Archives, Kheel Center, Cornell University.

First AFL-CIO convention, 1955. ER with (left to right) George Meany (AFL-CIO president), Charles Zimmerman (ILGWU), and Walter Reuther (UAW) at the first convention of the merged AFL-CIO. Photograph by Alexander Archer: IUE Records, Special Collections and University Archives, Rutgers University.

The Reuther family, 1958. ER with Walter Reuther, his wife, May, and their daughters Linda and Lisa (front) during a summer visit at Val-Kill. Walter P. Reuther Library, Wayne State University.

ACWA Training Institute, 1957. ER meeting with union students visiting Val-Kill as part of their program. Photograph by Sam Reiss: Robert F. Wagner Labor Archives, Tamiment Library, New York University. Reproduced courtesy of The George Meany Memorial Archives/RG 96-001, series 2, 19/91.

National Farm Labor Advisory Committee meeting, 1959. ER with (left to right) Frank Graham, president of the University of North Carolina; A. Philip Randolph, president of the Brotherhood of Sleeping Car Porters; former congresswoman Helen Gahagan Douglas; and Secretary of Labor James P. Mitchell. Photograph by Nate Fine: Franklin D. Roosevelt Presidential Library and Museum.

PRES. JOHN F. KENNEDY   **ARTHUR J. GOLDBERG**

DR. MARTIN LUTHER KING   **MRS. ELEANOR ROOSEVELT**

Kennedy Tops Guest List
For AFL-CIO Convention

(Continued from Page 1) the convention hotel, the Americana, on Dec. 6.

In the week prior to the convention, five AFL-CIO trade departments will hold their own conventions in Miami Beach. In addition, the Intl. Labor Press Association will hold its annual meeting in Miami Beach during the same period. The AFL-CIO Auxiliaries will meet Dec. 7-11.

A listing of speakers and a summary of programs for the departmental conventions follows:

BUILDING & CONSTRUCTION TRADES DEPT.

Some 350 delegates and an equal number of visitors are expected at the AFL-CIO Building & Construction Trades Dept. Convention to be held Nov. 29- Dec. 1 in the Balmoral Hotel, Miami Beach.

The convention will be preceded by meetings of the department's executive council Nov. 27.

The session will be opened by Pres. Joe E. Henry of the Miami Building & Construction Trades Council, who as temporary chairman will lead the pledge of allegiance to the flag and will present the Most Rev. Coleman F. Carroll, Catholic Bishop of Miami, for the opening invocation. Permanent chairman is BCTD Pres. C. J.

the AFL-CIO Maritime Trades Dept. scheduled for the Hotel Americana in Miami Beach for Dec. 4-6 and will act on a series of resolutions dealing with the maritime industry and with the labor movement generally.

A long list of speakers headed by AFL-CIO Pres. George Meany will be heard. Others scheduled are Pres. C. J. Haggerty of the Building & Construction Trades Dept.; Pres. James A. Brownlow of the Metal Trades Dept.; National Dir. James L. McDevitt of COPE; Maritime Administrator Donald Alexander; George P. Delaney, special assistant to the assistant secretary of labor for international affairs; H. H. Bookbinder, special assistant to the Secretary of Commerce.

Also Deputy Dir. George Brown of the Labor Dept.'s Bureau of Labor Standards; Pres. John L. Weller of Seatrain Lines, Inc.; Max Harrison of the American Maritime Association; Gordon Chapman, special assistant to the Secretary of State as coordinator of international labor affairs and former secretary-treasurer of the State, County & Municipal Employes; Dir. Nelson Cruikshank of the AFL-CIO Dept. of Social Security, and Donald V. Geoffrion, labor relations advisor

The delegates, expected to number between 100 and 150, will hear 10 speakers headed by AFL-CIO Pres. George Meany.

Other speakers listed include Oscar Smith, director of industrial relations for the Atomic Energy Commission; Adm. M. J. Lawrence, head of the Navy's Office of Industrial Relations; Sec. of Labor Arthur J. Goldberg; Assistant Sec. of Labor Jerry R. Holleman; Edward E. Goshen, director of the Labor Dept.'s Bureau of Apprentice Training; Pres. C. J. Haggerty of the AFL-CIO Building & Construction Trades Dept.; Pres. Paul Hall of the AFL-CIO Maritime Trades Dept.; National Dir. James L. McDevitt of COPE, and Andrew J. Biemiller, director of the AFL-CIO Dept. of Legislation.

AFL-CIO AUXILIARIES

About 100 delegates representing some 50 local units and city and state councils will attend the convention of the AFL-CIO Auxiliaries, to be held Dec. 7-11 in the Americana Hotel.

They will hear addresses by AFL-CIO Pres. George Meany, Sec.-Treas. William F. Schnitzler; Sec.-Treas. Joseph Lewis of the Union Label & Service Trades Dept.; Wesley Reedy, assistant to Schnitzler, and three COPE officials—National

AFL-CIO News, 1961 (detail). Speakers announced for the AFL-CIO convention include President John F. Kennedy, Secretary of Labor Arthur Goldberg, the Reverend Martin Luther King Jr., and Eleanor Roosevelt. The George Meany Memorial Archives/RG 20-001.

IBEW education program, 1959. ER meets with the IBEW Local 3 education program, Bayberry, Long Island. Photograph by Sam Reiss: Sam Reiss Photographs Collection, Robert F. Wagner Labor Archives, Tamiment Library, New York University.

President John F. Kennedy and the ILGWU, 1961. ER attending the opening of an ILGWU housing program, Penn Station South, with President John F. Kennedy speaking, Governor Nelson Rockefeller (left), and David Dubinsky, president of the ILGWU (right of JFK). Franklin D. Roosevelt Presidential Library and Museum.

Meeting of the President's Commission on the Status of Women, 1962. ER with Esther Peterson (ACWA), executive director, and Kitty Ellickson (AFL-CIO), secretary, at the third meeting of the commission just months before ER's death, Hyde Park. Franklin D. Roosevelt Presidential Library and Museum.

AFL-CIO poster. After ER's death a memorial fund was established by the U.S. Congress to carry on her work. The AFL-CIO raised money to support the fund. The George Meany Memorial Archives/RG 99-001.

5

An Essential Element of Freedom

The right to form and join trade unions [is] an essential element
of freedom.
ELEANOR ROOSEVELT to the UN Human Rights Commission, 1948

The fall of 1948 found Eleanor Roosevelt in Paris attending the United
Nations General Assembly at the ornate Palais de Chaillot on the banks of the
Seine. As a U.S. delegate, she served as chair of its Human Rights Commission. The U.S. delegation took up residence in the majestic Hôtel de Crillon,
on the Place de la Concorde. Amidst formal meetings and negotiations, ER
invited fellow delegates to her suite for tea where they could discuss issues in
a more collegial atmosphere. As always, despite her overwhelming schedule,
between meeting diplomats and dignitaries, the press and the politicians, in
palaces and elegant hotels, Eleanor Roosevelt made time to see at firsthand
programs for workers. On a Monday afternoon in October she hurried from
her committee meeting, almost an hour late, to spend the afternoon at a technical school run by ORT (Organization for Rehabilitation through Training),
for which she had helped the American unions raise funds. The adult students were war refugees, the youngsters orphans, enrolled in trade and academic classes. One woman in a dressmaking course "had been a doctor in the
Russian army during the siege of Stalingrad." The director had spent time in
the Nazi concentration camp at Buchenwald. She explained in "My Day" that
the school was "located in a building in the Montreuil area of Paris—the workmen's area. It formerly was an old factory, and there is a plaque in the entrance
corridor that states that it is a gift of the International Ladies Garment Workers Union through their president, David Dubinsky, whose picture hangs in
the school's canteen."[1]

Known not only as the widow of the president of the United States but also as an advocate for international cooperation and humanitarian causes, ER brought her considerable political and organizational skills to the task of defining human rights for the world, including workers, both women and men, of all colors and nationalities. More than most seasoned diplomats and politicians, she understood how intertwined domestic and international policy had become. During the war she had fought to preserve and strengthen the social and economic polices of the New Deal. When she praised the clothing workers' contributions to the war effort, however, she not only acknowledged that many of their fellow citizens were badly nourished and lacked adequate medical care and education but also urged them to think of helping poor and exploited people around the world. Economic problems were global in scope and required international solutions. As she looked ahead, ER called for "fresh thinking." The most important lesson of recent history, she affirmed, is that the way to prevent more destructive wars is "by giving people all over the world hope for better economic conditions." This lesson became a central part of her work as she moved forward.[2]

During the first months following her husband's death, ER sought to redefine her place in the world. She was free of the constraints imposed by her role as first lady, but she was also without the power base that she had carefully developed through her partnership with FDR. As she adjusted to the many emotional and practical changes in her life, work was one of her strongest anchors. Just days after the president's funeral she resumed writing her column, explaining to her readers that the only two jobs she considered herself obligated to do were her column and her magazine page: "Now I am on my own, and I hope to write as a newspaper woman." Being a columnist gave her an independent forum through which she acknowledged she could shape public opinion on important policies and social issues, including labor issues.[3]

While friends counseled her about what else she could do, ER dismissed the speculation about elective and appointed political offices she might consider. Like many of her friends, labor leaders tried to influence her decisions. One offer that she did not dismiss out of hand combined her labor and political interests: she met with Sidney Hillman and discussed the possibility of chairing the National Citizens' Political Action Committee. The criteria she laid out included accepting no pay, coming to the office five half-days a week, and doing no fund-raising. She sought a clear understanding of her authority and support. She met with Jim Carey in Hyde Park as well as with the NCPAC board. They offered her the job, but in the end she decided it was unwise to take a prominent position with any organization. She was well aware that her presence could bring controversy; she also worried that such a position could limit her new independence. In this case she did not want to alienate the Democratic Party. David Dubinsky was relieved to hear of her decision, because this position would have complicated New York party politics. ER resumed her advisory roles, attending the Women's Trade Union League discussions about union problems and teaching classes on current events at the League's clubhouse. She agreed to join the board of the NAACP, where she would work with A. Philip Randolph, Walter Reuther, and other leaders on civil rights issues, including employment discrimination and a permanent Fair Employment Practices Commission.[4]

With a delicate mix of respect for the new president's authority and differences with his policies, ER offered Harry Truman her advice. She had serious reservations about his commitment to a liberal policy agenda but wanted to help him succeed. Truman felt strongly that he needed Eleanor Roosevelt on his side and looked for the right position for her in his administration. When he asked her to serve as one of five American delegates to the General Assembly of the United Nations, ER initially declined, citing her lack of background and experience in foreign diplomacy. Friends and family encouraged her to accept. Still, she faced political opposition. Senator Theodore Bilbo of Mississippi voted against her confirmation because he vehemently disapproved of her commitment to racial equality, suggesting at one point that she be deported to Liberia. Westbrook Pegler called the appointment a political job for which the government was not getting its money's worth. Looking back, she remarked that had she realized the job required Senate confirmation, she might not have accepted. On reflection, however, she believed that the United Nations was the one hope for a peaceful world. As often happened with ER, her sense of responsibility overcame her fear. She accepted the appointment and joined Secretary of State James F. Byrnes, UN Ambassador Edward Stettinius, and Senators Tom Connally, Democrat of Texas, and Arthur Vandenberg, Republican of Michigan, on the U.S. delegation.[5]

As ER worked to achieve a consensus about fundamental human rights in the international arena, she defended those rights from conservative attacks at home. The tension between domestic and international goals framed her work after she left the White House. This struggle played out visibly on the labor front. A lack of postwar planning led to rising unemployment, massive strikes, and new legislation, most notably the Taft-Hartley Act, which rescinded key protections for labor won under the New Deal. Still, with new colleagues from around the world, and with advice from her longtime friends in the labor movement, ER guided the Universal Declaration of Human Rights through the volatile international obstacle course that was the United Nations during the early days of the cold war. In the meetings leading up to its passage, she informed others on the commission that the United States "considered that the right to form and join trade unions was an essential element of freedom," a statement that was quite remarkable given the state of labor relations in the country. Her own views were well known, but the delegation included representatives of those who had passed the Taft-Hartley Act. Her first principle of just and orderly labor relations, collective bargaining, had been weakened at home, but at the same time firmly placed on the international agenda because both ER and U.S. labor leaders understood the interrelatedness of domestic and international issues.[6]

Peacetime Strife

As hostilities in Europe and Asia ended during the summer of 1945, celebrations of the Allied victory were tempered by anxieties about the future. Union membership had grown dramatically during the war, and the labor movement had gained new political organizations, but corporate America also reached new heights of industrial power, controlling half of the world's manufacturing capacity and monetary reserves, the largest merchant fleet, a near-monopoly on the aerospace and electronics industries, and the potential for the peacetime use of atomic power. Few industrial or military leaders were eager to develop a peacetime system of shared power with labor unions, continued wage and price controls, or government oversight of their activities, and political forces shifted significantly to their side. As the soldiers returned home, the problems of economic reconversion became acute. Billions of dollars in war contracts were canceled. In Michigan alone an estimated 300,000 war workers lost their jobs, and there were ninety unauthorized strikes in the Detroit area by the end of September. The number of days lost to strikes doubled that month and redoubled in October.[7]

Eleanor Roosevelt quickly resumed her advocacy of economic policies that included full employment legislation and wage and price controls. These issues were central in the struggle between President Truman, liberal leader Henry Wallace, and ER over the direction of economic policy and the focus of the Democratic Party in the postwar period. While striving for a planned economy, ER defended striking workers, opposed legislation to curtail strikes, praised public-minded labor leaders such as Sidney Hillman and Walter Reuther, and criticized the militant John L. Lewis. Reuther was her closest labor ally, for she shared his broad vision of social policy. She sought his advice on issues, defended him to the general public, promoted him to the new president, and supported him within his union.[8]

In the midst of the strikes, ER was urged to resign from her CIO union as a patriotic gesture. One reader complained that "it was terrible for the workers to strike when the industrialists were trying so hard to give jobs." She publicly declined to give up her union membership and decided it was time to set the record straight on the economics of reconversion. ER acknowledged that unions were not perfect, but argued that industrialists' desire to destroy the unions and return to lowering production costs by cutting jobs and wages was destructive and intolerable. Employees as well as employers should benefit from new technologies that raise productivity, and workers must have steady jobs with good wages in order to consume enough manufactured goods to avoid a postwar depression. She concluded: "There should have been set up, long ago, labor management committees. . . . We need a big national income with money kept in circulation if we are not to go through another depression in which both employer and employee will suffer." Her economic reasoning was roundly criticized by Henry Hazlitt, financial editor of the *New York Times,* and attributed to Walter Reuther. Reuther proudly sent her the article and included a new UAW pamphlet, "How to Raise Wages without Increasing Prices."[9]

Balancing the interests of returning veterans and wartime workers who would be competing for a limited or even declining number of jobs was a subject of serious debate. The principle of seniority was central to unions' policies on job security. When layoffs were necessary, workers who had been employed the longest had rights that superseded those of workers hired more recently; fairness replaced arbitrary managerial decisions. Applying this formula mechanically to industries such as auto manufacture, however, would pit returning veterans against wartime workers and push out many newly hired women and African Americans. In order to solve the problem without setting different groups of workers against one another, some labor leaders espoused a full employment policy. ER sought Reuther's opinion on material from the newly formed American Veterans Committee arguing for full employment and emphasizing the need to combat management initiatives to split veterans from unions. After receiving his positive response and additional information from the UAW, ER addressed the issue in her column. She contended that only full employment would eliminate the problem. She told her readers: "The unions are more interested than any other group in seeing that returned veterans get every possible benefit and protection. . . . [T]his fight for seniority for all war workers is not a fight against the veterans. It is a fight eventually to protect all workers, whether they are veterans or not, and it should be understood in this way by the public."[10]

When Victor Reuther, Walter's brother, won control of the union education department, he invited ER to speak at the educational conference in Cleveland because she was a favorite among the auto workers, and black workers held her in particularly high esteem. Afterwards he wrote that "Mrs. Roosevelt saw in Walter more than a bright young trade union leader. She recognized the social visionary who always related his trade union commitments to other broad social responsibilities, which all Americans should share. . . . Her attendance at our conference and her praise of Walter had a profound effect on the twelve hundred delegates and increased his influence within the union." For her part, ER wrote a column explaining the importance of the closed shop, which was based on one of the talks she heard there.[11]

Truman initiated a month-long labor-management conference, but no progress was made on a cooperative system, and the president's support for continued wage and price controls was weakening. The Reuther brothers prepared a new strategy. They would call a companywide strike against General Motors, seeking a substantial wage increase without an increase in the price of cars and challenging the company to open its books for inspection so the validity of its claims that it could not afford to raise wages could be assessed. ER began to advise President Truman behind the scenes. She suggested that a survey of resources be made to aid in planning the national economy, and assured him that someone like her old friend Bernard Baruch would be acceptable to the industrialists and that "even the young labor leaders, like Walter Reuther and James Carey, believe in his integrity." The crisis brewing in Detroit could, she hoped, be postponed for as much as a year if the parties were guaranteed a fair report in a timely manner.[12]

Truman agreed, but before he responded, more than 200,000 auto workers walked out of GM under Reuther's leadership and stayed out for 113 days. ER supported the strike indirectly, explaining in "My Day," "I did all I could to help the women and children whose men were on strike in the UAW recently, because I believe that in our country we want to alleviate suffering wherever it is possible to do so." In addition to sending a check to Reuther to help the striking families, she joined a national Committee to Aid the Families of GM Strikers. ER argued that the problems of peace needed the same kind of economic planning that had been so successful during the war. Unreasonable demands should not be met, "but, if the demands are reasonable, then their refusal is not in the public interest." She asked how Americans could expect the nations of the world to sit down together and solve disputes if "we do not use the same mechanisms successfully in settling our domestic problems?" ER underlined the need for people to keep their ultimate objectives in mind but for compromise to move forward: "The strike, which is a weapon of force, should be renounced. But that cannot be until we set a limit on the time allowed for arbitration and until we say that all interests shall be equally considered and that concessions shall never be expected from one side only."[13]

When President Truman asked Congress for legislation to end the strikes, ER objected. She thought that the UAW's demands were reasonable and that government intervention on the side of the corporation was dangerous. Under his proposal the president could prohibit a work stoppage for thirty days and establish a fact-finding board to make recommendations. While ER acknowledged in her column the importance of having business prosper, she feared that without rent and price ceilings, the country would return to the depressed conditions of the early 1930s. She strongly defended organized labor as essential to a democracy. She thought that a turn to fascism was possible in this country, and pointed out that Germany had curtailed the rights of labor. In clear terms she warned her readers that "taking away the right of any man to stop work at any time he wishes to do so, except with his agreement, is abrogating a right." She reminded them that employer organizations wielded extensive powers and that the gains of organized labor eventually benefited all workers. Imposing a ban on strikes seemed to her "an abrogation of fundamental rights which eventually would do harm to every citizen."[14]

Congress did not act on the Truman proposal, and the strike at General Motors continued. As working families were squeezed between rising prices and stagnant wages, the strike wave spread. Early in 1946 the autoworkers were joined by over 400,000 electrical and meatpacking workers, and on 21 January Phil Murray led over a half million steelworkers off the job. According to Robert Zieger, by 1 February over a quarter of the CIO's entire membership was on strike. Truman sent in fact-finding boards, but he retreated from establishing wage-price controls; instead a system of pattern bargaining, which led to regular increases in wages and prices, was put in place. ER was uncharacteristically critical of both management and labor as she put these events into the context of what was happening in Europe. She lamented that "between them, they are adding to the sum total of the greatest misery the world has ever seen.... This is no time for men and women of narrow vision." Other nations were watching "the great democratic capitalist nation," and some, including the European allies, were shifting toward socialism. "It is not so much our Government which has failed to understand our world situation," she concluded. "It is our industrialists who have failed to give leadership in the economic field. Labor, too, should have had the world point of view ... the only one which will benefit the United States of America as a whole."[15]

Antiunion legislation was wending its way through Congress with support from southern Democrats despite Truman's opposition. Southern politicians' vehement objections to unions were exacerbated by the CIO's organizing drive in the region. Operation Dixie primarily targeted the textile industry, in which poor whites toiled under deplorable conditions. Lucy Mason, who had a key role in Operation Dixie, wrote to ER about violations by employers and law enforcement officials of workers' rights of free speech and assembly, as well as their violent attacks on black workers across the largely segregated industries. ER noted the link between labor troubles and race, concluding: "Racial minorities always are the first to suffer when there are strikes or layoffs, and when our people, instead of working toward full employment, are indulging not only in labor strikes, but in management strikes. Management seems to be trying to bring about less strong workers' organizations and a lower labor cost."[16]

Southern Democrats charged that the CIO-PAC was a communist-front organization. The AF of L, worried that it might lose its base among southern textile workers to the CIO, contributed to the red-baiting. Eleanor Roosevelt responded by demanding, "Just what makes the CIO-PAC a Communist organization?" She allowed that there were communists in some labor groups, and she believed they should not hold leadership positions, but she saw no problem in overwhelmingly democratic organizations having communist members. She challenged white southerners to look beyond their parochial interests and respond to the needs of the majority of citizens. In private she urged Truman to find someone to advise him who actually knew which labor leaders and organizers were communists and which were not.[17]

In the spring Walter Reuther was elected president of the UAW by a narrow margin. When the opponents he defeated tried to limit his power, ER defended him as an "honest labor leader who has at heart the interests of the majority of the rank and file." By May 1946 what was left of the labor-Democratic coalition was severely tested by a showdown between two other unions and the president. Once again the powerful John L. Lewis led the coal miners out on strike over demands to create a health and welfare fund. Then the Railroad Brotherhoods walked off the job, seeking the eighteen-and-a-half-cent raise already secured by steel, auto, and electrical workers. Fearing a national emergency, Truman addressed a joint session of Congress to request temporary authority to draft striking workers into the armed forces; he proposed permanent legislation to prevent stoppages in essential industries.[18]

ER opposed the draft privately and publicly. She supported the railway workers but also voiced strong objections to Lewis's militancy. For the UMW the strike seemed to be a first response rather than an act of last resort. Lewis lacked any larger social vision for the country; he did not subscribe to a liberal agenda or work within the Democratic Party, but single-mindedly pursued what he saw as in the best interests of his miners, without necessarily consulting them. She condemned "his arrogant attitude as regards the public interest," but the miners generally supported militant action whether or not it was arrived at through an internally democratic process. ER found herself simultaneously opposing Truman's drastic legislative initiatives, criticizing Lewis, and defending the miners—a most awkward position. She objected that drafting workers to stop them from striking would "interfere with men's fundamental liberty to work or not to work." Never losing sight of the suffering of ordinary working people, she argued that mining companies had done little to ensure the health and safety of the miners. The public had a responsibility "to see that organized labor has a fair deal."[19]

For ER these conflicts between labor and management were troublingly similar to problems in international relations. She declared: "Sometimes, when I see how inadequate we are at settling these disputes among ourselves reasonably, I despair about a peaceful world. . . . If we can't do this in labor disputes at home, how on earth do we expect to do it when the people concerned belong to different nations?" She chastised business executives who "have shown themselves incapable of real leadership in the economic and moral field in this great world crisis." But she did not spare Lewis, who, she said, "does not even trust his own followers enough to tell them how he intends to administer the welfare fund he is asking for their benefit." She suggested solutions that would conciliate the warring parties, such as a plan for labor courts or a system of mediated national bargaining like that in Great Britain.[20]

The contentious debate about the role of government in labor-management relations pervaded national politics. Even Hillman publicly condemned the president as "autocratic." Renewed rumblings about a third party were heard from Reuther and Dubinsky, and there were fears that labor might sit out the midterm elections. On the other side, southern Democrats threatened to leave the party if Truman continued to support labor and civil rights. Congress passed the Case bill, which attempted to gut the Wagner Act. Using Phil Murray's analysis, ER called on the president to veto the bill, saying that it was "permanently harmful, not just to labor but to labor relations, which include business and the country as a whole." In the end, Truman did veto the law. But he could find no way to resolve the economic issues that fueled the wave of strikes or develop effective means of conciliation.[21]

On 10 July 1946 Sidney Hillman died at the age of fifty-nine, his heart problems exacerbated by the stresses of union leadership and public service. Mourned as a "labor statesman," he lay in state at Carnegie Hall as thousands filled the streets of the garment district. President Truman praised him as a "great humanitarian and an outstanding statesman in the field of labor-management relations." Eleanor Roosevelt expressed shock and a sense of personal loss. In her eulogy she emphasized the importance of his foreign background, which his critics had often used against him, to his ability to understand and solve problems. "For the people in his own union, he always worked unselfishly, with a broad vision both of the needs of labor and of the responsibility of labor to the community as a whole as it gained power." Implicit in this praise was criticism of Lewis.[22]

Labor turmoil continued through the summer of 1946. Rising rents and food prices eliminated the wage gains secured earlier in the year, and working people began to picket and boycott grocery stores. Truman dismissed liberal leader Henry Wallace from his cabinet for his criticism of the president's foreign policy, thereby alienating labor leaders. Then Lewis led the coal miners out on strike even though the mines were under federal control, directly challenging the U.S. government. Voicing suspicions about his political motivations, ER wondered aloud: "Is he expecting recognition from the Republican Party if they should win in 1948? . . . Has he entered into an understanding with the owners of the mines?" Lewis put both the AF of L and the CIO in a difficult position. They had to support the right to strike, but, she predicted, that stance might cost them the political support and government protections that labor had gained over the last fifteen years. The AF of L and CIO considered combining their efforts to back up the strike and paralyze the country. ER cautioned that the United States was absolutely critical to worldwide economic recovery, yet "we seem to go our way blithely indifferent to the effect our actions have on the rest of the world."[23]

Truman obtained a temporary restraining order to bar the walkout. The courts found the United Mine Workers in contempt and fined the union $700,000. Lewis was personally fined $10,000. "Even the United Mine Workers, which is said to be a fairly rich union, must be a little appalled at the size of the fine imposed upon it for contempt of court," wrote ER. She disliked the injunction but sensed from the letters she received that Lewis was losing support even from his members. She expressed her fear that labor as a whole would suffer from this action. Every day more people were unemployed as the shutdown in the mines affected other industries and a "rising tide of misery" threatened to engulf the country. For the first time since the Great Depression ER found a destitute man waiting for her as she arrived at her apartment, saying he had lost his job, and his mother was sick, and asking if she could call the steel company. Such scenes were commonplace in 1933, but they should not be repeated in 1946, she declared. ER supported ordering the miners back to work. Finally, on 9 December the strike in the coalfields was settled as the miners negotiated a health and pension fund. ER questioned whether any one man, such as Lewis, should have so much power. She saw labor relations as the number-one domestic problem and praised a proposal for a mediation system made by an advisory committee to the U.S. Conciliation Service. Antilabor forces, however, gathered strength in the new Congress, aiming not to improve the system but to roll back New Deal labor laws.[24]

Taft-Hartley

The 1946 midterm elections were a stunning defeat for the Democratic Party and organized labor. The Democrats lost control of both houses of Congress for the first time since 1930. Some attributed the huge loss to voters' weariness with labor strife, inflation, and food shortages. Others worried about charges of communism. According to Nelson Lichtenstein, "young ex-servicemen, like Richard Nixon in California and Joseph McCarthy in Wisconsin, unhesitatingly identified the CIO and its political action committee as near-synonyms for Communist. In the South an orgy of red-baiting and race-baiting stopped the CIO's postwar organizing campaign, Operation Dixie, dead in its tracks." The new Congress lost no time in putting together its antilabor agenda. In the first four months, seventy-three labor bills were introduced to amend the Wagner Act. ER wondered "really whether the gentlemen in Congress want our system of private enterprise to be a success.... Perhaps they hope to establish an economy which will keep up large incomes for certain great business corporations but cut down on small business, gradually reducing the living standard for the average individual while keeping it high for the few favored people. This is not a democratic theory."[25]

The most damaging legislation, which was introduced in the Senate by Robert A. Taft of Ohio and in the House by Fred Hartley of New Jersey, stipulated that the National Labor Relations Board was to serve unions, workers, and employers equally. Strikes were restricted, secondary boycotts and the closed shop were prohibited, and foremen were not allowed to join unions since they were supposed to serve as managers. Section 14(b) allowed states to pass "right-to-work" laws prohibiting contracts requiring union membership as a condition of employment. The bill made permanent the ban on union— but not employer—contributions to political campaigns. Union officials were required to sign affidavits swearing that they were not communists. Labor leaders testified against the legislation before congressional committees. The AF of L conducted a $1.5 million publicity campaign to defeat the bill, while the CIO declared April "Defend Labor Month" and organized rallies, distributed literature, broadcast radio programs, and encouraged letter writing. ER commented that if the bill accurately represented the views of the majority of citizens, "then the people have done a somersault in their thinking since 1944, when they elected as president a man who believed in the Wagner Act."[26]

Despite labor's campaign, Congress passed the Labor Management Relations Act of 1947, known as Taft-Hartley. While the Wagner Act still stood, it had been severely weakened. ER acknowledged that labor leaders, especially Lewis, had brought some of these problems on themselves. She agreed that communists had no place in labor leadership. Yet in the end it was "a bad bill...weighted in favor of the employer" and would have a negative effect on working people. Union members wrote to ER, and she put their words before her readers. The Chicago Typographical Union wrote: "We [are] alarmed and resentful, being a realistic as well as an idealistic organization, at the fact that Sen. Taft would deprive us of things which we possessed fifty years before the Wagner Act was adopted. For example, power to bargain for foremen and assistant foremen." ER concluded that the bill struck "at the fundamental rights and protection of labor," and would lead to "unending agitation and unrest." On a Friday, President Truman vetoed the Taft-Hartley bill, claiming that it would cause long-term damage to the labor movement and the country. By Monday both the House and the Senate voted to override the veto.[27]

"My Day"
14 June 1947
United Feature Syndicate, Inc.

New York, Friday—I wonder if members of Congress are getting anything like the communications which I am getting on the Taft-Hartley Labor Bill. If they are, they must begin to be conscious of the fact that quite a number of people are not in favor of that bill. Sen. Robert A. Taft keeps insisting that it is really a bill designed to give both management and labor equal rights, but a great many people seem to think that it takes away rights which organized labor groups had acquired even before the Wagner Act was passed.

I have before me a telegram of several hundred words from the Chicago Typographical Union, and it reads as though it had been written by some men who were in a fighting mood.

They say: "Our members are aroused today as they never have been aroused before . . . Still more are we alarmed and resentful, being a realistic as well as an idealistic organization, at the fact that Sen. Taft would deprive us of things which we possessed fifty years before the Wagner Act was adopted. For example, power to bargain for foremen and assistant foremen [and] . . . periodical elections to determine whether a majority of the employees in a given printing office wish to continue it as a so-called union shop, thereby compelling us to match resources in propaganda warfare with belligerent employers who wish to seduce our members from their natural allegiance to the oldest union in America."

If I were in the House or the Senate, I think it would trouble me a good deal that so many workers feel this legislation is going to be harmful and take away protection in the earning of their livelihood—which is, after all, something very important even to non-union workers.

As I have said before, I think that many average people in this country have been embittered by the actions of labor leaders which have endangered their home comforts and frequently their jobs. A coal stoppage, for instance, is a very serious thing. But I am told on very good authority that this bill will not make it any more possible to prevent John L. Lewis from bringing on a strike in the coal industry than it has been before. I think individual regulations made by unions for their members sometimes irritate the public. But I think these things are not fundamental and could be taken up and negotiated, whereas this bill seems to me to strike at the fundamental rights and protection of labor.

To pass it will, I think, lead to unending agitation and unrest; and it will not achieve the one thing which we need above all else to achieve—namely, increased production. The more goods we produce, the more the prices will come down. Labor is both a producer and a consumer, and it is of paramount importance that all over the world people get to work, produce jobs, produce goods, and begin to fill the needs of the people. This bill will not help to achieve this essential factor in our return to a normal situation under our present free-enterprise system.

E. R.

ER, after protesting that she would not presume to give the president advice, congratulated Truman for being courageous and wise. In the end she told her readers: "No one likes the abuses in labor unions which have been ably pointed out by Westbrook Pegler and others, but such abuses are a tiny percentage of the labor movement. And organized labor does benefit all labor, whether organized or unorganized." ER found much to criticize in the bill. Telling unions on what basis they could expel members was high-handed; dictating how to run their health, welfare, and pension funds was an infringement on their liberties. She argued forcefully in her column and in private correspondence that management as well as unions should be held accountable. If unions' books were to be open for examination, then companies' books should be open too.[28]

As the cold war began, the most controversial provision of the bill proved to be the requirement that union leaders sign affidavits declaring that they were not communists. If a leader refused to sign, then the union was denied access to the National Labor Relations Board (NLRB), which even in its weakened state provided crucial protections. Unions faced insoluble dilemmas. Many labor leaders were strongly anticommunist but bitterly resented being forced to sign such a declaration, regarding it as an infringement on their civil liberties, and one that managers were not subjected to. Some CIO unions had communists in leadership positions, as well as among the membership, and they faced charges of perjury if they signed. Some refused to purge leaders who would not sign the affidavits, both because they regarded the communists as good unionists and because they found government intervention into their internal affairs undemocratic. If unions called strikes over this issue, however, they would be breaking their hard-won contracts. Lewis had returned to the AF of L and urged a boycott of the NLRB. When this strategy was rejected, he again pulled the UMW out of the federation. The UE and the Mine, Mill, and Smelter Workers forfeited NLRB protection. Most unions, both CIO and AF of L, signed the affidavits and turned to political organizing in an attempt to elect pro-labor politicians and amend Taft-Hartley.[29]

ER did not hesitate to take a position on this contentious issue, writing: "There are certain things in this act which, as an American citizen, I resent. Why should the head of a union be asked to declare that he is not a communist? It will shortly become necessary, before we start out to earn a living, to declare all sorts of things about ourselves which we considered nobody's business in the past." She reiterated her 1930s argument that the best defense against both communism and fascism was a strong democracy. These ideologies are dangerous, she declared, only "if we allow democracy to fail."[30]

Her worries about labor strife were compounded by an appalling act of violence. On 20 April 1948 Walter Reuther was at home with his wife, May, having a late dinner in the kitchen, when a blast from a shotgun ripped through the window, smashing his right arm and entering his chest. The newly elected president of the UAW almost died. He was rushed to the hospital, where blood transfusions led to infections and months of surgeries; he spent a year in a cast. ER wrote: "The recent dastardly attack on Walter Reuther of the United Automobile Workers was a shocking occurrence. No matter how great our disagreements are[,] if we are to continue to be a country ruled by law and not by violence, we must try to bring the whole force of public opinion against actions of this kind." The assailant was never identified, despite much speculation about the mob, factions within the union, other unions, communists, and complicity on the part of the police.[31]

The presidential election of 1948 was a referendum on the Democratic Party's postwar policies. Henry Wallace, the liberal former vice president, launched a bid for the presidency as the nominee of the Progressive Party, with support from some CIO unions on the left, as well as isolationists. He agreed with the communists in opposing the Marshall Plan, which was designed to provide substantial economic aid to help European countries recover from the war and keep them from turning to Soviet-style communism. At the same time, southern Democrats, dubbed "Dixiecrats," broke with Truman over the civil rights plank in the party platform and supported the States' Rights Democratic Party, which nominated Governor Strom Thurmond of South Carolina for president. Fearing defeat, some Democrats considered drafting the wildly popular General Dwight Eisenhower. Rose Schneiderman wrote to ER about the "political mess" in New York, where many in the state federation were supporting the Republican presidential candidate, Governor Thomas E. Dewey.[32]

ER tried to stay out of partisan politics because of her role as a UN delegate and her doubts about the president, but she was a powerful voice within the party, and neutrality was taken as support for the Republicans. Finally, Frances Perkins called her in Paris and persuaded her to send a letter of support to

Truman, although her lack of enthusiasm was apparent. Dubinsky nonetheless immediately used her letter and picture in a Liberal Party campaign ad for Truman. In the end, the AF of L did not endorse any candidate for president, and the CIO reluctantly endorsed Truman, who subsequently gave organized labor a great deal of credit for his upset victory over Dewey. Wallace and Thurmond were held to single digits. Many congressmen who had voted for Taft-Hartley, including nine senators and fifty-seven representatives, were defeated, while all those who had supported Truman's veto won reelection. Control of Congress returned to the Democrats. But Taft-Hartley was domestic law, while the fight for trade union rights had moved to the international stage.[33]

Human Rights, Labor Rights

At the end of the war, international affairs were at the forefront of the agendas for both the CIO and the AF of L, but the divisions between the two organizations shaped their differing foreign policy positions. The CIO, led by Murray, Hillman, Carey, and Reuther, saw the strength of the labor movement in the United States linked to the development of strong labor movements in Europe and Asia, largely through economic policies. They were anti-Soviet but cooperated with Russian and socialist unions in Europe when feasible and joined ER in supporting the Marshall Plan. The AF of L, led by Green, Meany, Dubinsky, and its longtime vice president Matthew Woll, sought to promote a strong democratic labor movement in opposition to communism and refused to work with communists or socialists, whether within unions or in governments. While they supported the Marshall Plan to rebuild the economy of war-torn Europe, they emphasized the Truman Doctrine, with its anti-Soviet framework and emphasis on military aid. ER saw this unilateral doctrine as undermining the United Nations and enlisted Reuther and Carey to join 100,000 others in reaffirming their faith in the international organization.[34]

The cold war was well under way within the U.S. labor movement as well as internationally. In 1944 Murray had asked FDR to allow the CIO to have a representative at the International Labor Organization along with the AF of L. The federation so strongly opposed the idea that Murray eventually withdrew the request. The CIO then called for the formation of an international labor federation. In February 1945, 204 delegates, representing 60 million workers from thirty-five countries, met in London for the founding meeting of the World Federation of Trade Unions (WFTU). The AF of L, which refused to join any body in which the Soviets participated, aligned with the UMW to boycott the meeting.[35]

Despite these differences, American labor leaders supported the United Nations and worked with ER to secure trade union rights in the human rights declaration. Given the antiunion character of labor relations and national politics, ER was possibly the only person who could work with both the AF of L and the CIO on this important matter and then guide the articles on trade union rights through the State Department, her colleagues on the U.S. delegation, and the UN Human Rights Commission. Much of this was accomplished through her personal friendships with Jim Carey and David Dubinsky. Both men provided draft language for the human rights document and met with her formally and informally to discuss the issues.[36]

James B. Carey was a critical player in the international arena for the CIO. He was known as "labor's boy wonder" for his rapid ascent within the union at a very young age. Born in Philadelphia in 1911, he grew up in a progressive Irish Catholic home where social issues were discussed around the dinner table. He was the first of John and Margaret Carey's eleven children to graduate from high school. He wanted to become an electrical engineer, but this was 1929, so he hired on at Philco Radio Corporation and was soon involved in union organizing. A wiry young man with curly brown hair, Carey had enormous energy and enthusiasm but was also seen as mercurial and combative. In 1933, at the age of twenty-three, he led a strike, formed a union, and negotiated his first contract. Three years later he was elected president of the new United Electrical, Radio and Machine Workers of America (UE). He led the union to affiliate with the CIO, became a close confidant of Lewis and Murray, and was chosen secretary of the CIO in 1938. Carey was drawn into conflict with the communists who were actively organizing production workers in the electrical industry. In the late 1930s the union became embroiled in disputes over the Soviet Union's shifting stance toward Nazi Germany, and when Carey ran for reelection as UE president in 1941, he was defeated by a left-wing rival. He continued to serve as secretary-treasurer of the CIO and maintained close ties with the anticommunist faction in the UE while representing Phil Murray internationally.[37]

Carey also assumed leadership on youth and civil rights issues for the CIO; in fact he recalled first meeting ER at an American Youth Congress event. Over the years they developed what he described as "an excellent personal relationship." He and his wife, Margie, enjoyed dinners at the White House and with their two children spent weekends at Val-Kill. When Elliott Roosevelt asked him for any letters he had from the president for a book he was editing, Carey replied that he had only a few thank you notes, saying, "You will easily appreciate the reason why there is no correspondence, in as much as our office is within 250 yards of the Executive Mansion." In her letters to Carey, ER often asked about Margie and the children. After FDR's death, Carey and his family spent a weekend at Val-Kill. He thanked ER warmly for the visit and the opportunity to buy a car from her at a good price, described a short stay with his parents on the way home, and added a note about the dog. This was a thank you note from a friend.[38]

Carey attended the founding meeting of the WFTU in London and became secretary of the U.S. delegation. He arranged to meet with ER on his return and sent her a copy of the conference report. The conference declared its support for the elimination of political, economic, and social discrimination based on race, creed, color, or sex, the establishment of equal pay for equal work, full employment, and the freedom for working people to "organize themselves in Trade Unions and to engage freely in all normal Trade Union activities, including that of collective bargaining." The recommendations fit closely with her agenda.[39]

ER's friendship with David Dubinsky was equally important. In the summer of 1945 she went with Dubinsky to Unity House, the ILGWU's family resort in the Poconos, to address a war fund drive. While she and Dubinsky did not always agree, they had a bond of trust and friendship, and a mutually productive working relationship. In her column ER praised the ILGWU's innovative programs and the active participation of the members. Dubinsky in turn appreciated her firm support for labor's political agenda. He told her he was delighted with her comments and also arranged to transfer a freezer to Val-Kill for her. Although he did not share her willingness to work with the Soviets internationally, he appreciated her critique of communists' roles within trade unions. Evidently recalling her experiences with communists in the American Newspaper Guild and the American Youth Congress, she declared in "My Day" that the Communist Party espoused the "philosophy of the lie," adding, "Because I have experienced the deception of the American Communists, I will not trust them." ER's importance to Dubinsky in labor-political matters was summed up by the chairman of New York State's Liberal Party, who admonished Dubinsky after he and ER had had a disagreement that he should be working to "foster her goodwill and understanding, not to alienate her.... [S]he belongs with us, and our aim must be to keep our solidarity with her."[40]

Carey and Dubinsky held key roles in the United Nations deliberations. At the San Francisco conference in 1945, over forty nongovernmental organizations were invited as consultants and observers for the U.S. delegation. Religious, legal, labor, and peace organizations joined forces to seek a human rights guarantee. Included were representatives of the AF of L and the CIO, as well as the Chamber of Commerce and the Federal Council of Churches. A small group representing these organizations met with Secretary of State Edward Stettinius. After making powerful presentations on the need to address human rights from the very beginning, the consultants were asked if anyone disagreed. Phil Murray rose. Some were not sure exactly where the labor leader stood; he had not yet signed the letter they had presented. According to historian William Korey, Murray got to his feet and with power and authority said to the secretary, "I am here to tell you that I believe I am speaking not only for the CIO but for all labor when I say that we are 100 percent behind the argument which has just been made."[41]

The secretary of state took these recommendations to the delegation, and with U.S. leadership, seven major references to human rights were incorporated into the UN Charter. The United States supported establishing the Human Rights Commission as well. When asked at her last White House press conference about the role of nongovernmental organizations at the UN, ER replied that the objective was to create the machinery for joint action. "They will report back to their own organizations and as far as possible publicize the meeting's reports in every channel they have. They may use radio, newspapers, and magazines. They may have town meetings to reach as many as possible." Mobilizing public support for the UN was complemented by ensuring that the UN endorsed workers' rights. Of the seven NGOs given consultative status with the UN Economic and Social Council, which were allowed to attend meetings and present positions, three were labor groups: the AF of L, the World Federation of Trade Unions, and the International Federation of Christian Trade Unions, a group of mainly Catholic unions allied with Europe's Christian Democratic parties. Dubinsky and Woll were the official consultants from the AF of L, while Carey represented the CIO through the WFTU. As she advised others to do, ER began using her "My Day" column, her speeches, and articles to explain the UN and to gather support for labor positions.[42]

On 1 January 1946 the U.S. delegates embarked on the HMS *Queen Elizabeth* for the transatlantic voyage to the opening meeting of the UN General Assembly in London. Senator Vandenberg asked ER to serve on the Third Committee on Social, Humanitarian and Cultural Affairs. While she suspected that the men considered this a "safe" committee where little of importance would happen, the plight of more than a million refugees quickly became the center of contentious debate in the General Assembly. With her usual intense level of effort and hard work, she mastered the substantive issues and spoke forcefully, though diplomatically, before the assembly. Delegates quickly learned to respect and admire ER. She was smart, hardworking, politically astute, an accomplished pubic speaker, and an experienced committee member. She facilitated helpful informal exchanges by inviting people to meetings in her apartment, and her fluency in French enabled her to hold some discussions in a neutral language. At one meeting, after a very long speech by a French delegate, the translator left the room in tears; ER promptly summarized the remarks for her English-speaking colleagues.[43]

Her "My Day" columns often described the UN proceedings in detail. On 19 January, for example, ER discussed the WFTU's request for a representative in the General Assembly and voting rights on the Economic and Social Council (ECOSOC), based on the WFTU's representation of over 60 million workers. The request was included in the material that Carey had given her the previous year and was reinforced by the Russians. The U.S. delegation was seated next to the Russian delegation, and ER received a warm welcome from V. V. Kuznetsov, president of the All-Union Central Council of Trade Unions in the USSR and part of the WFTU. They had met the previous year through Carey, and she remarked how "a little opportunity like this of seeing someone in your own home, even for a little while, makes you feel much more friendly with them." The request was referred to a subcommittee.[44]

The Economic and Social Council asked ER to join a small group to make recommendations for a permanent Human Rights Commission. When she returned to New York, the group met at Hunter College and immediately elected ER chair. The effort to define human rights, reach a worldwide consensus, and incorporate these principles into the fabric of the United Nations began in earnest. At an early hearing Rose Schneiderman was the only woman to testify. She sought to include rights for women, such as the right to work at profitable employment, to receive equal pay, to vote, and to bargain collectively, and supported a subcommission on the status of women. Schneiderman declared, "The workers of any one nation can make or maintain their gains only if the women all over the world have their rights under an International Bill of Rights."[45]

ER was well aware of her position as the only woman on the U.S. delegation. If she failed, it would look as if "all women had failed." There were only eighteen women from eleven countries among the delegates and advisers. She invited them to tea in her sitting room at the Hotel Claridge to get to know one other and to discuss their concerns. Representatives from feminist groups came to see her, seeking support for a women's commission. While ER had long supported women's organizations domestically, she was not in favor of a separate women's commission at the international level, arguing that women should be represented on all of the commissions rather than by a special body. Two leading proponents of the commission were the Danish delegate Bodil Begtrup and India's Hansa Mehta. A separate women's commission was in fact established, and its officers were present, though not in a voting capacity, when the rights of women were discussed by the Human Rights Commission.[46]

In August 1946 Jim Carey and his family arrived at Hyde Park for the weekend. Carey had just returned from a trip to Russia, Germany, Paris, and London. He brought greetings from Russian friends and sent ER a copy of the CIO delegation's report on the executive committee meetings of the WFTU in Moscow. ER was eager to hear about his travels, she told Carey, no doubt including his ideas for the Human Rights Commission. Later that year she received a letter from Matthew Woll seeking a meeting for himself and Dubinsky to discuss the AF of L's proposed International Bill of Rights, a copy

of which he included. ER was short with Woll and referred him to the Secretariat, where drafts and proposals were being assembled. Nonetheless, she
read the AF of L's statement on trade union rights and soon met with him.[47]

On Wednesday, 22 January 1947, Dubinsky and Woll came to see ER
about the human rights bill they had presented to the commission, for as she
told her readers, "it is natural, of course, that labor unions should be interested in human rights. And one of the things that I hope will evolve from any
bill of this kind is the right of people to economic as well as political freedom."
Dubinsky and Woll were the official consultants and had the right to submit materials and attend meetings of the Economic and Social Council, the
Human Rights Commission, and other UN organizations. The AF of L soon
hired Toni Sender as a full-time representative to participate in such meetings
on a regular basis and report back.[48]

Sender was a German journalist who had been active in social democratic
politics and served in the Reichstag. After the Nazis seized power, she fled
to Belgium and came to the United States in December 1935. She had much
in common with Eleanor Roosevelt as a journalist, lecturer, politician, labor
supporter, and specialist on refugees and forced labor. She wrote articles and
traveled the country giving speeches and in 1939 published *The Autobiography of a German Rebel.* ER later praised Sender and Woll for their work on
documenting the extent of forced labor in communist countries. During the
formation of the Human Rights Commission, Sender had the authority to put
items on the agenda and participate in the discussions, though not to vote,
and was able to attend the many social functions where delegates and consultants met informally.[49]

By January 1947 the United Nations had found a temporary home on Long
Island, setting up offices in a building where gyroscopes had been made during the war. It was a reasonable drive from Hyde Park or from ER's apartment
in the city. John Humphrey, an expert in international law from Canada, had
been named director of the Human Rights Division of the UN Secretariat and
was given staff to help with the necessary research and technical assistance.
He later remarked that early in its history the Human Rights Commission
gathered strength and influence from Eleanor Roosevelt's world-renowned
stature, both because she reminded people of FDR and because she was a
well-known advocate of humanitarian causes.[50]

That summer the UN referred trade union matters to the International
Labor Organization for advice. In the fall the ILO proposed ten principles
to the Economic and Social Council, but because the ILO dealt with employer and worker organizations on an equal basis, it did not support the
specific provisions for union recognition that organized labor was seeking.
The Economic and Social Council and the General Assembly voted to trans-
mit the documents to the Commission on Human Rights to decide if there

were labor rights that could be considered essential for all people who work. ER assumed that the issue of trade union rights would be settled quickly and thought the ILO was already well on the way to safeguarding the freedom of association for trade unions. The basic question posed by ER was simply "Where is the proper place to discuss trade union rights?" As the debate continued, a subcommittee was established to gather all of the resolutions and amendments. The WFTU had only a part-time staff representative there, but ER was conscious of the divide within the U.S. labor movement and "repeatedly insisted that if any mention of the WFTU was adopted the AF of L must be given the same place," according to Sender. The debate moved to the full Human Rights Commission and was the subject of discussion for the next year.[51]

Mounting international tensions complicated the process of consensus-building for delegates to the commission. In China, Mao Zedong was leading the Communist Party to victory over the U.S.-supported government forces led by Chiang Kai-shek. In eastern Europe, Stalin had ended multiparty government and seized control of Czechoslovakia. The Middle East was in turmoil. Communist parties were gaining electoral strength in Italy and France. When General Charles de Gaulle proposed that trade unions be replaced by associations where employers and employees had equal rights, ER noted dryly that "trade unions were the first organizations to be dissolved" under Hitler. She saw the State Department's efforts to have the CIO withdraw from the WFTU as shortsighted. She believed it was important for American unionists to engage in dialogue with their counterparts in other countries and "find points of agreement on which to work together." ER became increasingly frustrated with Truman's turn toward a militant and unilateral approach to the Soviets, based more on fear than on strength.[52]

The work on human rights moved forward amid these upheavals. ER prepared for the drafting committee meetings. Trade union rights were on the agenda. She found the Russian delegates, following a strict party line, particularly difficult. Each article was debated, and the committee was unable to complete the review of the new economic and social rights. Then the full Human Rights Commission reviewed the entire draft, one article at a time. Contentious and often emotional debates turned especially on the relationship between political and civil rights, which were well understood in countries with constitutional legal traditions, and social and economic rights, which varied greatly across nations and were seldom understood as fundamental rights rather than as privileges granted or withheld by the state. ER began with a strong endorsement of these new rights, affirming that the United States "favored the inclusion of economic and social rights in the Declaration, for no personal liberty could exist without economic security and independence. Men in need were not free men."[53]

The specific mention of trade unions was removed from the article on association and elevated to a separate paragraph in the article on work. Strong arguments for the inclusion of trade unions were made by Auguste Vanistendael for the International Federation of Christian Trade Unions and Toni Sender for the AF of L, who emphasized that trade unions were a new form of association "in existence for only some sixty years." ER stated that from the perspective of the United States, trade union rights were an essential element of freedom, the recent passage of the Taft-Hartley law notwithstanding. "While other associations had long enjoyed recognition," she remarked, "trade unions had met with much opposition and it was only recently that they had become an accepted form of association. The struggle was, in fact, still continuing, so her delegation thought, therefore, that trade unions should be specifically mentioned." The commission also took up the issues of the closed shop and the right to strike. In the interest of reaching an agreement on principles, however, it was decided to divide the work into two phases. The declaration would be a statement of principles with no legal status or enforcement mechanisms, enabling countries to agree on the language. The second phase was implementation; here covenants would be developed that had legal implications.[54]

Both the closed shop and the right to strike were designated as implementation issues. The U.S. delegation appeared to favor language guaranteeing the open shop, which Taft-Hartley had provided. Delegates from other countries, however, noted that Truman had vowed to restore the rights that Taft-Hartley had curtailed, and ER had publicly supported the closed shop. The U.S. delegates must have had lively debates about what stand to take on this issue. Amendments were offered and withdrawn until they agreed on the wording "Everyone has a right to form or join a trade union," but left the decision on open as opposed to closed shops for the implementation phase. A similar debate was held on the right to strike, and again a resolution was postponed by agreeing to treat the matter as one of implementing the right to form and join unions. A final resolution was not reached until the November meeting of the Third Committee at the General Assembly in November. Other debates were held on equal pay, discrimination, remuneration, family allowances, and rest and leisure. Eleanor Roosevelt and Toni Sender were active participants.[55]

Throughout 1948 ER was in contact with Jim Carey and the WFTU. In February Carey felt so confident about ER that he asked her to take his place as the speaker at a CIO dinner. After he attended the WFTU executive committee meeting in May, he met with ER at the 1 June dinner to raise money and awareness for the Hudson Shore Labor School, run by Hilda Smith. Just ten days later Carey asked ER to visit his wife, Marge, who was in the hospital in White Plains. In September, when ER, her eighteen-year-old grandson, and the entire U.S. delegation crossed the Atlantic to Paris on the SS *America*,

Carey was also on board. Together she and the labor leader answered questions about issues such as the Marshall Plan and the United Nations from a group of students from the United States and Europe. ER told her readers about socializing with Carey and several other delegates, including the Russians, in the comfort of a Parisian home. Carey brought movies he had taken of labor meetings in Russia, Czechoslovakia, and Italy. These gatherings were opportunities for ER and Carey to share information beyond what the State Department or Toni Sender provided.[56]

When the UN General Assembly convened in Paris on 21 September 1948, the international situation was deteriorating rapidly. The Soviets had set up a blockade around the sections of Berlin occupied by the United States, Britain, and France, and around-the-clock airlifts were bringing food and supplies into West Berlin. Korea remained divided along the truce line, but rival regimes had been established in the North and South. Palestine was under a truce imposed by the UN. Refugees, forced labor, and the reconstruction of Europe were being addressed in many committees and commissions. This increasingly unstable, even explosive atmosphere both impeded the work of the UN and justified the need for its existence. ER's staff noted a new urgency on her part. Durward Sandifer, her State Department aide, observed a very different demeanor from ER's tentative approach in London in 1946. The Third Committee on Social, Humanitarian, and Cultural Affairs took up the draft declaration, and debate began anew on each article, much to the frustration of many of the delegates and staff. ER reported on these negotiations but also took time to meet with others, including trade unionists and people from the ORT training center.[57]

Paris was rainy and gray the week of 15 November, when the committee took up discussion of work-related rights. The debates were long and contentious, and weary delegates grew irritated as they scrutinized the language of these fundamental principles again and again. Yet the process was necessary to arrive at a consensus; every nation wanted to be heard, and each needed to understand the others' perspective. As they took up the article on work in its original form, ER told her readers that it "gave everyone the right to work under favourable conditions and at fair wages, with protection against unemployment." Everyone had the right to equal pay for equal work and a decent standard of living. The article stated that "everyone is free to form and join trade and labor unions for protection of his rights and interests." The Russians again insisted on amendments barring discrimination on the basis of race, nationality, and sex, which ER thought "unwise and unnecessary"; the article was sent to a subcommittee. On Thanksgiving Day they took up the related issues of workers' family responsibilities, meeting until 11 pm. Between sessions the Americans shared a holiday dinner; ER had managed to acquire two turkeys from the U.S. embassy.[58]

On Friday the article on work was finally completed. ER's "My Day" column focused on the first two paragraphs: the right to work with just and favorable conditions and protection from unemployment, and the right to equal pay for equal work without any discrimination. The final version also included paragraph 3, the right to just and favorable remuneration for the worker and his family, and paragraph 4, the right to form and join trade unions. Eleanor Roosevelt objected to paragraph 3 because she believed that pay should be based on work, not family status, but acknowledged that the article as a whole was acceptable. A subcommittee on style was appointed to put everything in final form. It was in this subcommittee that Hansa Mehta, the delegate from India, argued most effectively for the inclusive language of "Everyone has the right" throughout the entire document. ER understood "All men have the right" to include men and women, but Mehta countered that in many societies it would be understood as limited to men. The "everyone" language was included, although ER maintained that there were circumstances that required differential treatment. The committee had held more than eighty-one meetings and considered almost 170 resolutions containing amendments. A concise final document contained thirty articles.[59]

With ER's gentle but firm guidance and close collaboration with the delegates from France, China, and Lebanon, the Universal Declaration of Human Rights was presented to the General Assembly late in the evening of 9 December. The mood in the Palais de Chaillot was somber. Charles Malik, the tall, broad-shouldered delegate from Lebanon who chaired the Committee on Social, Humanitarian, and Cultural Affairs, introduced the document, which for the first time clearly articulated the principles of human rights, including social and economic as well as political and civil rights. This Harvard-educated philosopher, an Arab leader of Muslims and Christians, pointed out where each country could find its contributions and the influence of its culture. Delegates from many parts of the world, including India, China, Greece, France, the Soviet Union, the United Kingdom, the United States, and Latin America, had drawn on their own documents, experiences, and wisdom over several years of careful deliberations. Thirty-four delegates followed Malik to the podium.[60]

"When her turn came," writes legal scholar Mary Ann Glendon, "Mrs. Roosevelt, in a simple, long-sleeved blue dress, stepped up to the bank of microphones and donned her reading glasses. The golden brooch at her neck, resembling a fleur-de-lis, was a replica of the three-feathered Roosevelt crest that FDR had given her on their wedding day. In a high, clear voice, she announced: 'We stand today at the threshold of a great event both in the life of the United Nations and in the life of mankind.'" The document set a high standard, and while acknowledging the differences and deficiencies of all the member nations, she called on the General Assembly to approve the declaration overwhelmingly. On 10 December, when the speeches came to an end, the delegates were polled on each article. Just before midnight the roll call began on the entire document. The Universal Declaration of Human Rights passed the General Assembly with forty-eight votes in favor and none against. The Soviet-led bloc, as well as South Africa and Saudi Arabia, cast eight abstentions. Honduras and Yemen were absent. Herbert Evatt, president of the General Assembly, ended the meeting with a special tribute to Eleanor Roosevelt, and the General Assembly responded with a standing ovation.[61] The final article on work reads:

The Universal Declaration of Human Rights Article 23

1. Everyone has the right to work, to free choice of employment, to just and favourable conditions of work and to protection against unemployment.
2. Everyone, without any discrimination, has the right to equal pay for equal work.
3. Everyone who works has the right to just and favourable remuneration ensuring for himself and his family an existence worthy of human dignity, and supplemented, if necessary, by other means of social protection.
4. Everyone has the right to form and to join trade unions for the protection of his interests.

ER returned to Hyde Park as quickly as possible, knowing all too well what challenges lay ahead for the declaration and the United Nations. She gave only small hints suggesting the role of the labor movement in what would become her most acclaimed accomplishment. She thanked Mathew Woll of the American Federation of Labor for his kind words on her work in Paris, telling him simply, "Your draft was a great help." One of her first commitments in the new year was to speak about the Universal Declaration at a meeting of the Women's Trade Union League, and to begin translating words into facts. Soon, however, the unions acknowledged how much they valued her contributions. For progressive labor leaders, ER had developed from an intermediary who had access to powerful people to a political and diplomatic power in her own right. She was able to take their cause to the highest political levels and to the general public in ways that they were unable to do themselves. They also recognized the important way she connected with their members, who were the critical base of their own power. Even more conservative labor leaders saw her as a force to be reckoned with; her letters were answered and her calls returned. Now she had helped take their cause to the entire world through the United Nations. In 1949 Phil Murray showed the esteem in which many labor leaders held her by writing a letter to the Norwegian parliament supporting Eleanor Roosevelt's nomination for the Nobel Peace Prize.[62]

When asked why a document with no power of enforcement was important, ER responded, "One should never belittle the value of words, . . . for they have a way of getting translated into fact, and therein lies the hope for our universal declaration." She was very proud of the declaration and worked tirelessly to translate the words into action the rest of her life. She argued forcefully that the right to form and join trade unions was an essential element of freedom on the international level, while at the same time that right was being attacked at home, making her achievement all the more significant and the need for action in the very near future that much more crucial.[63]

6

POINTING THE WAY

You have started a great change which will bring about a better life
to all of our people and a better life and greater hope ... to all the
peoples of the world.
ELEANOR ROOSEVELT to the first AFL-CIO Convention,
4 December 1955

On 4 December 1955 Eleanor Roosevelt, now seventy-one years old, left
her apartment on East Sixty-second Street in Manhattan and began her public
day as a guest on the radio program hosted by Margaret Truman and Mike
Wallace. Her topic was the meaning of Human Rights Day, to be observed
on the eighth anniversary of the UN's adoption of the Universal Declaration.
After the broadcast ended, she hurried over to the grand old Pierre Hotel
across from Central Park, where two hundred of Adlai Stevenson's supporters were gathered for a private luncheon. She and the governor gave brief
talks, and $100,000 was pledged for Stevenson's second presidential cam-
paign. New York's Liberal Party was represented by Alex Rose, president of
the Hat, Cap and Millinery Workers Union. As lunch ended, ER was met by
her friend Jim Carey, who escorted her downtown to the old Seventy-first
Regiment Armory at Thirty-fourth Street and Park Avenue.[1]
    There, in the cavernous hall, 1,500 delegates of the newly merged AFL-
CIO were waiting for Eleanor Roosevelt. The delegates, representing 15 million members from 141 unions, were accompanied by 4,500 guests and 250
members of the media. *Time* magazine described it as "the greatest assem-
blage of free labor's many mansions in one house." The merger convention
was the culmination of persistent efforts to resolve conflicts and get the two
great labor organizations to work together. ER considered this historic occasion "significant for the labor movement and for our country." Behind the
speakers' podium hung a huge red, white, and blue banner displaying the logo

of the new federation, hands clasped across the continent. Among the cluster of stars at the very top was the heading "All Trades–All Crafts–All Colors–All Creeds–Together! Below it, an artist's image of working men and women of every color and trade dwarfed the speakers standing in front of the banner. ER was worried about addressing the delegates. "The hall is so big and so bare," she remarked, "that I was a little troubled for fear I would not be able to hold their interest when it came to my turn." When AFL-CIO president George Meany announced, "Ladies and Gentlemen, to me this is the highlight of this Convention—the opportunity to present to you the No. 1 lady, the first lady of the entire world, Mrs. Franklin Delano Roosevelt," the crowd rose to its feet, applauded, and cheered. ER, in a dark tailored dress and small hat with three strands of pearls around her neck, stood radiant before the audience.[2]

"Mr. Chairman, ladies and gentlemen," she began, "I feel very much at home with this Convention because, as you know, I am a union member too. I belong to the American Newspaper Guild." ER went on to recall her early education in labor issues. A Miss Wray, a worker from the box makers' union who had welcomed the distinguished speaker in her role as a member of the reception committee, reminded ER that they "had once walked a picket line together. . . . [I]t gave me a nice and friendly feeling to remember that little incident, when Rose Schneiderman was educating me. . . . [she] had been a good teacher." Today Schneiderman was standing just behind ER on the podium. ER reflected on the progress workers had made since the days of tenement sweatshops, but she quickly laid down her challenge for the future: "First, of course, we have to set our house in order. We cannot hold up to the world either standards of race equality or of equal opportunity or of better conditions of labor unless we have them." Next she called on the workers to be politically engaged. In a democracy, she said, "we have to be active to get the right candidates. We have to support them once they are in office and we have to know about the issues." Finally, she emphasized the importance of understanding the problems of the world. Taking disarmament as an example, she called for the United Nations to be strengthened and people of different nations to listen to one another rather than be frozen into one position.[3]

As the cold war escalated and new international crises emerged, ER increasingly saw the labor movement as a model not only for civic engagement but for international relations as well: "If we can find a way to obviate strikes[,] it may well serve as a basis for obviating wars, since industrial difficulties are not so very different from the difficulties that face nations." She became discouraged about the fate of the world, however, when workers did not elect good leaders and when employees and managers could not work out agreements and avoid strikes. In the midst of the steel strike in 1952, she had wondered how nations in conflict could resolve their complex difficulties if the United States could not settle its own labor problems. Addressing the newly merged AFL-CIO, she warned the delegates that they would encounter difficulties, but she was optimistic that that they would work them out because of the intelligence of their leaders and their determination to remain united. In short, for ER the merger meant more power for the people, who, with education and understanding, could become a beacon of light for the world.[4]

ER's optimism and her restraint reflected her experiences during the transitions leading up to the merger convention. In 1950, eager to embrace innovations, she quickly added the new medium of television to her public education tools, starting with her own show about current events. As fear of the Soviet Union and communism gripped the nation, political resistance to the United Nations grew. ER sought union support for the international body as she made the transition from being a diplomat in the Truman administration to a private citizen after the Republican landslide in 1952. She defended civil liberties and opposed the repressive tactics of McCarthyism, but ER had grown increasingly concerned about communists after her own tense confrontations with the Soviets at the UN. She understood when the CIO, complying with the Taft-Hartley Act, insisted that its member unions either remove those accused of communist affiliations from leadership or leave the organization.

As conservatives gained power in Washington, ER supported a shift in industrial collective bargaining to negotiate for health and welfare benefits while challenging the government on wage and price control policies. After veteran labor leaders of Rose Schneiderman's generation retired, ER worked with the emerging women leaders. She had high hopes for the transfer of leadership in the AFL and CIO to George Meany and Walter Reuther. Still, she knew that the newly unified labor movement would continue to struggle in the face of employer hostility, political attack, and internal disputes. Eventually, she hoped, settling differences by negotiation would become a habit, and force would not be needed. Both at home and abroad, democracy, human rights, and the peaceful resolution of conflicts were her highest aspirations. "Perhaps," she cautiously concluded her speech to the AFL-CIO, "you are pointing the way."[5]

About the United Nations

In the years following ER's achievement with the Human Rights Commission she continued to defend labor rights at the United Nations and to seek union support for the international organization within the United States. Believing that democracy depended on individual participation, she felt that the success of the UN ultimately rested on the support of citizens who took a global perspective rather than pursuing purely personal ends. With growing hostility in the Congress, ER turned to the unions to deliver the message about international cooperation. Her early audiences included the Women's Trade Union League, the International Ladies' Garment Workers' Union, and the International Chemical Workers' Union.[6]

ER spelled out the connections in a speech to the convention of the International Union of Electrical Workers (IUE), a newly formed anticommunist CIO union led by Jim Carey. She praised the union's education programs and compared them to international programs sponsored by UNESCO (the United Nations Educational, Social, Cultural, and Scientific Organization). Stressing a recurring theme, she said that the people of the world were looking to see if Americans "accept[ed] the responsibility of actually being citizens in a free world of democracy." Foreign governments were quick to point out the contradictions between American ideals and actual practice as they read about it in the newspapers. ER told the five hundred delegates about her experience of trying to write the UN covenants for human rights and asked for their help in persuading the United States to become a signatory. The convention responded by unanimously endorsing the covenants and calling on the U.S. government to sign the document, sending the resolution to both the secretary of state and the UN secretary-general. Local unions were also asked to send statements supporting international human rights to the ambassadors who represented undemocratic nations, including the Soviet Union. She reached thousands more as the convention was televised and reported in the newspapers.[7]

IUE Third Annual Convention
18 September 1951
Mrs. Eleanor Roosevelt

Part of ER's speech at the convention addressed the United Nations Human Rights Covenants:

> Democracy counts on what each one of us does. . . . I never thought much about it until I began my long education in what can constitutionally go into a covenant on human rights which the United States could ratify. Now, as you know, the American Bar Association has already said that this international document is a Communistic document and that we should not ratify it. Of course, it is not ready to be ratified. The articles aren't really finally written yet, and there are things now in that covenant which are not there because we voted for them, but it happens of course that in writing an international document, while we ourselves may not vote in the affirmative, we can be outvoted by the majority, and thus witness a result with which we do not agree. . . . However, the document is yet unfinished. . . .

Wait, first of all to see what is in the document when it finally is submitted, and then study carefully how, in ratifying it, we can safeguard our rights. I assure you that your representatives have gravely considered all the constitutional questions involved in a document on human rights—a document to help the world to obtain some of the rights and freedoms that we enjoy.... We must never forget either that we have a great deal of work to do here at home in safeguarding and extending our own human rights and freedoms. We must constantly keep in mind this fact—that what we are doing here at home is being watched by all the other nations of the world.

The convention did not wait. After ER finished, the chairman of the Resolutions Committee requested: "Will the members of the Resolutions Committee please appear in the room at my right immediately? We have a resolution we wish to consider shortly in the light of Mrs. Roosevelt's address."

Convention Resolution on Human Rights

The convention unanimously adopted a Resolution on Human Rights, calling on the United Nations and the U.S. government to approve the covenant and work toward the objectives it set forth. They further resolved "that not only the IUE-CIO International Office, but also IUE-CIO local unions send statements in support of this resolution to the Ambassadors in the United States of all the dictator countries, including those of the Soviet Union, Poland, Czechoslovakia, Argentina and Spain."

IUE, *Proceedings of the Third Annual Convention.* Used with permission of the IUE-CWA, Industrial Division of the Communications Workers of America, AFL-CIO, CLC (Canadian Labour Congress).

As work on the documents proceeded slowly at the UN, ER invited several labor leaders to meet at her apartment "to discuss the present and future course of our international endeavors for human rights." She considered unions among the "foremost of the groups to be consulted" because they had so much national and international experience that was relevant to the discussions and because of the "increasingly apparent need for better and full understanding by the American people of the human rights program." Unions, she hoped, could form a grass-roots response to the increasingly hostile stance taken by Congress.[8]

The Human Rights Commission eventually developed two covenants, one on economic and social rights and one on civil and political rights. For her readers ER used trade union rights as an example of the difficulties the documents were addressing. One article declared, "The states, parties to the Covenant, recognize the right of everyone, in conformity with Article 16, to form and join local, national and international trade unions of his choice for the protection of his economic and social interest." After the technical problem of where to place trade union rights in the articles and covenants was resolved, the Soviet Union had wanted to spell out what each state should do, including a paragraph that read, "The right to strike should be guaranteed." ER found herself in a difficult position. She told her readers that it was hard to vote against that one provision in the Soviet amendment, because while people in the United States believed in the right to strike, that right "is resorted to only after collective bargaining has failed. Other nations have other provisions, but it is obvious that in a covenant of human rights we cannot incorporate any of these details and still have the covenant acceptable to the majority of nations." In the end, the article set forth the brief statement of principles, and the more detailed Soviet amendment was rejected.[9]

Increasingly ER looked at domestic problems with an eye toward how they were seen internationally and how they affected U.S. foreign policy. When President Truman asked her to address the 1952 Democratic convention, she was reluctant, but Truman persuaded her to tell the country what the United Nations meant to world peace. She stressed how important domestic issues had become to foreign policy, taking civil rights and labor as her examples. She said, "Our attitude on labor is of vital importance as it will be used by the Soviets, if possible, to prove that we do not have a real interest in the working class which forms a majority of our population." Her reception at the convention was overwhelmingly positive. The political landscape, however, shifted dramatically in November, as Eisenhower won the White House in a landslide, and the Democrats lost control of both the House and Senate. ER had offered some advice to Adlai Stevenson, and defended him against labor critics, but she was not actively involved in the campaign. Both the AF of L and the CIO had worked hard for the Democrats, with massive efforts at voter registration and PAC support. Stevenson carried the labor vote, but by smaller margins than Democrats had in the past. Political analysis in the 1950s found that many union members were not registered to vote, did not show up at the polls, or opposed the unions' political activities.[10]

After twenty years Eleanor Roosevelt's Democratic Party was no longer in power. She sent her letter of resignation from the United Nations to the president-elect, and on 30 December she received Eisenhower's response accepting her offer to step down. Shortly before Eisenhower's inauguration, ER went to see Clark Eichelberger, director of the American Association for the United Nations, and offered her services as an educational volunteer. This offer did not diminish her ties with labor. Jim Carey was on the board of the association, and Walter Reuther soon joined the membership committee at ER's request. The isolationist campaign was gaining strength in Congress, and Eisenhower's new secretary of state, John Foster Dulles, announced that the United States would no longer seek adoption of the two covenants on human rights. ER countered by traveling the country and the world speaking in support of the United Nations. In Salt Lake City labor leaders from the AF of L and the CIO representing all of labor in Utah met with her. In Seattle union members came from across the Pacific Northwest, and others joined her in Huron, South Dakota. She told her readers, "We owe a vote of thanks to Mr. Meany and Mr. Reuther and the head of the brotherhoods for the way they have alerted their groups so that they have felt an obligation to come to these organizational meetings." ER continued this call to action on behalf of the UN at the AFL-CIO merger convention.[11]

The Cold War at Home

As ER fought for the human rights covenants, the country was once again gripped by fear of communism. The determination to contain the Soviet Union abroad was accompanied by a drive to purge dissent and enforce conformity at home. White working-class Americans, many of whom were union members, were moving to the suburbs, buying houses, and starting families. While they hoped to enjoy the "American dream," their children were learning to duck under their desks in case of nuclear war, and some families were building bomb shelters in their backyards. In the name of national security, union leaders and members even vaguely suspected of communist affiliation were effectively attacked by a wide range of people using multiple tools. Charges of "un-American" activities were investigated by federal agencies and congressional committees, became the subject of articles and sermons, were pursued by employers as well as rival labor leaders, and led to courtrooms and ruined reputations. While Communist Party membership was not illegal, by 1954 three out of four Americans thought that members of the party should lose their citizenship.[12]

Under enormous legal, political, and public pressure the CIO moved away from its previous tolerance of left-wing unions. These unions had defied CIO policy by supporting Henry Wallace's third party presidential campaign and refusing to comply with the Taft-Hartley Act's requirement that unions file affidavits attesting that they had no communists in leadership positions. At the CIO executive board meeting in May 1949 Phil Murray began the effort to expel unions that did not file affidavits, and the convention that year established a series of three-man trial committees to assess charges of communist affiliation against member unions. Some leaders, including Carey, collaborated with federal agencies and congressional investigating committees.

When the left-led unions went to court to argue that the affidavit requirement was unconstitutional, the U.S. Supreme Court ruled against them. Simultaneously the CIO executive board voted to withdraw from the WFTU because of Soviet dominance and joined with the AF of L to form the International Confederation of Free Trade Unions (ICFTU), which excluded unions in communist-led countries. The CIO came into compliance with federal law and helped lay the groundwork for the merger with the AF of L, but the price was high. By the time the CIO was finished, eleven unions had been expelled and it had lost almost one-third of its membership. Many of the left-wing members who were purged or chose to depart included African Americans, women, and white men who were effective shop floor organizers committed to equality in the workplace.[13]

During that summer the largest of the left-leaning unions, the United Electrical, Radio and Machine Workers (UE), withdrew from the CIO. Murray chartered a new union, the International Union of Electrical, Radio and Machine Workers (IUE), and appointed Jim Carey, longtime secretary of the CIO and former president of the UE, to head the organization. The UE refused to cede control, and bitter struggles for the allegiance of local unions broke out around the country. Carey fought for every local, not only against the UE but also against other unions that saw the split as an opportunity to raid the UE. Mary Callahan, secretary-treasurer of Local 105 in Philadelphia, reported that her local had unanimously voted to join the IUE. In other locations the NLRB held contested elections in the factories of General Electric, Westinghouse, Delco, Frigidaire, Philco, RCA, and many smaller companies. The atmosphere was charged with anticommunism, as the IUE portrayed the UE as communistic and unpatriotic, implying that staying with the UE carried a risk of losing government contracts in national security facilities. There was a growing Catholic anticommunist movement, and priests preached in favor of the IUE on the grounds that communists were atheists.[14]

During this difficult period ER spoke out forcefully in support of civil liberties and in opposition to such rising anticommunist crusaders as Senator Joseph McCarthy, the Wisconsin Republican. Her position on communists within the labor movement, however, shifted with that of the CIO. Initially ER was quiet on the struggle engulfing the CIO, but her relationship with Carey, both public and private, was a sign of her support for the CIO's decision. She continued to seek Carey's advice on labor questions. When Carey invited her to address the first convention of the new IUE, he wrote: "I know you have followed with personal interest the startling recent events in the CIO and you know too how active I have been in the struggle.... A message from you would add tremendously." She did not attend the November meeting, but she noted in "My Day" that one afternoon just before Christmas she had driven with Carey to his home "to see his wife and children whom I had not seen for a long time." She often asked about his family, expressing her concern when the Careys' daughter was injured. In 1950 ER embraced the new medium of television. When NBC began broadcasting *Today with Mrs. Roosevelt,* a half-hour Sunday afternoon program about current events, ER invited Carey to be one of her first guests, giving him a national platform to defend the CIO's policies.[15]

Anticommunism took an ominous political form when Senator McCarthy claimed in a speech delivered on 9 February 1950 in Wheeling, West Virginia, that he had a list of known communists working in the State Department who should have been fired as potential traitors. His heated rhetorical attacks on President Truman, the federal government, and the Democratic Party for aiding and abetting the "enemy within" fueled a round of red-baiting and persecution that exceeded the 1919 "Red Scare" led by Attorney General Palmer. In retrospect the term "McCarthyism" has become synonymous with reckless and unsubstantiated accusations and attacks on the patriotism of political opponents. At the time, however, it represented a major threat to civil liberties and to postwar liberalism. Recognizing the danger, ER invited a group of liberal leaders to Hyde Park to discuss ways to strengthen a positive liberal program, including means to combat "the dangerous misuse of the fear of Communism by reactionary forces in order to destroy the liberal movement." Carey represented Murray and the CIO.[16]

Labor leaders saw McCarthy's assault on suspected communists who had infiltrated government and the media as quite different from their own anticommunist actions, and ER seemed to agree. In 1952, addressing students at Howard University in Washington, DC, Carey justified his anticommunist position within the labor movement and distinguished it from McCarthy's views. Carey argued that his mission as president of the IUE was a daily war to drive a communist-controlled union out of the plants and shops in an important defense industry for the nation. McCarthy, by contrast, was leading a broad right-wing attack on civil liberties in Congress and across the country. Carey charged that "professional anti-Communists" were creating a "national hysteria" with their attacks against public schools, book publishers, the entertainment industry, the United Nations, and the State Department. Turning to an allegation that was guaranteed to shock his audience at the nation's premier university serving African Americans, he reminded them that Senator McCarthy had accused Eleanor Roosevelt of the "promotion of Communism and immorality and indecency among so-called minority groups in Washington." He called for a new liberalism, "no longer susceptible to the extremes of the left or right, but militant in its own democratic courage." Carey sent the printed speech to ER, and she congratulated him. The AF of L would not tolerate neutrality in the cold war at home or abroad, but even George Meany disavowed McCarthy, declaring, "We are not going to gain anything in the fight on Communism if, in these Congressional investigations such as are carried on by the McCarthy committee, we throw to the winds all semblance of American fair play." Dubinsky offered alternatives to what he called the McCarthy way.[17]

This was not the only crisis in which ER came to the public defense of the CIO. The unexpected outbreak of the Korean War in 1950 and Truman's rapid commitment of U.S. armed forces had sent the nation back to war in the Pacific. ER reluctantly agreed that force was a necessary response to aggression. The Truman administration expected a short-term conflict and only slowly moved the economy onto a war footing. The Office of Defense Mobilization was not created until six months after the war began; Truman appointed Charles E. Wilson, president of General Electric, director. Wilson had been unbending in his dealings with the IUE and made no distinction between the CIO and the left-wing members it had expelled.[18]

When the defense mobilization effort reached a crisis over controlling wages but not prices and labor leaders walked out of the government meetings in protest, ER placed part of the blame on the employers' history of redbaiting. In her defense of the patriotism of the remaining CIO unions, she used Carey as an example. "The labor unions have had a long struggle to rid themselves of Communists," she wrote. "One of the people who has carried on a most difficult fight within his own union is James B. Carey of the CIO. He finally had to form a new electrical workers' union and there is no question about the bitterness he must have experienced when Mr. Wilson insisted that there was no difference between the two electrical workers' groups." Carey would have to overcome his bitterness, she argued, but Wilson would also have to abandon his former antiunion position.[19]

In the fall of 1951 ER offered her full support for the IUE-CIO by addressing its third convention. She flew to Buffalo in time to have lunch with Carey and the executive board before speaking at the afternoon session. Five hundred delegates filled the ballroom of the Statler Hotel. Carey explained the procedures for televising the address and then introduced Eleanor Roosevelt as the CIO's most distinguished member. Having the "first lady of the world" address the convention was an important endorsement for Carey and his union, sending a strong message to government leaders and employers that Jim Carey and the IUE were not the same as the UE. "I am very much honored to be with your Union at this Convention," she began, "because I feel that you stand for the very best in the labor movement. I think you have done a magnificent job, and in your hands is so much that is vital to the interests of the country today when so many things have to be done for our safety."[20]

While the speech focused on the UN, ER concluded her remarks by addressing the threat of international communism. She argued that the best insurance against communism was for the country to be strong economically and to help other nations. She cautioned, much as FDR had in 1933, that people should not make decisions out of fear. Rather, "we must make our decisions on the national level and on the international level because we have a vision of what we want to achieve at home and abroad.... We are not perfect," she concluded, "but we move forward and the nation that moves forward can never be conquered." Both Carey and ER used this speech to reach broader audiences through television and newspaper articles.[21]

As the number of people whose names were smeared and careers were ruined by allegations of their being communists or communist sympathizers grew, ER was among the few unintimidated liberals who defended people such as Virginia Foster Durr, a white activist who had worked with interracial unions in the South. She wrote in "My Day" that Durr "did not like Ku Klux Klan or vigilante methods," and if people "wanted to have a union, they had a right to have it." ER was beginning to think that "if you have been a liberal, if you believe that those who are strong must sometimes consider the weak, and that with strength and power goes responsibility, automatically some people consider you a Communist." Labor, she wrote, now shared the responsibilities that strength and power entailed, but this had not always been the case, and the rights of labor had to be fought for. Expressing a sentiment shared by grass-roots activists in labor and civil rights, she declared, "If everyone who fought for those rights was Communist, then there are more Communists than we can count in this country."[22]

The anticommunist crusade maintained its focus on organized labor. New federal legislation was proposed allowing employers to dismiss people from defense plants who they feared might be likely to engage in sabotage or espionage. More hearings were held to determine if unions were controlled by the Communist Party and to prohibit workers from paying dues to organizations that were communist-led. ER wondered aloud "if these bills are not aimed more at weakening labor unions than actually at protecting us from communism." Finally, Senator McCarthy went too far by challenging the patriotism of the U.S. Army. In nationally televised hearings, the country watched as he attacked the reputation of men in uniform and sparred with the army's able defense lawyer, Joseph Welch, who repudiated McCarthy's attempts at character assassination with the stunning question, "Have you no sense of decency, sir?" McCarthy rapidly lost favor with the public. On 12 December 1954 McCarthy was censured by his colleagues in the U.S. Senate.[23]

Just days before the censure vote, ER returned to Los Angeles to address the sixteenth and last CIO convention. Reuther introduced her effusively, saying, "In a time when the apostles of fear and hatred and hysteria are dividing America, hers has been the voice of courage and of common sense calling upon the people and urging that as free people, we unite." ER praised the CIO's accomplishments and growing strength. She urged the unions and the nation to recapture the attitude that allowed people to experiment with new ideas and not be afraid of the unknown. Communism could be defeated only by showing the world what democracy could achieve, which depended on the efforts of every individual in the hall. "We can't just talk," she argued. "We have got to act.... [W]e must see improvement for the masses of people, not for the little group on top." Union members could help make this vision a reality, but she warned the delegates and her readers that it would not be easy.[24]

After the CIO had expelled the left-led unions, the remaining unions, like the newly formed IUE, actively recruited their members. The CIO unions grew during the Korean War, while the expelled unions were besieged with lawsuits, organizing raids, government investigations, and corporate hostility. The UE was one of the few left-led unions to survive, winning elections in a few large electrical plants. Labor's cold war, however, was not limited to the domestic front. Internationally, after the CIO joined with the AF of L to form the ICFTU, they were unable to agree on policies toward countries and unions that were social democratic, socialist, or communist. According to Reuther biographer Nelson Lichtenstein, the CIO, and particularly the Reuther brothers, were more willing than either the State Department or the AF of L "to subordinate grand strategy to the unique history and character of each national labor movement." In some situations strengthening social democratic unions was critical to defeating the alternative communist model; eventually CIO leaders met with the communists. George Meany and the AF of L strongly disagreed. These differences over foreign policy intensified after the merger.[25]

ER remained aligned with the Reuthers. Victor Reuther worked closely with the ICFTU and the social democratic trade unions in Britain, the Netherlands, West Germany, and Sweden. He lived in Paris representing the CIO in the early 1950s and later recalled taking his wife and children to visit ER at her hotel when she arrived for UN meetings, as if they were going to see their grandmother. He made clear, however, that the important discussions on both foreign and domestic issues were between ER and his brother. While working internationally, ER never lost sight of labor issues at home and the need to educate the public. She was particularly concerned with labor relations in the large industrial sectors so important to national security and economic progress.[26]

Bargaining for Benefits, Fighting Inflation

In the postwar years the focus of bargaining for the large industrial unions expanded from wages and working conditions to include pensions and health care. While ER defended strikes over these issues, and Walter Reuther became one of the strongest union champions of such benefits, both advocates preferred a system similar to that of Sweden, where representatives of labor, industry, and government met on a regular basis to prevent work disruptions, and full employment was national policy supported by a generous welfare state. Leaders such as Reuther and Murray initially thought that once companies undertook large pension and health insurance costs, they would soon join with unions to seek a national system that would cover everyone. Combating inflation and establishing wage and price controls were also on the agenda.[27]

In the summer of 1949 a strike over pensions was brewing in the steel industry. From Hyde Park at the end of August ER noted, "Mr. Philip Murray dropped in to see us yesterday with some of his co-workers." Murray was not only president of the CIO but also led the United Steelworkers of America (USWA). Her Labor Day column was devoted to questions raised in the steel negotiations, which were also being considered by Congress. In the steel situation, she wrote, "the basic question is how much the participation of labor in the over-all earnings of a company should actually be. If you discuss wages or a pension plan this sharing of over-all earnings is still the basic question." She argued that unions had become much more aware of the importance of rewards for managers and investors. Nonetheless, the worker knew that the "wheels of industry could not turn at all without his active participation." While some cried that this thinking "was leading us down the road to socialism," she demurred and suggested, "Perhaps what we are really doing is to save capitalism." Even businessmen and steel company stockholders were urging companies to accept the union's proposed pension plan, but the industry endured a strike first. ER defended the steelworkers, arguing that most businesses provided adequate pensions for their executives, and workers "wanted the same kind of insurance." She found it "imperative that the companies come to some kind of arrangement with the unions" because strikes had worldwide implications. By early November, ER was expressing gratitude that the strike had finally been settled.[28]

In the auto industry that year Reuther negotiated the first pension plan with Ford Motor Company. In May 1950 General Motors agreed to a model contract that was hailed as the "Treaty of Detroit." In exchange for a contract that lasted for five years, the autoworkers gained a pension plan, an improved cost of living formula for wage increases, and a subsidy for half of the costs of a new health insurance plan. At the same time, however, Chrysler refused the union's demands. While the negotiations were going on, ER was in Michigan and was told about bonuses awarded to highly paid auto executives. She chided top management, declaring their ideas outmoded, and affirmed, "The people have decided ... that they intend to share more equally in the fruits of their labor." The UAW went on strike. After 104 days and at a cost of over

$1 billion, a settlement was reached. It was a victory for the union, although Reuther didn't get the full pension funding that he had wanted. ER expressed relief but found the price discouraging. While strikes cost the company money, firms could often afford a work stoppage, but the employees suffered more because the worker "has to replace the long weeks of idleness by weeks of even harder work."[29]

ER was proud of Reuther's accomplishments and outraged at the attacks against him, his family, and the union. In March 1949 she wrote in support of his proposal to reduce unemployment and provide much-needed housing by "producing inexpensive homes for the people by using idle airplane factories." Reuther himself was still in the hospital recovering from the failed assassination attempt. He used his time to good advantage, devising a complicated system of pulleys to facilitate his care. ER remarked amusedly, "If he can do the two jobs of improving the running of the hospitals as well as devising ways to give us more homes, and employ more people, we will profit greatly by the time for thinking which he acquired in such an unpleasant way!"[30]

The "unpleasantness" continued, however. On the evening of 24 May a shotgun blast ripped into Victor Reuther's face as he sat in his living room reading the *New York Times,* with his wife, Sophie, mending some clothing nearby and the children asleep upstairs. Although Victor was blinded in one eye, both Reuther brothers recovered and continued their union work, but guards went up around their houses and their families. The investigations of the assassination attempts were bungled at several points. ER wrote: "It seems unthinkable that the police have never been able to discover who shot Walter Reuther and because of that, in all probability, the same person perhaps has felt he could get away with shooting another brother. . . . [W]e have a right to protect men who are working in the interests of their fellow men." Just three days before Christmas a box wrapped in candy cane–striped paper and tied with a blue bow was left at a side entrance to the UAW headquarters. A tip to a *Detroit Times* reporter kept the box of dynamite from destroying the four-story building when "the big guy" was there. Neither the Detroit police nor the FBI were ever able to solve the mystery of the attacks and in fact showed little interest in doing so.[31]

In December ER attended a testimonial dinner honoring Walter Reuther for his "distinguished service to democracy and to greater justice for human beings anywhere in the world." Reuther had just returned from London, where the CIO and the AF of L had joined forces to help form the anticommunist ICFTU. She soon praised Reuther for his understanding of economic situations and his ability to view issues from an international perspective. She thought his work around the world gave him an understanding of economies that the industrialists could not see from their particular vantage point. His speech that night made a deep impression on ER. What she wanted people to remember first and foremost was "that democracy has to prove itself, and that each individual, and not the government, is responsible for that proof." She herself made this point again and again, but the former first lady and chair of the UN Human Rights Commission found that "it was inspiring to listen to Walter Reuther."[32]

In 1950, shortly after the Treaty of Detroit was signed, the Korean War brought a resumption of rampant inflation. Workers demanded wage increases, and strikes followed. While the unions supported the war, they once again sought a substantive role in the planning process, only to be rebuffed by Truman administration officials and their corporate appointees. In a new show of labor unity the CIO joined forces with the AF of L and other unaffiliated unions to form the United Labor Policy Committee. Labor was once again balancing its role in the Democratic Party, its agreement with the president's foreign policy, and the need to maintain fair wages despite wartime inflation. While explaining the difficulties for the railroad workers, ER emphasized the importance of including not only labor but also farmers, women, and youth in advising on wartime economic policies.[33]

When the Wage Stabilization Board tried to limit wage increases but not price increases, the unions rebelled. Organized labor was reluctant to take responsibility for decisions made without their advice and with which they disagreed. The United Labor Policy Committee, ER argued, could not comply with demands to stabilize wages in the absence of any guarantee that prices would stabilize, and it was safe to say that the country had "completely failed so far in keeping prices down. . . . After all, this group is responsible to its members[,] and the vast numbers who make up our unions are the ones who are paying the prices and to whom the prices are more important than they may be to the management group." ER devoted five columns largely to the wage and price debate as Truman rearranged his wartime economic planning agencies to include labor. She invited Jim Carey of the CIO and Michael V. DeSalle, the director of price stabilization, to debate the issues on her television show.[34]

Work stoppages in the steel industry and rail service continued during the war. In 1952, with a presidential election in the offing, the steel companies put up strong resistance to union demands. When Truman intervened and seized the mills to avert a strike, the Supreme Court invalidated the seizure, and the longest strike since 1919 followed. ER reflected on her country's "lamentable poverty in the art of dealing with human relations." She argued that antagonists such as Israel and the Arab states, Pakistan and India, and the Soviet Union and the United States would all be better off if they could settle their differences, but, she asked, "how can we expect to iron out difficulties in these situations where so many different questions of nationality, of creed, or customs enter into the picture if here at home we cannot settle our simple labor problems?" She turned to Sweden for an example of labor, industry, and government working together to prevent problems and asked for a study of how that system might be adapted to save the loss of wages, production, and comfort to those affected by the strikes.[35]

The problems of the labor relations system were exemplified for ER by the mining industry and her old adversary John L. Lewis. She frequently declared that as unions became more "mature," they assumed more responsibility. Defining what those terms meant in practice, she wrote: "Strikes are the last resort.... [T]he more mature we grow[,] the more we should perfect our machinery to avoid strikes which are costly to the workers, to the industry and to the consumer." When the miners once again went out on strike, she described the policy Lewis was pursuing as shortsighted. In the words of Lewis biographers Melvyn Dubofsky and Warren Van Tine, "coal strikes occurred as predictably as the seasons," compelling government intervention. In an industry so crucial to the national economy, and in the ever more hostile political climate, the strategy became more harmful than beneficial, they argue. Lewis depended on government intervention but remained antagonistic to the Democrats and had no broader social vision. ER remained a staunch supporter of the coal miners but a critic of Lewis and the companies, suggesting that coal be made a public utility, "operated with a sense of responsibility to the public."[36]

After the Korean War ended with a cease-fire in July 1953, a recession predictably followed. ER took time in September to praise the labor movement and called, as she often did, for recognition of unions' increased responsibilities both nationally and internationally. Wages, hours, and working conditions had been improved, she observed, and union leaders were becoming aware of both the strengths and limitations of business. Emphasizing the global economy, she concluded, "It is not just a question today of seeing that high tariffs keep out the goods made by sweated labor in other countries, but it is a question of helping to change conditions so that our labor does not compete with sweated labor anywhere in the world." At the end of the month she noted, "There is no longer any question that labor has a right to organize and to protect itself, just as capital has."[37]

ER's Labor Day columns reflected on the struggles and successes of the labor movement. In one she reminded readers: "Without organized labor the unorganized groups would slide back quickly to poor conditions, which would hurt the prosperity of the nation. So when we celebrate Labor Day we should have in our minds the things for which we are really grateful—a strong labor movement and increased knowledge, wisdom and honesty among its leaders." She felt strongly that the costs of economic policies had to be shared, and to "expect more from labor than from any other source was an unfair proposition." She did, however, have higher expectations for labor than for employers when it came to advancing equality for women workers.[38]

A New Era for Women

ER reached the peak of her career just as the women who had introduced her to the labor movement began to retire. In the early 1950s Rose Schneiderman, Lucy Mason, and Hilda Smith all stepped down. The Women's Trade Union League and the Hudson Shore Labor School closed their doors. At the same time, women from the shop floors of auto and meatpacking plants, electrical workers, and waitresses joined clothing workers, teachers, and telephone operators to become union members in unprecedented numbers. Women such as Mary Callahan from the IUE and Addie Wyatt from the Packing House Workers were elected local officers and then executive board members. Maida Springer traveled from the shop floor through positions as business agent and local educational director to the international staff of the AFL-CIO. In 1953 eleven union research departments were directed by women. Esther Peterson, probably the most influential of the new generation of union women, moved from the education staff of the Amalgamated Clothing Workers to become a lobbyist for the Industrial Union Department of the newly merged AFL-CIO.[39]

ER bridged this transition well. She never lost contact with the close friends who had inspired her to join labor's cause, but she was soon working effectively with the new generation of union women. Early in 1949, at the January meeting of the WTUL, Rose Schneiderman was eager to hear about the Universal Declaration. ER also used the occasion to reflect on the remarkable accomplishments of women workers. Increasingly she felt that "the day may come when women will be so well organized and integrated with men in their various occupations and organizations that the working women will not need separate organizations but will form a strong and influential part of a joint organization of workers." But that time had not yet come, she warned, and women workers still had particular problems to solve.[40]

The WTUL, however, was increasingly less able to help. The group's legislative agenda was stalled by the most conservative Congress in years. Hard-won protective legislation banning night work for women workers was being used to displace women from wartime employment. As rigid as ever in its rejection of the ERA, the League began to work on an alternative constitutional amendment that would preserve protective legislation, but nothing moved forward. The AF of L insisted on expelling CIO members but provided few resources to support the organization. The surge of anticommunism in the late 1940s left few wealthy allies willing to contribute money to help working women unionize. Unions increasingly provided their own education programs, and many thought that labor no longer needed the services of a women's organization that operated outside of labor's control. WTUL leaders who had devoted their lives to the organization found it difficult to make room for younger leaders with different priorities. Women new to the union movement, especially in the CIO, looked elsewhere for leadership.[41]

On 6 April 1949 Schneiderman called reporters to the clubhouse and announced that she was retiring as president of the New York League. She was sixty-seven years old and was tired of the struggle. While pointing to the League's accomplishments, she warned that much of its progress was in danger. On 2 June ER left her duties at the United Nations and joined three hundred guests at a luncheon to pay tribute to her friend. She praised Schneiderman's ability to communicate working women's problems to others and acknowledged her personal debt. "The opportunities which she gave me to work with her and her co-workers were of inestimable value to me in many of the ensuing experiences of my life," wrote ER.[42]

WTUL leader Elizabeth Christman argued forcefully for the League's continued relevance; women workers in agriculture, domestic service, and white-collar positions still desperately needed help organizing. There was no national equal pay law, and minimum wage, hour, and safety standards were far from universal. Women occupied few leadership positions in the unions. In the ILGWU, for example, by 1952 women formed the majority of its membership, and almost one-third were black and Puerto Rican, but Dubinsky continued to rely on Jewish and Italian men as leaders, showing little change from 1932. Jennie Matyas in San Francisco replaced Rose Pesotta as the lone woman on the executive board, and there were no black or Hispanic board members. Schneiderman blamed the lack of progress on discrimination but also lamented the failure of women to pursue leadership positions aggressively. Christman lost the argument for continuation of the WTUL: the national organization shut its doors in 1950 and the New York League closed in 1955. After the WTUL disbanded, its remaining assets went into a scholarship fund for working women. ER agreed to serve as a trustee, hosting the first meeting at her home at 211 East Sixty-second Street.[43]

Others of ER's generation were passing from the scene. In her foreword to Lucy Mason's autobiography, *To Win These Rights,* ER praised her courageous work with the CIO in the South. Mason retired in 1953, but she soon became ill, and in 1959 she died. Since the end of the war Hilda Smith had devoted herself full-time to the national Labor Extension Services bill, designed to set up education programs for workers similar to agricultural extension programs for farmers. She continued to involve ER, but the legislation was defeated in 1949, condemned by some in Congress as communist. No longer able to maintain the Hudson Shore Labor School, Smith turned her attention to programs for the elderly and worked with ER on political events in the Hudson Valley.[44]

As these intrepid women retired from the labor front, a new generation of union women emerged from the shop floors and local halls, as well as from education and research departments. Described by historian Dorothy Sue Cobble as "labor feminists," these new leaders were firmly committed to working within their unions and actively pursued an agenda of "equality *and* special treatment" to enable them to combine decent paid employment with full family and community lives. They opposed the ERA, were committed to strategies of unionization and legislation, took an active part in the Democratic Party, and enthusiastically participated in the Labor Advisory Committee of the Women's Bureau established at the end of the war. Seeking to reach out to women in other groups, they also formed coalitions with organizations such as the National Council of Negro Women.[45]

These women developed agendas and new structures within their unions. In 1946, for example, Caroline Davis became director of the UAW Women's Bureau, and local and regional women's committees and conferences became active, forming their own department by vote of the national convention in 1955. ACWA's 1954 convention passed a "Resolution on Women's Rights" calling for child care tax deductions and federal legislation prohibiting discrimination and guaranteeing equal pay. At the IUE's first national conference in 1957, the delegates called for equal pay for work of equal value, equal job and promotion opportunities, civil rights legislation, and more tax exemptions for working mothers. As they set their new agenda, these women acknowledged the accomplishments of the generation before them. Maida Springer reflected on the influence that Rose Schneiderman and a host of other women had had on her. "They touched my life and mind," she said, remarking that she had "come up at a time of great transition."[46]

Many of these new women leaders welcomed ER's support through her consistent defense of the labor movement in her "My Day" columns and in her radio and television appearances, her speeches at their national conventions, and her participation in their labor education programs. New York City and the garment workers remained her base. Evy Dubrow, the ILGWU lobbyist, talked about how accessible "Mrs. R" was when she went to her apartment in New York and made arrangements for her to speak at events. Springer accompanied her friend Pauli Murray, the young black civil rights lawyer, on visits to "Mrs. R" in New York and organized a local education program, as well as a Madison Square Garden event where ER spoke on behalf of the Fair Employment Practices Committee. Mark Starr and Fannia Cohn, with the ILGWU's Education Department, wrote to ER directly to arrange visits to Hyde Park and talks in New York City for hundreds of members. Starr told her, "You are so often happily assisting the educational activity of the ILGWU, that President Dubinsky would be well advised to invite you to join the staff."[47]

ER's efforts on behalf of equality for union women often intertwined with her support for racial equality. In 1957 Starr asked her to participate in a large meeting in Newark, New Jersey, to discuss the importance of civil rights to workers. Increasing numbers of African Americans were moving to Newark, and he wanted to create a sense of mutual appreciation between Newark's union members and the city's newest residents. "We know that the cause of Civil Rights is very close to your life work," he wrote. Women in union families, as well as women in the factories, were active in the cause. By the mid-1950s women's auxiliaries claimed almost 2 million members. Author Tillie Olsen, who later wrote so movingly about working-class women's lives and the silence of their voices, served as president of the California State CIO Women's Auxiliary; she named one of her daughters Eleanor. Jim Carey spoke to the newly merged AFL-CIO women's auxiliary on the subject of "Women and the Future of Civil Rights." He saw women's rights and minority rights as inseparable and sent a copy of the speech to ER because of her "intense and active interest both in women's rights and racial democracy."[48]

Still central to the debate about women's rights was the Equal Rights Amendment. As an alternative to the ERA, in 1947 two of ER's closest allies in Congress, Democrats Mary Norton of New Jersey and Helen Gahagan Douglas of California, introduced the Women's Status Bill with the support of union women. The bill called for a review of state legislation to eliminate laws that discriminated against women but to keep those of true benefit, similar to a proposal ER had recommended to Schneiderman. The increasingly conservative Congress, however, put the bill on hold. By 1951 ER had quietly dropped her opposition to the ERA, believing that women in industrial jobs could finally secure their rights through unions. She told her readers that "women can be as well organized as men and are certainly able to fight for their rights." She acknowledged that "perhaps it does add a little to the position of women to be declared equal before the law and equal politically and in whatever work a woman chooses to undertake." This was the position of the UN Commission on the Status of Women as well.[49]

Still, ER declined to work actively for the ERA, citing her lack of enthusiasm for the amendment, which was no doubt related to her respect for those union women and their strong congressional allies who still opposed the idea. When writing about the National Woman's Party convention in 1951, she showed her disdain for the group of feminists who had introduced the ERA and were still headed by Alice Paul. An equal rights amendment, "to which these dear ladies of the National Woman's Party have been devoting themselves these past several years," would not have much effect whether or not it passed, she predicted. Although, as historian Virginia Scharf writes, ER moved beyond the patronizing advocacy of the upper-middle-class women on both sides of the debate and turned to the growing labor movement as the place for working women to define their own priorities, her most active efforts remained focused more narrowly on women's political participation.[50]

ER challenged the all-male hierarchy of the labor movement in letters and speeches, but not nearly as forcefully as she challenged the Democratic Party and successive Democratic administrations, for here changes could be achieved to a great extent by appointing women to positions of authority and responsibility. Changes within the labor movement depended on working women organizing, voting, and moving their own agenda forward, as she constantly urged, and ER saw the women making progress, especially in the CIO. In retrospect, it is apparent that she underestimated how difficult women's progress was going to be. In the mid-1950s, however, with the rapid growth and increasing power of the newly merged labor movement, she and many union women thought it would finally be possible for women to achieve a new level of parity in the workplace and in the union hall.

ER's connection with the newly emerging women union leaders can be seen most clearly in her work with Esther Peterson. The granddaughter of Danish immigrants, Esther Eggertsen was raised in a Mormon family on a farm in Provo, Utah, where her father was the state superintendent of education and her mother took in boarders from Brigham Young University. After graduating from the university, she moved to Columbia University Teachers College in New York, where she met Oliver Peterson, a socialist who introduced her to the labor movement. They married and moved to Boston, where she taught at a private girls' school and volunteered at the YWCA, which offered evening classes for both white and black working women. There Peterson met Hilda Smith; she soon began teaching at the Bryn Mawr Summer School for Working Women.[51]

Peterson first met Eleanor Roosevelt while working on a political campaign with Rose Schneiderman. "In those days," she remembered, "one of my jobs was to go and get a group going at a street corner and sing and harangue, and then we would all crowd around and the others would come in for the union like Bessie Hillman and Frances Perkins and Eleanor Roosevelt. We were all women who were working for the Roosevelt election." In the summer of 1940 she was teaching at the Hudson Shore Labor School and took a group of women students to Val-Kill for a Sunday picnic. When she told them ER was in Chicago giving the acceptance speech for FDR, the girls started to cry, lamenting that she wouldn't be there the next day. Still, Peterson recounted, they "ironed their best dresses, their Sunday best, and they go over to Val-Kill. And there is Eleanor. She greeted us in a wet bathing suit. She said, 'I thought I invited you to a picnic.' She found bathing suits for everybody and she served hot dogs."[52]

Peterson first became a union organizer for the American Federation of Teachers, then joined the education staff of the ACWA. When her husband's work took them to Washington, DC, she became a lobbyist representing Sidney Hillman on Capitol Hill, joined the Labor Advisory Committee of the

Women's Bureau, and supported the Women's Status Bill. After the war ended, Oliver Peterson was asked to become one of the State Department's new labor attachés; the day after the 1948 election, he and Esther left for Sweden, with four young children in tow.[53]

Two years later ER visited Sweden. She frequently explored labor issues in her travels abroad, often after UN meetings. Oliver Peterson most likely arranged her visits with the Swedish Federation of Employers and the Federation of Unions, as well as her tours of factories and cooperatives. ER encouraged a study of Swedish employer-employee relationships, which she described for her readers as "more mature and better integrated than ours." On 9 June the Petersons joined ER at a small embassy dinner. Esther arranged for ER to meet some of the Swedish students who had attended the Hudson Shore Labor School, and she sent Hilda Smith a picture and an article about the event from the front page of a Swedish newspaper.[54]

Other connections between the women were less direct. In 1945 ER had suggested that Phil Murray have more women included in the delegation to the World Federation of Trade Unions. The CIO was represented by nine vice presidents from the executive board, all of whom were men. He assured her "that our women are going to play an extremely important part in the building of the World Federation of Trade Unions." It was not until 1949, however, that Jacob Potofsky, president of the ACWA, asked Peterson to travel from Sweden to attend a meeting in London of the newly forming ICFTU. She was an alternate for one of the male delegates, and the first and only woman in the U.S. delegation, as is dramatically illustrated in a photograph published in *Life* magazine. Peterson also hosted trade unionists known to ER, including Maida Springer, in her Swedish home.[55]

During this time abroad Oliver Peterson was called before Congress to respond to accusations that he was a communist, based in part on his wife's union associations. Union leaders rallied to his defense, and his name was cleared, but the ordeal took a heavy toll. Esther later wrote a pamphlet for the ICFTU encouraging women to get involved in the fight against communism, and noted the irony of her becoming an anticommunist spokeswoman. After the family returned to the United States in 1958, when Oliver was ill with cancer and their finances were tight, she was invited by Jim Carey to join the new Industrial Union Department of the AFL-CIO as a lobbyist. Esther Peterson assumed a new leadership role in the labor movement. She soon convened a group of top women labor leaders to discuss state labor laws; they advocated the formation of a women's conference and a permanent women's committee at the AFL-CIO.[56]

Dorothy Sue Cobble has defined these new labor feminists as sharing a liberal anticommunist agenda and favoring close ties to the Democratic Party. This stance was clearly aligned with Eleanor Roosevelt's political position.

In the summer of 1958 Peterson and her daughter Karen traveled to Val-Kill with the ACWA Training Institute. Afterward she wrote to thank ER for her hospitality and expressed the hope that ER would be able to talk with Mrs. Ulla Bodorff of Sweden about refugee camps. Her renewed connection with Eleanor Roosevelt grew into the last sustaining relationship ER had with a union woman now representing the newly merged AFL-CIO.[57]

Labor Unites

Shortly after Stevenson's defeat in 1952 a major transition occurred within the leadership of the labor movement. Exhausted from the steel negotiations and an arduous campaign on Stevenson's behalf, Phil Murray died of a heart attack on board a train for California, where he had planned to preside over the fourteenth annual convention of the CIO. Eleanor Roosevelt extended her sympathy to his family and the unions and told her readers, "His leadership and wisdom will be sadly missed in the days to come." Then William Green, the octogenarian president of the AF of L, passed away. ER again extended sympathy to his family and paid tribute to his "wise and calm counsel" and his years "well spent in the service of his fellow men."[58]

ER took this opportunity to call for reconciliation, saying, "Now when the two great labor movements of the country, the CIO and the AF of L, are waiting to choose a new head, those of us who feel that labor would be stronger if it came together under one head cannot help wishing that this might be a time when factional difficulties would be conciliated and labor might once again present a united front." George Meany, from the plumbers' union in the Bronx, was elected president of the AF of L with virtually no opposition. The fifty-eight-year-old Meany was a seasoned administrator and labor politician with no large international union to manage. Merging with the CIO was a high priority for him. ER praised his election as a "very good choice. He has already suggested that the CIO and the AFL join hands again."[59]

The succession process in the CIO was not so smooth. Walter Reuther had long been expected to succeed Murray, but he was challenged by Allan Haywood, the director of organizing, who was well known around the country, especially among the smaller unions. Haywood was backed by David J. McDonald, Murray's successor as president of the USWA, who was known to dislike the UAW leader intensely. Reuther won with just 52 percent of the vote. He spent most of his time and effort in Detroit on UAW matters, but with McDonald constantly threatening to withdraw the Steelworkers from the CIO, he had little choice but to begin merger talks with Meany. On 6 December Eleanor Roosevelt devoted her entire column to Walther Reuther. She acknowledged his able opponent but stressed Reuther's understanding of economics, his international experience, and his ability to dream. As she offered her congratulations and her prayers, she again expressed her wish for the unification of the labor movement.[60]

Organized labor was in a strong position despite the election results and antilabor sentiments. The CIO reported a membership of close to 4.6 million; the core industries were almost 70 percent organized. The AF of L had twice as many members and had made some progress among clerks, public employees, and service workers. The two organizations had moved closer together on foreign policy through the ICFTU, their support for the Marshall Plan, and the Korean conflict. They were solidly anticommunist on the domestic front, though critical of the extreme measures undertaken by McCarthy and his followers. An agreement to stop the jurisdictional disputes and union raids was a joint goal, as was the need to curb corruption. Differences, however, remained. Reuther hoped to renew an emphasis on organizing, and his foreign policy goals remained focused on economic growth and assistance. Meany, by contrast, saw organizing as strictly an international union responsibility, and his foreign policy was staunchly one of anticommunist containment. Reuther did not seek the presidency of the new organization, but he was optimistic about the possibility of the merger and was willing to bide his time and wait for leadership of the federation.[61]

In 1955 ER alerted her readers to a new survey by *Look* magazine on the question of "bigness." Particularly troubling was the finding that many more people feared the power of labor unions than that of business. ER attributed this view to scandals that had exposed corruption in some unions, and she was hopeful that the right balance of responsibility and power would eventually be struck. In May she urged everyone to read the new AFL-CIO constitution carefully. She highlighted the sections that dealt with wrongdoing and racial segregation, which she thought were strong, though not perfect. The year closed on a note of strength for the labor movement. On the Saturday night of the convention, 3 December 1955, Robert F. Wagner, mayor of New York City, hosted a dinner to honor George Meany and Walter P. Reuther. ER was present. The two labor leaders' speeches, she reported, reflected their increased sense of responsibility to the nation, and she looked forward to their growing influence as representatives of a broad segment of Americans.[62]

ER addressed the convention on Thursday afternoon. Maida Springer, then a business agent for Local 22 of the garment workers' union, was in the audience. Since her meeting with ER in 1945 before going to England, Springer had studied in Sweden and then at Oxford, where she developed strong ties with African trade union leaders. Early in 1955 she represented the AF of L as a delegate to the first ICFTU meeting in Africa. On the day of the merger convention she reported to her friend Pauli Murray that ER had risen to great heights in addressing the crowd; she was "warm and vibrant," and her speech

was "the high point of the AFL-CIO convention." ER saw the merger as giving labor more power to exert "a great influence in American life, and...an
influence for the well-being of all the people of the world." There was "a warm
feeling of comradeship" with her audience as she left the podium.[63]

The newly formed AFL-CIO rested on fragile compromises forged in the
earliest days of the cold war. ER supported a complex strategy of opposing
communism and Soviet expansion while defending civil liberties at home and
encouraging the peaceful resolution of international disputes through the
United Nations. Her call to the convention delegates that December day to set
their house in order, to work actively on behalf of racial equality, to improve
labor conditions, and to take political action on broader policy questions
articulated issues that she would champion in the coming years, while she
joined with Walter Reuther and steadfastly challenged what would become
the dominant cold war foreign policy of George Meany and the AFL-CIO.

7

WE HAVE SOMETHING TO OFFER

I am always encouraged and inspired by the example that you and
others have shown in the face of difficulties and adversities.
WALTER REUTHER to Eleanor Roosevelt, 29 July 1958

The Reuthers made the thirteen-hour drive from Paint Creek, Michigan,
to Hyde Park in a single day. On 15 August 1958 Walter and May were taking daughter Linda to school in Putney, Vermont, with a two-day stop to visit
Eleanor Roosevelt. The ever-present bodyguard drove, his gun bulging from
his waistband. May Reuther sat next to him in the front seat because her back
problems made traveling painful. Eleven-year-old Elisabeth, called Lisa, and
Linda, five years older, scrambled for the window seats in the back of the Olds-
mobile 98. Walter Reuther, dubbed the "most dangerous man in Detroit," sat
in the backseat between his daughters reading the *New York Times,* which for
them made the long car trip more like a library visit than a vacation.[1]

Waking up in Val-Kill was "magical," Lisa remembered. She admired the
exotic details of the lovely home. The library was her favorite room; they
would settle there for tea after dinner, with lively discussions between her
father and ER. Their days were spent by the swimming pool; as Lisa dove
into the water, she recalled, her "father and Mrs. R would dive back into the
issues of the day." According to ER's daughter, Anna, Walter Reuther and
her mother, despite a generation gap, "had mutual concerns about humanity
throughout the world. When they met, no time was wasted in reminiscences
as they laid plans for further action." Reuther shunned the fancy hotels where
Meany and the AFL-CIO met, uncomfortable with card playing and cigar
smoking, just as Eleanor Roosevelt had shunned the social cocktail hour that
her husband so enjoyed. What a pleasure to walk and talk and plan for the

world in the summer warmth of Val-Kill. Reuther's daughter wrote, "Their relationship touched my heart."[2]

The agenda that warm August weekend included the Republicans' continuing attack on unions as they geared up for the congressional midterm elections. The Republican National Campaign Committee produced a 216-page book, *The Labor Bosses: America's Third Party,* which attacked Walter Reuther and the UAW. In a remarkably long and unguarded letter before the visit, Reuther wrote to "My dear Mrs. Roosevelt" about the increasing amount of hate mail they were both receiving. He was negotiating with the Big Three auto companies and actively engaged in the national political campaign, a combination he thought always brought out the worst in his opponents. According to his latest missive, he was under attack for his work with the "communist-NAACP," and the "socialist" Americans for Democratic Action, his leadership of the AFL-CIO, and his work in the Soviet Union years before. What was new, he suggested, was the number of mainstream Republicans who openly joined the attacks on organized labor. He reported on one Republican politician who had told reporters that because of new scandals, increasing debt, and rising unemployment, the only issue the Republicans had left was labor.[3]

Reuther further argued that the Democratic Party needed to point out that the labor leaders who were guilty of corruption and abuse were, in fact, most closely tied to the Republican Party, especially Dave Beck, Jimmy Hoffa, and the Teamsters. Republicans, he wrote, "fear honest labor leadership and a labor movement with a sense of social vision that would elevate the labor movement above the status of a pressure group and which would assume its broader economic, social and political responsibilities to the whole community." Reuther admitted to being annoyed by the volume of propaganda. He told ER: "I am always encouraged and inspired by the example that you and others have shown in the face of difficulties and adversities.... I trust I have not burdened you unduly about this matter, but I suppose I had the need for talking to someone."[4]

ER drew strength from close personal bonds of friendship, and while she continued to work with labor leaders on a wide variety of issues and to comment on the activities of many different unions in her columns, Reuther emerged as one of her strongest allies on the international and domestic fronts. Central to their shared world vision was an international policy based on economic aid and negotiation, reflected in their dealings with India and Russia. Their liberal domestic policy agenda was closely related to this vision: the United States would become an example of democracy and equality to the rest of the world. ER took a leadership role in defeating the antiunion state right-to-work campaigns, argued for a united labor movement free of internal corruption, and advocated for a strengthened civil rights program to organize black workers and migrant farm laborers. Neither she and Reuther, however, fully appreciated the emergence of public-sector unionism. ER openly struggled with whether public employees had the right to join unions. The 1950s ended much as the decade had begun, shadowed by recession and an approaching presidential election, but ER and Reuther were more determined than ever to show the world that they had "something to offer."[5]

Strategies for Democracy: India and the USSR

The strains between the leaders of the AFL and the CIO were palpable immediately after the merger convention. ER and Reuther agreed on the importance of economic aid in the global contest with communism, the need for the United States and the labor movement to approach Asia and other parts of the world differently from the way they approached Europe, and the importance of talking to people with whom they disagreed. They publicly presented their positions in clear opposition to George Meany and the conservative branch of the labor movement. ER realized that Congress was not convinced that economic aid to foreign countries was critical, yet she contended that in the long run it could well be more important than military aid. Reuther sounded similar themes. If conflict were waged by military means alone, he feared that democratic trade unions would disappear and communism would fill the vacuum. The situation in Asia, in particular, required different policies; he lamented that Meany's position was "based upon the assumption that Europe is Asia and Asia is Europe." These differences played out in the two labor leaders' conflicting approaches to India and in their dealings with Nikita Khrushchev's rise to power in the USSR.[6]

Following the merger convention, the National Religion and Labor Foundation hosted a luncheon to present its annual social justice award to Meany and Reuther. In his speech Reuther declared that for the United States to be a "symbol of moral power" the country had to end its immoral race relations: "We must be as courageous in fighting what goes on in Mississippi as in fighting tyranny behind the Iron Curtain." According to ER, who was in the audience of 1,200 clergy and unionists from around the world, he appealed for "high ethical standards" and "stirred his listeners deeply." Meany took the opportunity to reiterate his anticommunist worldview, leaving "many in his audience somewhat stunned," by one reporter's account. Embedded in communism, Meany declared, were "savagery, slavery, feudalism and life-sapping exploitation." He condemned racism but castigated liberals for being weak in their fight against communism and silent about "Soviet concentration camps." Declaring that no one could be neutral in this fight, he lashed out against President Josip Broz Tito of Yugoslavia and Prime Minister Jawaharlal Nehru of India, who had just hosted a visit from Khrushchev: "Nehru and

Tito are not neutral. They are aides and allies of communism in fact and in effect, if not in diplomatic verbiage."[7]

Both ER and Reuther were the targets of Meany's speech. ER had praised Nehru on her earlier trip to India, interviewed communist President Tito, and reported positively on Nehru's visit to the Soviet Union. She wasted no time in responding to Meany. In her column she acknowledged that being "soft" on communism was an error but argued that communism did not mean the same thing everywhere. Yugoslavia and China might develop differently from Russia. More important, it "is a sad mistake...to give the impression to the people in India that their Prime Minister, because he wishes to remain neutral between the Soviet Union and the U.S., must therefore be a Communist. Nehru is trying to keep his country a democratic one." Making "an untrue statement about the leader of another great country" could make it harder for America's democratic labor movement to assist India's struggling trade unions. She challenged Meany to recognize shortcomings at home and not be "frightened into exaggerated statements which can only antagonize, and cannot help us build friends for our own desired aims of peace and justice."[8]

Reuther responded with his own trip to India. Meany's attack had made headlines in India as well as in the United States. K. P. Tripathi, general secretary of the Indian National Trade Union Congress, charged that Meany sounded like a representative of the War Department and predicted "unfortunate repercussions" across Asia. Even Eisenhower's State Department saw the speech as harming this important bilateral relationship. John Sherman Cooper, the U.S. ambassador to India, personally asked Reuther to make a trip that he had previously postponed. Victor Reuther worked with Nehru and the Indian National Trade Union Congress to have a formal invitation issued to his brother.[9]

Eleanor Roosevelt had toured India in 1952. Arriving in New Delhi she declared, "I have come here to learn." The crowd responded, "Eleanor Roosevelt *Zindabad!*": Long live Eleanor Roosevelt! She was greeted by Nehru's sister Madame Vijaya Lakshmi Pandit, whom she had come to know well when they were both delegates to the United Nations, and her friend Chester Bowles, the U.S. ambassador. Traveling the country, she spoke about the need for more economic aid and less military support for newly independent nations. To friends, government officials, and the public at home she praised Nehru's leadership and tried to explain why he wanted India to remain neutral between the communist and Western superpowers. ER maintained that it was essential to understand that other peoples brought different experiences and beliefs to political discussions and that other democracies would not look exactly like the United States.[10]

Four years after ER's visit and four months after Meany's attack on Nehru, Walter Reuther toured India, making numerous speeches to cheering crowds across the country. He got along well with Nehru and had met Madame Pandit through ER. In keeping with ER's advice to Meany, Reuther admitted that American society was not perfect and addressed the problems of African Americans. His resounding Lincolnesque declaration that "peace and freedom cannot endure with the world half well fed and half starving" placed India's problems in global perspective. In a news conference that was rebroadcast by the Voice of America, Reuther openly repudiated Meany's indictment of Indian neutrality and called Nehru a great statesman. U.S. diplomats were pleased, but Meany was furious. He rejected Reuther's arguments and resented the public challenge to his leadership. The next AFL-CIO executive council meeting reportedly degenerated into a "knock-down, drag-out affair."[11]

Just a few weeks later ER addressed the twentieth convention of the Amalgamated Clothing Workers of America in Washington, DC. It was held on the tenth anniversary of Sidney Hillman's death, and ER was pleased to be seated next to his widow, Bessie Hillman, a vice president of the union, an advocate for liberal causes, and a friend. When ER rose to speak, the delegates cheered and whistled. She urged union leaders to support the UN and carry that message to their locals so that members "know where your interests lie in the United Nations." Aligning herself with Reuther, she urged that to achieve peace and progress, Americans must resist the temptation "to think that we can dictate to other people, that we can make people accept our point-of-view." Her examples were all drawn from her observations of India: "I had never imagined what poverty could really mean until I saw what Indian people endure, and still have hope. And yet India is a great nation."[12]

In her address on receiving the twentieth anniversary UAW Freedom Award, ER focused primarily on foreign policy, bolstering Reuther's approach and promoting the UN. On 9 April 1957 four thousand UAW delegates filled the enormous convention center ballroom on the Boardwalk in Atlantic City. Reuther offered a warm introduction and then ER, in her most teacher-like fashion, explained to the autoworkers how she saw the problems in the Middle East after her recent visit. She argued that the United States should have taken a stronger leadership role to prevent the Suez Canal crisis and that the Eisenhower administration's policies had weakened U.S. allies, leaving Americans alone to keep the peace. In a democracy, she declared, union members all had a responsibility to learn about these international problems and to hold the U.S. government accountable, making sure it did "not fall short and leave a vacuum in which the only possible way to have it filled would be by the Soviet Union." The United Nations was a useful institution, but the member nations had to make it operate. She also told her audience about her visit to Algeria, Tunisia, and Morocco, Arab states recently freed from colonialism.[13]

Another high-profile area of agreement on foreign policy between ER and Reuther was the Soviet Union. Shortly after the ACWA convention, ER invited the Reuthers to Hyde Park for a weekend, telling them, "I am sure you cannot have many more things to talk to me about than I have to talk over with you." Afterwards ER told her readers that she "enjoyed every minute of their visit. Mr. Reuther is concerned, as the Quakers say, about many of the things which concern me." In his thank you letter Reuther wrote, "Having an opportunity to visit with you and compare notes on the many matters that we have in common was a most rewarding experience which will long be remembered." Their discussions ranged from the effects of automation and workers' leisure time to ER's travel. Most of Reuther's letter was devoted to her planned trip to the Soviet Union. As ER reflected in her autobiography, she did "feel that we, as individuals, or as a nation, gain neither in dignity or in prestige by refusing to know the people who lead the great opposition to our way of life." On this trip, as on many others she had undertaken, she met not only with leaders but also with the people. From his own experiences Reuther had marked a map with several recommended routes, including Leningrad (formerly and currently St. Petersburg), Tashkent, and Samarkand (now in Uzbekistan), the Black Sea resort of Sochi, and Yalta, where FDR had met with Churchill and Stalin in 1945.[14]

When Joseph Stalin died in 1953, he was succeeded by Nikita Khrushchev and ER was the first Westerner to secure an interview with him. On her trip, which she made as a journalist for the *New York Post,* she visited factories, farms, and medical centers. At the end of her journey she spent three hours talking with Khrushchev at his summer residence in Yalta. Afterwards they agreed that they had had a friendly conversation but differed on many things. To her readers ER reported on the ordinary people she had met, as well as on her interview with the premier. Reuther assured her: "I am certain that your articles are being widely read and are helping to develop a greater understanding and awareness of the problem and the need for a more positive approach to this world situation." When she returned from her trip, she joined the Reuther family for dinner at their home in Detroit.[15]

ER expressed great faith in Reuther's views on international issues. During the year after the Russians launched Sputnik, the first satellite, she encouraged the idea of summit meetings with the Soviets, "even though a great deal may not come out of them," but felt that they should include more than politicians. The only two people she thought could successfully negotiate with Khrushchev were her friends Chester Bowles and Walter Reuther. When he heard this, Reuther jokingly responded that since John L. Lewis had suggested that Reuther and Khrushchev become members of the crew on the first rocket to the moon, "perhaps we might have the preliminary negotiations on our way to the moon." ER objected, "I don't think I go along with Mr. Lewis' suggestion of a trip to the moon, so please remain here!"[16]

Soon Reuther was invited by Willy Brandt, the social democratic mayor of West Berlin, to address a May Day Freedom Rally organized there by the trade unions. Speaking in German to over 600,000 people, Reuther assured them that the United States would help in their defense against the Russians. ER wrote, "Dear Walter, I have been so proud of all you did abroad and want to hear about your trip." Arrangements were made for the Reuther family to visit Hyde Park, where Reuther and ER could discuss Berlin and compare notes "on a number of other important developments." After the visit his thank you letter included both detailed instructions on how to handle the algae in the Val-Kill pond and a note about the AFL-CIO executive council meeting stating, "Mr. Meany unfortunately still insists upon hiding his head in the sand and you have no doubt seen reports of the action of the Executive Council with respect to Mr. Khrushchev's visit."[17]

Nikita Khrushchev had accepted President Eisenhower's invitation to visit the United States in September 1959, but George Meany refused to talk with the Russians. During his widely publicized tour the premier frequently asked, "Where are the workers?" The State Department had hoped that he might attend the AFL-CIO convention in San Francisco, but Meany turned down the request. Diplomats contacted Victor Reuther, who put together a dinner for several union presidents at the Mark Hopkins Hotel. Fueled by whisky and cognac, the discussion was frank and sometimes angry as American trade unionists criticized the Soviet system unsparingly and defended their own unions. When the premier noted that Reuther was not actually drinking with each toast, Reuther replied, "Mr. Chairman, I think you should know that when the revolution comes to America, there will be at least one sober trade unionist." This comment would surely have pleased ER.[18]

Just three days before his arrival in San Francisco, Khrushchev had visited Hyde Park. He laid a wreath on the grave of President Roosevelt, and ER invited him to her Val-Kill cottage for tea. Like Reuther, she was criticized for showing hospitality to the Soviet leader. Just four days after the dinner in San Francisco, ER was an overnight guest in the Reuthers' home at Paint Creek. Lisa, who had been helping her mother prepare for the visit, described their breakfast of waffles and syrup, fruit salad, and "Mrs. R's favorite herbal tea," adding, "I was struck by her grace, her appreciation for small things, and her admiration for father's union work."[19]

The Reuther brothers' dinner with the premier was generally thought to have ended amicably. After Khrushchev's return to Russia, however, a series of critical stories appeared in *Trud,* the Soviet trade union newspaper, based on interviews with people who had worked with the Reuther brothers decades earlier in the Gorky plant. They portrayed Walter as stingy and self-absorbed, and claimed that he had married a young Russian woman and then left her when he returned home. Worse still, they likened him to Meany. ER once again came to Reuther's defense, telling her readers, "The labor leaders who met...with Soviet Premier Nikita Khrushchev certainly did manage to get under his skin." She suggested that Khrushchev was resentful because American workers preferred the democratic freedoms they enjoyed under capitalism to the "security under compulsion" that communism offered; the fact that Khrushchev feared the influence of the American labor movement on his own people should "make us grateful to our American labor leaders," she wrote. As ER and Reuther addressed these international concerns, however, they were very aware of the connections between international and domestic issues. Labor and civil rights problems at home weakened labor's international position and the United States' standing in the world.[20]

Union Rights and Responsibilities

When responding in her *McCall's* magazine column to a question asking her to identify the two biggest changes in her thinking over the years, ER replied that one had been learning that unions must demonstrate increased responsibility to match their growth in rights and power. This included responsibility for ethical behavior within unions as well as awareness of the implications of the unions' actions beyond their own members. Protecting the right to organize and taking responsibility for corruption became major issues, as labor slowly sought to regain the political power it had lost in the 1956 presidential election, when ER and Reuther had actively campaigned for Adlai Stevenson. Antiunion forces were advocating union-busting laws on the state level, while union corruption became headline news when Senator John McClellan of Arkansas opened public hearings and labor leaders were called to testify.[21]

On the political front, ER supported Stevenson in 1956 even though he was not strong on union issues. She thought that the labor plank in the 1956 Democratic Party platform was sound, although Stevenson did not favor repeal of the Taft-Hartley Act. Meany had shown support for him at the merger convention, and after Stevenson won the California primary, Dubinsky urged liberals to unite behind him. At the Democratic National Convention, the five New York delegates from Dubinsky's Liberal Party joined with ER to back Stevenson rather than native son Averell Harriman and the Tammany delegation. ER's strong political ties with Dubinsky were reinforced by their mutual dislike of Tammany boss Carmine DeSapio, who had helped derail Franklin Jr.'s run for governor of New York. In the end, Reuther felt that Stevenson was more electable than Harriman or Senator Estes Kefauver, and UAW delegates helped swing the convention in favor of Stevenson.[22]

During the campaign ER addressed civil rights audiences as well as labor groups across the country in support of the Democratic Party ticket. She received reports from the labor leaders, and after she spoke in Detroit, Reuther wrote her, "We are all so proud and grateful for the tremendous contribution which you are making in the present campaign." The UAW, the IUE, and the AFL-CIO all endorsed Stevenson. In a swing through West Virginia, ER praised a hospital run by the UMW and was pleased to report that although Lewis had backed Harriman rather than Stevenson in the primary, he did not support Eisenhower's bid for reelection. Dubinsky invited her to address the Harlem meeting of the United Labor Committee, a group he told her had been formed "to abolish discrimination within the labor movement and our general community life." Unable to attend, she nevertheless sent a strong message conveying Stevenson's commitment to civil rights.[23]

On election day, before the results were in, Carey wrote to ER, "I want you to know how much Marge and I and literally dozens of union leaders I've talked to have admired your superb and indefatigable work during this campaign." ER responded, "Thanks, but we couldn't beat Ike!" Stevenson's margin of defeat was even larger than in 1952, but the Democrats maintained control of the House and Senate. The election had particularly serious consequences for Eleanor Roosevelt. Objecting to her political activities, coupled with her outspoken advocacy of civil rights and her defense of labor unions, the Scripps-Howard newspaper chain canceled her column. "My Day" would now appear in only forty rather than eighty newspapers, reducing her income from the columns from $28,000 in 1956 to $9,630 in 1957.[24]

ER and the cause of labor rights would face new challenges under Eisenhower and his vice president, Richard Nixon. The contest over the right to join a union took a dramatic turn after the 1956 election, offering a classic example of ER's active cooperation with unions on legislative initiatives. Ten years after the Taft-Hartley Act became law, eighteen states had taken advantage of Section 14(b) and passed what are still called "right-to-work laws," including eleven southern states plus Arizona, Indiana, Iowa, Nebraska, Nevada, and North and South Dakota. Under the national labor law, unions could negotiate a "union shop," that is, contractual clauses requiring a worker to join the union after working for a set number of days in workplaces where the union had won an election. Section 14(b) allowed states to override the union shop and create an "open shop." Under these laws, no worker was required to join the union or pay dues, but the union was still required to represent that worker. In 1958 six more states had right-to-work laws on the ballot: California, Colorado, Idaho, Kansas, Ohio, and Washington.[25]

On 9 July 1958 ER and former New York senator Herbert H. Lehman announced the formation of the National Council for Industrial Peace to oppose right-to-work legislation. In a joint press release they proclaimed that it was time "for all right-thinking citizens, from all walks of life, to join in protecting the nation's economy and the working man's union security from the predatory and misleading campaigns now being waged by the U.S. Chamber of Commerce and the National Association of Manufacturers." Now seventy-four years old, ER plunged into the fray of a hard-fought political campaign. Labor and employer groups used what the *New York Times* called a "hard sell approach to the electorate by television, radio, motion picture, billboard, pamphlet, comic book, newspaper advertisement, bumper sign, button, matchbox, shopping bag and even Halloween trick-or-treat kit." Labor estimated that in Ohio alone, 4 million cups of coffee were poured at gatherings designed to "drown a proposed constitutional amendment in a sea of hostile votes."[26]

ER was on familiar ground. This issue had been debated at the Human Rights Commission, and a few years earlier she had told her readers that government should not force people to join unions, but when collective bargaining was in place, a majority of the workers should be able to decide on a requirement to join the union to protect their hard-won status. There was no right to be a "free rider," to "expect to get the benefits of the union without paying for them." If a worker did not want to join a union, he or she could find a job at a nonunion workplace. "To protect collective bargaining and the interests of the workers are, in my view, the right thing to do and when state laws oppose this, I think the state laws are wrong." Her support was not unconditional. The Louisiana AFL-CIO Labor Council met sharp criticism when it succeeded in getting a right-to-work law repealed but in exchange supported a similar measure for some 200,000 agricultural workers earning only fifty or sixty cents an hour. The deal hurt field hands and migrant workers, refinery workers, and cotton press, cotton gin, and rice mill workers, as well as small farmers. Industrial and agricultural labor divided instead of standing together, weakening both.[27]

Now, she dedicated an entire column to the issue, pointing out that "the 'right to work' laws have confused this situation." A survey in Indiana, ER reported, found that only four university students knew what a "right-to-work" law actually was. Her 1958 Labor Day column was devoted to explaining the misnomer. She began with a brief history lesson, showing how the labor movement had improved wages and working conditions. While acknowledging some abuses within organized labor, she contended that right-to-work laws were a "political maneuver of employers" and were being deceptively presented as protecting workers' rights. The misnomer was close to ER's heart. Article 23 of the Universal Declaration of Human Rights began with the carefully crafted words "Everyone has the right to work." As the 1958 elections drew near, Irene Dunne, an actress, Republican activist, and member of the U.S. delegation to the UN General Assembly, accepted the honorary chairmanship of a right-to-work advocacy group. ER quickly denounced Dunne's position, saying that the laws were aimed at the destruction of human rights. The proposal "does not concern itself one iota with human rights or the right to work," she wrote, but rather is a "calculated and cunning smoke screen to beguile the innocent and unknowing."[28]

ER's most scathing comments came when the State of California, in the official document mailed to all voters giving the pros and cons of ballot initiatives, included a statement that made it appear that President Roosevelt had supported the principle of a compulsory open shop, or right-to-work laws. She called the pamphlet a "shameful fraud on the public." By the use of "weasel words," proponents "sought to give the impression that my husband did, during his lifetime, support the concept embodied in the so-called 'right-to-work laws.'... The American public understands very well that Franklin Delano Roosevelt would never have supported such a reactionary doctrine." The Democrats won a sweeping electoral victory, and the right-to-work ballot measures were defeated in all the states but Kansas. For her efforts with the National Council for Industrial Peace, ER received a "flood of favorable mail." Charlotte Walker, from Seattle, wrote, "In your long service to mankind you have performed many outstanding services, but this Council will some day be the greatest tribute of a gracious lady."[29]

The "right-to-work" issue, however, did not go away. ER followed up the elections with an article in the *American Federationist,* the premier publication of the AFL-CIO, explaining, in the words of the title, "Why I Am Opposed to Right To Work Laws." She wrote:

> I am opposed to this legislation because it is narrow in concept, punitive and discriminatory against wage-earners, and is designed solely to benefit employers.
>
> I am opposed to it because its real aim is to destroy American labor.
>
> I am opposed to it because the campaign to enact "right to work" laws is based on dishonesty and deception.
>
> I am opposed because it would upset the present balance between labor and management that has become a basic guarantee of a prosperous national economy.
>
> I am opposed to "right to work" laws because they promote industrial strife instead of industrial peace. It is true that unions have become powerful over the years. But we should not forget that the power of the unions is puny compared to the power that goes with the enormous wealth of Big Business. And business had power first. Whether unions have grown and with this growth have become powerful is not the problem today. The problem, rather, is to make both labor and business feel the responsibility that goes with power, and to use this power mutually for the benefit of all.[30]

Her final points about the power of "big labor" and the need to exercise that power responsibly indicate another political issue labor faced during this period: the problem of union corruption. In 1957 Senator John McClellan began a series of high-profile hearings on the labor movement. Corruption, autocracy, and nepotism were the most common problems uncovered among local trade union leaders on the New York docks and in the short-haul trucking industry, some construction trades, and bakeries, restaurants, and bars. As Reuther had indicated to ER, most of these unions were members of the AFL. While Dave Beck, Jimmy Hoffa, and the International Brotherhood of Teamsters were the primary target of chief committee counsel Robert Kennedy, many union leaders were brought forward to testify and defend their records, and none of them was perfect. Large pension and welfare funds had become particularly susceptible to corruption.[31]

ER was outspoken on the need for labor to meet the highest standards of honesty and integrity. While condemning the unions found guilty of corruption, she also pointed out that the leaders, whether national or local, were not alone in such transgressions. She called for the unions to police themselves but acknowledged that "with so much publicity about unfaithful stewardship within the unions, it is certainly going to be difficult not to undergo examination from without." Her positive columns about unions, on issues large and small, began to serve as alternative stories to counter charges of corruption as well as red-baiting.[32]

The AFL had taken some measures to curb racketeering and mob influence before the merger, and the new AFL-CIO constitution established a Committee on Ethical Practices, to which both David Dubinsky and Jacob Potofsky were appointed from the garment trades. Collusion between employers and subcontractors had long plagued the garment industry, and Dubinsky had made cleaning it up a condition of his return to the AFL in 1940. The committee was authorized to investigate affiliates and established a code of conduct stating principles and guidelines. The CIO was mainly preoccupied with combating accusations of communism, but it also faced charges of corruption. The UAW offered a new, proactive approach. At its sixteenth annual convention in 1957, the union established a public review board; seven prominent community members, including clergy, jurists, and academics, would hold the power to review appeals from aggrieved workers dealing with internal union affairs.[33]

Some union leaders, however, ended the decade by invoking the Fifth Amendment against self-incrimination on corruption charges before the committee. The AFL-CIO executive council adopted a policy prohibiting union officials from holding office if they took this route for personal protection. ER informed her readers about the conflict at the Miami Beach meeting and she agreed that the AFL-CIO policy was correct. While she believed in the constitutional right to claim Fifth Amendment protection, where union racketeering was concerned "there can be no proper reason why the government cannot have truthful answers." Dave Beck invoked the Fifth Amendment over two hundred times in his testimony before the McClellan committee, which found that he had misappropriated Teamsters Union funds and shown contempt for unions and working people. The AFL-CIO executive council voted to expel him. ER agreed, but she also suggested that sometimes union funds were misused or unaccounted for through ignorance, simply because labor leaders were not necessarily good businessmen. She nevertheless concluded that "to deliberately use the union funds for one's own purposes is dishonest and disloyal and cannot be countenanced by any labor union." With Beck gone, the union elected vice president James Hoffa to take his place. Although Hoffa did not take the Fifth before the committee, there was substantial evidence linking him to what the historian Robert Parmet called "financial skullduggery, racketeering, violence, and disdain for union democracy." At the AFL-CIO convention in Atlantic City, the delegates voted overwhelmingly to expel the Teamsters.[34]

In view of the scandalous headlines about rampant corruption in certain unions, Reuther sent ER a copy of the pamphlet "A More Perfect Union," which set forth the purposes and functions of the UAW's public review board. She devoted a column to explaining why big unions were needed to counterbalance big business. Praising the review board, she said that the union went beyond "technical legalities" and lived up to the "spirit of service to the community as a whole." Reuther's innovative measure provided a positive alternative to business as usual and to investigations by hostile outside bodies. Reuther himself testified before the McClellan committee for three days. The major labor dispute that the Republicans hoped to use against him was the UAW strike against the Kohler Company in Sheboygan, Wisconsin. The bathroom fixtures manufacturer had been militantly antiunion since the 1890s. UAW staff took the union's entire Kohler file to Robert Kennedy's office and urged him to visit the company. Kennedy was skeptical, but the level of deep-seated animosity toward the union that he found among managers at the company's headquarters led him and his brother, Senator John Kennedy, to support Reuther and the UAW in the hearings. Reuther ably held his own against the Republican attack.[35]

The wife of one of the Kohler workers wrote to ER to say that the strike for union recognition had been going on for four years and she wanted the government to stop buying Kohler products. ER concluded that such a protracted strike "shows a real desire by the workers for unionization." She welcomed the McClellan committee's hearings on the UAW, which posed problems for the Republicans because they could find no evidence of wrongdoing by the UAW. She concluded:

> The UAW is one of the unions that has done very excellent work in removing
> Communists from any positions of influence, and no one has been stronger

than Mr. Reuther in insisting that labor must clean house itself and have the highest possible standards. Otherwise, he rightly contends, labor would lay itself open to government regulation of a kind that would prevent the growth of unions, for instance in the South, which is one of the things that the new labor reform bill seems likely to accomplish.[36]

Reuther communicated his concerns about potential antilabor legislation to ER. Shortly after the midterm elections in 1958, he sent her some of the propaganda the Republicans had put out about him and declared that the election had reinforced his faith in the "judgment of free people and the strength of our democratic form of government." But, he wrote, "the Democratic majority in Congress must, even though with great difficulty, try to fill the leadership vacuum by a bold and adequate legislative program equal to meeting the unfilled needs of all the people at home and capable of meeting the challenging dimensions of our responsibilities in the world." He included in this "effective and workable corrective legislation dealing with the problem of corruption in the field of labor-management relations." He attached a copy of the first annual report of the UAW public review board. ER was amused by the propaganda and agreed about the role of the Democratic Party in Congress but wondered, "Will [Senate Majority Leader] Lyndon Johnson let the party do it?"[37]

The McClellan hearings uncovered abuse and corruption within unions, while also linking big labor with corruption and organized crime, as well communism, on the national level. There were powerful consequences. Ten years after the Taft-Hartley Act was passed, the second major piece of legislation restricting unions became law, despite intense lobbying by organized labor. Couched in the language of protecting workers' "rights," the 1959 Labor-Management Reporting and Disclosure Act, known as the Landrum-Griffin Act, further restricted democratically elected unions. The act began with a "Bill of Rights" to protect union members from their own elected leaders, established regulations for managing internal union affairs, including standards for the election of union officers and requirements for financial reporting, and increased the investigative powers of government. Members of the Communist Party and convicted felons were barred from holding union office. This was not the kind of reform called for by Eleanor Roosevelt or initiated by Reuther, Dubinsky, and the AFL-CIO.[38]

Striving for Civil Rights

The second major issue on which ER called on labor to take more responsibility was civil rights. ER was increasingly outspoken in her opposition to racial discrimination, moving as Allida Black documents from favoring legislative and legal strategies to counseling civil disobedience, from "patience to protest." She also continued to support legislative protection and unionization of migrant workers, many of whom were racial and ethnic minorities. ER carefully selected her goals and tactics, working with a wide range of unions, many with left-wing histories but strong civil rights credentials. She worked with the NAACP, the National Sharecroppers Fund, and the Democratic Party, all of which shared common goals but did not always agree on tactics. While collaborating closely with A. Philip Randolph, she also made the transition to working with younger black leaders, just as she had with the emerging women trade unionists. She called on labor to lead on civil rights within the international framework of the United Nations.[39]

As ER told Meany, and Reuther acknowledged in India, leaders in the United States had to admit the country's failure to achieve equal rights and do something about it. Labor's leadership around the world was challenged by discrimination at home. When antidiscrimination measures were taken up in the ILO, American trade unions had little influence because others were well aware of discrimination in the ranks of labor in the United States. The Soviets and socialists regularly pointed out this contradiction. ER told her readers, "I am afraid the free trade unions have a real fight on their hands, because . . . labor unions must try to provide leadership in these countries and show that they do not countenance discrimination anywhere, including the U.S." She encouraged the unions to "bestir themselves in their own unions, for the free trade unions have an important role to play in this whole situation by acting properly in their own organizations."[40]

The ACWA convention in 1956 passed a civil rights resolution urging the implementation of *Brown v. Board of Education,* the landmark 1954 Supreme Court decision ending discrimination in education, and calling for legislation to guarantee other civil rights, including fair employment. One of ER's goals was to see that the resolution was put into practice. She reminded delegates that two-thirds of the world's population were people of color, and their UN representatives "are particularly sensitive to how a great nation like ours is striving to meet the problem of civil rights, of equality for all its citizens, justice and fair dealing everywhere throughout our land." She felt that the union's espousal of civil rights was "tremendously important" and could be influential because "it is through [union] strength . . . that we will help the world to accept our leadership and understand that, under our form of government and through our way of life, we have something to offer [the world's people] which cannot be offered by the communists. But we have to demonstrate it. We have to show it, and prove it." ER, like other leaders, black as well as white, turned cold war anticommunism into a reason to advance civil rights.[41]

When District 65 of the Retail, Wholesale, and Department Store Union in New York City held its annual "Brotherhood Rally," ER joined noted

NAACP lawyer Thurgood Marshall and the Honorable Manuel Gomez, the city's first judge of Puerto Rican descent, to speak about the local, national, and international meaning of "brotherhood" and how it might be achieved. The union's membership was almost two-thirds women and predominantly black and Puerto Rican. When the Transport Workers Union of America asked for publicity to help end the Pennsylvania Railroad's discriminatory racial practices against employees, she urged her readers to write to the railroad's president. When she received complaints about racial discrimination by unions as well as employers, she sent them on to be answered by the people involved. For example, when Lynn Oscar Dixon, a black man, wrote to her about collusion between the Teamsters and employers to "deprive Negroes of their jobs" in Memphis, she referred the letter to Reuther, who asked Arthur Goldberg, then general counsel for the Industrial Union Department of the AFL-CIO, to look into the case.[42]

During this period ER played an integral role in helping the NAACP develop and implement the litigation strategy to desegregate public education. As a board member she brought not only financial and public relations resources but also expert organizational experience and political skills to the struggle leading to the *Brown v. Board of Education* decision ruling that separate was not equal and that school segregation must end with "all deliberate speed." Randolph, also on the board, was concerned with the vexing problems of implementation. He asked for ER's help with the National Trade Union Committee for Racial Justice, a new organization he was forming to support those who were being harassed and penalized for daring to claim their rights. Forceful economic pressures were being used to drive African Americans from their farms, businesses, and homes. He stressed: "There are organizations, such as NAACP, filling many of the political and legal action needs. This new group will concern itself solely with the unmet needs for welfare and resistance to economic reprisals." He wrote asking ER to serve as honorary chairman, given the public's "deep respect for and warm confidence in the integrity and wisdom of your leadership." She agreed to help and arranged a meeting. ER and Reuther offered the NAACP technical advice on legislative strategy. Congressman Adam Clayton Powell introduced a rider to a school construction bill that denied federal funds to any school that refused to comply with the Supreme Court decision. While ER and Reuther supported the idea, they feared that adding the amendment in committee ensured that the bill would never get to the floor for debate. This advice was rejected, and they went on to support the Powell Amendment.[43]

On the national political scene in 1956, Adlai Stevenson's appeal for moderation on civil rights alienated those civil rights and labor leaders who had supported Harriman in the primary. When NAACP leaders suggested abandoning Stevenson ER threatened to resign from the board. At the same time, the southern delegates were threatening to walk out of the Democratic National Convention to protest desegregation. A key point of contention was the use of federal action to enforce the *Brown* decision. The issue became so divisive that Paul Butler, chairman of the Democratic National Committee, turned to ER to draft the civil rights plank and chair the session. According to Black, she took on this task to help Stevenson, "but also because of the opportunity to define the civil rights issue in a way that both expanded party support and strengthened its commitment to racial justice."[44]

Meany, Reuther, and Randolph all testified before the committee in favor of a strong civil rights plank. The compromise plank that finally passed by a narrow majority did not please either of the contending factions—ER admitted, it "does not say everything I would like it to say"—but it kept the convention together. In general terms, it called for equal rights in employment and voting as well as education and objected to the use of force to interfere with the implementation of court decisions. Without mentioning *Brown*, it recognized decisions of the U.S. Supreme Court as the law of the land. Reuther and the UAW helped move the Michigan delegation behind the plank in the crucial vote. In the end, ER told her readers that "anyone who reads the platform will concede that the labor plank is a good one," but the civil rights plank took far more explaining.[45]

The liberal community faced these challenges with a new leader rising from their midst. Opening one of the six days of hearings with a prayer and also testifying before the platform committee at ER's request was the Reverend Martin Luther King Jr. The twenty-five-year-old preacher had become pastor of the Dexter Avenue Baptist Church in Montgomery, Alabama, in 1954 and at the time of the convention was the most visible leader of the Montgomery bus boycott. An awareness of ER in both his thinking and his rhetoric is attested to by one of the early handwritten note cards for his speeches, which quotes a 1951 "My Day" column about working for peace which ended with, "Pray God for the ability to dream and the determination to seek the realization of our dream."[46]

In early May 1956 Rosa Parks, the NAACP activist whose refusal to move to the back of the bus in Montgomery had triggered the boycott, was in New York at a fund-raising event with Myles Horton, director of the Highlander Folk School. At ER's request, Horton accompanied Parks to ER's apartment so that the two women could meet. Describing Parks as "a very quiet, gentle person," ER told her readers: "It is difficult to imagine how she ever could take such a positive and independent stand.... [But] human beings reach a point when they say 'This is as far as I can go' and from then on it may be passive resistance, but it will be resistance." Horton wrote to King to tell him about the meeting with ER. The summer before her act of civil disobedience, Parks had attended a workshop on desegregation at the Highlander Folk School in

Tennessee, her first such experience "with people of another race." ER had a long history with Highlander; her friend Lucy Mason had introduced her to its first director, James Dombrowski, in 1940. Castigated by the right for her contributions to the "communist" school, she countered that those who opposed Highlander for communist activities were in fact opposed because the school provided "a meeting place for colored and white to discuss subjects of mutual interest to both races, and particularly [because] it has helped to train people in the labor movement... [and was] strengthening the cause of integration in the South and strengthening the cause of Labor."[47]

As the CIO unions expanded their own labor education programs, they often disagreed with Highlander's goals and strategies. In 1950, when the CIO withdrew its support at the same time it was expelling unions for alleged communist leanings, ER courageously stood with Highlander. By 1953 the staff concluded that racism was the major obstacle to economic and political reform in the United States and began to develop workshops for black and white community leaders; eventually they developed education programs to aid the campaign to register black voters across the South. It was through this civil rights work that ER visited Highlander in June 1958 and worked with King to defend it against a new onslaught of anticommunist attacks and attempts to close the school.[48]

On 24 May 1956 a rally packed Madison Square Garden to honor "Heroes of the South," including Autherine Lucy, the first black student to enter the University of Alabama, and Martin Luther King Jr. Harlem congressman Adam Clayton Powell joined in this salute with Eleanor Roosevelt and A. Philip Randolph. ER challenged the audience to recognize that racism was a problem in the North as well as the South. She called on New Yorkers to "integrate housing and otherwise set a pattern of community life for the rest of the nation."[49]

ER paid a price for her commitment. Anticommunist smear tactics were increasingly turned against civil rights activists, and white violence was increasing. In 1955 Emmett Till, a fourteen-year-old Chicagoan who was visiting relatives in Mississippi, was lynched; Lamar Smith, a black farmer, and the Reverend George Lee were murdered for registering to vote in the state. The violence touched ER personally. She continued to be threatened when she appeared at civil rights events in the South. A bomb exploded near a church where she was speaking in North Carolina; the Texas White Citizens Council threatened to run her out of town on a rail. When she went to visit the Highlander School in Monteagle, Tennessee, the Ku Klux Klan planned a raid and the county sheriff agreed to look the other way. The FBI told her to stay away, but to no avail. ER was joining a growing list of leaders who endorsed civil disobedience and nonviolent resistance.[50]

Both civil rights and labor rights were denied to migrant farm workers, many of whom were African American, and Randolph asked for ER's help.

She and other advocates continued to see legislation and unionization as the best strategy for these marginalized workers. Her old friend Frank Graham, president of the University of North Carolina, became chair of the National Sharecroppers Fund, which had grown out of earlier efforts to support the Southern Tenant Farmers' Union. He asked her to co-chair the fund's National Advisory Committee with Randolph. ER was trying to reduce her commitments, but she agreed to attend hearings and to write about the farm workers in her column. Soon after she reminded her readers that the migrant workers had families in need of education and care but few legal protections and no unions. She asked citizens in New York and across the country to consider legislation that would help these workers in the farming industry, which was basic to the economy and security of the country.[51]

Choosing to highlight the working conditions of migrant laborers by challenging a powerful U.S. senator, she wrote about conditions for workers who picked apples for Senator Harry F. Byrd, the biggest grower in Virginia. One-room shacks built before Pearl Harbor were being replaced with cinderblock apartments consisting of "a room 25 feet square in which 40 Bahamians sleep in double-deck bunks less than a foot apart." African American laborers and their wives and children, mostly from Florida, also occupied these one-room dwellings. The lack of plumbing and water, the long hours and low pay, and the costs of illness were all reminiscent of conditions during the 1930s, when ER had toured the migrant workers' camps. The following month she gave a positive example of conditions by reporting on the apple farm owned by her friend Henry Morgenthau, whose labor practices and accommodations met the standards established by New York State. Employers trying to do the right thing faced hardships, however, in part because their competitors were exploiting workers. She called for hearings to be held in which "all interested parties are represented in an effort not only to meet the needs of the growers whose crops are necessary to the people of the country, but also to safeguard the workers in every possible way." Graham thanked her for the columns and noted their contribution toward a workable program for agricultural labor.[52]

On 4 February 1959 ER attended the meeting of the National Farm Labor Advisory Committee in Washington, DC, with Secretary of Labor James Mitchell and A. Philip Randolph. She introduced the labor secretary's speech and co-chaired the first afternoon session. While conceding that "even" organized labor had been slow to recognize the problems of migrant labor, she felt that unions were coming to understand them. In the spring Secretary Mitchell circulated proposed changes in the regulations for farm workers. The proposal met strong opposition from the farm lobby, which represented large-scale farmers and agribusiness, and ER urged those who supported change to press for the hearings. In June "My Day" readers learned that the advisory committee had recommended that farm workers "be included in Federal and

State laws requiring union recognition and collective bargaining, setting fair standards for wages and hours of work and providing for unemployment compensation." The report also put forward special measures for migrant workers, both domestic and foreign, and recommended the establishment of a Bureau of Migratory Labor in the Department of Labor to improve standards. Employer standards and worker protections were a familiar combination of unionization and legislation to address workplace problems.[53]

In October ER illustrated the need for federal protections by writing about twelve-year-old Christine Hayes, whose "scalp and most of her face were ripped off by a potato-digging machine while she and other child laborers were helping to harvest the potato crop on a farm near Blackfoot, Idaho." Exempted from the Fair Labor Standards Act, many thousands of rural and migrant farm workers' children between the ages of ten and thirteen were legally allowed to work in dangerous conditions, while thousands more, some as young as six, were illegally employed. This situation needed to be "corrected by law immediately," wrote ER. On 7 December ER was the first witness at the hearing of the Senate Subcommittee on Migratory Labor. She noted the needs of small farmers, farm workers, and their children. One of the problems she highlighted was the exclusion of farm labor from federal legislation protecting the rights of workers to organize and bargain collectively. When public employees soon advocated for this same right, however, they proved a challenge for ER.[54]

Workers in Public Service

ER struggled with the question of organizing service workers and those employed in the public sector. Workers in municipal and state government, including firefighters and police officers, as well as clerks and garbage collectors, were largely unorganized and specifically exempt from existing labor laws. Yet their numbers were rising dramatically, and their wages and benefits were falling behind those of their blue-collar counterparts in the private sector. These jobs were increasingly filled by nonwhite workers, many of whom were Spanish-speaking; in many service occupations women predominated. Organizing these workers created a dilemma for Eleanor Roosevelt.[55]

When the Teamsters Union announced that it would try to organize New York City's 24,000 policemen, ER questioned the wisdom of unionizing workers critical to the public safety and worried about the possibility of a union usurping the powers of government. Hoffa, she concluded, "[is] getting a little bit arrogant and somewhat dangerous!" She opposed the drive in part because of the Teamsters' well-known links with organized crime but also because of her concern about the unionization of public safety jobs. She had addressed this question earlier in the decade, discussing the need for no-strike clauses, and continued to feel strongly that police officers should be able to have group representation among themselves and be protected by law from arbitrary acts by their superiors. Shocked that New York's police commissioner had refused to meet with a grievance committee, she promised to register her concerns with City Hall. Still, she deemed public policy more appropriate than union representation for handling these problems.[56]

ER's struggle continued when a different version of the public-service union question developed in New York City. African American and Puerto Rican men and women were still excluded from many better-paying private-sector jobs and were treated as a distinct workforce that could be paid less than white workers for toiling under more difficult conditions. Most of the established unions saw them as "unorganizable." Exceptions emerged in the 1950s. New labor leaders such as Jerry Wurf of the American Federation of State, County, and Municipal Employees began to organize them in New York City. In 1958 Mayor Robert Wagner Jr. issued a municipal order recognizing collective bargaining rights for city workers. A major organizing drive was undertaken for hospital workers—those in the laundry and kitchen, the maintenance and housekeeping staff, and nurses' aides and orderlies. Under the leadership of Leon J. Davis pharmacists, clerks, and other drugstore workers had formed Local 1199, Retail Drug Employees Union, AFL-CIO. They had a strong record of organizing and fighting discrimination, and when black porters from the Montefiore Hospital asked for help, Davis decided the time was right to organize the voluntary hospitals.[57]

These hospitals posed a unique set of problems. Neither public nor private, the majority, some eighty-five hospitals, were chartered as nonprofit institutions and run by wealthy philanthropists and businessmen who functioned through boards of directors. As employers they were exempt from federal and state labor laws; in fact laws prohibited strikes by hospital workers. The nonprofessional workers at Montefiore voted overwhelmingly to join Local 1199, but the hospital board members argued they had no obligation to negotiate. Finally, threatened with a strike by 90 percent of the support staff, they recognized the union and signed a historic contract including a wage increase, overtime pay, a forty-hour, five-day workweek, paid sick leave, dues check-off, and a grievance system with arbitration. ER found this "permissible," but cautioned that strikes must be avoided so that patients were not left to suffer and perhaps die without proper care. She also acknowledged the institutions' budget problems but asked, "Must employees of voluntary hospitals be kept at starvation wages?"[58]

The organizing drive moved into high gear. As the historian Philip Foner describes it, "on May 8, 1959, 3,500 workers at six voluntary hospitals—nurses' aides, orderlies, porters, elevator operators, kitchen workers, and other 'housekeeping' employees, the majority of them women, and 85 to 90 percent of them black or Puerto Rican—walked off their jobs." Despite a New York State Supreme Court order, picket lines went up all around the city. Harry Van Arsdale, who came from the building trades to lead the newly merged New York City Central Labor Council, saw an opportunity to unite the unions and backed the strike. Davis recognized the importance of community support and called on civil rights leaders like Martin Luther King Jr. and A. Philip Randolph, who assigned Bayard Rustin to work full-time on the campaign. He also sought the support of public figures such as Eleanor Roosevelt.[59]

ER was uncharacteristically hesitant. Within a week of the walkout, she used her column to consider the complex issues involved. Reviewing the legal questions, she thought that the laws might prohibit unions. But the situation had been "very stupidly handled" when the hospital directors refused to meet with their employees. She argued, "Employees who are quite evidently not receiving a living wage and are dissatisfied with their conditions of work would simply be slaves if they were obliged to work on without being able to reach their employers with their complaints and demand negotiation." She chastised hospital boards for not resolving the problems earlier: "You cannot just refuse to meet people when they want to talk about their basic human rights." No one had more standing to talk about human rights than Eleanor Roosevelt.[60]

A few days later her hopes that a settlement was close proved unfounded, and she was disheartened as the strike dragged on. She unequivocally blamed management for the situation, thought that the city could have done more, and deemed hiring parolees for low wages utterly unacceptable. Yet the strike posed a profound dilemma. ER had long argued that every worker had a right to join a union, and she was an unquestioned champion of poor and minority working women. This strike was about poor minority women trying to improve their working lives by joining a union. Her colleagues in both the labor and the civil rights movements were supporting the strikers. Yet, she told her readers, "I am opposed to the unionization of employees in such vital areas as hospitals, police, fire, and municipally owned power plants." She sympathized with the workers and blamed management, but did not support the strike.[61]

ER discovered that her interpretation of the legal situation had been incorrect; unions were acceptable under state law. Still she preferred "hospitals to have their employees safeguarded in other ways than through representation," since they provided essential services to "helpless individuals." Yet she came around to believing that "the same reason that compelled us to put so much strength into union leaders' hands where industry was concerned is going to compel us to do the same thing where hospital boards are concerned." She could not fathom why the "able men and women on these hospital boards "could not work out an acceptable plan" with the employees. On 22 June an agreement was signed. Management refused to recognize the union but agreed to impartial grievance machinery and arbitration, a minimum wage, a wage increase, a forty-hour week, time-and-a-half for overtime, seniority rules, and a system of job grades and wage rates.[62]

The day after the strike was settled, "My Day" reflected ER's lingering unease, but ultimate support. She reported on how uncomfortable she felt in a conversation with a doctor who supported the hospital administrators and dismissed the workers as illiterate and unskilled. She thought that most were likely literate in their native Spanish. "But, illiterate or not, it is impossible for a family, or even a single individual, to live decently in New York City on the wages the hospitals paid.... [A] business has no right to exist which cannot pay every employee a living wage." In the end, she agreed that the union would have to be recognized. Union organizing drives gained momentum in hospitals and the public sector, and directors of hospitals and government services turned out to be little different from their counterparts in privately owned businesses. As this new direction in organizing was moving forward, conditions in the industrial sector worsened, and tension between Meany and Reuther increased.[63]

Labor Politics in a Recession

The deepest recession in two decades began in 1957, and unemployment remained above 6 percent for the next several years. Cities like Detroit, Cleveland, and Buffalo were particularly hard hit as foreign autos such as the Volkswagen made their debut in the American market. The UAW alone lost 400,000 members by 1960. ILGWU membership was down slightly from its peak of 445,000, and garments made overseas were being imported at an increasing rate. Between 1953 and 1961 employment in the New York dress industry dropped 31.5 percent in Manhattan and 17.5 percent throughout the state. Comparing 1958 to 1929, ER reminded her readers of times during another Republican administration when "we kept hearing that prosperity was waiting for us just around the corner and, therefore, we were besought to buy to bring this slow-moving lady around that corner. Somehow the lady never came!" In this postwar slump she called for a fundamental redirection of the economy.[64]

Despite the Democrats' smashing electoral success in 1958 congressional races and against the right-to-work-laws, 1959 was a grim year for labor. The recession deepened, the steelworkers went out on strike for 116 days, and industrial organizing came to a standstill. Neither the UAW's efforts to organize professional and technical workers in the Midwest nor its attempt to negotiate higher wages in the aircraft industry in the West showed much progress. The Eisenhower administration refused to stimulate the economy, fearing inflation. Under the leadership of Lyndon Johnson in the Senate, the Republican-Dixiecrat coalition blocked labor's reform efforts. Initiatives to promote civil rights, increase unemployment payments, provide economic aid for distressed areas, set up a public works program, and furnish health insurance for the elderly were all stalled in committees.[65]

Internal labor peace was also elusive. The AFL-CIO merger was increasingly frustrating for Reuther and the industrial unions. There were no plans for a major organizing initiative, and jurisdictional disputes continued to rage. Reuther declared the AFL-CIO "totally paralyzed." On rare occasions ER mixed in labor's internal politics, but more often than not she served as a mediator between factions. For example, she wrote to Meany and Reuther about ten people claiming that they were denied job opportunities and had suffered other abuses by the officers of Local 138 of the International Union of Operating Engineers on Long Island. Reuther used her inquiry as a basis to raise the issues again with the executive council. Meany may have considered ER a nuisance, as had many others before him, but when she asked a question, he answered. In this case he requested a special report, and was able to explain to her that none of the men had lost his job and a monitor had been appointed to oversee the local. In strictest confidence, Reuther asked ER to share Meany's response with him, and she did.[66]

The overarching labor issue was the strike by the USWA against thirteen steel companies, which shut down 90 percent of the steel industry for 116 days. The union was asking for a wage increase, a cost-of-living adjustment, and improved fringe benefits. Critical to the negotiations was the employers' demand to eliminate what ER referred to as "certain wasteful work practices." The company wanted to break the idea of an automatic wage increase and reassert control over work assignments and plant rules, provoking militant union resistance. The *New York Times* called it the key labor fight of the last twenty years. ER followed the strike in detail. She again saw the labor dispute as a discouraging sign, writing, "Differences between nations lead to war and we want peace, but if we cannot come to agreement within our own country, where we speak the same language, know how we live and how we want to live, what can we look for among nations?"[67]

ER detailed the costs of the strike: 1.5 million tons of steel production lost, pay losses for half a million steelworkers amounting to $50 million, and a total loss of eighty thousand jobs in steel, transportation, and coal. Amidst accusations on all sides, she agreed with her friend Chester Bowles, now a member of Congress from Connecticut, that President Eisenhower needed to appoint a fact-finding board. Because of the strike, she hoped that people might recognize what she saw as a "rather false prosperity" in the country." The Board of Inquiry that Eisenhower appointed under the national emergencies section of the Taft-Hartley Act was only a temporary fix, and she doubted it would produce the information needed for a just decision. "The public is entitled to know what these facts are," she argued. She looked to a system of impartial investigations and mediation by judges to avoid these breakdowns as the need for steel became more acute. By the end of the year an eighty-day truce was in place. Still, recognizing the precariousness of postwar prosperity and the structural problems of inflation and what is now called globalization, ER worried about renewed labor-management conflict and the absence of public mediation.[68]

At the close of the decade ER traveled to Bayberry, Long Island, the training center of the powerful New York Local 3, International Brotherhood of Electrical Workers. Journeymen, foremen, and superintendents participated in a week-long program that was, she said, "designed to make you think." She delivered a lecture that stressed "the importance of understanding the world in which we live, and the role America must play as a leader of the free nations." The union members asked questions and chatted informally with ER. Josephine Telesco, a business representative of Local 3, who brought a delegation of ten women trade union leaders from New York City, renewed an acquaintance with ER which had started in 1940, when Telesco "was a striking employee of the Leviton Company and Mrs. Eleanor Roosevelt visited the picket line, to encourage the strikers in their long bitter struggle for union recognition and improved conditions." ER would soon take up the cause of working women as her last official responsibility. As she and Reuther headed into another year of presidential politics, the steelworkers were on strike, and unemployment was a central issue. Many of the policy positions that unions had adopted to end corruption and racial discrimination were not carried out on the shop floor, and African Americans and women were becoming better organized and active in expressing their grievances. The election of the young President Kennedy brought new opportunity for their shared social vision, and once again they would show that labor had something to offer.[69]

8

A REVOLUTIONARY PERIOD

We are living in a revolutionary period which requires the
maximum contribution of men and women.
ELEANOR ROOSEVELT to the President's Commission on the Status
of Women, 16 June 1962

Eleanor Roosevelt convened the third meeting of President Kennedy's
Commission on the Status of Women at the Roosevelt home in Hyde Park
on 16 June 1962, almost exactly thirty-three years after the Women's Trade
Union League had celebrated its anniversary on the Hudson. In an event
reminiscent of that earlier one, members and staff gathered for a picnic on
the sprawling lawn of ER's home at nearby Val-Kill. Esther Peterson circulated among the guests. The labor educator and lobbyist for the Amalgamated
Clothing Workers union was now an assistant secretary of labor and executive director of the commission. Kitty Ellickson, on leave from the AFL-CIO
research department, was executive secretary. There was no time, however,
for a leisurely boat ride up the Hudson River. The members flew in from all
over the country for a two-day meeting, representing business, labor, government, churches, civil rights groups, academia, and women's organizations.
Commission members officially representing the labor movement were Mary
Callahan, from the executive board of the International Union of Electrical
Workers, and William Schnitzler, president of the Bakery and Confectionary
Workers Union and vice president of the AFL-CIO.[1]

ER led the group on a tour of the Roosevelt family home, telling familiar
stories about FDR, the children, and her mother-in-law. The main house had
become a historic site, owned by the federal government. For work sessions,
the group assembled around the large table in the Ship Model Room, beneath
FDR's beloved seafaring pictures. Despite her declining health, ER, at age

seventy-seven, chaired the meeting. The commission members listened to committee reports and endorsed minimum wage legislation. At ER's request they authorized her to send a progress report to the president. At her suggestion they left the question of public hearings up to the officers and staff, after consultation with relevant committees and evaluation of the costs. At one point during the meeting Peterson thought ER looked quite tired and had perhaps fallen asleep. But when they came to a very difficult point, "she sat up and made a statement that brought the entire discussion into focus," Peterson recalled. "She had been listening to everything and absorbing it." During the discussion of new and expanded services, ER noted that "the whole point of having a Commission of this kind is because we are living in a revolutionary period. It is a revolution in economic life, in all of our relations to the world, in our social and cultural life." Revolution, not political or military but economic and social, was very much on her mind.[2]

At the beginning of the 1960s, after a tumultuous presidential primary, an aging ER reluctantly joined with labor in support of the young John F. Kennedy. Their efforts were important to his narrow victory over Richard Nixon. As president he offered opportunities to bring new life to ER's long-standing commitments to labor causes, which were linked closely with racial justice and gender equity. She understood that jobs, housing, poverty, and discrimination were complex interrelated factors affected by elections and the government policies that followed. She never lost sight of the need to address these problems from an individual as well as an international perspective. Her comprehensive approach demanded a great deal from the citizens of a democracy, and she demanded no less of herself. Organized labor worked closely with the Kennedy administration. ER praised Kennedy's appointment of a labor-management committee to address workplace issues, while Reuther, Dubinsky, and Meany took their seats at the table.

As the country embraced what Kennedy called the "New Frontier," familiar challenges were complemented by new opportunities. Unemployment was high, and racial tensions escalated within the labor movement. Migrant workers were not yet protected by legislation or represented by unions. Women were increasingly vocal about the lack of equality in the workplace and in their unions. Reuther and Meany continued to clash over internal union procedures. ER addressed them all. She worked most closely with Reuther on political and economic issues, and he continued to turn to her for advice and support. True to her core principles, she publicly defended A. Philip Randolph and challenged the AFL-CIO to live up to its standards for racial minorities and migrant workers. When she agreed to chair the President's Commission on the Status of Women, a lifetime of collaborating with union women to address working women's problems came full circle. In the last years of her life ER worked with her labor allies on politics, economics, civil rights, and women's rights: organizing, educating, lobbying, and voting in a revolutionary time.

Presidential Politics

News of a new contract in the prolonged steel strike came early in 1960. While this was a relief, ER found it "disquieting" to note that the contract stated only that the price of steel would not go up in the "immediate future," leaving open the prospect of a price rise. She showed sharp political vision in the light of the upcoming presidential campaign, predicting that "the price will not be raised until after this year's Presidential election, for the steel magnates are so close to the Administration that they would not want to hurt the Republican chances by putting an increase into effect before the election." With an increase in pay and cost-of-living adjustments, some blamed labor for a contract that might prove inflationary. ER defended the industrial workers, writing that the steel companies' "published profits and the salaries of management at the top certainly give a justification for labor to feel that it should have a greater proportion of the wealth created, since the end product is produced by labor's daily contribution." Labor alone could not be "held responsible for inflation."[3]

As ER and labor leaders were concerned about strikes, inflation, automation, and unemployment, the 1960 presidential campaign became a top priority. The Democrats thought they could take back the White House, but the liberal wing of the party wanted a candidate who would address unemployment and strongly advocate for the rights of labor, minorities, and women. Tensions between liberals and conservatives in the party were running unusually high. Despite her age and failing health, ER remained a political force within the Democratic Party strongly aligned with labor, and she was active behind the scenes during the primary season. She was not happy with John Kennedy as the potential Democratic candidate and encouraged Adlai Stevenson to seek the nomination again, despite his two losses to Eisenhower. ER felt that Kennedy had neither taken a stand against Senator Joseph McCarthy nor understood how damaging McCarthyism had been; he was not strong on civil rights, his Catholicism would be a problem, she didn't like his father, and she worried about the power the Kennedy machine would exert. Several encounters in the 1950s had made the tension between them public.[4]

There was no consensus among labor leaders. Kennedy and Senator Hubert Humphrey of Minnesota had both spoken at the 1959 UAW convention, and Humphrey seemed the clear favorite. Although Reuther shared some of ER's misgivings about Kennedy, Dubinsky had met with Kennedy early in the year and had quickly become a strong supporter. Meany and the AFL-CIO were officially neutral but informally supported Kennedy, in part out of fear of one alternative, Lyndon B. Johnson, the Senate majority leader from Texas, whom Meany regarded as "horrible" on labor issues. Esther Peterson, despite warnings from ACWA officials not to stick her neck out, was one of the first labor leaders to support Kennedy. As a labor lobbyist she had met the young congressman in 1945. When the union lobbyists got together after Esther had left the room, someone asked, "What are we going to do with her?" Another answered, "Oh, assign her to that new congressman Jack Kennedy, he isn't going to amount to much." So Peterson began a long and productive working relationship with the congressman from Massachusetts.[5]

After Kennedy won the Wisconsin primary, he began to move more to the left on civil rights and other issues, and Reuther tried to get Humphrey to withdraw. At the end of April, Reuther went to see ER and reported that he thought things were looking better for Stevenson, who had not entered the race. He was worried, however, that a bitter primary fight would help the Republicans, especially in West Virginia, and asked ER to call Kennedy and Humphrey and ask them not to make charges that would be damaging later on in the national election. She wrote to Reuther that she had called Humphrey "but had absolutely no effect upon him." He and Kennedy, she thought, "both seem to feel they have no chance in the nomination unless they go on with these primaries. There is a chance they may be less enthusiastic after the West Virginia primary, though this is only a chance!"[6]

Kennedy's victory in West Virginia was a turning point for his campaign. Now Stevenson could win the nomination only if the convention became deadlocked. Despite pleas from ER, Reuther, and others to declare quickly, Stevenson continued to deny that he was a candidate. When the *New York Times* reported that Reuther was going to announce for Kennedy, ER wrote Reuther a confidential letter asking him to "consider waiting until the Convention to find out what Stevenson's chances are before making your decision." Reuther assured her that he had "no immediate plans for announcing for any candidate" and sent her the statement he had issued. When he and his family came to visit, he told her, they would "have an opportunity to compare notes . . . about the political situation."[7]

In the midst of the primaries Reuther reaffirmed to ER his faith that the Democratic Party, "despite all of its deficiencies," was the only "political instrument capable of providing America with the leadership and program essential to preparing us to meet our needs at home and to be equal to our responsibilities in this period of change and challenge." Yet he cautioned that it was "imperative . . . that the liberal forces within the Democratic Party go to the Convention united and prepared to act together," for "wishful thinking among liberals," he wrote, "will not meet the challenge of cold, power politics which will motivate the conservative bloc." Several other leading liberals and former Stevenson supporters, such as Arthur Schlesinger Jr. and John Kenneth Galbraith, endorsed Kennedy. After the Reuthers' visit in June, ER told Joseph Lash: "Walter feels we are lost unless Stevenson & Kennedy agree before the convention that whichever one can't win will throw his votes to the other, which means if Kennedy starts a band wagon he'll win. Walter's argument is that unless they are agreed, they will elect the Republicans."[8]

ER joined the New York Draft Stevenson Committee, writing to her daughter, Anna, "Politics are very active…and now I have to go out to the convention." Advocating liberalism as staunchly as ever, she worked tirelessly on Stevenson's behalf. At the convention she held three press conferences, met with women delegates and fifteen state leaders, pressured Stevenson to become more involved, plotted strategy, and planned floor demonstrations. Meany maintained a neutral position, but his wife wore a straw hat with a Kennedy ribbon throughout the proceedings. Peterson helped deliver the Utah delegation for Kennedy. Reuther came to ER at the convention and told her that if Stevenson would support Kennedy, he could have the position of secretary of state. No longer willing to act as intermediary, she advised him to talk directly with Stevenson himself, but nothing came of the conversation. Kennedy won on the first ballot. ER left the convention immediately, greatly disappointed in Stevenson. She reluctantly congratulated Kennedy in a telephone call from the airport but had no say in the vice presidential selection. Dubinsky saw Johnson as a winning choice. He calmed Meany and Reuther so they would not protest the addition of a southern conservative to the ticket.[9]

After the convention the labor movement united behind Kennedy. The general executive board of the AFL-CIO voted to endorse him. Meany directed an effort to organize new voters and made speeches for the Kennedy-Johnson ticket. The UAW raised half a million dollars for "educational" activities, and Roy Reuther directed the Democratic Party's voter registration drive. His brother Walter crossed the country on the campaign trail, along with hundreds of UAW staff and thousands of rank-and-file members from their union's 1,250 locals. The ILGWU was by their side. More than a quarter of a million dollars was raised from member contributions for voter registration and advertisements on radio and television and in the newspapers. Esther Peterson joined Arthur Goldberg from the Industrial Union Department as key liaisons at the labor desk in Democratic Party headquarters. She called a meeting of women labor leaders and formed the Committee of Labor Women for Kennedy and Johnson, some two hundred strong, with ties to thousands of labor groups across the country.[10]

ER was slow to jump onto the Kennedy bandwagon. Instead of siding with the unions, she was critical of them. She worried that union education on citizenship and campaign issues was reaching only union members and not all their family members of voting age. In August she deplored the political apathy of union members. Although the candidates were actively seeking the labor vote, she reported that "nationally, about 37 percent of male union members and about 44 percent of their wives do not vote." In New York City the labor vote was not very important because "less than a third of the male union members are registered for voting and only from 10 to 15 percent of their wives." She encouraged both parties to help union members with the required literacy tests and ensure they were registered and well informed on the issues: "Here is a group that can be reached easily, yet no effort apparently has been made in New York City to see that they participate actively in their citizenship."[11]

Kennedy went to Val-Kill in August to seek ER's active support. She offered campaign advice, and they came away from that meeting with an improved relationship. She agreed to be honorary co-chair of the New York Committee for Kennedy. Dubinsky asked ER to record an eight-minute nationwide ABC radio broadcast for the campaign, and she gladly agreed. She had seen Kennedy grow during the campaign, especially on civil rights issues, and he was clearly supported by her friends in labor. When ER returned from a trip to Europe in late September, she campaigned for Kennedy from New York to California. She appeared with him on television, taped radio and television ads in support of the ticket, and offered informal advice. When Rose Schneiderman sent belated birthday greetings, she said she thought Kennedy would win. ER hoped her friend was right.[12]

The pollster Louis Harris declared that there was not merely a labor vote but a UAW vote, and it helped Kennedy carry Detroit by the largest margin of any industrial city in the nation. Labor's influence was also felt in New York: Kennedy and Johnson received almost half a million votes on Dubinsky's Liberal Party line, more than the margin by which they won the state's forty-five electoral votes. The AFL-CIO executive board credited Kennedy's narrow win to its voter registration program. By the end of the campaign ER felt that Kennedy would make a good president, and both she and labor made substantial contributions to his narrow victory over Nixon.[13]

Labor's New Frontier

On the day John F. Kennedy was elected, Eleanor Roosevelt had just celebrated her seventy-sixth birthday. She had come to admire Kennedy's strengths and to offer advice in areas of disagreement, both privately and publicly. Her health was declining, and she was writing her column three days a week rather than six, but when asked by the president, she agreed to serve in several new positions while continuing vociferously to critique his performance and the administration's policies. Both Meany and Reuther had respect and genuine fondness for the Kennedys and were enthusiastic about working with the new administration, though aware of the limits of his narrow victory and the power of Congress. Before the inauguration the first order of labor business was choosing a secretary of labor. Arthur Goldberg, a lawyer originally from Chicago who had worked as general counsel for the CIO and the USWA, was supported by both Dubinsky and Reuther, and they worked hard to convince Meany. When he was selected, ER praised the Goldberg appointment as on the "same high level" of the president-elect's other cabinet appointments.[14]

President Kennedy invited ER to join his family for the inauguration, but she declined and sat in the bleachers instead. On that bitter cold January day, wrapped in a fur coat and an army blanket, ER was enormously hopeful. Lash described her as hearing the sound of youth and fearlessness in Kennedy's speech. The severe weather prevented the Reuthers from meeting with ER as planned, but later Reuther shared his thoughts in a long letter. In his opinion, Kennedy's inaugural address and his State of the Union speech were important first steps, but the real problem, he told her, was "going to be on the legislative front.... [L]iberal forces will need to mobilize the broadest possible support among the people if we are to get the needed margin for essential social legislation." His primary concern was putting people back to work. He feared that unemployment would get worse, with severe layoffs in the automotive industry, which already had, her told her, "in excess of one million cars in inventory."[15]

ER continued to enjoy the close company of her labor colleagues. Rose Schneiderman was like a sister, Dubinsky an old friend, and Reuther like a beloved son. On 15 February 1961 Reuther joined her for breakfast in New York City. He appreciated the opportunity to discuss several current problems and receive the benefit of her point of view. "I left your house so exhilarated in spirit," he wrote her, "and so well nourished in body and the morning was so beautiful that I enjoyed the luxury of a walk from your place back to my hotel on 45th Street." After his wife, May, had surgery at Presbyterian Hospital in Manhattan, he told ER that her visits to May had "lifted her spirits and helped her back on the road to recovery." When ER was once again appointed a member of the UN delegation, Rose Schneiderman congratulated her, saying, "You'll do a superb job," and suggested that she need not come to the next meeting of the WTUL scholarship committee. ER confirmed that she would be there, though perhaps a little late, and sent flowers when Schneiderman was recovering from an injury. ER and Reuther were both strong supporters of Kennedy's Peace Corps initiative and agreed to participate on an advisory committee. When Schneiderman wrote about providing workers' compensation and medical insurance for the Peace Corps volunteers, ER forwarded the letter to the director and was assured that he was working on the problems. When the failed Bay of Pigs invasion left 1,200 men captured and thrown into

Cuban jails, Kennedy turned to Reuther and Eleanor Roosevelt to help secure their release in an unsuccessful effort that became known as the tractors-for-freedom deal.[16]

Dubinsky and the ILGWU saw some immediate success with the new administration. Together with his legislative director, Evelyn Dubrow, Dubinsky reinforced the campaign for an increase in the minimum wage. Kennedy signed a bill in the spring of 1961 raising wages from $1.00 to $1.25 an hour over three years. As part of a new consumer campaign ER sewed the eleven billionth label into a garment to show it was union made. That summer Dubinsky again joined forces with ER in New York reform politics when they finally defeated Carmine DeSapio, the leader of Tammany Hall, who had opposed both Stevenson and FDR Jr.'s run for governor of New York and earned ER's wrath. She campaigned against him all summer and regaled her family with stories of how she was able to give speeches in Italian while the Italian American DeSapio was not. When ER joined President Kennedy, Governor Rockefeller, and Dubinsky for the dedication ceremonies of the new ILGWU housing project at Twenty-sixth Street and Eighth Avenue, she thanked Dubinsky for his vision and imaginative leadership in education, health care, vacation time, and, above all, the great housing projects. She thought it noteworthy that President Kennedy had fit this dedication into his busy schedule, for he understood "the value of better housing and of good leadership in the union field."[17]

ER also welcomed Goldberg, the plainspoken secretary of labor, who was touring the country, acknowledging a full-fledged recession and calling for government, business, and labor to collaborate on full employment and renewed prosperity. Photographs of unemployed men reminded ER of the haunting days of the Great Depression. She asked the president to speak to the nation, explain the problems, and call on everyone to make sacrifices so that no one group of people would bear the brunt of economic change. She was hopeful about the new Labor-Management Committee charged by the president to bring about "voluntary" agreements and provide him with consensus views on unemployment, production, wages, prices, export competition, and inflation. Reuther, Dubinsky, and Meany, along with four other union leaders, represented labor. Reuther suggested to her that the committee should direct its attention to full employment and the "whole question of how our free society can harness the abundance of automation and share this abundance in . . . [a] rational social manner." He shared ER's concern that without full employment "our deficits in education, medical care, civil rights—all these do serious damage to the image of American democracy in the eyes of the uncommitted people of the world." They planned to talk further at the AAUN board meeting as they once again took up the conflict between full employment and a shorter work week.[18]

The building trades accepted the premise that the number of jobs was limited, so the solution of sharing the work through shorter hours with no loss in total pay seemed reasonable. Reuther was committed to a full-employment, full-production economic strategy that would be achieved through national planning, government job creation, and other economic controls. Unemployment and the underutilization of plants and equipment was an "economic waste." ER joined Reuther in supporting full production and rejected the short work week favored by the construction trades. After the Reuthers visited Hyde Park in the summer, Walter sent ER copies of the economic charts he had shown her, as well as two booklets, "The Margin of Survival," which contained data on the overall economy, and "UAW 1961 Negotiations with the Automotive Industry," which was specific to his industry. He had an appointment to spend an evening with President Kennedy, and hoped it would provide the "opportunity of discussing with him in considerable depth" the matters that Reuther and ER had talked about. He promised to let her know the outcome of the conversation.[19]

Reuther then turned his full attention to his collective bargaining responsibilities, working closely with Kennedy, Goldberg, and Walter Heller, chairman of the Council of Economic Advisers. He agreed to a profit-sharing plan with the struggling American Motors Company and sent ER a copy of his statement declaring it a "most significant and historic step in labor-management relations which opens up new and promising possibilities as we search to find answers to human compelling problems in the age of automation." Contract negotiations with General Motors immediately followed. After agreeing to appear on ER's television show *Prospects of Mankind,* Reuther had to withdraw because of the negotiation schedule. Promising to give her a full report on his "interesting" two hours with the president, he went into some detail about the negotiations:

> I have been at the bargaining table almost continuously around the clock trying to avert a GM strike, which would involve 350,000 directly and several hundred thousand indirectly. At four o'clock this morning, I succeeded in getting an agreement on the broad national economic issues and persuaded the National Negotiating Committee to extend the contract until Monday, September 11th, at 10:00 a.m. This will give us an opportunity to work out many complex problems in the working agreement and the many knotty problems in the 130-odd GM plants.[20]

A strike was averted, and the negotiations led to a small wage increase and supplements for short workweeks. Negotiations with Chrysler continued through October. Reuther was painfully aware that these agreements did nothing to create much-needed jobs. He hoped that a policy solution could be worked out in Washington, but the first year of the Kennedy administration produced few results.[21]

As she had done so many times before, ER continued to call on business, labor, and government to come together to solve the problems of the "revolutionary period in which we live as it affects both our economic and political life.... The longer we delay the more difficult the situation will be." In response to the corporate call for immediate tax reductions for high-income earners and corporations, she suggested that businessmen "search out their allies among the intelligent leaders in labor and in government and stop finding fault with each thing the President does, regardless of whether it is good or bad for them." Still, she did not spare the Kennedy administration from criticism for its economic policies. On one occasion she passed along the wisdom of Walter Lippmann, who pointed out similarities with the last administration and called for increased production through government spending.[22]

ER recognized that for some unions the demand for a shorter workweek was only a stopgap measure to prevent unemployment. "This trend toward unemployment can be met basically only by increased production in all of our big industries. We should make this clear to our people as a whole," she told Reuther, "and tell them the basic truth that perhaps we should be stimulating production through government incentives rather than holding off, hoping that private incentive will do a job that perhaps only government can do." Later she and Reuther discussed the labor movement's concerns about the short workweek. Unemployment created great insecurity among workers. Corporations scheduled excessive overtime, while tens of thousands of workers stood idle. A special UAW report offered alternatives such as a flexible workweek, though Reuther believed that "with our tremendous unmet needs in the fields of education, health, housing, resource development and the many other things that need doing in America, there is obviously no need for a reduction in the workweek if we will but find a way to full employment and relate the abundance of our developing technology to the satisfying of these basic and unmet needs." ER promised to use the material he sent her in a column, but she was soon in the hospital suffering from a high fever, recurring pain, and exhaustion that were symptoms of a more serious misdiagnosed illness.[23]

Reuther's ideas did find their way into her writing. Their shared vision for an economy based on planning and achieving full employment was central to a portion of ER's final book, *Tomorrow Is Now*, published after her death in 1963. In the chapter on the economic revolution, she raised the recurring problems of underproduction, unemployment, and automation. She called for the analysis of workforce needs, long-range planning, and teaching new skills for new jobs. She rejected the demands of some union leaders for the "panacea of shorter hours and higher wages." Instead she called for "fresh thinking, long-range action, full production on all fronts instead of curtailing work and hours. It is not more vacation we need—it is more vocation." She also saw the basic economic transformation that was under way as directly connected to the emerging social revolution.[24]

Shifting Coalitions on Civil Rights

The concerns voiced by minority workers were intensifying tensions within the labor movement. A. Philip Randolph, the elder statesman of civil rights, mentored and cooperated with younger leaders who were adopting new strategies. Labor leaders like Reuther and Dubinsky continued their outspoken support for civil rights, but at the same time more pressure was being put on the unions by black organizations. The NAACP called for an end to racial discrimination within the unions, while the National Advisory Council on Farm Labor sought more organizing in the fields. At the 1959 AFL-CIO convention in San Francisco, Randolph and several colleagues introduced another resolution to eliminate segregated locals. Meany took the position that this issue was not the AFL-CIO's business. He argued that there were African American locals that wanted to stay that way. As the debate heated up, Meany is reported to have demanded of Randolph, "Who the hell appointed you the guardian of all the Negroes in America?"[25]

Both white liberals and black leaders sprang to Randolph's defense. ER took on the fight. While granting that Meany was not contending that segregation was right, she lamented, "Since there was great opposition to setting a time when segregation should be wiped out[,] he was vociferously opposed to forcing a specified date on these unions for doing this." She saw this foot-dragging as akin to the argument that was used to delay school desegregation. She told her readers, "It seems to me that Mr. Randolph is not asking anything unreasonable in saying that the union, just like the states, should specify a time when they would accomplish compliance with the Supreme Court order." Despite their heated disagreement, Meany and Randolph maintained a working relationship. *New York Times* reporter Abe Raskin later wrote that their "differences have never been over which way the federation should go, but over how fast its progress should be and how much pressure it should exert to make it faster."[26]

A few months later Martin Luther King Jr. invited ER to participate in a salute to A. Philip Randolph at Carnegie Hall, telling her, "Unquestionably your presence as America's First Citizen will heighten the significance of the occasion and serve to dramatize the profound meaning for all Americans of Mr. Randolph's dedicated decades of service." It was Randolph's seventieth birthday, and the hall was packed. The event was chaired by Harry Van

Arsdale Jr., president of the New York City Central Labor Council, and speakers included Republican and Democratic politicians, religious leaders, civil rights leaders, musicians, and actors; Langston Hughes wrote a poem for the occasion. Randolph, King, and ER once again appeared together, as they had at the Madison Square Garden rally in 1956.[27]

Randolph remained active in the civil rights movement. That year alone he headed a national committee that raised more than $50,000 to defend the students using the sit-in strategy in the South and in support of King against charges of perjury in Alabama. At the same time he traveled the country in his role as president of his union. He helped to form a new organization, the Negro American Labor Council, and was elected chairman at the founding convention. Like ER, he argued that democratic unions were an essential part of a democratic society and that racial discrimination was unacceptable. The council was formed to end racially segregated unions because, while the AFL-CIO was committed to this goal on a national level, the policy of voluntary implementation at the union level had failed. Younger militants in the organization were far more critical of the AFL-CIO, and despite Randolph's assurances, Meany declined an invitation to speak to the opening convention in Detroit.[28]

Randolph maintained his pressure from inside the house of labor. In the spring of 1961 he sent a memorandum to the AFL-CIO executive council charging that while only one union still had a color clause, others continued to segregate blacks into separate locals or exclude them by "tacit consent." He again demanded that all forms of discrimination be abolished. Unions could be expelled from the body for corruption, but Meany maintained that they could not, or would not, be expelled for discrimination. In an unexpected move, the executive council issued a twenty-page report censuring Randolph for discriminatory acts and causing the division that had emerged between the unions and the African American community. Meany thought that Randolph was too close to militant civil rights groups. The NAACP was furious. King called the report "shocking and deplorable." Reuther was not at the meeting that produced the censure, but Jim Carey was and he organized a rebuttal to the charges from the Industrial Union Department. Randolph remained calm.[29]

Following this outcry, on Friday, 8 December 1961, Eleanor Roosevelt flew to Miami Beach, where she once again addressed an AFL-CIO convention. She joined an illustrious list of speakers, including President John F. Kennedy, Secretary of Labor Arthur Goldberg, and Martin Luther King Jr. "She came in from the side, the lady everybody loves," reported the AFL-CIO *News*. "She was half-hidden by her escort of AFL-CIO vice presidents, but the convention knew she was there. Delegates and visitors hailed her with a roaring welcome that told better than words of the affection and esteem America's workers have for her." Arthur Rosenstock, president of the Newspaper Guild, presented "Sister Roosevelt" with a specially cast gold pin in honor of her twenty-fifth anniversary as a member of the union, and ER thanked the delegates for their fund-raising and education efforts on behalf of the Eleanor Roosevelt Cancer Foundation. Then she quickly turned to the serious plight of the agricultural workers and the unfinished business of racial discrimination.[30]

In a short speech ER reminded the delegates that they had a great role to play in the country and high ideals to live up to: "The labor movement—and perhaps I can say my movement, too, because I think sometimes I work as hard as any of you do—I feel that it is part of our job to keep alive the ideals that you started with, the ideals of really helping the people to better conditions, to a better way of life which is part of the basis of democracy." Highlighting the ongoing problems of discrimination and poverty, she expressed the hope that "we are going to continue to make of our movement the star in our country that leads the way in our country. We need it badly today." To the rest of the world, "we are going to show in the things that we do for people that democracy has something to contribute that communism never contributes." She closed, "So I thank you for the inspiration you give, for the great generosity and understanding you have shown."[31]

The messages the AFL-CIO convention heard about racial discrimination, however, were complicated and contentious. In his address King called the labor movement and the black freedom movement the "two most dynamic and cohesive liberal forces in the country." The labor movement "undeniably ... had done more than other forces in American society to wipe out discrimination," but that was not enough. He told his audience that unions must remedy their failings, such as racial barriers to membership and the exclusion of black workers from apprenticeship training. Union members must give "thoughtful examination" to the criticisms of labor brought by their own vice president, A. Philip Randolph, because "a man who has dedicated his long and faultless life to the labor movement cannot be raising questions harmful to it." African Americans, he went on, will be labor's staunchest political allies in order to "prevent automation from becoming a Moloch, consuming jobs and contract gains." He urged united political action so that "together we can bring about the day when there will be no separate identification of Negroes and labor." A politically active and racially integrated labor movement was part of King's dream for an inclusive democracy.[32]

Randolph, in his address to the convention, assured the delegates that "anyone who is in the labor movement and has gone through some 40 years of struggle ... is not thin skinned. Consequently, I am willing to go through the fires in order to abolish second-class status for black people in this country. It must be done, and it must be done now—not tomorrow." From Randolph's perspective, the convention's resolution on civil rights was the strongest the AFL-CIO had ever adopted, and it was the first to pass unanimously.[33]

The plight of farm workers was also very serious. ER had written to President Kennedy about it, and he assured her that he was working on legislation to protect the migrant workers. Just before the convention she had written to Meany, concerned that the AFL-CIO had ended its support for the Agricultural Workers Organizing Committee. As a member of the National Advisory Committee on Farm Labor, she had also joined Randolph in signing a letter to the AFL-CIO executive council asking that the members continue their organizing efforts. At the convention she reminded the delegates that the situation of the farm workers was an important problem; she hoped that "those of us who are better off" would "give real thought and real help to all the areas of blight, and we have some in our country." The Agricultural Workers Organizing Committee was off to a promising start, she said, but she asked for more help.[34]

ER also told readers of "My Day" that investment by the labor movement could help "in improving the living standards of those among us who seem too weak to bring about the necessary changes for themselves." The National Advisory Committee on Farm Labor was very pleased with her remarks and her column. Reports from Miami Beach confirmed that her message had been well received, and the convention passed an excellent resolution "recognizing [labor's] moral responsibility to help farm workers." Later, also on behalf of the advisory committee, ER wrote to Frank Stanton, president of CBS, asking that *Harvest of Shame*, a documentary on the conditions for migrant farm workers, be rebroadcast to remind the public of the dismal conditions and lack of progress for those who toiled in the fields. CBS commissioned a new program on the farm workers.[35]

Having seen her only briefly in Miami, Reuther wrote to ER to say that the convention had gone well, "considering all of the difficulties and complications." First on his list of achievements was a rational and workable internal dispute mechanism, hammered out in an all-night session of the executive council. Second was the civil rights resolution, which "should prove a useful instrument in our effort to accelerate the wiping out of the last vestige of discrimination in certain of the unions and to mobilize the white labor movement in the overall civil rights fight." Third was a resolution committing the AFL-CIO and its affiliates to "continue the drive on both the organizational front and the legislative front as it relates to the problems of the agricultural and migratory workers."[36]

Signs of impatience were evident, however, in King's speech, as well as in Randolph's demand for justice "now—not tomorrow." White workers were moving to the suburbs, with access to union jobs and decent housing and education, while black workers were confined to the inner cities with fewer job opportunities, deteriorating housing, and inadequate schools. Hints of the economic transformation to come were visible as automation led to unemployment, adding to the racial strife over what were rapidly becoming scarce resources. It was not long before labor unions and leaders previously considered the most progressive also faced criticism for the inadequacy of their actions to redress discrimination. In the mid-1950s Herbert Hill, the tenacious labor director of the NAACP, turned his considerable investigative skills toward the unions. In 1961 he issued a report charging institutional racism in both craft and industrial unions. Joined by increasingly unhappy and vocal union members, he specifically charged the ILGWU and the UAW with racial discrimination. His research and analysis not only appeared in reports and articles but also formed the basis of complaints before state fair employment commissions, congressional hearings, and eventually lawsuits against the labor unions.[37]

Hill charged that the ILGWU was directly responsible for African Americans being concentrated in low-paid, unskilled jobs in the garment industry. The conflict was intense. Both Hill and Dubinsky testified at congressional hearings. In October 1962 the NAACP board of directors approved a resolution calling for a thorough investigation of the ILGWU. The vote was taken late at night, when only twelve of the thirty-six members were still in attendance. Dubinsky condemned this as a communist tactic and resorted to red-baiting, criticizing Hill for his leadership of the Socialist Workers Party in New York City during the 1940s. The ILGWU trustee for the NAACP Legal Defense Fund resigned. In agreeing to testify before a hearing on behalf of the ILGWU, Maida Springer, though a friend of Hill's, defended her union, saying, "This is an industry I know, would never deny its sins but know enough of its virtues to be able to stand up and be counted as a member and former officer of this union." Randolph came to Dubinsky's defense as well, and Dubinsky wrote to ER for help, charging that Hill was abusing congressional investigating powers. We have no copy of her response, but we know that one of the last letters ER sent from her hospital bed just a month before she died was to Dubinsky.[38]

As the civil rights struggle grew more heated, ER was increasingly outraged by the growing violence in the South and saw organized labor as a resourceful ally. When asked by the Southern Nonviolent Coordinating Committee and the Congress of Racial Equality, which led direct action for voting rights, she agreed to chair a public commission investigating violations of civil rights and civil liberties when groups of white citizens attacked Freedom Riders in Mississippi and Alabama. She chaired the hearings in Washington and was angered by the failure of the government to protect its citizens, faulting the Kennedy administration and the Democratic Congress. In the chapter on social revolution in *Tomorrow Is Now*, ER described this experience as one of the most difficult she had ever been through. Reuther was unable to accept her request to join the commission, but the rising levels of protest and violence, and the outspoken leadership on civil rights by one of labor's champions, made the fight against racial discrimination within the labor movement all the more urgent for the unions.[39]

Conflicts and Celebrations

As labor's internal problems were intensifying, ER responded as she always did: by listening to what the parties had to say, referring problems to those responsible, and publicly supporting those who shared her worldview. When ER received a letter from a woman who was having trouble with the Teamsters Union on the West Coast, she passed it along to Reuther. His staff looked into the problem, talked to the woman, and gave her the regional contacts that she needed. When a group of airline workers sought her help in securing a charter from the AFL-CIO, she consulted with Reuther, and he advised her to send the information on to Meany. When Reuther turned to ER to help define a broader social vision for labor, she responded publicly. On behalf of the UAW he invited her to the union's twenty-fifth anniversary celebration, saying that her participation would "provide encouragement to and strengthen the efforts of those forces in the labor movement who view the labor movement as an instrument of responsible social action harmonious with the needs and the aspirations of a whole free people." Though unable to attend the event because she was ill, ER soon joined Supreme Court Justice Douglas at a luncheon to honor Reuther in Washington. She told her readers:

> Mr. Reuther is one of the few labor union leaders who has been able to think and plan for the well-being of all the members of his union and, at the same time, to remember that unions also have a responsibility to understand the whole economic set-up of the country and to be a part of it . . . , as well as the problems of their industry in the context of the world industrial and economic picture. . . . Unions must have unusually well-trained and educated leaders, a requirement Walter Reuther has met extraordinarily well.[40]

When ER praised Reuther and worked with him, providing public support, she was well aware of his escalating internal disputes with Meany. Reuther and Meany continued to disagree on international issues, domestic policy, and the internal workings of the federation, the animosity often deteriorating to a personal level. Behind their contest for power lay a debate over whether unions should serve their members' narrow economic interests or join coalitions to advance broader social policies, and over the federation's role in relation to the member unions in these decisions. Reuther explained his position to ER and sought her help. When the Industrial Union Department passed a resolution seeking internal procedures to resolve disputes, he explained it had done so because Meany's friends in the building trades, who were also friends of the suspect Jimmy Hoffa, had failed to create an equitable dispute resolution system with final and binding arbitration. The internal strife, he argued, "dissipates the goodwill and the resources which the labor movement should be committing to useful and constructive purposes." For him the situation was becoming impossible owing to Meany's "willingness to submit to the pressure of the most backward forces in the labor movement instead of joining with those who want to make the labor movement more than a narrow economic pressure group." Seeking further public support, he sent copies of the letters and wrote, "You are free to use any of this material any way you choose since we have decided that to continue to cover up for Mr. Meany's shortcomings is a disservice to the labor movement."[41]

While the internal tensions escalated, strikes in the public sector continued to worry ER. One of the last strikes that she informed her readers about involved the teachers in New York City. The state was reducing the amount of educational aid to the city, limiting its ability to meet the demands of the United Federation of Teachers. She thought that the state should be held accountable, and she could not blame the teachers "for wanting to improve their conditions of work as well as their salaries." ER argued that vital government employees, including teachers, needed alternative mechanisms, such as mediation, but concluded that "if we do not provide adequate machinery for them to right their wrongs[,] then they have no other way to meet the situation" and must use the possibility of a strike. Teachers should not have to work two jobs to provide for their families or police the lunch hour instead of helping children in need. She agreed with the public sentiment that "under the present set-up teachers have no other recourse but to strike to draw attention to their legitimate complaints. If the school board can do nothing about these complaints, then the city and state must bear the burden."[42]

At the same time, strikes in New York City ranged from the private hospital workers to the musicians at the Metropolitan Opera. Labor disputes and looming strikes in industries that were central to the national economy, such as the airlines, worried ER as much as strikes involving public-sector workers. Although Secretary Goldberg tried to intervene, arbitration was staunchly resisted. As the system of labor-management relations seemed to break down too often, ER began to question the future of collective bargaining, "which is based on the reasonable give-and-take of human beings with equal power but who have an interest to come to decisions that will allow them to serve the national interest and the interest of the public as a whole." Strikes, she believed, did not improve the situation. She thought that organized labor had reached a position of such strength that militant action was no longer necessary. Ever hopeful, she encouraged the public to press for the development of arbitration because she believed that "strikes in the world in which we now live are becoming obsolete as a method of settling our difficulties in much the same way that war is becoming obsolete. In both cases we must find reasonable ways to settle the normal difficulties that arise among individuals, among groups and among nations."[43]

ER's health was failing, and she reluctantly cut back on her activities, but she found the strength to attend celebrations, from which she derived great hope. In Atlantic City in May 1962 she joined authors and social activists Upton Sinclair and Mary Heaton Vorse to receive the UAW Social Justice Award. She wrote: "The nearly 6,000 delegates do not seem to be interested only in wages and hours and working conditions for themselves. Over the years in this union they have developed a social conscience. . . . Leaders and members dare to think as statesmen and consider the future economic development of our own country and of the world." She reminisced in "My Day" about her early work in the tenement houses, telling her readers: "We have moved forward, certainly. And perhaps the labor unions need to be reminded occasionally that they must grow in statesmanlike ways, but I also wish that organized labor could grow in membership to far greater proportions, too. The standards for working conditions are really established by what in America is still only a handful of the total number of workers. Other workers are profiting by the dues paid by organized labor and their bargaining powers." Following the pattern of a lifetime, ER encouraged more people to join unions.[44]

The President's Commission

As Eleanor Roosevelt neared the end of her life, she devoted her limited energies to the causes that were dearest to her. Her personal history repeated itself when, in the summer of 1961, she agreed to serve as chair of President Kennedy's Commission on the Status of Women, working closely with union women.

After the election, when the White House asked Esther Peterson what job she wanted in return for her early support of Kennedy, she chose the Women's Bureau of the Department of Labor because she thought that with her strong union base, she could do her best work there. Her goal was to implement the policy agenda that union women had developed in the 1940s and bring back the spirit of former labor directors Mary Anderson and Frieda Miller. She immediately revived the Union Women's Labor Advisory Committee, which had been dormant under the Republican administration. At the first meeting a small group began to draft a proposal for a commission on women. This idea was not new. Union women had been advocating such a commission since the end of World War II, and Peterson recalled that Representative Emanuel Celler of Brooklyn had "introduced legislation calling for a congressional commission on the legal status of women annually throughout the 1950s, but he never got to first base."[45]

Such a commission would draw on the past. On 25 March 1961 hundreds of people gathered for the fiftieth anniversary ceremony honoring the women and men who had died in the Triangle Shirtwaist Factory fire. Outside the building, just off Washington Square in Manhattan, Esther Peterson joined Eleanor Roosevelt, Frances Perkins, Rose Schneiderman, David Dubinsky, and twelve survivors of that tragic day on the speakers' platform. They not only remembered the 146 workers who had lost their lives and the worker safety laws that resulted but they also denounced a new bill that would delay fire safety measures for current workers. Shortly after that, ER described a small gathering in her home for six young women who had been awarded scholarships by the Women's Trade Union League Fund. They were struggling with questions of employment and care for the children of working mothers. ER was amused by the "expression on the young people's faces when one of the older working women, at my request, told of conditions when she first went to work. She spoke of a 10 hour day, six days a week for a child of 13, with $2 a week as pay. The young things could hardly believe it."[46]

Esther Peterson provided encouragement and support to the women within their unions. Without the agreement of the full AFL-CIO, the Industrial Union Department, led by Reuther and Carey, finally sponsored the first national inter-union women's conference to focus on how women could best contribute to the growth and security of industrial unions. Planned by union leaders including Caroline Davis of the UAW, Gloria Johnson of the IUE, Evy Dubrow of the ILGWU, and Kitty Ellickson of the AFL-CIO, the theme shifted to the problems of working women. Gathered in the Mayflower Hotel in Washington, DC, 175 women from twenty-one different international unions laid out their demands in three categories: economic, legislative, and social issues. They made very clear that their problems were not limited to employers but were deeply embedded in the labor movement itself. Just as African Americans were calling for leadership positions in the UAW and the AFL-CIO, women such as the ACWA's Bessie Hillman now called for women to assume leadership roles in their unions.[47]

While aware of the challenges still facing working women, Eleanor Roosevelt put her faith in the labor movement and women's ability to organize to right those wrongs. Her primary focus was on the lack of women in political office. In the first three months of his administration, Kennedy had appointed only nine women out of 240 executive positions filled. ER went to the Oval Office and handed the president a three-page list of women she considered qualified for high office. The highest-ranking woman in the administration was Esther Peterson. One of the first things she did was propose an executive order creating a President's Commission on the Status of Women to Goldberg in June. She wanted Eleanor Roosevelt appointed chair "to give the commission the highest status," but Kennedy apparently still held a grudge against her for supporting Stevenson. Kennedy wasn't willing to ask ER to serve but said he would welcome her participation. "I asked her, and she agreed," recalled Peterson. The official invitation came from the White House.[48]

Esther Peterson was an engaging and charismatic leader with a strong labor background in organizing, education, legislation, and politics. Representing the new generation of union women, she offered ER an opportunity to reflect on the progress that women had made, as well as the problems they still faced. Rejecting narrow interests, the commission promised to be inclusive in scope and practical in approach and to address the concerns of housewives as well as workers. How could Eleanor Roosevelt say no? President Kennedy signed Executive Order 10980 on 14 December 1961, establishing the commission that would be chaired by Eleanor Roosevelt.[49]

The commission convened in February 1962 in Washington, DC, with twenty-six members: eleven men and fifteen women. Cabinet secretaries and members of Congress joined business executives, academics, leaders of nationwide women's organizations, and, representing labor, IUE executive board member Mary Callahan and William Schnitzler, president of the Bakery and Confectionary Workers International Union and secretary treasurer of the AFL-CIO. Eventually the advisory committee totaled over 250 members. Advisers with backgrounds in the labor movement included Caroline Davis, UAW; Addie Wyatt, United Packing House Workers of America; Bessie Hillman, ACWA; Esther Johnson, American Federation of Government Employees; and historian-sociologist Caroline Ware. Eleanor Roosevelt's good friend Pauli Murray, the outspoken black civil rights activist and attorney, served on the committee for civil and political rights, advising the commission and challenging the administration on civil rights for women and African Americans.[50]

Scholars have given ER little credit for the work of the commission, but the commission staff disagreed. Although she was getting weaker, they described ER as more than a figurehead. Peterson recalled that during the first year ER was "actually very influential in keeping the Commission on its course." She attended planning meetings, reviewed documents, talked frequently on the phone, and approved nominations. When given the list of commissioners, she immediately wrote to Reuther asking for more information on Schnitzler. She attended press conferences, appeared on television, and testified at hearings. The staff met in her apartment in New York, and ER spent an entire weekend in Washington reviewing papers and plans. Princeton economist

Richard Lester, vice chairman of the commission, recalled ER's skills at running a meeting, writing that she "was masterful in keeping the meetings moving along in a constructive manner, avoiding pitfalls and getting sidetracked." Peterson attributed the commission's focus on minority women to the work of Dorothy Height, president of the National Council of Negro Women, and to Eleanor Roosevelt. "She was so great on that," Peterson remembered of ER's commitment to improving conditions for minority women. "She said that that should be a concern of every committee. And as it is it runs through all the reports.... This was part of her philosophy and we adopted it." ER brought a lifelong commitment to equality and justice to the commission as well as the ability to run meetings, develop consensus, and communicate to policy makers and the public.[51]

ER chaired the first two-day meeting on 12 and 13 February 1962, just before she left for Europe. She told her readers about the event, beginning with President Kennedy's welcome at the White House, explaining, "The commission will try to make its influence felt concerning women's problems not only in the Federal area, but in state and local areas and in industry as well as in women's home responsibilities." She framed the work of the commission as finding ways to make the best use of "all of our manpower—and that includes womanpower," while caring for families and communities. ER described a world undergoing rapid economic and social changes, and she highlighted the problem of unemployment for women and men as the economy remained unstable and manufacturing became automated. She called for full employment. The first responsibility of the commission, however, was to investigate the situation and educate the public about its findings. ER stressed that the commission report should make concrete recommendations for action. Harking back to her early days with the consumer movement, she saw the commission as a source of much-needed facts. She held no illusions that a report would change the world. Rather, the information the commission gathered would act as "a stimulus...to all the people who are already working and who want to work in the future."[52]

The commission's mandate was broad, covering six designated areas. John W. Macy, chairman of the Civil Service Commission, spoke to the subject of federal employment. In this area immediate action could be taken, and indeed was already under way. Members agreed to consider employing women in the foreign service and the armed forces and to review an 1870 law that permitted "government agencies to specify the sex preferred in filling positions." Under Macy's second area of concern, government contracts, fell three intertwined topics: equal opportunity in hiring; equal opportunity for training, advancement, and promotion; and equal pay for the same or comparable work. The commission had to grapple with implementation through persuasion, publicity, counseling, education, and the use of executive orders and related enforcement mechanisms. The third area, federal tax and social insurance laws, covered discrimination in social security and welfare policies, including old-age insurance benefits, tax liabilities for married women, and disproportionately low benefits for widows, as well as proposals for maternity benefits. This policy arena was complicated by the tangled relationships between the federal government and the states in social legislation.[53]

The question of protective labor legislation was considered one of the most difficult, with strong divisions within the women's community. The commission had to reconcile the views of those who saw the laws as an obstacle, often women in professional and high-paid occupations, and those who desired legal protection, often women in low-paid occupations. Some wanted to eliminate the laws altogether, while others hoped to expand coverage to men as well as women. Not all the union women agreed with one another. Caroline Davis of the UAW challenged protective laws that discriminated against women, while Mary Callahan of the IUE supported laws that were truly protective. ER no longer opposed the ERA, but she did not make this clear to the union women. Ellickson interpreted the discussions as indicating ER's continued support for protecting low-income working women at the state level. The debate on civil and political rights followed these divisions closely, and Murray began work on a compromise to challenge state laws under the Fourteenth Amendment. The commission called for an up-to-date study of the legal differences among states on granting these rights and an analysis of property and contract laws. Finally, in the area of new and expanded services, the commission considered counseling and vocational education, day care for children, school lunch programs, housing arrangements, and community planning.[54]

At a second meeting on 9 April in Washington, DC, chaired by ER, the commission continued to work out its organizational framework, budget, committee structure, and staff responsibilities. Members heard committee reports, and education was added as the seventh area of focus. A public information program was outlined, and members were encouraged to make speeches and participate in radio and television appearances. ER engaged in all of these activities when she could. She appeared on the television public affairs show *Issues and Answers* with Peterson and devoted one of her own *Prospects of Mankind* programs to the commission. She challenged President Kennedy in a television interview in which she complained about the paucity of women in policymaking positions, and she testified on the behalf of the equal pay legislation.[55]

Commission members and staff pursued a legislative agenda at the same time that they were preparing the report. Most prominent was the Equal Pay Bill, introduced by Representative Edith Green of Oregon in January 1961. On her return from a trip to California in late April 1962, ER went with Esther Peterson to the Foley Square Court House in Manhattan to testify at hearings on equal pay for equal work chaired by Herbert Zelenko, a Democratic congressman from New York. Gladys Tillett from the UN Status of Women Commission also appeared. ER informed her readers, "The dignity of women's equality when they meet in government, professional and industrial work is important the world over, not just in the U.S." A few days later Rose Schneiderman wrote to ER that she had read about the hearings: "When you have time, I should like to discuss equal pay with you. You know of course that we have such a law in New York State—few people know about it and there is no attempt to enforce it." Schneiderman also mentioned that she was looking for a collaborator on her autobiography. ER immediately sent her the name of someone who was interested. "My everlasting thanks to you dear friend," wrote Schneiderman.[56]

After the commission's third meeting at Hyde Park, where ER talked about the current economic, social, and cultural revolution, she spent the summer days writing her columns and trying to finish the manuscript of her book *Tomorrow Is Now*. At the end of July she was rushed to the hospital with a fever of 105, delirious and in need of a blood transfusion. She returned to Val-Kill and then made her final trip to the family home at Campobello. When Rose Schneiderman learned of ER's illness, she wrote immediately; her last words to her friend of over forty years were: "Get well.... Hearts best love, Rose." In her last book, ER expressed gratitude to Rose Schneiderman and the Women's Trade Union League for teaching her the importance of individuals working together to spur public action.[57]

In early September, on their way back from taking their daughter to school in Vermont, May and Walter Reuther stopped at Val-Kill. As always ER was inspired by the articulate labor leader and asked if she could use some of his ideas on the importance of economic rather than military aid for containing communism. She accurately predicted that the rapid economic and social changes she had observed would have unforeseen effects on women and men in the coming years. She drew on Reuther for her chapter on economic revolution. Still, she confessed to being ill. She had agreed to speak at the IUE's tenth convention and asked that Reuther tell her friend Jim Carey that she would not be able to come. Despite her fever, on Sunday morning she insisted that Reuther take her to church, which of course he did.[58]

It was "Dear May" who had the last communication with ER. She wrote a thank you note and expressed her concerns about leaving her daughter Lisa at school. ER responded with understanding and sympathy. Always concerned for others, ER thanked both May and Walter for "giving me a little of your time" and offered her "apologies for being so miserable." The members of the President's Commission on the Status of Women met again in early October, but much to her regret, ER was not able to be with them. Soon diagnosed with a rare bone-marrow tuberculosis, she wrote, "[A] rather bad set-back which has kept me practically in bed for the last ten days makes the doctors want me not to go to Washington next Sunday for the Status of Women meeting." Responsible to the end, she arranged for the vice chairman to preside. When the commissioners replied, "You are very much in our thoughts today," they knew that no ordinary illness could keep her from their work. Eleanor Roosevelt died in her New York City apartment on 7 November 1962. She was deemed irreplaceable, and her chair was left vacant.[59]

The President's Commission on the Status of Women presented its final report to President Kennedy on 11 October 1963, which would have been Eleanor Roosevelt's seventy-ninth birthday. In its report *American Women* the commission recognized the ability of unions to improve working conditions, increase workers' dignity, and provide essential protections. They acknowledged that the right to organize and bargain collectively was established under federal law, and recommended that state laws should also "protect the right of workers to join unions of their own choosing and to bargain collectively."[60]

Epilogue

Close to Home

Eleanor Roosevelt's death was mourned by workers across the country. Photographs of her at labor events, surrounded by rank-and-file members, and speeches praising her words and actions filled union newspapers. Her labor spirit was captured in the tributes they paid her. The AFL-CIO declared: "Nowhere will her loss be more keenly felt than in the ranks of labor. No one can ever tabulate the lives that were brightened, the slums cleared, the sweatshops eradicated, the suffering mitigated through her unflagging battle against misery and oppression." The electrical workers spoke of "her ability to ignite enthusiasms for life and living"; the garment workers simply "knew her well and loved her." Union presidents were invited to join world leaders to show their respect as she was laid to rest beside her husband in the Rose Garden at Hyde Park.[1]

Forty years later Esther Peterson declared that she would be honored to be mentioned in the same breath with Eleanor Roosevelt. She remembered a warm, friendly, easygoing person, never putting herself above anyone else, who "was always with us [in the labor movement]. She could always communicate with whomever she was talking to, connecting the little problems that they were having and fitting them into a pattern of larger legislative issues.... Her work continues to inspire me." Evelyn Dubrow spoke for many in the rank and file. A young journalist when she first met Eleanor Roosevelt, she said that ER "was one person who seemed to be able to meet every level of person. She could talk to labor people, she could talk to company officials, it was always a very quiet kind of thing, but very solid in what her position was.... [S]he made me feel right at home."[2]

Historians rate Eleanor Roosevelt as the most influential first lady. Her critical role in defining human rights has been well established. On behalf of people everywhere, Eleanor Roosevelt's most lasting contribution to public discourse has been the Universal Declaration of Human Rights. Scholar Mary Ann Glendon has concluded that the ending of apartheid in South Africa and the fall of totalitarian governments in eastern Europe can be attributed more to the "moral beacon of the Declaration" than to the UN's covenants and international treaties. Nations have translated these principles into their legal systems and used the declaration as a model for their constitutions.[3]

The article on labor in the declaration remains a central goal for workers today, as it was for Eleanor Roosevelt. She made clear to those at home and in the international community that workers' rights are human rights. Everyone has the right to gainful employment, to the free choice of a job, to just conditions at work, to a living wage, and to protection against unemployment. Everyone has the right to equal pay for equal work, without discrimination. The right to form and join a trade union is fundamental to the achievement of economic and social rights. Although the world of work has changed dramatically since ER's death, many of the problems remain: low wages, rising inequality, employer hostility, racial and gender discrimination. Twelve million union members represent only 12 percent of the workforce in the United States. Just over 7 percent of workers in the private sector belong to a union, a level not seen since 1929.[4]

ER argued persuasively that all working people are better off with a strong and unified labor movement and that the core of that labor movement is democracy at work. She called on union members not only to be active in their unions but also to vote in local and national elections and to lobby politicians to support labor at home and social justice around the world. She demanded that leaders be honest and insisted that neither corruption nor discrimination on the basis of race or gender had any place in the labor movement or the workplace. Both union leaders and employers, she believed, must be held accountable.

In the face of difficulties both domestic and foreign, from the Great Depression through World War II and the cold war to the economic challenges posed by automation and globalization, Eleanor Roosevelt allied herself with workers who sought to advance economic and social justice. Her dedication to labor-management negotiations went hand in hand with her commitment to resolving international conflicts through cooperation. The labor movement, whose concerns extended from the shop floor to city hall and into national politics and public policy, could exemplify democracy in action and provide a model for others to follow.

In ER's view, everything depended on educated, organized, and active citizens participating in their democracy and acting collectively in the workplace and in the community to secure the changes necessary to bring about a fair and equitable world. When asked, "Where after all do universal human rights begin?" she answered, "In small places, close to home...the neighborhood...the school...the factory, farm, or office." Individuals, men and women, of all colors and creeds, must practice what they preach and secure their rights close to home. For Eleanor Roosevelt that meant joining a union, because, she continued, "unless these rights have meaning there, they have little meaning anywhere. Without concerted citizen action to uphold them close to home, we shall look in vain for progress in the larger world."[5]

Source Abbreviations

ACWAR   Amalgamated Clothing Workers of America Records, Kheel Center, Cornell University

AERP   Anna Eleanor Roosevelt Papers, FDRL

ALUA   Archives of Labor and Urban Affairs, Wayne State University, Detroit

APRP   A. Philip Randolph Papers, BSCPR, LOC

ARMS   Archives and Records Management Section, UN

BSCPR   Brotherhood of Sleeping Car Porters Records, LOC

CIO Carey   CIO Secretary-Treasurer Collection, James B. Carey Files, ALUA

COHC   Oral History Collection of Columbia University

DDPR   International Ladies' Garment Workers' Union, David Dubinsky, President's Records, 1932–1966, Kheel Center, Cornell University.

ERPP   Eleanor Roosevelt Papers Project, George Washington University

FDRL   Franklin D. Roosevelt Presidential Library and Museum, Hyde Park

GMMA	George Meany Memorial Archives, National Labor College, Silver Spring, MD
HWSP	Hilda Worthington Smith Papers, Schlesinger Library, Harvard University
IUE Carey	Records of the President's Office of the International Union of Electronic, Electrical, Salaried, Machine & Furniture Workers, 1938–1965, SCUA
Kheel Center	Kheel Center for Labor-Management Documentation and Archives, Martin P. Catherwood Library, Cornell University
LOC	Library of Congress
MLKP	Martin Luther King Jr. Papers, Stanford University
NSFC	National Sharecroppers Fund Collection, ALUA
NYNG	New York Newspaper Guild Records, TL
NYWTULP	New York Women's Trade Union League Papers, Cecil H. Green Library, Stanford University
OPGM	Office of the President, George Meany, GMMA
RFPDC	Roosevelt Family Papers Donated by Children, FDRL
RSP	Rose Schneiderman Papers, TL and WTULP
SCUA	Special Collections and University Archives, Rutgers University
SHP	Sidney Hillman Papers, ACWAR, Kheel Center, Cornell University
TL	Tamiment Library/Robert F. Wagner Labor Archives, New York University
TSP	Toni Sender Papers, WHS
TUWOHP	Twentieth Century Trade Union Woman: Vehicle for Social Change, Oral History Project, University of Michigan
WHS	Wisconsin Historical Society, Madison
WPRC	UAW President's Office, Walter P. Reuther Collection, ALUA
WTULP	Women's Trade Union League Papers, Cecil H. Green Library, Stanford University

NOTES

Prologue

1. *New York Times,* 6 January 1937. American Newspaper Guild, *Guild Reporter,* 15 January 1937.
2. AFL-CIO, *Proceedings: Fourth Constitutional Convention,* Miami, December 1961, 139.

1. Why Women Should Join Unions

1. The description of the WTUL party is based on Schneiderman's autobiography, Rose Schneiderman and Lucy Goldthwaite, *All for One* (New York: P. S. Eriksson, 1967), 175–76; *New York Times,* 8, 9 June 1929; Joseph P. Lash, *Eleanor and Franklin: The Story of Their Relationship, Based on Eleanor Roosevelt's Private Papers* (New York: Norton, 1971), 328–29; and Annelise Orleck, *Common Sense and a Little Fire: Women and Working-Class Politics in the United States, 1900–1965* (Chapel Hill: University of North Carolina Press, 1995), 148–49.
2. Eleanor Roosevelt to Franklin D. Roosevelt, 15 May 1929, folder 3 ER to FDR 1929, Roosevelt Family Papers Donated by Children (RFPDC), Franklin D. Roosevelt Library (FDRL), Hyde Park, NY. *Life and Labor Bulletin,* July 1929, Women's Trade Union League (WTUL) Publications, Women's Trade Union League Papers (WTULP), reel 7, Microfilm Edition, 1981, Cecil H. Green Library, Stanford University, Palo Alto. For more on women's labor education, see Joyce L. Kornbluh and Mary Frederickson, eds., *Sisterhood and Solidarity: Workers' Education for Women, 1914–1984* (Philadelphia: Temple University Press, 1984).
3. FDR quotation in *New York Times,* 9 June 1929.
4. Rose Schneiderman to Franklin D. Roosevelt, 12 June 1929, quoted in Lash, *Eleanor and Franklin,* 329. *New York Times,* 9 June 1929.
5. For the WTUL answer see Schneiderman and Goldthwaite, *All for One,* 151.
6. ER quotation in *New York Times,* 15 February 1933.

7. ER's years at Allenswood and her days as a New York debutante are covered in detail in Blanche Wiesen Cook, *Eleanor Roosevelt* (hereafter Cook, *ER*), vol. 1, *1884–1933* (New York: Viking, 1992), chaps. 5 and 6. Lash, *Eleanor and Franklin*, 81. ER quotation in Cook, *ER*, 1:4.

8. The settlement house work is discussed in Cook, *ER*, 1:134–35. For moving descriptions of this period, see David Von Drehle, *Triangle: The Fire That Changed America* (New York: Atlantic Monthly Press, 2003); and Orleck, *Common Sense*. The number of settlement houses is found in Von Drehle, *Triangle*, 197.

9. For the description of ER, see Cook, *ER*, 1:135. The University Settlement House continues to serve immigrants today, although the staff no longer lives there, and the gym has become a children's play area; see Jeffrey Scheuer, "Legacy of Light: University Settlement's First Century" (New York: University Settlement House, 1985). (This pamphlet is available from University Settlement, 184 Eldredge St., New York, NY.) Jewish immigrant numbers are from Orleck, *Common Sense*, 23.

10. Many descriptions and analyses of the Roosevelts during this period are available. Here, as much as possible, ER's own words are used to describe what she saw and felt. Eleanor Roosevelt, *This Is My Story* (New York: Harper & Bros., 1937), 108. Eleanor Roosevelt, *You Learn by Living* (New York: Harper, 1960), 104. Also see Cook, *ER*, 1:138; and Lash, *Eleanor and Franklin*, 97–100.

11. Robert H. Wiebe, *The Search for Order, 1877–1920* (New York: Hill and Wang, 1967). Roosevelt, *You Learn by Living*, 104; Roosevelt, *This Is My Story*, 109; Roosevelt, *You Learn by Living*, 103–4.

12. Lash, *Eleanor and Franklin*, 99–100.

13. Ibid., 98–100. Cook, *ER*, 1:135–37 (ER to FDR, 6 January 1904, quotation 136).

14. ER's childhood is described in detail by biographers Cook and Lash, as well as by ER herself in her autobiographies, especially *This Is My Story*.

15. Lash, *Eleanor and Franklin*, 153. The Roosevelts' early married life is also covered in Lash and Cook.

16. This account of the Roosevelts' early days in Albany is drawn from Kenneth Sydney Davis, *FDR: The Beckoning of Destiny, 1882–1928; A History* (New York: Putnam, 1972), chaps. 8 and 9; and Frank Burt Freidel, *Franklin D. Roosevelt* (Boston: Little, Brown, 1952), chap. 7.

17. ER quoted in Cook, *ER*, 1:138. Also see Lash, *Eleanor and Franklin*, 171–74.

18. Davis highlights the change in FDR's attitude toward labor and suffrage in *FDR*, 263–65. James MacGregor Burns attributes the change to the influence of progressivism and TR's leadership in *Roosevelt: The Lion and the Fox* (New York: Harcourt Brace Jovanovich, 1984), 43. FDR's lack of engagement in progressive legislation was noted more recently in Kirstin Downey, *The Woman behind the New Deal: The Life of Frances Perkins, FDR's Secretary of Labor and His Moral Conscience* (New York: Doubleday, 2009), 88–89.

19. Cook details ER's role as adviser and critic, although ER downplayed her role in her own writings. See Cook, *ER*, 1:190–94; for ER on suffrage, see 195. Her independence and FDR's acknowledgment are described in Allida M. Black, *Casting Her Own Shadow: Eleanor Roosevelt and the Shaping of Postwar Liberalism* (New York: Columbia University Press, 1996), 8; Ruby Black, *Eleanor Roosevelt: A Biography* (New York: Duell, Sloan and Pearce, 1940), 27–28.

20. For more on FDR, TR, and the 1912 election, see James MacGregor Burns and Susan Dunn, *The Three Roosevelts: Patrician Leaders Who Transformed America* (New York: Atlantic Monthly Press, 2001), 136–40; ER's position is on 140.

21. Eleanor Roosevelt, *This I Remember* (New York: Harper, 1949), 23. Davis, *FDR*, 315. The importance of his navy experience to FDR's understanding of labor was suggested to the author by Harvard economist John Dunlop, who was active in the New Deal and later served as secretary of labor in the Ford administration. From his perspective, however, ER was not involved in labor policy. See John Dunlop, interview by author, 21 November 2002, Cambridge, in Eleanor Roosevelt Papers Project (ERPP), George Washington University, Washington, DC. On the importance of the war years to strengthening FDR's ties to the labor movement and their political implications, see Freidel, *Franklin D. Roosevelt*, 192–206 (quotation 197); Davis, *FDR*, 478–81.

22. Davis, *FDR*, 479. ER quotations in Roosevelt, *This Is My Story*, 263.

23. ER's early independence before the Mercer affair is persuasively argued by Black, *Casting Her Own Shadow*, 7–10. Also see Cook, *ER*, 1:215–36; Lash, *Eleanor and Franklin*, 220–27.

24. See Davis, *FDR*, 480, for labor during the war, and 576 for strikes after the war. FDR's claim, 18 August 1920, quoted in Freidel, *Franklin D. Roosevelt*, 192.

25. Cook, *ER*, 1:240–44. Lash, *Eleanor and Franklin*, 239–40. ER to Bob Ferguson, 16 September 1919, quoted in Cook, *ER*, 1:243–44; for race riots and staff, see 250–54.

26. For conference details, see *New York Times*, 6 October 1919. Dinners with the Lanes and others are found in Cook, *ER*, 1:208. For examples of ER's reporting, see ER to FDR, 22, 23 October 1919, in Lash, *Eleanor and Franklin*, 236. Samuel Gompers of the AF of L led the unions out of the conference; see *New York Times*, 23 October 1919.

27. All the conferences received newspaper coverage. See, for example, *Washington Post*, 28, 29, 30 October 1919; and *New York Times*, 27, 31 October and 4 November 1919.

28. Roosevelt, *This Is My Story*, 163, 304. ER to Sara D. Roosevelt, 28 October 1919, folder 9 ER to Sara D. Roosevelt, June–December 1919, RFPDC, FDRL; and Tuesday, 28 October, Daily Journal for 1919, RFPDC, FDRL. Schneiderman was at the conference, and was known in New York political circles, but neither Schneiderman nor ER mention meeting at this time, although Lash reports that ER hosted a lunch for the group, *Eleanor and Franklin*, 236. Cook suggests that ER was taken with the unusual marriage of Margaret Dreier Robins because she and her husband worked both together and separately; Cook, *ER*, 1:258–59.

29. Cook, *ER*, 1:265–87; Lash, *Eleanor and Franklin*, 249–58.

30. Burns, *Three Roosevelts*, 170–73; Frances Perkins, *The Roosevelt I Knew* (New York: Viking Press, 1946), 28. The FDR quotation is from Irving Bernstein, *The Lean Years: A History of the American Worker, 1920–1933* (Boston: Houghton Mifflin, 1960), 117. For ER's activities, see Lash, *Eleanor and Franklin*, 259–60.

31. Cook, *ER*, 1:308–309. Quotation from Frances Perkins in Perkins, *Roosevelt I Knew*, 30.

32. Cook, *ER*, 1:319–21; Lash, *Eleanor and Franklin*, 277–78.

33. Dorothy Sue Cobble credits historian William O'Neil with first using the term "social feminist" in a 1968 article, "Feminism as a Radical Ideology," cited in Cobble, *The Other Women's Movement: Workplace Justice and Social Rights in Modern America* (Princeton: Princeton University Press, 2003), 3–4, 232, fn. 12. The importance of this network in ER's development and the struggle to place her in the sometimes competing categories of reform and feminism are elaborated in Joan Hoff and Marjorie Lightman, eds., *Without Precedent: The Life and Career of Eleanor Roosevelt* (Bloomington: Indiana University Press, 1984). For more on the impact of this dual strategy for New Deal labor legislation and ER's key role, see Eileen Boris, "The Quest for Labor Standards in the Era of Eleanor Roosevelt: The Case of Industrial Homework," *Wisconsin Women's Law Journal* 2 (1986): 53–74. For the important roles these women went on to play in the New Deal, see Susan Ware, *Beyond Suffrage: Women in the New Deal* (Cambridge: Harvard University Press, 1981).

34. In addition to the founding of the Women's Trade Union League and its early history as described in Schneiderman and Goldthwaite, *All for One,* see Nancy Schrom Dye, *As Equals and as Sisters: Feminism, the Labor Movement, and the Women's Trade Union League of New York* (Columbia: University of Missouri Press, 1980); Gary Edward Endelman, *Solidarity Forever: Rose Schneiderman and the Women's Trade Union League* (New York: Arno Press, 1982); Philip Sheldon Foner, *Women and the American Labor Movement,* vol. 1, *From Colonial Times to the Eve of World War I* (New York: Free Press, 1979), 290–323; and Elizabeth Anne Payne, *Reform, Labor, and Feminism: Margaret Dreier Robins and the Women's Trade Union League* (Urbana: University of Illinois Press, 1988). While labor reform for women and children was part of the progressive agenda, Payne describes this partnership between unions and feminists as rare.

35. Schneiderman and Goldthwaite, *All for One,* 75. Payne provides analysis of the tension between Robins and Gompers in *Reform, Labor, and Feminism,* 102; also see, for example, Endelman, *Solidarity Forever,* 32.

36. Tensions between native-born skilled trades women and immigrant factory workers surfaced in 1914, when Melinda Scott narrowly defeated Rose Schneiderman to become president of the New York WTUL; see Endelman, *Solidarity Forever,* 50–53; Orleck, *Common Sense,* 106–7; Dye, *As Equals,* 50, 116–20; and Alice Kessler-Harris, *Gendering Labor History* (Urbana: University of Illinois Press, 2007), 77–78. For a vivid personal description of this period that includes these cross-class tensions, see Theresa Serber Malkiel and Françoise Basch, *The Diary of a Shirtwaist Striker* (Ithaca, NY: ILR Press, 1990). Robins retired in 1924 and was disappointed in the new union leadership, which she thought became distracted by the fight over the Equal Rights Amendment; see Payne, *Reform, Labor, and Feminism,* 156.

37. Schneiderman and Goldthwaite, *All for One,* 155, 150.

38. Here I have relied primarily on Schneiderman's autobiography, Schneiderman and Goldthwaite, *All for One.* Newman is quoted in Orleck, *Common Sense,* 32. For a focus on Schneiderman's eventual turn to government rather than unions to solve working women's problems and the complications this involved, see, for example, Endelman, *Solidarity Forever;* and Kessler-Harris, *Gendering Labor History.*

39. Schneiderman quoted in *New York Times,* 12 April 1911. Also see Schneiderman and Goldthwaite, *All for One,* 99–102; George Whitney Martin, *Madam Secretary, Frances Perkins* (Boston: Houghton Mifflin, 1976), 86–88. On the fire and its public impact, see Von Drehle, *Triangle.*

40. Little more is known about Maud Swartz; she left no personal papers, and Schneiderman destroyed much of her personal records. See Orleck, *Common Sense,* 134–36.

41. *New York Times,* 31 May 1920. The problems Schneiderman faced in this campaign are described in Endelman, *Solidarity Forever,* 83–93. The "Red Rose" epithet was first attributed to James Holland, president of the New York Federation of Labor, at hearings on a bill to reverse maximum hours for women workers which he supported and Schneiderman opposed; see Orleck, *Common Sense,* 138. The kite reference is from Holland's testimony before the New York State Joint Legislative Committee for the Investigation of Seditious Activities, known as the Lusk Committee, quoted in *New York Times,* 18 July 1919.

42. Schneiderman and Goldthwaite, *All for One,* 150–51.

43. Social unionism in the garment unions is defined in Robert D. Parmet, *The Master of Seventh Avenue: David Dubinsky and the American Labor Movement* (New York: New York University Press, 2005), 1; also see *A Power among Them: Bessie Abramowitz Hillman and the Making of the Amalgamated Clothing Workers of America* (Urbana: University of Illinois Press, 2008); Steve Fraser, *Labor Will Rule: Sidney Hillman and the Rise of American Labor* (New York: Free Press, 1991); and Schneiderman and Goldthwaite, *All for One.*

44. Schneiderman and Goldthwaite, *All for One,* 178–79.

45. Ibid., 180.
46. Minutes of Executive Board, 4 January 1923, Rose Schneiderman Papers (RSP), reel 2, Women's Trade Union League Papers, Microfilm Edition, 1981, Cecil H. Green Library, Stanford University, Palo Alto (WTULP). RS to ER, 14 February 1924, New York Women's Trade Union League Papers (NYWTULP), reel 11, WTULP. Executive Board, 27 March 1924, RSP, reel 2, WTULP. Executive Board, 3 December 1925, RSP, reel 3, WTULP. The Christmas party is described in Schneiderman and Goldthwaite, *All for One,* 156. Also see Lash, *Eleanor and Franklin,* 281; Report of Work, December 1924, RSP, reel 2, WTULP.
47. Executive Board, 8 October 1928, RSP, reel 3, WTULP. Report of Work, 3 May 1923, RSP, reel 2, WTULP. Club Reading, 8 December 1924, NYWTULP, reel 12, WTULP. Mabel Leslie to ER, 7 May 1924, NYWTULP, reel 11, WTULP. Schneiderman and Goldthwaite, *All For One,* 153. For Bryn Mawr see Rita Heller, "Blue Collars and Blue Stockings," in Frederickson and Kornbluh, *Sisterhood and Solidarity,* 107–45.
48. *Life and Labor Bulletin,* June 1923, May 1927, WTUL Publications, reel 7, WTULP.
49. Endelman, *Solidarity Forever,* 130. Rose Schneiderman to ER, 23 May 1924, NYWTULP, reel 11, WTULP. Orleck, *Common Sense,* 138.
50. *New York Times,* 12, 25 June 1924. The meetings (but not the union plank) are discussed by Cook, *ER,* 1:350; and Lash, *Eleanor and Franklin,* 290. For more about ER's development as a Democratic Party activist, see Susan Ware, "ER and Democratic Politics," in Hoff and Lightman, *Without Precedent,* 46–60; Black, *Casting Her Own Shadow,* 7–22; and Cook, *ER,* 1:288–301.
51. Endelman, *Solidarity Forever,* 132–41. Dye, *As Equals,* 150; Orleck, *Common Sense,* 139–41. *New York Times,* 12 June 1924.
52. Roosevelt, *This Is My Story,* 354; Cook, *ER,* 1:350–51.
53. Schneiderman to ER, 29 July 1924, NYTWULP, reel 12, WTULP. Lash, *Eleanor and Franklin,* 291–92.
54. Eleanor [Mrs. Franklin] Roosevelt, "How to Interest Women in Voting," *Women's Democratic Campaign Manual* (Washington, DC: 1924), 102–3; this pamphlet can be found at the Media Center, Cecil H. Green Library, Stanford. On the *Women's Democratic News,* see Maurine Hoffman Beasley, Holly Cowan Shulman, and Henry R. Beasley, eds., *The Eleanor Roosevelt Encyclopedia* (Westport, CT: Greenwood Press, 2001), 577–78.
55. *Life and Labor Bulletin,* December 1925, WTUL Publications, reel 7, WTULP; Cook, *ER,* 1:363. *New York Times,* 9 December 1926.
56. Pauline Newman, interview, Twentieth Century Trade Union Woman Oral History Project, Institute of Industrial Relations, Bentley Historical Library, University of Michigan, Ann Arbor (TUWOHP), 1978, 63. Perkins, *Roosevelt I Knew,* 30–31; Schneiderman and Goldthwaite, *All for One,* 176–77.
57. Perkins, *Roosevelt I Knew,* 30–31. Orleck concludes that the relationship was reciprocal, as the WTUL would have been finished without ER's financial help (*Common Sense,* 148).
58. Perkins, *Roosevelt I Knew,* 32.
59. This summary is drawn from Bernstein's thorough discussion in *Lean Years,* 47–82.
60. Ibid., 84; for the UMW, see 127.
61. Ibid., 85. For the Bok Peace Prize, a competition for a peace plan with a $50,000 reward, and the Senate hearings see Cook, *ER,* 1:342–45. For more about ER's FBI file see Cook, *ER,* 1:3, fn. 502. The file is available at http://foia.fbi.gov.
62. For a history of the NCF, see the National Civic Federation Records, 1894–1949, New York Public Library. NCF Papers are quoted in Ted Morgan, *Reds: McCarthyism in Twentieth-Century America* (New York: Random House, 2003), 121.

63. Morgan, *Reds*, 122.

64. Cook, *ER*, 1:376; Black, *Casting Her Own Shadow*, 14.

65. Maud Swartz to ER, 18 October 1929, folder WTUL, General Correspondence, 1928–1932, Anna Eleanor Roosevelt Papers (AERP), Franklin D. Roosevelt Library (FDRL), Hyde Park, NY. Frances Perkins Oral History Interview, vol. 4, part 2, 570, Oral History Collection of Columbia University, New York, (hereafter Perkins, COHC), 1955; also in Endelman, *Solidarity*, 159.

66. These events are reported in Elisabeth Israels Perry, "Training for Public Life," in Hoff and Lightman, *Without Precedent*, 44.

67. For Perkins's life story, see Downey, *Woman behind the New Deal;* and Martin, *Madam Secretary*. Perkins and ER had a complicated relationship, beginning in the 1920s. While there is evidence of jealousy on both sides, they were also friends and worked together, maintaining communication and correspondence until ER's death. While ER contacted Perkins about labor issues and Perkins sought ER's help with FDR, they had quite different and independent relationships with union leaders. Their relationship is worthy of a book in its own right but is not covered extensively here.

68. ER to FDR, 22 November 1928, quoted in Lash, *Eleanor and Franklin*, 323–24; Susan Ware, *Partner and I: Molly Dewson, Feminism, and New Deal Politics* (New Haven: Yale University Press, 1987), 152–53. Dewson quoted in Ware, "ER and Democratic Politics," in Hoff and Lightman, *Without Precedent*, 53.

69. *Life and Labor Bulletin*, March 1929, WTUL Publications, reel 8, WTULP.

70. *New York Times*, 9 April 1929; *Life and Labor Bulletin*, May 1929, WTUL Publications, reel 8, WTULP.

71. In *Common Sense*, Orleck provides more depth than other historians to the relationship between the Roosevelts and the union women, acknowledging that it was reciprocal, that the Roosevelts were eager to learn, and that they genuinely respected the outspoken union women. Her assertion that the "remarkable bond" grew in part because the tough socialist union women were "seduced and charmed" by the Roosevelts (148–50), however, overlooks the observation offered here that a fundamental basis of friendship is found in shared emotional and practical experiences. Schneiderman to Pauline M. Newman, 11 August 1917, quoted in Orleck, *Common Sense*, 300. ER to Lorena Hickok, 21 July 1938, quoted in Joseph P. Lash and Eleanor Roosevelt, *Love, Eleanor: Eleanor Roosevelt and Her Friends* (Garden City, NY: Doubleday, 1982), 1.

72. Downey, *Woman behind the New Deal*, 101–2; Martin, *Madam Secretary*, 234–35. Cook, *ER*, 1:329. Roosevelt, *You Learn by Living*, 59. Neither Schneiderman nor Maud Swartz shared these stories. Schneiderman destroyed most of the evidence about her personal life and there is little personal record of Maud Swartz. ER's correspondence with Schneiderman doesn't begin until 1928.

2. Here Comes Mrs. Roosevelt

1. Trip details are drawn from the *UMW Journal*, 1 June 1935; and the *New York Times*, 22 May 1935. Area information is found in "A History of Bellaire," www.bellaire.lib.oh.us. Robert Day, cartoon, "For gosh sakes, here comes Mrs. Roosevelt!" *New Yorker*, 3 June 1933, 13; Eleanor Roosevelt, "In Defense of Curiosity," *Saturday Evening Post*, 24 August 1935, 8–9, 64–66.

2. Lorena A. Hickok, Richard Lowitt, and Maurine Hoffman Beasley, *One Third of a Nation: Lorena Hickok Reports on the Great Depression* (Urbana: University of Illinois Press, 1983). ER is quoted in Blanche Wiesen Cook, *Eleanor Roosevelt*, vol. 2, *1933–1938* (New York:

Viking, 1999), 262. For the scene at the mine, see *UMW Journal,* 1 June 1935. Despite the new safety features, an explosion in this mine killed seventy-three miners on 16 March 1940; ER sent her condolences. See Dolores and Donald Davis Web page, www.geocities. com.

3. *New York Times,* 22 May 1935.

4. Cook draws this conclusion about the importance of unionization to economic security in *ER,* 1:422.

5. Biographer Ruby Black first defines ER's principles on labor in *Eleanor Roosevelt,* 179–80.

6. Roosevelt, "In Defense of Curiosity."

7. Martin, *Madam Secretary,* 213–14, 224; Bernstein, *Lean Years,* 492. For Schneiderman's support of unemployment insurance and the WTUL's resistance, see Endelman, *Solidarity Forever,* 166–67. Schneiderman to ER, 8 July 1930, folder WTUL, General Correspondence, 1928–1932, AERP.

8. *New York Times,* 18 November 1930. Alfred Steinberg, *Mrs. R: The Life of Eleanor Roosevelt* (New York: Putnam, 1958), 174, 164 (last two quotations).

9. Irving Bernstein, *A Caring Society: The New Deal, the Worker, and the Great Depression; A History of the American Worker, 1933–1941* (Boston: Houghton Mifflin, 1985), 277. Bernstein, *Lean Years,* 457.

10. Schneiderman quoted in *New York Times,* 18 November 1930, 21 December 1931. See Endelman, *Solidarity Forever,* 167–68.

11. Endelman, *Solidarity Forever,* 160–62. ER contributions in Orleck, *Common Sense,* 154 and n. 85.

12. On prison reform, for example, ER chaired a WTUL luncheon discussion, reported in *Life and Labor Bulletin,* March 1930, WTUL Publications, reel 7, WTULP. Appointments in the *New York Times,* 1 August 1930; FDR to Rose Schneiderman, 7 September 1929, 12 May 1930, box 1, folder 8 1929–1932, Correspondence 1915–1964, Rose Schneiderman Papers (RSP), TAM 018, Tamiment Library/Robert F. Wagner Labor Archives, New York University (TL). A defense of the respectability and value of domestic work appeared in Forum Article Draft, January 1930, Speech and Article file 1917–1962, AERP; and ER to Rose Schneiderman, 19 December 1930, folder WTUL, General Correspondence 1928–1932, AERP. For the defense of married women's employment, see ER, Seventh Radio Speech, "Woman's Career vs. Woman's Home," 20 January 1933, folder Pond's Radio Program Speeches, Speech and Article File 1917–1962, AERP (quotation). To put these activities in the perspective of ER's full schedule, see Cook, *ER,* vol. 1, chap. 15, 381–96. For more on unemployment and women during this period, see Kessler-Harris, *Out to Work;* and Philip Sheldon Foner, *Women and the American Labor Movement,* vol. 2, *From World War I to the Present* (New York: Free Press, 1980).

13. Local 22 in *Life and Labor Bulletin,* May 1930, WTUL Publications, reel 7, WTULP. Local 38 letter and quotations in *New York Times,* 4 October 1930.

14. FDR to Rose Schneiderman, 12 May 1930, in Alfred B. Rollins and Hendrien Kaal, *Roosevelt and Howe* (reprint, New Brunswick: Transaction Publishers, 2001), 281. Labor support in *New York Times,* 27, 28 August, 21 October 1930. See also Rollins and Kaal, *Roosevelt and Howe,* 294–95.

15. ER to Schneiderman, 11 November 1930, and Maud Swartz to ER, 18 December 1930, folder WTUL, General Correspondence 1928–1932, AERP. Orleck, *Common Sense,* 150.

16. FDR's speech in Cook, *ER,* 1:455–56. ER's speech in *Herald Tribune,* "Adequate Wage to All Asked by Mrs. Roosevelt," 8 July 1932, Scrapbook T785, AERP. Also see Lash, *Eleanor and Franklin,* 350–53. Lash reported that it was "considered unseemly" for ER to campaign for her husband (353).

17. For the campaign, see Bernstein, *Lean Years,* 511–12. Schneiderman endorsement in *New York Times,* 9 October 1932. Hillman's role in Steve Fraser, *Labor Will Rule,* 284–85.

18. Bernstein, *Lean Years,* 508. Schneiderman to FDR, 18 November 1932, RSP, reel 1, WTULP.

19. See Lorena A. Hickok, *Reluctant First Lady* (New York: Dodd, Mead, 1962). Schneiderman to ER, 18 November 1932, RSP, reel 1, WTULP. For the dinner, see Lash, *Eleanor and Franklin,* 357; *New York Times,* 15 February 1933.

20. *Scribner's Magazine* 93 (1933): 140. This section draws on Brigid O'Farrell, "A Stitch in Time: The New Deal, the International Ladies' Garment Workers' Union, and Mrs. Roosevelt," *Transatlantica* 1, Beyond the New Deal (2006), http://transatlantica.org.

21. ER to Herman Milgrim, 28 September 1933, and Milgrim to ER, telegram, 9 October 1933, folder Herman Milgrim, Personal Letters 1933–1945, AERP. For the press conferences, see Maurine Beasley, ed., *The White House Press Conferences of Eleanor Roosevelt* (New York: Garland Publishing, 1983); and Beasley, *Eleanor Roosevelt and the Media: A Public Quest for Self-Fulfillment* (Urbana: University of Illinois Press, 1987). Black, *Eleanor Roosevelt,* 177–88 (quotation 179–80). Among these issues, only apprenticeship was not actively addressed by ER.

22. Downey, *Woman behind the New Deal,* 114–27; Martin, *Madam Secretary,* 233–42. For labor's reaction, see Irving Bernstein, *Turbulent Years: A History of the American Worker, 1933–1941* (Boston: Houghton Mifflin, 1970), 8–11; Hillman in Fraser, *Labor Will Rule,* 284–85; and Dubinsky in David Dubinsky and A. H. Raskin, *David Dubinsky: A Life with Labor* (New York: Simon and Schuster, 1977), 296.

23. For Perkins's view on ER's role in her appointment see Downey, *Woman behind the New Deal,* 103; for ER's view of the appointment see Eleanor Roosevelt, *Autobiography* (New York: Harper, 1961), 132. Dewson's role is described in Ware, *Partner and I,* 176–80. Despite ER's denials, Cook documents the first lady's close relationship with Dewson on patronage issues for women in *ER,* 2:67–69. As noted in chap. 1, ER and Perkins had a complicated relationship not yet fully addressed by historians.

24. See Martin, *Madam Secretary,* 251–56, for the conference; and Perkins, *Roosevelt I Knew,* 194–95, for Perkins on the Black bill.

25. Schneiderman to ER, 17 April 1933, folder Rose Schneiderman, Personal Letters 1933–1945, AERP.

26. ER to Schneiderman, 26 April 1933, folder Rose Schneiderman, Personal Letters 1933–1945, AERP. Perkins, *Roosevelt I Knew,* 195–96. The crowd is described in Martin, *Madam Secretary,* 262. O'Farrell, "A Stitch in Time."

27. For the development of this bill from a labor perspective, see Bernstein, *Turbulent Years,* 27–31. For a broader account that minimizes labor's role, see David M. Kennedy, *Freedom from Fear: The American People in Depression and War, 1929–1945* (New York: Oxford University Press, 1999), 150–53. Also see Perkins, *Roosevelt I Knew,* chap. 17; and Martin, *Madam Secretary,* 263–69. For FDR's position, see Bernstein, *Turbulent Years,* 29. For Green, see Perkins, *Roosevelt I Knew,* 196, 199–200; and for Lewis, see Melvyn Dubofsky and Warren R. Van Tine, "John L. Lewis," in *Labor Leaders in America,* ed. Dubofsky and Van Tine (Urbana: University of Illinois Press, 1987), 193.

28. Schneiderman and Goldthwaite, *All for One,* 195–96; Endelman, *Solidarity Forever,* chap. 6; Orleck, *Common Sense,* 150–51. Other women such as Agnes Nestor of the Glovemakers Union were also involved as advisers; see Perkins, COHC, 4:310. Mary Anderson to Margaret Dreier Robbins, 11 May 1936, quoted in Endelman, *Solidarity Forever,* 192. Schneiderman's role with the NRA highlights the dual strategy of protecting women and extending wage and hour protection to men which the social feminists brought to the New

Deal. For more on their influence and ER's leadership role, see Boris, "The Quest for Labor Standards."

29. Beasley, *White House Press Conferences,* 12. Schneiderman and Goldthwaite, *All for One,* 9. Endelman, *Solidarity Forever,* 182, argues that Schneiderman did not see this benefit at the time but instead emphasized the role of the codes in the abolition of child labor and homework.

30. Bernstein, *Caring Society,* 277–78; Bernstein, *Turbulent Years,* 80 (Dubinsky quotation), 84. Parmet puts the membership as low as 23,876 in 1932 in *Master of Seventh Avenue,* 66.

31. Bernstein, *Turbulent Years,* 34, 85 (Dubinsky quotation).

32. This profile of Dubinsky, the ILGWU, and social unionism draws on Parmet, *Master of Seventh Avenue;* for Dubinsky's perspective, see Dubinsky and Raskin, *David Dubinsky.* For the view of longtime staff members, see Gus Tyler, *Look for the Union Label: A History of the International Ladies' Garment Workers' Union* (Armonk, NY: M. E. Sharpe, 1995).

33. Maida Springer quotation in Brigid O'Farrell and Joyce L. Kornbluh, ed., *Rocking the Boat: Union Women's Voices, 1915–1975* (New Brunswick: Rutgers University Press, 1996), 4. The challenges women faced in the ILGWU were the focus of some of the earliest studies in women's labor history; see, for example, "Organizing the Unorganizable," first published in 1976, in Kessler-Harris, *Gendering Labor History.* Rose Pesotta told her story as the only woman on the executive board in 1944; see Rose Pesotta and John Nicholas Beffel, *Bread upon the Waters* (Ithaca, NY: ILR Press, 1987). The intersection of gender and race is explored in Yevette Richards, *Maida Springer: Pan-Africanist and International Labor Leader* (Pittsburgh: University of Pittsburgh Press, 2000). Racial discrimination was seriously challenged by Herbert Hill and the NAACP beginning in 1958; see Parmet, *Master of Seventh Avenue,* 299–311. Bertnstein, *Turbulent Years,* 80–81, and Parmet, *Master of Seventh Avenue,* 206.

34. See O'Farrell, "A Stitch in Time." *Justice* (ILGWU), 1 September 1933.

35. *International Ladies' Garment Workers' Union Report and Proceedings of the Twenty-second International Convention,* Chicago, 1934, 120, quoted in Endelman, *Solidarity Forever,* 192.

36. For a full biography of Springer, see Richards, *Maida Springer;* chap. 1 covers her early years; a rich description of the New Deal is found on 43–44. The Springer quotation from TUWOHP is in O'Farrell and Kornbluh, *Rocking the Boat,* 89–90.

37. Bernstein, *Turbulent Years,* 172–73. For implementation strategies, see O'Farrell, "A Stitch in Time."

38. See Kessler-Harris, *Out to Work,* 262–72, for this period, and chap. 11, "The Radical Consequences of Incremental Change," 300–319. Philip Foner describes this meeting and credits ER with the change in *Women and the American Labor Movement,* 2:279–80.

39. *New York Times,* 12 April 1933.

40. Dubinsky quotation in *New York Times,* 12 April 1933. Schneiderman to ER, 24 April 1933; and ER to Schneiderman, 25 April 1933, folder Rose Schneiderman, Personal Letters 1933–1945, AERP.

41. David Kennedy, for example, concludes that the Blue Eagle badge "signaled the poverty of the New Deal's imagination and the meagerness of the methods it could bring to bear at this time against the Depression," in *Freedom from Fear,* 184.

42. Eleanor Roosevelt, *It's Up to the Women* (New York: Frederick A. Stokes, 1933), vii, 238, 249. O'Farrell, "A Stitch in Time."

43. ER reported that FDR asked her to go on the trip in part because labor conditions were so bad and he wanted to show his concern. Rexford Tugwell, a member of FDR's Brain Trust, was to make a study of these conditions for the Department of Agriculture, according to ER,

This I Remember, 138. For a full description of the trip, including the international context, see Cook, *ER,* 2:169–74. As with much else that ER did, there were as many reasons for the trip as there were people accompanying her. See Black, *Eleanor Roosevelt,* 296; and Doris Farber quoted in Orleck, *Common Sense,* 337, n. 82.

44. For Schneiderman's work in Puerto Rico, see Endelman, *Solidarity Forever,* 203–8. Labor issues and requests are discussed in correspondence: Schneiderman to ER, 3 January 1934; ER to Schneiderman, 20, 26 February 1934; and Schneiderman to ER, 14 April 1934, folder Rose Schneiderman, Personal Letters 1933–1945, AERP. FDR to ER in Cook, *ER,* 2:172.

45. Orleck, *Common Sense,* 153. Endelman, *Solidarity Forever,* 205 (Schneiderman quotation), 206 (Pesotta quotation). Pesotta and Beffel, *Bread upon the Waters,* 99. Pesotta later resigned as vice president in protest against the lack of women in leadership positions in the ILGWU and returned to her sewing machine. Also see Elaine J. Leeder, *The Gentle General: Rose Pesotta, Anarchist and Labor Organizer* (Albany: State University of New York Press, 1993).

46. *Justice* (ILGWU), 1 April 1934. The ILGWU film *Moving On* (Nation Picture Bureau, 1934) is available at the Kheel Center, Cornell University. The plaques are at FDRL.

47. Leeder, *Gentle General,* 66; Black, *Eleanor Roosevelt,* 297; Cook, *ER,* 2:173–74.

48. For colorful descriptions of Lewis, see Bernstein, *Lean Years,* 117–26; Dubofsky and Van Tine, "John L. Lewis"; Albert Fried, *FDR and His Enemies* (New York: St. Martin's Press, 1999), 78–87.

49. Bernstein, *Lean Years,* 123–126 (quotation, 124–25).

50. Bernstein, *Turbulent Years,* 41. Fried, *FDR and His Enemies,* 82–83.

51. *New York Times,* 7 June 1933. Greenway, a longtime family friend of the Roosevelts, had married John Greenway, owner of a company that would later become Phelps Dodge, in Ajo, Arizona. See Kristie Miller, *Isabella Greenway: An Enterprising Woman* (Tucson: University of Arizona Press, 2004); for the debate, see 191. Beasley, *White House Press Conferences,* 10–11.

52. Hickok, *Reluctant First Lady,* 136–42. Selected reports are found in Hickok, Lowitt, and Beasley, *One Third.* For ER's account, see Roosevelt, *This I Remember,* 127–33. ER's relationship with Hickok has been the subject of much debate; see, for example, Cook, *ER,* vol. 1, 2. Hickok, *Reluctant First Lady,* 138.

53. Arthurdale and the homestead communities have been examined at length by ER's biographers. In addition to Black, *Eleanor Roosevelt,* chap. 15, see Cook, *ER,* vol. 2, chap. 8; and Lash, *Eleanor and Franklin,* chap. 37. A short, more recent addition is Nancy Hoffman, *Eleanor Roosevelt and the Arthurdale Experiment* (North Haven, CT: Linnet Books, 2001). For an overview of the coalfields and local efforts at community improvement since the 1920s, see West Virginia Archives, *West Virginia History* 53 (1994): 1–119.

54. Eleaner Roosevelt, "They Keep Their Power to Dream," 10 December 1933; and "Why I Went to Bloody Run," 3 December 1933, McNaught Syndicate, Speech and Article File 1917–1962, AERP.

55. J. S. Dudley to ER, 3 December 1934; ER to John L. Lewis, 11 December 1934; John L. Lewis to ER, 17 December 1934; and Dudley to ER, 4 February 1935, folder Le 1934, file Dr–Dy 1935, Personal Correspondence 1933–1945, AERP. Ruby Black provides another example of ER's opposition to company towns in the textile industry in *Eleanor Roosevelt,* 180. Gardner Jackson Oral History Interview, 755, Oral History Collection of Columbia University (hereafter Jackson, COHC).

56. There is no biography of Hilda Worthington Smith, but there are insightful tributes to her in a small book of her poetry, *Selected Poems by Hilda Worthington Smith* (Ithaca, NY: Institute for Education and Research on Women and Work, School of Industrial and Labor Relations,

Cornell University, 1977); see especially those by Esther Peterson (vii), Caroline F. Ware (x), and Lynn Goldfarb (xvi). Smith's work with the Bryn Mawr Summer School can be found in Rita Heller, "Blue Collars and Bluestockings," in Kornbluh and Frederickson, *Sisterhood and Solidarity*, 107–45; and Joyce L. Kornbluh, *A New Deal for Workers' Education: The Workers' Service Program, 1933–1942* (Urbana: University of Illinois Press, 1987), 16–17, which also analyzes Smith, ER, and the New Deal.

57. Kornbluh, *A New Deal*, 5, 47; for ER's perspective, see 102.
58. Ibid., 17. Hilda W. Smith to ER, 20 October 1933, and "Why Support Affiliate Schools for Workers?" Event Program, 23 October 1933, Speech and Article File 1917–1962, AERP.
59. Kornbluh, *A New Deal*, 3, 46–48, 58.
60. Ibid., chap. 5, 79–95.
61. Ibid., 100–101; see "Reds" in *Washington Herald*, 24 February 1935. ER quoted in Cook, *ER*, 2:356–57.
62. *New York Times*, 5 May 1934. For descriptions of the San Francisco and textile strikes, see Bernstein, *Turbulent Years*, 259–317; Kennedy, *Freedom from Fear*, 293–96.
63. Black, *Eleanor Roosevelt*, 181–82. Beasley, *White House Press Conferences*, 28.
64. Kennedy, *Freedom from Fear*, 328 (FDR quotation). Cook, *ER*, 2:265–66.
65. Kennedy, *Freedom from Fear*, 290–91. For WTUL see Orleck, *Common Sense*, 159. For ER see Cook, *ER*, 2:258. Despite their relationship dating to their early days in Albany, there was little correspondence between ER and Wagner, and there is nothing specifically about the Wagner Act in either AERP or Wagner Papers, Georgetown University.
66. Cook, *ER*, vol. 2, chap. 14, 264–82; WTUL, 266. Schneiderman quotation in Schneiderman and Goldthwaite, *All for One*, 210.
67. James B. Carey Oral History Interview, 89, Oral History Collection of Columbia University (hereafter Carey, COHC), 1956–1958.
68. Bernstein, *Turbulent Years*, 396–97. Robert H. Zieger, *The CIO, 1935–1955* (Chapel Hill: University of North Carolina Press, 1995), 23.
69. Bernstein, *Turbulent Years*, 400–401; Zieger, *CIO*, 22–29.

3. Practicing What You Preach

1. Details of this meeting are taken from ER's account in "My Day," 27 September 1940; *New York Times*, 26 September 1940; and Lewis Gannett's recollections in the *Guild Reporter*, 23 November 1962.
2. Gannett in *Guild Reporter*, 23 November 1962.
3. "My Day," 31 December 1935. ER quotation from "My Day," 20 October 1937. George Carlin to ER, 7 August 1940, quoted in Lash, *Eleanor and Franklin*, 429.
4. Evelyn Dubrow, interview by author, 19 July 2002, Washington, DC; Douglas Fraser, interview by author, 30 May 2003, Detroit; Eula McGill, telephone interview by author, 8 October 2002. Rose Schneiderman to ER, 24 August 1936, folder Rose Schneiderman, Personal Letters 1933–1945, AERP. William Green to ER, 12 April 1936, Folder Gre–Gu 1936, Personal Letters 1933–1945, AERP.
5. "My Day," 21, 28 January, 2, 8 September, 20 December 1936.
6. *New York Times*, 6 January 1937; Black, *Eleanor Roosevelt*, 167. ER joined the Guild at the end of December 1936, the month when the union pulled out of the AF of L and joined the CIO. Her membership was announced in January 1937. Bernstein provides a summary of union organizing in the newspaper business and a description of Broun in *Turbulent Years*, 127–37.
7. Broun quotations from the *New York World Telegram*, February 1933, in Lash, *Eleanor and Franklin*, 356–57; and in Black, *Eleanor Roosevelt*, 141.

8. *Guild Reporter,* 15 January 1937. Letters between ER and her daughter are in Eleanor Roosevelt, Anna Roosevelt, and Bernard Asbell, *Mother and Daughter: The Letters of Eleanor and Anna Roosevelt* (New York: Fromm International, 1988), 84–87, 90–91.

9. Roosevelt Press Conferences, 9:276–307, quoted in Bernstein, *Turbulent Years,* 794–95. Bernstein does not mention ER or her union membership.

10. On Broun's death, see "My Day," 20 December 1939; *New York Times,* 21 December 1939. For ER as Broun's successor, see *New York Times,* 31 December 1939; Wohl to ER and ER to Wohl, both 29 December 1939, quoted in Beasley, Shulman, and Beasley, *The Eleanor Roosevelt Encyclopedia,* 9; Black, *Eleanor Roosevelt,* 167–68; and *Guild Reporter,* 1 January 1940.

11. For ER's support for Marian Anderson and for Harry Truman in 1948 when Henry A. Wallace offered a third party choice, see Black, *Casting Her Own Shadow,* 41–44, 76–84. Lash describes her relationship with and withdrawal from the American Youth Congress in *Eleanor and Franklin,* 597–611. When she asked Dubinsky for his opinion of the Youth Council, he sent a five-page letter explaining why he thought it was a communist organization; see ER to Dubinsky, 13 May 1940; and Dubinsky to ER, 20 June 1940, folder 1C, box 154, Requests A: Subject Files 1932–1951, ILGWU, David Dubinsky, President's Records, 1932–1966, Kheel Center for Labor-Management Documentation and Archives, Martin P. Catherwood Library, Cornell University (hereafter DDPR).

12. Zieger, *CIO,* 102–3. David Witwer, "Westbrook Pegler and the Anti-union Movement," *Journal of American History* 92, no. 2 (2005): 527–52. William Bioff, the West Coast representative of the International Alliance of Theatrical Stage Employees and Moving Picture Machine Operators, and George Scalise, president of the Building Service Employees International Union, were the two union officials who had gone to jail.

13. See Witwer, "Westbrook Pegler," 527–28; Alden Whitman, "Free-Swinging Critic," *New York Times,* 25 June 1969. Lash, *Eleanor and Franklin,* 428. ER's response is in Asbell, *Mother and Daughter,* 87.

14. Black, *Eleanor Roosevelt,* 185–86. Craig to ER, 29 July 1940; and ER to Craig, 31 July 1940, quoted in Beasley, Shulman, and Beasley, *Eleanor Roosevelt Encyclopedia,* 116–17. "My Day," 3 August 1940.

15. *New York Times,* 8 August 1940. "My Day," 9 August 1940. Black, *Eleanor Roosevelt,* 185–86 (Pegler quotations).

16. Lash, *Eleanor and Franklin,* 429. ER to Nat Einhorn, 10 August, Einhorn to ER, 16 August, ER to Einhorn, 19 August, and Einhorn to ER, 28 August 1940, folder 8, box 24, New York Newspaper Guild Records, series 1, General Files 1934–1950, TL (hereafter NYNG Records).

17. For Burke-Wadsworth, see Kennedy, *Freedom from Fear,* 459. ER's letter appeared first in the *Guild Reporter* and was reported in the *New York Times,* 15, 17 September 1940.

18. ER to Nat Einhorn, 25 October 1940, folder 8, box 24, NYNG Records. *New York Times,* 12 December 1940.

19. United Press dispatch quotation in Beasley, Shulman, and Beasley, *Eleanor Roosevelt Encyclopedia,* 10.

20. Zieger, *CIO,* 39.

21. For ER's role, see Lash, *Eleanor and Franklin,* 442–45. For women's issues, see Ware, *Partner and I,* chap. 13, 212–26. "Mrs. Roosevelt Writes for Miners' Wives," *United Mine Workers Journal,* 1 March 1936, 24.

22. Schneiderman to ER, 16 April 1936; and note to Farley, 16 April 1936, Rose Schneiderman file, Personal Letters, 1933–1945, AERP.

23. Lash, *Eleanor and Franklin,* 445, 449. *Justice,* 15 November 1936.

24. Cook, *ER*, 2:426–27; Kennedy, *Freedom from Fear*, 309–10. The Logan story is told in Je-rold S. Auerbach, *Labor and Liberty: The La Follette Committee and the New Deal* (India-napolis: Bobbs-Merrill, 1966), cited in Cook, *ER*, 2:427.

25. Much has been written about the sit-down strikes and the growth of the UAW. For an over-view, see Kennedy, *Freedom from Fear*, 308–15. For in-depth coverage, see, for example, Bernstein, *Turbulent Years*, chap. 11; Nelson Lichtenstein, *Walter Reuther: The Most Dan-gerous Man in Detroit* (Urbana: University of Illinois Press, 1997), chap. 6; Victor G. Reu-ther, *The Brothers Reuther and the Story of the UAW: A Memoir* (Boston: Houghton Mifflin, 1976), chap. 13.

26. Kennedy, *Freedom from Fear*, 313–14.

27. Black, *Eleanor Roosevelt*, 172; "My Day," 7 February 1937. For more of ER's perspective see Cook, *ER*, 2:428–30.

28. "My Day," 11 February 1937.

29. Zieger, *CIO*, 34–39, 54–65. Kennedy, *Freedom from Fear*, 314, 334–37. The KKK and Shreveport are cited in Cook, *ER*, 2:436.

30. Kennedy, *Freedom from Fear*, 317–18; Cook, *ER*, 2:451. The statue was commissioned by Henry Adams for his wife's tomb and created by Augustus Saint-Gaudens. Hickok described it as a place that made ER feel better when she was unhappy (*Reluctant First Lady*, 91–92).

31. Kennedy provides a vivid overview of these events, drawing on both Bernstein and Zieger, in *Freedom from Fear*, 318–19. For ER's response, see Cook, *ER*, 2:462–63. Both quote FDR's press conference, 29 June 1937.

32. ER to Hickok, 8 August 1937, cited in Cook, *ER*, 2:465; Lewis quotation, 466. Schneider-man to ER, 14 September 1937, folder Rose Schneiderman, Personal Letters 1933–1945, AERP.

33. Kennedy, *Freedom from Fear*, 350–51; Dubofsky and Van Tine, "John L. Lewis," 199–200. Schneiderman to ER, 2 March, 6, 24 May 1937; and ER to Schneiderman, 26 May 1937, folder Rose Schneiderman, Personal Letters 1933–1945, AERP.

34. Bernstein, *Turbulent Years*, 697–98 (CIO), 710–11 (ILGWU). Carey, COHC, interview 7, 206. Beasley, *White House Press Conferences*, 59.

35. Black, *Eleanor Roosevelt*, 178.

36. "My Day," 1, 18 March, 6 May, 6, 11 November 1939.

37. Five of her columns dealt with labor education programs and her work with Hilda Smith: 27 June, 2 August, 14, 26 October, 10 November 1939. CIO, *News*, 13 March 1939. Quotation from ER letter to Mrs. Bernstein, 21 June 1939, cited in Lash, *Eleanor and Franklin*, 595.

38. Cook, *ER*, 2:497.

39. This profile draws on Lucy Randolph Mason, *To Win These Rights: A Personal Story of the CIO in the South* (New York: Harper, 1952), as well as John A. Salmond's biography, *Miss Lucy of the CIO: The Life and Times of Lucy Randolph Mason, 1882–1959* (Athens: Univer-sity of Georgia Press, 1988). For women's labor history in the South, see Mary Frederickson, "'I know which side I'm on,'" in *Women, Work, and Protest: A Century of U.S. Women's Labor History*, ed. Ruth Milkman (Boston: Routledge & Kegan Paul, 1985), 156–80. For the Southern Summer School, see Frederickson, "Recognizing Regional Differences," in Korn-bluh and Federickson, *Sisterhood and Solidarity*, 148–86.

40. See Salmond, *Miss Lucy*, 17 (description of Mason), 57 (beginning of her relationship with ER). Mason tells the story of how she came to work for the CIO in Mason, *To Win These Rights*, 16–18.

41. John M. Glen, *Highlander: No Ordinary School*, 2nd ed. (Knoxville: University of Tennes-see Press, 1996). Approximately three thousand pages of correspondence between Mason, Roosevelt, and others from October 1937 to September 1952 are archived on microfilm. For

an analysis, see Abagail M. Shaddox, "From Back Bench to Oval Office: The Letters of Lucy Randolph Mason and Eleanor Roosevelt," *Southern Studies: An Interdisciplinary Journal of the South* 14, no. 1 (2007): 13–31. For ER forwarding Mason's reports, see Cook, *ER,* 2:fn. 510–11, 643.

42. Mason quotation cited in Cook, *ER,* 2:510. For the economic report, see Cook, *ER,* 2:564; and Salmond, *Miss Lucy,* 153–54. Mason to FDR, 25 March 1938, cited in Salmond, *Miss Lucy,* 153.

43. For SCHW, see Salmond, *Miss Lucy,* 152–54. Lunch was reported in "My Day," 31 March 1938. Cook, *ER,* 2:564–68. There is some question about Mason's exact role in arranging the conference with the White House, but there is no doubt she was involved.

44. Mason, *To Win These Rights,* 54–59 (quotation 58).

45. Mason quotation ibid., 59.

46. Salmond, *Miss Lucy,* 154; Cook, *ER,* 2:567–68. For more on SCEF, see Black, *Casting Her Own Shadow,* 40, 118–22.

47. "My Day," 28 November 1940. For Bass, see Mason, *To Win These Rights,* 109–13.

48. Mason, *To Win These Rights,* 112–13.

49. For Mason's long-standing relationship with Highlander, see Salmond, *Miss Lucy,* 148–52. The Grundy County example comes from Glen, *Highlander,* 75.

50. The convention was covered in the *New York Times,* 1, 5, 6, and 7 May 1936. *Justice,* 15 May 1936.

51. Eula McGill, interview, 1978, TUWOHP.

52. Quotations from Eula McGill, telephone interview with author, 8 August 2002.

53. Orleck, *Common Sense,* 163–65. "My Day," 23 February 1937. Schneiderman to ER, 2 March 1937, folder Rose Schneiderman, Personal Letters 1933–1945, AERP. If more intimate thoughts and feelings were shared between the two women over the loss of their dear friend, they left no record.

54. ER to Schneiderman, 4 March 1937, folder Rose Schneiderman, Personal Letters 1933–1945, AERP. Kessler-Harris, *Gendering Labor History,* 86–87. Quotation in Orleck, *Common Sense,* 165. Cook, *ER,* 2:457. Schneiderman to ER, 27 May 1937; and ER to McIntyre, 2 June 1937, folder Rose Schneiderman, Personal Letters 1933–1945, AERP. See Orleck and Kessler-Harris for discussion of the accomplishments and problems of women during this period. For the Fair Labor Standards Act, see Martin, *Madam Secretary,* 387–95

55. "My Day," 11 August 1937.

56. "My Day," 10 November 1936; *Justice,* 12 December 1936.

57. Harry Goldman, "When Social Significance Came to Broadway: 'Pins and Needles' in Production," *Theatre Quarterly* 7, no. 28 (1977–78): 25–41. See also the unpublished manuscript Harry Goldman, "Pins and Needles: When Social Significance Comes to Broadway" (Ithaca, NY: Kheel Center, Cornell University, 1977). The play's importance is discussed in Dubinsky and Raskin, *David Dubinsky,* 190–92; Tyler, *Look for the Union Label,* 201–2, 245–46; and Bernstein, *A Caring Society,* 223, 245.

58. Schneiderman to ER, 10 February 1938, folder Rose Schneiderman, Personal Letters 1933–1945, AERP. "My Day," 16 February 1938.

59. Malvina Scheider, Secretary to ER, to Dubinsky, 24 February 1938, box 376, F2D, DDPR. Goldman, "Pins and Needles: When Social Significance Comes to Broadway;" 156–59, 154; *Justice,* 15 March 1938. Dubinsky and Raskin, *David Dubinsky,* 191. Dubinsky and *Justice* record that "Four Little Angels of Peace" was performed for FDR, but Goldman disagrees. Goldman also suggests that black cast members were cut from the White House performance, but this appears to be more an assumption than a demonstrable fact.

60. See Goldman, "When Social Significance Came to Broadway: 'Pins and Needles' in Production," *32–33*.

61. For Schneiderman's family, see Orleck, *Common Sense,* 164. Léon Blum, the first socialist and Jewish prime minister of France, is discussed in Cook, *ER,* 2:557, 576; Kennedy, *Freedom from Fear,* 310, 398.

62. "My Day," 8 December 1938.

63. *Report and Proceedings: Twenty-fourth Convention of the ILGWU,* 335.

64. Ibid.

65. "My Day," 30 May, 4 June 1940.

66. Kennedy, *Freedom from Fear,* 346–49. Lewis in Bernstein, *Turbulent Years,* 717–19. Fraser, *Labor Will Rule,* 442–47. Parmet, *Master of Seventh Avenue,* 185–86.

67. Lewis quotation in Dubofsky and Van Tine, "John L. Lewis," 201. Jackson, COHC, 4:754–55.

68. For ER's address to 1940 Democratic convention, see Allida M. Black, ed., *What I Hope to Leave Behind: The Essential Essays of Eleanor Roosevelt* (Brooklyn: Carlson, 1995), 373–74. ER letter to Carey, 26 October 1940, cited in Lash, *Eleanor and Franklin,* 621. Mason to Lewis, 27 October 1940, cited in Salmond, *Miss Lucy,* 90. Fraser, *Labor Will Rule,* 451.

69. "My Day," 17 December 1940.

70. Bernstein, *Caring Society,* 1–5.

71. "My Day," 11 December 1940. *Stanford Daily,* 5 April 1940.

72. *New York Times,* 10 December 1940.

73. Ibid., 4 December 1940. "My Day," 11, 18 December 1940.

4. In Her Own Way

1. The description of the convention is drawn from *The Black Worker,* September, October 1940. The 1940 quotation is in A. Philip Randolph Oral History Interview 1, 29 October 1968, 5, LBJ Library, Austin; also available online at http://www.lbjlib.utexas.edu.

2. *The Black Worker,* October 1940. "My Day," 18 September 1940.

3. For these specific examples of discrimination, see Goodwin, *No Ordinary Time,* 165–66. Discussion of the racial situation and these events is found in Lash, *Eleanor and Franklin,* 529–32; Jervis Anderson, *A. Philip Randolph: A Biographical Portrait* (New York: Harcourt Brace Jovanovich, 1973), 242–46; Goodwin, *No Ordinary Time,* 165–72; Kennedy, *Freedom from Fear,* 763–66. Henry Stimson Diary, October 25, 1940, Yale University Library, quoted in Lash, *Eleanor and Franklin,* 532.

4. Lash, for example, draws this conclusion about ER's change in thinking from the events following the convention, but he does not mention the convention itself; Lash, *Eleanor and Franklin,* 532. Goodwin characterizes the convention as a pivotal event putting ER in the middle of the battle against racial segregation in the military and this battle as the beginning of a new civil rights movement; Goodwin, *No Ordinary Time,* 161. Kennedy, however, highlights the important change in Randolph's approach from meetings to marches but limits ER's role to representing her husband; Kennedy, *Freedom from Fear,* 764.

5. *Time* magazine, 17 April 1939, cited in Beasley, *Eleanor Roosevelt and the Media,* 121. Raymond Clapper, "The Ten Most Powerful People in Washington," *Reader's Digest,* May 1941, cited in Lash, *Eleanor and Franklin,* 472. Randolph to ER, 5 August 1943, file N-S 1943, box 25, A. Philip Randolph Papers, Brotherhood of Sleeping Car Porters Records, Library of Congress (hereafter APRP).

6. FDR quotation from the *Public Papers and Addresses of Franklin D. Roosevelt,* 1940, 633–44, cited in Kennedy, *Freedom from Fear,* 469; on military requests, draftees, and unemployment,

see 476–77. For unions, see Nelson Lichtenstein, *Labor's War at Home: The CIO in World War II* (New York: Cambridge University Press, 1987), 46.

7. "My Day," 13 March 1941.

8. *New York Times,* 6 February 1941; "Every Worker Should Belong to a Trade Union Says Mrs. Roosevelt," *American Federationist* 48 (1941): 14–15; text also available in Black, *What I Hope to Leave Behind,* 387–88; "Leviton Strikers Get Hope from Mrs. Roosevelt," *Journal of Electrical Workers and Operators* (March 1941): 126, 160–61. James Carey to ER, 5 November 1943, folder Correspondence: Mrs. Roosevelt 1943, box 3, CIO Secretary-Treasurer Collection, James B. Carey files, Archives of Labor and Urban Affairs (ALUA), Wayne State University, Detroit (hereafter CIO Carey).

9. Lichtenstein, *Labor's War at Home,* 45–46. The pressures that his government positions put on Hillman is discussed in Fraser, *Labor Will Rule,* chap. 6, 441–94; for OPM, see 452–53.

10. In addition to Fraser's biography of Hillman, see Steve Fraser, "Sidney Hillman: Labor's Machiavelli," in Dubofsky and Van Tine, *Labor Leaders in America,* 207–33; and Pastorello, *Power among Them.* The 1939 biography by George Soule is titled *Sidney Hillman: Labor Statesman,* cited in Fraser, "Sidney Hillman," 232.

11. For Hillman seeking ER's political advice, see Fraser, *Labor Will Rule,* 363. For ER seeking advice about labor disputes, for example, with the Phillips-Jones shirt factory at Arthurdale, see Phillips to Raymond Kenny, 3 November; ER to Hillman, 12 November; Hillman to ER, 23 November; and ER to Hillman, 28 November 1938, folder 35, box 83, Correspondence, Sidney Hillman Papers 1930–1946, Amalgamated Clothing Workers of America Records (ACWAR) 1914–1980, 5619, Kheel Center for Labor-Management Documentation and Archives, Martin P. Catherwood Library, Cornell University (hereafter SHP). For an interesting account of ER's subsistence homestead plans with the ILGWU and Highstown, New Jersey, which Dubinsky did not encourage, see Dubinsky and Raskin, *David Dubinsky,* 204–7.

12. Lichtenstein, *Labor's War at Home,* 44–51, quotation 51; Zieger, *CIO,* 106–7. Beasley, *White House Press Conferences,* 186–87.

13. *New York Times,* 2 April 1941. Beasley, *White House Press Conferences,* 186–87. For more on the strikes, see Zieger, *CIO,* 127–30; Goodwin, *No Ordinary Time,* 230–31.

14. The labor situation leading up to Pearl Harbor is covered in Zieger, *CIO,* chap. 6; and Lichtenstein, *Labor's War at Home,* chaps. 4 and 5, esp. 67–70. "My Day," 24 November 1941.

15. Hillman's struggles are detailed in Fraser, *Labor Will Rule,* 483–90. For a concise summary of war policies and their effect on unions, see Kennedy, *Freedom from Fear,* 640–43.

16. Topics of positive stories include apprenticeship in "My Day," 7 May 1941, and union label in "My Day," 9 July 1941. Gallup polls are cited in Zieger, *CIO,* 116. The dispute with Pegler is found in "My Day," 8 January 1942; Westbrook Pegler, "Fair Enough" (syndicated column), 8 January 1942; *Time,* 19 January 1942; Beasley, *White House Press Conferences,* 251–52; Pegler, "Fair Enough," 19 May, 3 July 1942; *New York Times* review of *Native Land,* 12 May 1942. Pegler columns in box 21, James [Westbrook] Pegler Papers, Herbert Hoover Presidential Library, West Branch, IA. Advice is in ER to Carey, 7 July; Carey to ER, 18 July; and ER to Carey, 22 July 1942, folder Correspondence: Mrs. Roosevelt 1942, box 3, CIO Carey.

17. Textile Workers Union of America–CIO, *Proceedings of the Third Biennial Convention,* Carnegie Hall, New York City, 10–14 May 1943, 110–14. "My Day," 14 May 1943.

18. Kennedy, *Freedom from Fear,* 642–44 (poll results 643); Goodwin, *No Ordinary Time,* 439–41.

19. *New York Times,* 30 April and 9 May 1943. "My Day," 1, 17 May 1943.

20. "My Day," 3 June 1943. FDR quotation in Louis Stark, "WLB Kept in Power," *New York Times*, 4 June 1943. Also see Kennedy, *Freedom from Fear*, 642–44; Goodwin, *No Ordinary Time*, 442–43.

21. "My Day," 15, 18 June 1943. ER to Joseph P. Lash, 20 June 1943, in Joseph P. Lash and Eleanor Roosevelt, *A World of Love: Eleanor Roosevelt and Her Friends, 1943–1962* (Garden City, NY: Doubleday, 1984), 27; related letters on 20, 24. Kennedy, *Freedom from Fear*, 644.

22. "My Day," 14, 17 July 1943. Roosevelt, *This I Remember*, 305–6.

23. "My Day," 15 July, 26 August 1943, 14 January 1944. CIO, *Proceedings of the Sixth Constitutional Convention*, 1–5 November 1943, 215–17.

24. An overview of women's war work and government policy is found in Kessler-Harris, *Out to Work*, chap. 10, 273–301. Claudia D. Goldin finds a modest impact of the war on women's employment in "The Role of World War II in the Rise of Women's Employment," *American Economic Review* 81, no. 4 (1991): 741–56. An important study of differences within industries is Ruth Milkman, *Gender at Work: The Dynamics of Job Segregation by Sex during World War II* (Urbana: University of Illinois Press, 1987).

25. For discussion of ER's position on women, war work, and community services, see Goodwin, *No Ordinary Time*, 365–70, 415–18. ER to Lash, 29 September 1942, quotation 369. For the perspective of a UAW woman on the Willow Run visit, see Dorothy Haener in O'Farrell and Kornbluh, *Rocking the Boat*, 166.

26. Goodwin, *No Ordinary Time*, 369; statistics 416. "My Day," 29 January 1944, 15 January 1945.

27. Foner, *Women and the American Labor Movement*, 2:355. For the auto and electrical industries, see Milkman, *Gender at Work*; for equal pay, see 74–83.

28. Orleck, *Common Sense*, 166–67. "My Day," 18 January, 4 February 1943. Quotation from "My Day," 27 February 1943. ER to Lash, 16 June 1943, in Lash and Roosevelt, *A World of Love*, 24.

29. Orleck, *Common Sense*, 256–61; Kessler-Harris, *Gendering Labor History*, 88–89.

30. Lois Scharf, "ER and Feminism," in Hoff and Lightman, *Without Precedent*, 238, 245. ER to Rose Schneiderman, 11 February (quotation); ER to Frances Perkins, 11 February; ER to Perkins, 21 February; all 1944, reel 4, correspondence, Frances Perkins Papers, Columbia University.

31. Statistics in Milkman, *Gender at Work*, 84–90. For a comprehensive overview of women and unions during World War II, see Foner, *Women and the American Labor Movement*, vol. 2, chap. 19; for union leadership, see 366–67. Milkman presents a detailed analysis of the gains and the limits for women in the CIO, particularly the UAW and the UE, in *Gender at Work*, chap. 6.

32. *Advance* (ACWA), November 1941:5, June 1944: 18–19.

33. ACWA, *Report of the General Executive Board and Proceedings of the Fourteenth Biennial Convention*, Chicago, 15–19 May 1944, 137–43; "My Day," 20 May 1944. For more on Bellanca, see Nina Asher, "Dorothy Jacobs Bellanca: Women Clothing Workers and the Runaway Shop," in *A Needle, a Bobbin, a Strike*, ed. Joan M. Jensen and Sue Davidson (Philadelphia: Temple University Press, 1984), 195–226.

34. For women in union leadership see Foner, *Women and the American Labor Movement*, 2:367–68. ER to Carey, 9 December; Carey to ER, 15 December; and ER to Carey, 17 December 1943, folder Correspondence, box 3, CIO Carey.

35. CIO, *Final Proceedings of the Seventh Constitutional Convention*, Chicago, 20–24 November 1944, 110–14.

36. Goodwin, *No Ordinary Time*, 370–71; Black, *Casting Her Own Shadow*, 87. Eleanor Roosevelt, *If You Ask Me* (New York: D. Appleton-Century Company, 1946), 83. Thompson

to Carey, 11 April; and Carey to Thompson, 17 April 1944, folder Correspondence, box 3, CIO Carey. The record does not show whether a change was made.

37. Descriptions from William H. Harris, "A. Philip Randolph, Black Workers, and the Labor Movement," in Dubofsky and Van Tine, *Labor Leaders,* 258–59; Goodwin, *No Ordinary Time,* 161; Kennedy, *Freedom from Fear,* 763. On his haughtiness, see Harris, "A. Philip Randolph," 260. The profile of Randolph draws primarily on Anderson, *A. Philip Randolph.*

38. The number of porters is from Harris, "A. Philip Randolph," 262. Working conditions, the use of the name "George," and the process of organizing the union are described in Anderson, *A. Philip Randolph,* 153–68.

39. Anderson, *A. Philip Randolph,* 216–25; Randolph telegram to Walter White quoted 221. See Melinda Chateauvert, *Marching Together: Women of the Brotherhood of Sleeping Car Porters* (Urbana: University of Illinois Press, 1998). There were a small number of female union members who worked as maids, car cleaners, and "porterettes," but the union focused on the men; the largest, most visible and influential group of women were in the Ladies' Auxiliary.

40. For Randolph's politics, see Anderson, *A. Philip Randolph,* 343. For his change in goals and strategy, as well as ER's response, see ibid., 246–52; Lash, *Eleanor and Franklin,* 534; Goodwin, *No Ordinary Time,* 248–50; Kennedy, *Freedom from Fear,* 766–68.

41. Anderson, *A. Philip Randolph,* 241. Goodwin, *No Ordinary Time,* 247. For details of this organizational effort, see, for example, Anderson, *A. Philip Randolph,* 247–51.

42. Goodwin, *No Ordinary Time,* 249; Bethune to ER, 4 April 1941, 228. For differences, see Zieger, *CIO,* 84.

43. For an overview of racial tensions, see Zieger, *CIO,* 154–61.

44. Lash, *Eleanor and Franklin,* 532–33; Fraser, *Labor Will Rule,* 478–79.

45. Lash, *Eleanor and Franklin,* 533; Fraser, *Labor Will Rule,* 479; Goodwin, *No Ordinary Time,* 249.

46. Events surrounding Executive Order 8802 and ER's involvement are found in Lash, *Eleanor and Franklin,* 533–35; Anderson, *A. Philip Randolph,* 251–61; Goodwin, *No Ordinary Time,* 249–53. ER's letter to Randolph, 10 June 1941, and the Randolph quotation are both in *Pittsburgh Courier,* 21 June 1941, microfilm reel 34, vol. 1: 1933–1942, APRP.

47. "My Day," 18 June 1941.

48. Anderson, *A. Philip Randolph,* 256–58.

49. For the complete text of Executive Order 8802, see www.eeoc.gov. Lash, *Eleanor and Franklin,* 535. McLaurin in Anderson, *A. Philip Randolph,* 260.

50. Randolph, *The Black Worker,* September 1941. Hillman to ER, 7 November; and FDR to Hillman, 12 November 1941, folder 38, box 83, SHP; Lichtenstein, *Walter Reuther,* 172.

51. Kennedy, *Freedom from Fear,* 770. Also see Goodwin, *No Ordinary Time,* 445–46; Black, *Casting Her Own Shadow,* 91–92. The importance of race problems in the North and the impact of events in the 1930s and 1940s are brought to the forefront of the civil rights struggle in Thomas J. Sugrue, *Sweet Land of Liberty: The Forgotten Struggle for Civil Rights in the North* (New York: Random House, 2008). Sugrue discusses Belle Isle in *The Origins of the Urban Crisis: Race and Inequality in Postwar Detroit* (1996; reprint, Princeton: Princeton University Press, 2005), 29.

52. "My Day," 14 July 1943. Newspaper quotation in Black, *Casting Her Own Shadow,* 92. CIO Canteen, a social meeting place for soldiers and sailors during World War II, is discussed on 92–93. "My Day," 16 February 1944. Salmond, *Miss Lucy,* 105.

53. "My Day," 15 January 1945. For more on the Springer trip, see Richards, *Maida Springer,* 77–83. Quotation from Springer, interview by author, Pittsburgh, 28 October 2002.

54. ER to W. Reuther, 28 August 1942, folder 5, box 14, UAW President's Office: Walter P. Reuther Collection, ALUA (hereafter WPRC). Roosevelt, *This I Remember,* 256. Reuther quotation in Reuther Oral History Interview transcript, 21 February 1968, file 35, box 2, Papers 1966–1972, Frank Cormier and William Eaton Collection, ALUA. Also see Lichtenstein, *Walter Reuther,* 173.

55. The Reuther profile draws on Lichtenstein, *Walter Reuther,* 1–24; and Reuther, *The Brothers Reuther.*

56. Lichtenstein, *Walter Reuther,* 47; also see chap. 3, 25–46.

57. Ibid., 158. For more on these proposals, see ibid., chaps. 8 and 10, 196–98; Nelson Lichtenstein, *Labor's War at Home,* chap. 6; Reuther, *Brothers Reuther,* 225–30, 233. "My Day," 9 April 1942.

58. "My Day," 3 August 1943. ER to Anna Roosevelt, 1 August 1943, in Asbell, *Mother and Daughter,* 163. Lash and Roosevelt, *A World of Love,* 51. Malvina Thompson to Walter Reuther, 19 August; and Reuther to Bernard Baruch, telegrams, 23, 24 August 1943, folder 5, box 14, WPRC.

59. Walter Reuther to ER, 13 August; and ER to Walter Reuther, 27 September 1943, folder 5, box 14, WPRC.

60. FDR's speech reported in *New York Times,* 12 January 1944. ER's response in "My Day," 13 January 1944.

61. "My Day," 14 January 1944; Beasley, *White House Press Conferences,* 329. For more about the speech, see Kennedy, *Freedom from Fear,* 784–86.

62. On reconversion, see Goodwin, *No Ordinary Time,* 557–60. ER response, for example, in "My Day," 20 September 1944. Reuther to ER, 11 July; Malvina Thompson to Reuther, 29 May; Bernard Baruch to James Byrnes, 12 May; ER to Reuther, 13, 19 June; and Reuther to ER, 19 June 1944, folder 5, box 14, WPRC.

63. For reconversion ideas, see Reuther to ER, 11 July 1944; Baruch in Reuther to ER, 11, 13 July, 7 August 1944; Baruch to ER, 28 July 1944; Brewster Plant in Reuther to ER, 11 July; and ER to Reuther, 13 July 1944; Veterans' employment in ER to Reuther, 4 September; and Reuther to ER, 13 October 1944, all in folder 6, box 14, WPRC. For the Peace Production Board idea going to FDR, Goodwin cites a note from ER to FDR, 21 September 1943, in *No Ordinary Time,* 466.

64. Reuther to Thompson, 11 July 1944, folder 6, box 14, WPRC.

65. Lash, *Eleanor and Franklin,* 708–9.

66. For CIO-PAC and NCPAC, see Fraser, *Labor Will Rule,* 503–14; Lichtenstein, *Labor's War at Home,* 171–77. Salmond, *Miss Lucy,* 106–8. *New York Times,* 29 July 1944.

67. Fraser, *Labor Will Rule,* 520–21. ER's support for Dubinsky is also reported in Parmet, *Master of Seventh Avenue,* 198.

68. Hillman to ER, 17 April; and Dubinsky to ER, 23 May 1944, folder 2C, box 376, DDPR.

69. Lash, *Eleanor and Franklin,* 710. Amalgamated's Women's Voters' Special Edition, *The Advance,* 27 October 1944. The ILGWU in "My Day," 28 October 1944; ER to Dubinsky, 27 September; Dubinsky to ER, 12 October; and ER to Dubinsky, 11 November 1944, folder F2C, box 376, DDPR. For an analysis of the 1944 election and Hillman's role, see Fraser, *Labor Will Rule,* chap. 17, "Clear It with Sidney," 495–538; also see Lichtenstein, *Labor's War at Home,* 171–77.

70. CIO, *Final Proceedings of the Seventh Constitutional Convention,* Chicago, 20–24 November 1944, 110–14.

71. Roosevelt, *This I Remember,* 339. "My Day," 25 January, 1, 2, 16, and 25 February 1945. For the WFTU, see Lash, *Eleanor and Franklin,* 719. Reuther to ER, 3 April 1945, folder 15, box 193, WPRC. For FDR's death, see Lash, *Eleanor and Franklin,* 721.

72. Elisabeth Reuther Dickmeyer, *Reuther: A Daughter Strikes* (Southfield, MI: Spelman Publishers Division, 1989), 172. *Newsweek,* 30 April 1945. Eleanor Roosevelt, *This I Remember,* 348.

5. An Essential Element of Freedom

1. ER describes her schedule in Roosevelt, *Autobiography,* 305. "My Day," 26 October 1948.
2. ACWA, *Report of the General Executive Board and Proceedings of the Fourteenth Biennial Convention,* Chicago, 15–19 May 1944, 137–43.
3. "My Day," 19 April, 1 October, 1945. On labor see, for example, "My Day," 26 May 1945.
4. NCPAC in ER to Hillman, 2, 27 July 1945, box 83, SHP. ER to Dubinsky, 9 August 1945, file Dubinsky, David 1945–1952, ER General Correspondence 1945–1962, AERP. WTUL in "My Day," 9 October, 9 November 1945; Beasley et al., *Eleanor Roosevelt Encyclopedia,* 580. NAACP in Black, *Casting Her Own Shadow,* 96.
5. ER tells the story of her appointment in Roosevelt, *Autobiography,* 299–300. For her concerns about Truman, see Black, *Casting Her Own Shadow,* 55–60. Pegler's opposition is found in Lash, *Years Alone,* 41. ER was vehemently attacked by anticommunists and Protestant fundamentalists, and racism was a consistent theme; see Black, *Casting Her Own Shadow,* 133–34.
6. Economic and Social Council, Summary Record, E/CN.4/SR.66, 14 June 1948, Archives and Records Management Section, United Nations, New York, 4 (ARMS). For a comprehensive overview of work-related rights in the Universal Declaration of Human Rights see Johannes Morsink, *The Universal Declaration of Human Rights: Origins, Drafting, and Intent* (Philadelphia: University of Pennsylvania Press, 1999), chap. 5, 157–90. For ER's writings and speeches during this period, see Black, *Eleanor Roosevelt Papers,* vol. 1, 1945–1958, (New York: Charles Scribner's Sons, 2007).
7. For industrial power, see Kennedy, *Freedom from Fear,* 857; for effects on workers, see Lichtenstein, *Labor's War at Home,* 221–22. Reconversion politics, and the 1945 strikes against General Motors and the steel industry are covered extensively in Lichtenstein, *Walter Reuther,* chap. 11, 220–47; and Zieger, *CIO,* chap. 8, 212–52.
8. See Black, *Casting Her Own Shadow,* 51–84, for an analysis of ER's struggle over full employment and wage and price control policies with Truman and Wallace. ER pushed Truman for strong liberal policies, but he was inconsistent at best, and she turned to others in the administration. When her personal communications produced no results, she took her criticisms directly to the public through her column.
9. "My Day," 19 September 1945. Criticism in Reuther to ER, 15 October; ER to Reuther, 25 October 1945, folder 15, box 193, WPRC.
10. ER to Reuther, 26 June; and Reuther to ER, 2 July 1945, folder 15, box 193, WPRC. Seniority and equal pay are addressed in "My Day," 10 July 1945.
11. Reuther, *Brothers Reuther,* 262–63; also see UAW *Ammunition,* January 1947. "My Day," 29 January 1947.
12. Lichtenstein, *Labor's War at Home,* 220–21. ER to Truman, 20 November 1945, in Steve Neal, ed., *Eleanor and Harry: The Correspondence of Eleanor Roosevelt and Harry S. Truman* (New York: Scribner, 2002), 45–47. See also Black, *Casting Her Own Shadow,* 71–73.
13. "My Day," 22 April 1946. ER to Walter Reuther, 18 December 1945, folder 15, box 193, WPRC; Reuther, *Brothers Reuther,* 254. "My Day," 20, 27 September 1945.
14. Black, *Casting Her Own Shadow,* 72–73. "My Day," 8, 10 December 1945.
15. Zieger, *CIO,* 223–25; Lichtenstein, *Labor's War at Home,* 228–30. Black, *Casting Her Own Shadow,* 73–75. "My Day," 23 February 1946.

16. For the South and Operation Dixie, see Zieger, *CIO,* 227–41; Pastorello, *Power among Them,* 138–44. For Mason's role, see Salmond, *Miss Lucy,* chap. 7, 124–45. "My Day," 13 December 1945.

17. Fraser, *Labor Will Rule,* 571. "My Day," 5 April 1946. ER to Truman, 27 April 1946, in Roosevelt, Truman, and Neal, *Eleanor and Harry,* 69.

18. "My Day," 22 April 1946. Black, *Casting Her Own Shadow,* 75; Lichtenstein, *Walter Reuther,* 254. Truman's speech can be found at www.historymatters.gmu.edu.

19. ER to Truman, 27 May 1946, in Neal, *Eleanor and Harry,* 70–72, and "My Day," 28, 29 May 1946. ER devoted seven "My Day" columns to these two strikes in May 1946.

20. "My Day," 20, 9, 25 May 1946.

21. Fraser, *Labor Will Rule,* 567. Lichtenstein, *Walter Reuther,* 254–55, 304–5. "My Day," 5 June 1946.

22. Fraser, *Labor Will Rule,* 573. "My Day," 13 July 1946.

23. Lichtenstein, *Walter Reuther,* 255–57. "My Day," 19, 23, 27 November 1946.

24. Archie Robinson and George Meany, *George Meany and His Times: A Biography* (New York: Simon and Schuster, 1981), 143. "My Day," 7, 9, 10, 17 December 1946.

25. Neal, *Eleanor and Harry,* 82. Lichtenstein, *Walter Reuther,* 257. Zieger, *CIO,* 245–46. "My Day," 12 April 1947.

26. Parmet, *Master of Seventh Avenue,* 215–16; Zieger, *CIO,* 249. "My Day," 24 April 1947. See Taft-Harley Act, Labor-Management Relations Act, 80 Pub.L. 101; 61 Stat. 136 (1947).

27. "My Day," 10, 14 June 1947. Parmet, *Master of Seventh Avenue,* 217.

28. "My Day," 24, 26 June, 25 August 1947. For correspondence regarding Taft-Hartley, see ER and Albert Harris in Allida M. Black, ed., *Courage in a Dangerous World: The Political Writings of Eleanor Roosevelt* (New York: Columbia University Press, 1999), 240–43.

29. For overviews of the impact of Taft-Hartley, see Ellen Schrecker, "Labor and the Cold War, the Legacy of McCarthyism" in *American Labor and the Cold War: Grassroots Politics and Postwar Political Culture,* ed. Robert W. Cherny, William Issel, and Kieran Walsh Taylor (New Brunswick: Rutgers University Press, 2004), 7–24; Nelson Lichtenstein, *State of the Union: A Century of American Labor* (Princeton: Princeton University Press, 2003), 114–18; and Zieger, *CIO,* 249–52. For the AF of L, see Robinson and Meany, *George Meany,* chap. 8, 140–61; on Dubinsky and the ILGWU, see Parmet, *Master of Seventh Avenue,* 217; on Reuther and the UAW, see Lichtenstein, *Walter Reuther,* 261–69; on the UE, see Ronald W. Schatz, *The Electrical Workers: A History of Labor at General Electric and Westinghouse, 1923–1960* (Urbana: University of Illinois Press, 1983), 178–86.

30. "My Day," 25 August, 6 September 1947.

31. Reuther, *Brothers Reuther,* 276–78; Lichtenstein, *Walter Reuther,* 271–75. "My Day," 29 April 1948. There is no correspondence between ER and Reuther at this time, but she was surely in touch with her friend and his family. Her correspondence with "Dear Walter" ends in 1947 and does not resume until 1954.

32. Zieger, *CIO,* 266–77. Parmet, *Master of Seventh Avenue,* 219–21. Schneiderman to ER, 19 August 1948, General Correspondence 1945–1962, AERP.

33. Lash, *Years Alone,* chap. 6, 138–54; Neal, *Eleanor and Harry,* 149–50; Black, *Casting Her Own Shadow,* 82–83. For the ad, see *New York Times,* 1 November 1948. Election results in Lichtenstein, *Walter Reuther,* 305–6; Robinson and Meany, *George Meany,* 156–57.

34. For the early years after the war, see Zieger, *CIO,* 264–66; Robinson and Meany, *George Meany,* 133–37. For more on ER and the Truman Doctrine, see Lash, *Years Alone,* 94–100. ER to Reuther, 29 April; and Reuther to ER, 13 May 1947, folder 1, box 464, WPRC.

35. Fraser, *Labor Will Rule,* 543–44.

36. Lash, *Years Alone*, 62. Also see Mary Ann Glendon, *A World Made New: Eleanor Roosevelt and the Universal Declaration of Human Rights* (New York: Random House, 2001), 43. Both authors acknowledge ER's importance in persuading the State Department to include economic and social rights in the document. John Humphrey, director of the UN Human Rights Division, concluded that ER was the most important person in the human rights program during its formative years; see Glendon, *World Made New*, 33. Johannes Morsink has concluded that the sections on work-related rights took a "socialist shape," which he attributes to the Latin American and communist delegations, Humphrey's socialism, and French delegate René Cassin's being a trade unionist. He does not mention ER's trade union status or ties. Morsink, *Universal Declaration of Human Rights*, 157. To put ER's work during this period in perspective, see Black, *Eleanor Roosevelt Papers*, vol. 1.

37. There is no full biography of James B. Carey despite his central role in the labor movement, the CIO, and the electrical workers' unions. This profile draws on Carey, COHC; Bob Golon, Biography of James B. Carey, www.smlr.rutgers.edu/library; and IUE Administrative History, Records of the President's Office of the IUE, 1938–1965, International Union of Electronic, Electrical, Salaried, Machine & Furniture Workers Collection, SCUA, Rutgers University (hereafter IUE Carey).

38. Carey, COHC, interview, 96–97. Carey to Elliot Roosevelt, 26 August 1949, folder Correspondence: Mrs. Roosevelt 1949; and Carey to ER, 11 September 1945, folder Correspondence: Mrs. Roosevelt 1945, box 3, CIO Carey. Carey's correspondence with ER doesn't begin until 1942, but her letters are addressed to "Dear Jim," with frequent references to his family. There is limited correspondence between 1946 and 1948, yet this is the largest personal correspondence file in the Carey collection at Wayne State University.

39. Carey to ER, 13 March; Carey to ER, 27 June; ER to Carey, 5 July 1945; and Declarations of the World Trade Union Conference, 5–17 February 1945, 19, all in box 3, CIO Carey.

40. "My Day," 20, 21, 22 June 1945. Dubinsky to ER, 28 June; ER to Dubinsky, 20 June; Dubinsky to ER, 24 July; ER to Dubinsky, 9 August; and John L. Childs to Dubinsky, 24 August 1945, all in folder 2, box 376, DDPR.

41. Murray's remark is taken from Joseph M. Proskauer, *A Segment of My Times* (New York: Farrar, Straus, 1950), 225, cited in William Korey, *NGOs and the Universal Declaration of Human Rights: A Curious Grapevine* (New York: St. Martin's Press, 1998), 37–42. The only other reference to unions in Korey's book is to the International Confederation of Free Trade Unions in 1960. Also see Glendon, *World Made New*, 17.

42. Beasley, *White House Press Conferences*, 335–36. Reports on Nongovernmental Organizations, box 65, folder 50-4-2-2-5-1, RAG 1, Central Registry 1946–1947, ARMS. The other organizations included the International Chamber of Commerce, the International Cooperative Alliance, the International Federation of Agricultural Producers, and the Inter-Parliamentary Union.

43. Glendon, *World Made New*, 27–31; for the importance of informal gatherings, 114–15; French translation, 31. ER describes these events in Roosevelt, *Autobiography*, chaps. 30–32, 299–323.

44. "My Day," 19 January 1946, 13 February 1945.

45. *Life and Labor Bulletin* (WTUL), June 1946, 1, 5.

46. Roosevelt, *Autobiography*, 305. Lash, *Years Alone*, 49. Lois Scharf, "ER and Feminism," in Hoff and Lightman, *Without Precedent*, 243–44. Morsink, *Universal Declaration of Human Rights*, 116–17.

47. Carey to ER, 17 July; ER to Carey, 23 July 1946, box 3, CIO Carey. Woll to ER, 27 November; ER to Woll, 4 December; Woll to ER, 10 December 1946; and AF of L International

Bill of Rights, August 1946, all in file W–Z, November–December 1946, United Nations Correspondence and Publications 1945–1955, AERP.

48. "My Day," 24 January 1947. Woll to Tryvge Lie, 9 August 1946; and UN Press Release, 27 February 1947, in S-0544-0018-01, Department of Economic and Social Affairs, Committee-Non Governmental Organizations, ARMS. For an example see "Report on the AF of L Activities as Consultants to the Economic and Social Council of the United Nations," 12 May 1947, box 52, folder 13, Record Group 2-027, Office of the President, George Meany 1947–1960, George Meany Memorial Archives, Siler Spring (hereafter OPGM).

49. I found no correspondence between Sender and ER, but there was one picture of them together published in *Tony Sender, 1888–1964: Rebel, Democrat, Cosmopolitan,* exhibition catalogue (Frankfurt am Main: Historisches Museum, 1992). For more information on Sender, see Toni Sender Papers 1934–1964, Wisconsin Historical Society, Madison (TSP). Also see Richard Critchfield, "Toni Sender: Feminist, Socialist, Internationalist," *History of European Ideas* 15, no. 4–6 (1992): 701–5. Her first name is spelled both Tony and Toni in different official forms. ER's reference to Sender is found in Eleanor Roosevelt and William A. De Witt, *UN: Today and Tomorrow* (New York: Harper, 1953).

50. Glendon, *World Made New,* 32–33.

51. "My Day," 18, 20 October 1947. Sender, "Further Report on Trade Union Rights," 31 October 1947, 2, folder 1947–49, box 13, TSP.

52. Glendon, *World Made New,* 99–102. "My Day," 13 January 1948.

53. For preparation, see Hendrick to ER, 9 April; Winslow to ER, 17 April; and Schwelb to ER, 15 April 1948, draft response, all in file General Correspondence January–May 1948, United Nations Correspondence and Publications 1945–1955, AERP. Glendon, *World Made New,* 107–11, 115–16. Glendon does not specifically discuss trade union rights. ER quotation, Human Rights Commission Third Session, E/CN.4/SR.64, 17 June 1948, 5–6, ARMS.

54. Sender quotation in United Nations Economic and Social Council, Summary Record, E/CN.4/SR.61, 23 June 1948, 10, AERP. ER quotation in E/CN.4/SR.66, 14 June 1948, 3–4, ARMS.

55. For a full discussion of the open shop and strike debates, see Morsink, *Universal Declaration of Human Rights,* 174–90.

56. Mann to ER, 27 February; Carey to ER, 4 May; ER to Carey, 11 May; and Carey to ER, 11 June 1948, all in box 3, CIO Carey. "My Day," 3 June, 22 September, 1 October 1948. The CIO and the AF of L were also meeting in Europe at conferences to support the Marshall Plan; see Parmet, *Master of Seventh Avenue,* 232.

57. Glendon, *World Made New,* 130–31. For the full fall session, see ibid., chap. 8, 123–142; Lash, *Years Alone,* 77–81. For staff views of ER, see Glendon, *World Made New,* 134–35. Unions discussed in "My Day," 19, 26 October, 13, 15 November 1948.

58. "My Day," 19, 22 November 1948. Glendon, *World Made New,* 159–60. ER devoted fifteen "My Day" columns to the UN negotiations between 18 November and 10 December 1948; see Black, *Eleanor Roosevelt Papers,* 1:939–71.

59. "My Day," 29 November 1948. For a discussion of women and the language in the declaration, see Morsink, *Universal Declaration of Human Rights,* 116–29; Lash, *Years Alone,* 70. Also see Glendon, *World Made New,* 90–91, 111–12; number of meetings on 161–62.

60. Details of the final vote on the declaration are drawn from Glendon, *World Made New,* 163–71; and Lash, *Years Alone,* 78–79.

61. Glendon, *World Made New,* 166–67. For ER's statement before the General Assembly, see Black, *Eleanor Roosevelt Papers,* 1:972. Glendon, *World Made New,* 170; Lash, *Years*

Alone, 79. For the complete Universal Declaration of Human Rights, see Black, *Courage in a Dangerous World,* 149–55.

62. ER to Mathew Woll, 20 December 1948, file Miscellaneous, General Correspondence 1945–1962; and Schneiderman to ER, 15 December 1948, file Schneiderman, Rose 1947–52, AERP. Philip Murrary to Nobel Committee, Norwegian Parliament, 19 August 1949, folder Correspondence Mrs. Roosevelt, box 3, CIO Carey. No peace prize was awarded for 1948.

63. "My Day," 22 December 1948.

6. Pointing the Way

1. "My Day," 12 December 1955. "The Marksman," *Time,* 19 December 1955.
2. The convention description is drawn from "Armistice at the Armory," *Time,* 19 December 1955; Zieger, *CIO,* 369. "My Day," 12 December 1955. George Meany quoted in AFL-CIO, *Proceedings from the First Constitutional Convention,* New York, 1–5 December 1955, 143. A video of ER's speech is available at the Franklin Roosevelt Presidential Library, Hyde Park, NY.
3. AFL-CIO, *Proceedings from the First Constitutional Convention,* 143–45.
4. "My Day," 25 September, 20 June 1952. AFL-CIO, *Proceedings from the First Constitutional Convention,* 145.
5. AFL-CIO, *Proceedings from the First Constitutional Convention,* 145.
6. "My Day," 13 January 1949 (WTUL); "My Day," 1 January 1951, 23 May 1952 (ILGWU); "My Day," 10 September 1952; *Chemical Worker* (ICWU) 12, no. 9 (1952).
7. IUE-CIO, *Proceedings of the Third Annual Convention,* Buffalo, 17–21 September 1951, 83–89. IUE-CIO *News,* 10, 24 September 1951; "My Day," 21 September 1951.
8. ER to Murray, 19 May 1952; Carey to ER, 2 June 1952; and ER to Carey, telegram, 3 June 1952, folder Correspondence Mrs. Roosevelt 1951–1952, box 3, CIO Carey. Others invited to the meeting at her apartment included William Green, AF of L; David Dubinsky, ILGWU; Jacob Potofsky, ACWA; and George Harrison, Railway and Steamship Clerks.
9. "My Day," 21 May 1952. A similar dilemma was posed when some wanted to repeat an article declaring that men and women have equal rights. The technical problem had to do with reiterating already declared rights, but it again put ER in the position of voting against something that she supported.
10. For the description of the convention, see Lash, *Years Alone,* 209–11; and "My Day," 23 July 1952. A defense of Stevenson is in "My Day," 20 September 1952. Lash says it is unknown why she was not asked to campaign in *Years Alone,* 213. Zieger, *CIO,* 309–10. During this period ER's close political involvement with labor was demonstrated when two of her sons ran for political office. In 1949 Franklin Jr. won a congressional seat in Manhattan on Dubinsky's Liberal Party ticket; see Lash, *Years Alone,* 176; and "My Day," 19 May 1949. She worked even more closely with Dubinsky after 1954, when Franklin lost his bid for governor of New York in the primary and for attorney general in November in a fight with Tammany Hall boss Carmine DeSapio; see Parmet, *Master of Seventh Avenue,* 256–57; and Lash, *Years Alone,* 274–75. ER helped her son James secure labor support in his unsuccessful bid for governor of California in 1950; see "My Day," 20, 21, 23 January 1950. This was the same election in which her friend Helen Gahagan Douglas lost her Senate race against Richard M. Nixon. James went on to win a congressional seat from Los Angeles in 1954.
11. Lash, *Years Alone,* 217, 220–24. For Reuther's relationship to the American Association for the United Nations, see Reuther, *Brothers Reuther,* 358. ER to Walter Reuther, 8 February 1954; and Reuther to ER, 15 February 1954, folder 1, box 464, WPRC. "My Day," 11, 17 November 1953.

12. Containment of the Soviet Union dominated U.S. foreign policy. The transfer of that containment theory to the protection of the home in domestic policy is persuasively argued by Elaine T. May, *Homeward Bound: American Families in the Cold War Era* (New York: Basic Books, 2008). The relationship between the cold war, McCarthyism, and the labor movement continues to be a complicated and controversial subject among labor historians. For a concise review of the issues, see Ellen Schrecker, "Labor and the Cold War: The Legacy of McCarthyism," in Cherny, Issel, and Taylor, *American Labor and the Cold War,* 7–24; for the comprehensiveness of the containment approach, see 10. For an extensive bibliography, see John Earl Haynes, "American Communism and Anti-Communism: A Historian's Bibliography and Guide to the Literature," chap. 5, on *Communism and the American Labor Movement,* www.johnearlhaynes.org. Poll numbers are cited in Black, *Casting Her Own Shadow,* 152.

13. For discussion of the CIO's decision to expel the left-led unions and the process that was used, see Zieger, *CIO,* 277–93 (Carey, 285, fn. 94); Schrecker, "Labor and the Cold War," 10–12; Ronald W. Schatz, "Philip Murray," in Dubofsky and Van Tine, *Labor Leaders in America,* 252–53. Also see Peter Weiler, "The United States, International Labor, and the Cold War: The Breakup of the International Federation of Trade Unions," *Diplomatic History* 5, (Winter 1981): 1–22. One of the most controversial chapters in labor's cold war history involves the extent to which the FBI, the CIA, and the State Department secretly transferred money to unions for covert support of U.S. foreign policy. Much of the debate and evidence deal with the AF of L's foreign operations under Jay Lovestone, whose relationship with Reuther and the CIO was vitriolic; see, for example, Ted Morgan, *A Covert Life: Jay Lovestone, Communist, Anti-communist, and Spymaster* (New York: Random House, 1999). Yevette Richards concludes that Maida Springer was unaware of any money for her programs in Africa being channeled from the CIA through the ILGWU or AFL-CIO and suggests a more complex view of international labor relations; Richards, *Maida Springer,* 6–11. I found no evidence that ER was aware of government payments in domestic or foreign affairs.

14. For the UE-IUE confrontations at the local and company levels, see, for example, essays in Cherny, Issel, and Taylor, *American Labor and The Cold War;* and Schatz, *Electrical Workers.* Mary Callahan in O'Farrell and Kornbluh, *Rocking the Boat,* 124. For an example of the Catholic movement, see Richard Gid Powers, *Not without Honor: The History of American Anticommunism* (New Haven: Yale University Press, 1998), 193–97.

15. Allida Black provides a strong case for ER's defense of civil liberties, in which she was often at odds with other liberals; see Black, *Casting Her Own Shadow,* 151–76. She does not address ER's support for the CIO's expulsion of left-led unions. For an example of ER's asking Carey for advice, see the issue of the Waltham Watch Company in ER to Carey, 11 January 1949; and Carey to ER, 4 February 1949, folder 1949; or the response to an "If You Ask Me" column by ER in *McCall's* magazine, ER to Carey, 13 April 1950; and Carey to ER, 24 April 1950, folder 1950, both in box 3, CIO Carey. Carey to ER, 22 November 1949, folder 1949, box 3, CIO Carey. For the family visit, see "My Day," 23 December 1949. For the television show, see ER to Carey, 27 March 1950; and *Today with Mrs. Roosevelt* transcript, 26 February 1950, both in folder 1950, box 3, CIO Carey.

16. At the time McCarthy was unable to substantiate his accusations, although many of those charged had been associated in some way with the Communist Party. New scholarship and data from the Soviet archives have vindicated some of those charges, but innocent people were caught up in the anticommunist net, and careers and lives were ruined. See Ellen Schrecker, "Comments on John Earl Haynes' 'The Cold War Debate Continues,'" www.fas.harvard.edu. Historian Richard Gid Powers draws a helpful distinction between cold war

anticommunism, including liberal anticommunism, and the destructive excesses of McCarthyism, in *Not without Honor,* chap. 8, 191–233, and chap. 9, 235–72. ER's meeting is in Justine Polier to Philip Murray, 9 June 1950; Carey to Polier, telegram, 3 July 1950; and Polier to Carey, 3 July 1950, folder 1950, box 3, CIO Carey. Invitations were sent by Justine Polier, a friend of ER's from her days at the Women's Trade Union League, as well as a New York City children's court judge; see Beasley, Shulman, and Beasley, *Eleanor Roosevelt Encyclopedia,* 406–7.

17. Carey speech and ER note, "A Time to Get Angry: A Counter Offensive to the Attack on American Education," 2 March 1953, folder CAP-Carey, General Correspondence 1945–1962, AERP. Meany quotation in Robinson and Meany, *George Meany,* 127. David Dubinsky, "Instead of the McCarthy Method," *New York Times,* 26 July 1953.

18. For ER's position, see Neal, *Eleanor and Harry,* 173. For more on Wilson, see Zieger, *CIO,* 295–96.

19. "My Day," 7 March 1951.

20. IUE-CIO, *Proceedings of the Third Annual Convention,* 83–89.

21. Ibid., 88. *News* (IUE-CIO), 24 September 1951; "My Day," 21 September 1951.

22. "My Day," 25 March 1954; also see "Virginia Foster Durr," in Beasley, Shulman, and Beasley, *Eleanor Roosevelt Encyclopedia,* 148–51, for their differences during this period.

23. "My Day," 15 April 1954. Welch quotation in Powers, *Not without Honor,* 270. A summary of McCarthy's career and link to the 1953–54 congressional committee hearings can be found at www.senate.gov.

24. CIO, *Proceedings of the Sixteenth Constitutional Convention,* Los Angeles, 6–10 December 1954, 465. "My Day," 10, 11 December 1954.

25. Schrecker, "Labor and the Cold War," 14–15. Lichtenstein, *Walter Reuther,* 331–33; quote from 331.

26. Victor Reuther, interview by author, 18 July 2002, Washington, DC.

27. The failure of the larger social welfare system to develop and the limits of bargaining for benefits company by company are discussed by Lichtenstein, *State of the Union,* 125–28; Zieger, *CIO,* 305, 322. For views on Sweden, see Lichtenstein, *Walter Reuther,* 337–38; "My Day," 13 June 1950, 20 June 1952.

28. "My Day," 30 August, 5 September, 24 October, 3 November 1949.

29. For analysis of the consequences of the treaty, see Lichtenstein, *Walter Reuther,* chap. 13, 271–98. "My Day," 4 February, 6 May 1950.

30. "My Day," 24 March 1949. There is little correspondence between ER and Walter Reuther from 1949 to 1954. Her columns, coupled with the increase and content of their correspondence and visits after 1954, however, suggest that correspondence from the earlier period may have been lost, or perhaps they were in more direct contact. In contrast, with Jim Carey there is a personal correspondence but little mention in her columns of the labor issues involved in the electrical products industry, despite Carey's elevation to head the new IUE and their mutual concerns about communist influence.

31. Reuther, *Brothers Reuther,* 284–91. Lichtenstein, *Walter Reuther,* 272. "My Day," 24 December 1949.

32. "My Day," 19, 24 December 1949.

33. Zieger, *CIO,* 294–97. "My Day," 9 February 1951.

34. "My Day," 7, 9 (quotation), 13, 15, 19 March 1951. Preparation for television appearance, 8 March 1951, folder 1951, box 3, CIO Carey.

35. "My Day," 4, 20 June 1952.

36. "My Day," 3 November 1949. Dubofsky and Van Tine, *Labor Leaders,* 204. "My Day," 4 March 1950.

37. "My Day," 7, 21 September 1953.
38. "My Day," 6 September 1954, 31 December 1951.
39. Dorothy Sue Cobble's pathbreaking history provides a critical continuity to union women's progress and leadership that is missing from earlier works on women's labor history; see Cobble, *Other Women's Movement,* 27–49. While the number of women in the labor force declined for a short time after World War II, women workers soon surpassed their wartime peak of representing 36 percent of the labor force. The number of women union members tripled from fewer than 1 million in the late 1930s to over 3.5 million by the mid-1950s. By 1956, 18 percent of all union members were women, doubling the proportion in 1940. Statistics cited in Orleck, *Common Sense,* 253; and Cobble, *Other Women's Movement,* 16–17. To learn more about the limits of this progress during World War II, see Milkman, *Gender at Work.*
40. "My Day," 13 January 1949.
41. For an analysis of the decline of the WTUL, see Orleck, *Common Sense,* 258–67.
42. "My Day," 6 June 1949. Even the retirement lunch was controversial. League leader Elizabeth Christman opposed the fancy location, midday timing, and $6 fee, all of which made it inaccessible to working women. Part of the funds, however, went to help pay for Schneiderman's retirement, for, ironically, she was not eligible for Social Security benefits. See Endelman, *Solidarity Forever,* 251.
43. Orleck, *Common Sense,* 265. Parmet, *Master of Seventh Avenue,* 244; Orleck, *Common Sense,* 267. Endelman, *Solidarity Forever,* 252–53. Gerel Rubien to ER, 29 April 1955, folder WTUL, General Correspondence 1945–1962, AERP.
44. Mason, *To Win These Rights;* Salmond, *Miss Lucy,* 168–71. For Smith's activities, see Kornbluh, *A New Deal,* 113, 116; Lyn Goldfarb, "Hilda Worthington Smith, a Tribute," in Smith, *Selected Poems,* xvii. Smith wrote to ER about the school, the labor education bill, and her political activities; see, for example, Smith to ER, 13 November 1947 and 10 March 1948 (school and labor education); Smith to ER, 3 January and 23 February 1956; ER to Smith, 2 March 1956; and press release, 14 April 1956 (political activities), all in folder 413, box 25, Hilda Worthington Smith Papers, Schlesinger Library on the History of Women in America, Radcliffe Institute, Harvard University (HWSP).
45. Cobble, *Other Women's Movement,* 7, 50.
46. Ibid., 19, 40–42 (UAW); 148 (IUE, ACWA). The Springer quotation is in O'Farrell and Kornbluh, *Rocking the Boat,* 99.
47. Evelyn Dubrow, interview by author, 19 July 2002, Washington, DC. Maida Springer-Kemp, interview by author, 28 October 2002, Pittsburgh; Fair Employment Practices Committee event in O'Farrell and Kornbluh, *Rocking the Boat,* 94–95. Mark Starr to ER, 11 October 1955, folder ILGWU 1953–1956, General Correspondence 1945–1962, AERP.
48. Mark Starr to ER, 12 February 1957, folder ILGWU, 1951–1961, General Correspondence 1945–1962, AERP. For the importance of the women's auxiliaries, see Cobble, *Other Women's Movement,* 23–25; Chateauvert, *Marching Together.* Tillie Olsen, interview by author, 22 May 2003, Berkeley; see, for example, Tillie Olsen, *Yonnondio* (New York: Delacorte Press/Seymour Lawrence, 1974), and *Silences* (New York: Delacorte Press/Seymour Lawrence, 1978). Carey to ER, 11 December 1957, box 11 Correspondence, January 1957–December 1960, IUE Carey Papers.
49. Cobble, *Other Women's Movement,* 63–66. "My Day," 25 May 1951.
50. Scharf, "ER and Feminism," in Hoff and Lightman, *Without Precedent,* 245–46. "My Day," 7 June 1951. Scharf found ER's position unique, but also ironic, because it was male union leaders who sought protective legislation to protect men's jobs. ER's narrow focus was lamentable, writes Scharf, but understandable for the time. The women Cobble introduces offer

a missing perspective, supporting ER, as they pursued multiple strategies to accommodate complex problems that they thought the ERA would not resolve; Cobble, *Other Women's Movement.*

51. This profile draws on Esther Peterson and Winifred Conkling, *Restless: The Memoirs of Labor and Consumer Activist Esther Peterson* (Washington, DC: Care Publishing, 1995); Kornbluh and O'Farrell, "You Can't Giddyup by Saying Whoa," *Labor's Heritage* 5, no. 4 (Spring 1991): 38–59; and O'Farrell and Kornbluh, *Rocking the Boat,* 58–83. For a summary of her life and analysis and discussion of her contribution to the "other" women's movement, see Cobble, *Other Women's Movement.* Four interviews were also conducted with Peterson in 2003 and 2004 by the author, Joyce L. Kornbluh, and J. Suzanne Moore, available in the Esther Peterson Papers, Schlesinger Library on the History of Women in America, Radcliffe Institute, Harvard University.

52. Peterson in O'Farrell and Kornbluh, *Rocking the Boat,* 65.

53. Ibid., 79–80.

54. Lash, *Years Alone,* 192. "My Day,"13 June 1950. Peterson did not mention ER's visit in her autobiography, nor did ER comment on meeting Peterson in Sweden. The guest list for the embassy dinner is in Trips File Sweden 1950, United Nations Correspondence and Publications 1945–1955, AERP. A letter from Peterson to Hilda Smith written from Bromma, Sweden, is undated but appears to be from this trip; see folder 413, box 25, HWSP.

55. Phil Murray to ER, 9 August 1945, folder 15, box 173, Philip Murray Papers, American Catholic History Research Center and University Archives, Catholic University, Washington, DC. Peterson and Conkling, *Restless,* 81, 84–85. "Anti-Communist Workers of the World Unite," *Life* 27, 12 December 1949, 54–55. Kornbluh and O'Farrell, "You Can't Giddyup by Saying Whoa," 50–54; Richards, *Maida Springer,* 95–96.

56. Peterson and Conkling, *Restless,* 93–94. Peterson was warned by friends about the problems facing women within the unions, and she fought Carey's initial offer to pay her less than the man who had previously held the job. Cobble, *Other Women's Movement,* 147–48.

57. Esther Peterson to ER, 22 July 1958, Folder Esther Peterson 1958–1962, General Correspondence 1953–1962, AERP.

58. Ronald W. Schatz, "Philip Murray," 256. "My Day," 13, 24 November 1952.

59. "My Day," 24 November, 4 December 1952.

60. Lichtenstein, *Walter Reuther,* 322. "My Day," 6 December 1952.

61. Zieger, *CIO,* 304, 359; the merger process is discussed 360–69.

62. "My Day," 29 January, 5 May, 9 December 1955.

63. O'Farrell and Kornbluh, *Rocking the Boat,* 99–103; Pauli Murray to ER, 16 December 1955, file Murray, Folder A–Mz WE 1953–1956, ER General Correspondence 1953–1962, AERP. AFL-CIO, *Proceedings:* 143. "My Day," 12 December 1955.

7. We Have Something to Offer

1. Walter Reuther's daughter Lisa describes the trip to Val-Kill in Elisabeth Reuther Dickmeyer, *Putting the World Together,* chap. 24, 170–77.

2. Ibid., 172–73, Halsted quotation 172.

3. Reuther to ER, 29 July 1958, folder 16, box 193, WPRC. The Republican attacks are described in Lichtenstein, *Walter Reuther,* 346–49; and John Barnard, *American Vanguard: The United Autoworkers during the Reuther Years, 1935–1970* (Detroit: Wayne State University Press, 2004), 348–49.

4. Reuther to ER, 29 July 1958.

5. ER quotation from ACWA, *Twentieth Biennial Convention: GEB Report and Proceedings,* Washington, DC, 21–25 May 1956, 199. The extent of ER's relationship with Jim Carey is less clear than her relationship with Reuther. While she continued to seek Carey's advice (they maintained their correspondence and he visited Val-Kill with his family), ER did not comment on his collective bargaining and organizing successes, for example, the strike he won in 1956, or the disastrous one he lost in 1960. He did not appear to participate in her political and international discussions at this time. Carey had a volatile relationship with George Meany, and he increasingly alienated the strong local leaders in his union as he sought more control by questionable means and created hostile bargaining situations. Correspondence between ER and Marge Carey, as well as with May Reuther, suggests a great deal of family stress and instability. ER appears sympathetic in private, but not involved publicly. See IUE Administrative History, IUE Carey; May Reuther to ER, 19 September 1958, folder Mr. & Mrs. Reuther 1957–1959, General Correspondence 1945–1962, AERP. Marge Carey to ER, 7 April, 7 May, 7 August 1958, 27 August 1959, file Capannell–Caribbean 1957–1962, General Correspondence 1945–1962, AERP.

6. ER summarized her position on the importance of economic aid in Eleanor Roosevelt, *India and the Awakening East* (New York: Harper, 1953), 225–26. For Reuther's position, see Lichtenstein, *Walter Reuther,* 335; from the UAW executive board minutes, 3 May 1956, quotation 342. Other peace programs Reuther proposed are discussed in Barnard, *American Vanguard,* 343–44.

7. Abe Raskin, "Meany Says Nehru and Tito Aid Reds," *New York Times,* 14 December 1955; "My Day," 19 December 1955. Also see Lichtenstein, *Walter Reuther,* 340–41.

8. Roosevelt, *India,* 101–207 (Nehru). Lash, *Years Alone,* 231–32 (Tito); and "My Day," 31 July 1953. For Nehru's visit to Moscow, see "My Day," 10 June 1955. "My Day," 19 December 1955.

9. Raskin, *New York Times,* 14 December 1955. Morgan, *A Covert Life,* 288. Lichtenstein, *Walter Reuther,* 341.

10. In addition to India, this trip included Lebanon, Israel, Pakistan, and Indonesia; see Lash, *Years Alone,* 199–202. Roosevelt, *India,* chap. 5, 101–207; see, for example, 207 (Nehru), 225 (aid). The India trip was chronicled in "My Day" columns from 3 to 25 March 1952.

11. For Reuther's trip, see Lichtenstein, *Walter Reuther,* 341–42; Reuther, *Brothers Reuther,* 386–89; Barnard, *American Vanguard,* 343. UAW executive council meeting, 3 May 1956, quotation in Lichtenstein, *Walter Reuther,* 342.

12. "My Day," 24 May 1956. ACWA, *Twentieth Biennial Convention: GEB Report and Proceedings; Advance* (ACWA), 1 June 1956. For ER's friendship with Bessie Hillman, see Pastorello, *Power among Them,* 129–30.

13. United Automobile Workers, *Proceedings of the Sixteenth Constitutional Convention,* Atlantic City, 9 April 1957, 179–84. For ER's trip to North Africa, see Roosevelt, *Autobiography,* 364–67.

14. "My Day," 10 July 1957. ER to Reuther, 29 April, 17 May, 13 June 1957; and Reuther to ER, 25 June 1957, folder 15, box 193, WPRC. Roosevelt, *Autobiography,* chap. 37, 369–80; ER quotation 435. Also see Lash, *Years Alone,* 266–71; Lash attributes much of her itinerary to the advice of Supreme Court Justice William O. Douglas.

15. Beasley, *Eleanor Roosevelt Encyclopedia,* 531–32; Lash, *Years Alone,* 266–71; Roosevelt, *Autobiography,* chap. 38, 381–86. "My Day," 15 October 1957, for example, describes health programs, including union-owned sanitariums, in Sochi. Reuther to ER, 15 October 1957; and ER to May Reuther, 11 October 1957, folder 17, box 296, WPRC.

16. "My Day," 11 March 1958. Lash, *Years Alone,* 278. Reuther to ER, 9 June 1958; and ER to Reuther, 13 July 1958, folder 16, box 193, WPRC.

17. Lichtenstein, *Walter Reuther*, 343–44. ER to Reuther, 2 June 1959; Reuther to ER, 28 May, 1, 16 July 1959; ER to Reuther, 12 August 1959; and Reuther to ER, 24 August 1959, folder 16, box 193, WPRC.

18. Lichtenstein, *Walter Reuther*, 344–45; Reuther, *Brothers Reuther*, 394–99, Reuther quotation 397; Dickmeyer, *Putting the World Together*, 200–203.

19. Lash, *Years Alone*, 272–73. ER to May Reuther, 18 August 1959; and May Reuther to ER, 24 August 1959, folder 16, box 193, WPRC. Dickmeyer, *Putting the World Together*, 191–98, quotation 197.

20. Osgood Caruthers, "4 In Soviet Label Reuther Traitor," "Soviet Continues Reuther Attack," *New York Times*, 30, 31 October 1959. "My Day," 3 November 1959.

21. *The Wisdom of Eleanor Roosevelt*, June 1954–November 1962 (New York: McCall Publications, 1963), 13, box 135 FDR, Photos and Memorabilia, Frances Perkins Papers, Rare Books and Manuscript Library, Columbia University.

22. "My Day," 18 August 1956. Parmet, *Master of Seventh Avenue*, 282–83. Lichtenstein, *Walter Reuther*, 371–72.

23. Reuther to ER, 4 October 1956; and ER to Reuther, 9 October 1956, folder 17, box 296, WPRC. Carey to ER, telegram, n.d., file IUE, General Correspondence 1953–1962, AERP. On miners, see "My Day," 5, 6, 8 October 1956. ER to Dubinsky, 27 October 1956, file 3B, box 347, ILGWU, DDPR.

24. Carey to ER, 6 November 1956, file IUE, ER General Correspondence 1945–1962, AERP. Lichtenstein, *Walter Reuther*, 372. Consequences for ER are found in Lash, *Years Alone*, 266; Black, *Casting Her Own Shadow*, 117.

25. A. H. Raskin, "Right-To-Work Laws at Issue in Six States," *New York Times*, 26 October 1958.

26. *New York Times*, 10 July and 26 October 1958. Press release, 9 July 1958, folder 28, box 33, IUE Carey.

27. "My Day," 17 December 1954, 13 August 1956.

28. "My Day," 22 September 1956, 3 March, 1 September 1958. *New York Times*, 6 October 1958.

29. AFL-CIO News Service, 18 September 1958, folder 28, box 33, IUE Carey. NCIP Progress Report, 15 August 1958, folder 22, box 106, IUE Carey. Political scientist Totton J. Anderson concluded that supporting the right-to-work initiative cost the Republicans the election in California; see Anderson, "The 1958 Election in California," *Western Political Quarterly* 12, no. 1, pt. 2 (1959): 276–300.

30. *American Federationist* 66 (February 1959): 5–7; available in Black, *Courage in a Dangerous World*, 286–90.

31. For a summary of the McClellan committee, see Lichtenstein, *State of the Union*, 162–66.

32. "My Day," 5 February 1957. ER's columns in 1957 included positive stories about the settlement of a dock strike (25 February), labor press awards (17 June), an ILGWU celebration (19 June), two ILO issues (21 June, 2 July), union help during a storm (8 August), and two columns on teachers' associations (5 January, 23 October).

33. Parmet, *Master of Seventh Avenue*, 276–77. Lichtenstein, *Walter Reuther*, 325.

34. Parmet, *Master of Seventh Avenue*, 278–80. "My Day," 5 February, 23 May 1957. For more about the Teamsters, see, for example, David Witwer, *Corruption and Reform in the Teamsters' Union* (Urbana: University of Illinois Press, 2003).

35. Reuther to ER, 15 October 1957, folder 17, box 296, WPRC. "My Day," 4 November 1957. Lichtenstein, *Walter Reuther*, 347–48; Barnard, *American Vanguard*, 345–49.

36. "My Day," 31 July 1958; 22 August 1959. ER publicized the woman's request, but there is no record of further follow-up.

37. Reuther to ER, 21 January 1959; and ER to Reuther, 27 January 1959, folder 16, box 193, WPRC.

38. Parmet, *Master of Seventh Avenue,* 281; Lichtenstein, *State of the Union,* 164–65. For an argument that the law has not been as detrimental as expected, see, for example, Alton R. Lee, *Eisenhower and Landrum-Griffin: A Study in Labor-Management Politics* (Lexington: University Press of Kentucky, 1990). Landrum-Griffin Act, Labor-Management Reporting and Disclosure Act, 86 Pub.L. 257; 73 Stat. 519–546 (1959).

39. For ER's evolution on race relations, see Black, *Casting Her Own Shadow,* 85–129.

40. "My Day," 15 May 1958.

41. ACWA, *Twentieth Biennial Convention: GEB Report and Proceedings,* 199.

42. "My Day," 1 March 1958. District 65 membership in Foner, *Women and the American Labor Movement,* 2:419–20. "My Day," 26 April 1958. ER to Reuther, 31 March 1958, folder 16, box 193, WPRC.

43. Black, *Casting Her Own Shadow,* 107–9. A. Philip Randolph to ER, 4 February 1955, 31 January 1956, BSCP-APR Correspondence, box 26, APRP. Legislative strategy in ER and Reuther to Roy Wilkins, 22 April 1955; and Alfred Baker Lewis to ER, 27 April 1955, folder 5, box 76, WPRC. See Lash, *Years Alone,* 247–48; Black, *Casting Her Own Shadow,* 109–10.

44. For the platform, see Lash, *Years Alone,* 250–56; Black, *Casting Her Own Shadow,* 112–15 (quotation 113).

45. For the names of those who testified before the platform committee, see "Testimony to the Democratic National Convention, Committee on Platform and Resolutions," 10 August 1956, in *The Papers of Martin Luther King, Jr.,* vol. 3, *Birth of a New Age, December 1955–December 1956,* edited by Clayborne Carson, Stewart Burns, Susan Carson, Peter Holloran, and Dana L. H. Powell (Berkeley: University of California Press, 1997), 335. For the UAW, see Lichtenstein, *Walter Reuther,* 371–72. "My Day," 18 August 1956.

46. Carson et al., *King Papers,* 3:335–38. Personal Notecards on "P" Topics (1948–1954), Morehouse College Martin Luther King Jr. Collection, Robert W. Woodruff Library, Atlanta University Center (referred by the Martin Luther King Jr. Papers Project [MLKP]). For extensive resources relating to Martin Luther King Jr., see The Martin Luther King Research and Education Institute, Stanford University, http://mlk-kpp01.stanford.edu.

47. Myles Horton to Martin L. King Jr., 24 May 1956, in Carson et al., *King Papers,* 3:274–75. Horton discussed introducing the two women in "Rosa Parks, Myles Horton, and E. D. Nixon, Interview by Studs Terkel," 8 June 1973, box 14, folder 4, Highlander Research and Education Center Records, Wisconsin Historical Society (referred by MLKP). "My Day," 14 May 1956, 10 March 1959.

48. See Glen, *Highlander,* 2–3; Archival Summary, Highlander Research and Education Center Records, 1917–1978, Wisconsin Historical Society, Madison. For ER's visit, see "My Day," 21 June 1958. ER's account of the continuing anticommunist attacks and her defense of the racially integrated school can be found in "My Day," 10 March, 14 September, and 9 November 1959.

49. *New York Times,* 25 May 1956; Black, *Casting Her Own Shadow,* 116.

50. Black, *Casting Her Own Shadow,* 120–21, 117–18.

51. Frank Graham to ER, 20 March, 15 April, 17 June 1958; ER to Graham, 27 March, 17 April 1958; Fay Bennett to ER, 28 April, 21 October, 3 November, 3 December 1958; ER to Bennett, 24 October 1958, all in file 33, box 2, National Sharecroppers Fund Collection, Papers 1942–1969, ALUA (NSFC). Randolph to ER, 13 May 1958, BSCP-APR Correspondence, box 26, APRP. "My Day," 12 March 1958.

52. "My Day," 30 October, 21 November 1958. Bennett to ER, 3 November, 13 December 1958, box 2, NSFC.
53. Bennett to ER, 8, 13, 21 January 1959, box 2, NSFC. "My Day," 13 March, 27 April, 5 June 1959.
54. "My Day," 28 October 1959. Bennett to ER, 3 December 1959, box 2, NSFC. Charles Gratzner, "New Laws Asked on Migrant Labor," *New York Times,* 8 December 1959.
55. For this analysis of the rise of public sector unions, see Lichtenstein, *State of the Union,* 181–85.
56. "My Day," 6 September 1951, 31 December 1958, 3 February 1959.
57. Lichtenstein, *State of the Union,* 182–83. Hospital organizing is from Foner, *Women and the American Labor Movement,* 2:419–35.
58. Foner, *Women and the American Labor Movement,* 2:423, 426. "My Day," 3 February 1959.
59. Foner, *Women and the American Labor Movement,* 2:428–30 (quotation 428).
60. "My Day," 13 May 1959.
61. "My Day," 15, 23 May 1959.
62. "My Day," 3 June 1959. Foner, *Women and the American Labor Movement,* 2:431.
63. "My Day," 23 June 1959.
64. Lichtenstein, *Walter Reuther,* 349–50. Parmet, *Master of Seventh Avenue,* 297–98. "My Day," 16 April 1958.
65. Lichtenstein, *Walter Reuther,* 349–53.
66. Ibid., 351–52. ER to Reuther, 18 February 1959; Reuther to ER, 26, 27 February 1959; ER to Reuther, 5 March 1959; and Meany to ER, 8 April, 27 May 1959, all in folder 16, box 193, WPRC.
67. A. H. Raskin, "Steel Strike Fought over Basic Concepts," *New York Times,* 16 August 1959. "My Day," 17 July 1959.
68. She discussed the strike in eight "My Day" columns: 22 July, 3 and 6 August, 6, 16, 17, and 30 October, and 29 December 1959.
69. "My Day," 28 July 1959; *Electrical Workers' Journal* (IBEW), October 1959, 37.

8. A Revolutionary Period

1. The meeting is described in Minutes of Third Meeting, 16–17 June 1962, file 3, President's Commission on the Status of Women (PCSW), General Correspondence 1953–1962, AERP.
2. Ibid., 5. Peterson and Conkling, *Restless,* 108.
3. "My Day," 7, 8 January 1960.
4. On the liberal debate and ER's challenge to Kennedy, see Black, *Casting Her Own Shadow,* chap. 6, 171–97, in particular 175 (opposition), and 180–81 (public tension). See also Lash, *Years Alone,* chap. 14, 277–301.
5. Lichtenstein, *Walter Reuther,* 354–56. Parmet, *Master of Seventh Avenue,* 284–85 (Meany quote 284); Dubinsky and Raskin, *David Dubinsky,* 290–93. Robinson and Meany, *George Meany,* 217–20. Peterson and Conkling, *Restless,* 94–95; O'Farrell and Kornbluh, *Rocking the Boat,* 79–80.
6. Lichtenstein, *Walter Reuther,* 355. ER to Reuther, 25 April 1960, folder 16, box 193, WPRC.
7. Black, *Casting Her Own Shadow,* 182–83. ER to Reuther, 25 May 1960; Reuther to ER, 2 June 1960; and ER to Reuther, 9 June 1960, folder 16, box 193, WRPC.
8. Reuther to ER, 16 June 1960, folder 16, box 193, WPRC. ER to J. Lash, 15 June 1960, in Lash, *Years Alone,* 291.

9. ER to Anna Roosevelt, 19 June 1960, in Asbell, *Mother and Daughter*, 342. Black, *Casting Her Own Shadow*, 184–86. Lash, *Years Alone*, 294–95. Robinson and Meany, *George Meany*, 218–19. Peterson and Conkling, *Restless*, 95. Lichtenstein, *Walter Reuther*, 355–56. Dubinsky and Raskin, *David Dubinsky*, 290–91; Parmet, *Master of Seventh Avenue*, 285. Black portrays Reuther as a Stevenson scout at the convention (*Casting Her Own Shadow*, 185), while Lichtenstein reports that Reuther was trying to break the "stop Kennedy" effort led by ER (*Walter Reuther*, 355). It is not clear when, but during the convention Reuther threw his support to Kennedy: Douglas Fraser, interview by author, 30 May 2003, Detroit.

10. Robinson and Meany, *George Meany*, 220. Lichtenstein, *Walter Reuther*, 356. Parmet, *Master of Seventh Avenue*, 285–86. Peterson and Conkling, *Restless*, 95–96; Cobble, *Other Women's Movement*, 152.

11. "My Day," 28 July, 12 August, 1960.

12. Black, *Casting Her Own Shadow*, 188–92; Lash, *Years Alone*, 297–99. Dubinsky to ER, 8 August 1960, file IGWU 1951–1961; ER to Reuther, 28 September 1960; Reuther to ER, 5 October 1960, file Mr. & Mrs. Reuther 1960–62; Dubinsky to ER, 4 October 1960, file IGWU 1951–1961; and Schneiderman to ER, n.d. [October 1960], file Schneiderman (Schr–Schn) 1957–1962, all in General Correspondence 1953–1962, AERP.

13. Lichtenstein, *Walter Reuther*, 356. Parmet, *Master of Seventh Avenue*, 285–86. Robinson and Meany, *George Meany*, 220.

14. Black, *Casting Her Own Shadow*, 174. Dubinsky and Raskin, *David Dubinsky*, 291, 295–300. "My Day," 19 December 1960. Much has been written about the Kennedy administration, but an informative firsthand account remains Arthur M. Schlesinger Jr., *A Thousand Days: John F. Kennedy in the White House* (1965; reprint, Boston: Houghton Mifflin, 2002).

15. Black, *Casting Her Own Shadow*, 193; Lash, *Years Alone*, 300. ER to Reuther, 23 January; Reuther to ER, 2 February; and ER to Reuther, 7 February 1961, folder 16, box 193, WPRC. For the importance of unemployment as a UAW issue, see Lichtenstein, *Walter Reuther*, 360.

16. Reuther to ER, 8 March 1961, folder 16, box 193, WPRC. Schneiderman to ER, 5 March, 23 October 1961; Schneiderman to ER; and Morris Abram to ER, n.d. [1961], all in file Schneiderman (Schr–Schn) 1957–1962, ER General Correspondence 1953–1962, AERP. The correspondence between ER and Reuther on labor in Cuba began in January 1961. Correspondence on the Tractors for Freedom Committee is in both AERP and WRPC, along with several "My Day" columns. Also see Thomas G. Smith, "Negotiating with Fidel Castro: The Bay of Pigs Prisoners and a Lost Opportunity," *Diplomatic History* 19, no. 1 (Winter 1995): 59–86.

17. Parmet, *Master of Seventh Avenue*, 287–88. Dubinsky and Raskin, *David Dubinsky*, 306. Lash, *Years Alone*, 276. "My Day," 21 May 1962.

18. ""My Day, 13 February, 24 March 1961. Reuther to ER, 2 February 1961, folder 16, box 193, WPRC.

19. Lichtenstein, *Walter Reuther*, 360–65. Walter Reuther to ER, 7, 18 August 1961, file Mr. & Mrs. Reuther 1960–1962, ER General Correspondence 1953–1962, AERP.

20. Reuther to ER, 28 August, 6 September 1961, folder 17, box 193, WPRC.

21. For the limitations of the agreements and Reuther's hope for the new administration, see Lichtenstein, *Walter Reuther*, 361–362.

22. "My Day," 15 June, 11 July, 1 June 1962.

23. "My Day," 1 June 1962. Reuther to ER, 22 June; and ER to Reuther, 26 June 1962, folder 18, box 193, WPRC. Lash, *Years Alone*, 324–25. Aplastic anemia was later diagnosed as a rare bone-marrow tuberculosis, 331.

24. Eleanor Roosevelt, *Tomorrow Is Now* (New York: Harper & Row, 1963), 38–39, 42, 46.

25. Anderson, *A. Philip Randolph,* 302.
26. "My Day," 2 October 1959. A. H. Raskin, "A Loss for Jim Crow," *New York Times,* 21 January 1960.
27. King to ER, 4 December 1959, General Correspondence, 1952–1962, AERP (as referenced by MLKP). Salute Program, 24 January 1960, folder Birthday Wishes, Tribute 1954–77, box 30, APRP.
28. Salute Program Preface. Anderson, *A. Philip Randolph,* 304–6.
29. Anderson, *A. Philip Randolph,* 307–8. Harris, "A. Philip Randolph," in Dubofsky and Van Tine, *Labor Leaders in America,* 275. Ralph Katz, "AFL-CIO Chiefs Attacked for Voting Randolph Censure," *New York Times,* 14 October 1961. IUE Administrative History, IUE Carey.
30. *News* (AFL-CIO), 16 December 1961; "My Day," 11 December 1961.
31. AFL-CIO, *Proceedings of the Fourth Constitutional Convention,* Miami, 1–6 December 1961, 134–42.
32. "King's Address to the Delegates," *News* (AFL-CIO), 16 December 1961, 5.
33. Randolph quotation in Anderson, *A. Philip Randolph,* 308–09; quotation 308.
34. ER to Kennedy, 21 April; Kennedy to ER, 28 April 1961, file Kennedy, John F., 1957–1962, General Correspondence 1953–1962, AERP. ER to George Meany, 26 October 1961, file AFL-CIO, General Correspondence 1953–1962, AERP. *New York Times,* 16 December 1961. Fay Bennett to ER, 4 December 1961, box 2, National Sharecroppers Fund Collection, ALUA. AFL-CIO, *Proceedings of the Fourth Constitutional Convention,* 139–40.
35. "My Day," 11 December 1961. Fay Bennett to ER, 19 December 1961; ER to Fay Bennett, 28 July 1962; and Fay Bennett to ER, 30 August 1962, box 2, National Sharecroppers Fund Collection.
36. Reuther to ER, 18 December 1961, folder 17, box 193, WPRC.
37. Employment issues were integral to the civil rights movement during this period. See, for example, Sugrue, *Sweet Land of Liberty;* and Nancy MacLean, *Freedom Is Not Enough: The Opening of the American Workplace* (Cambridge: Harvard University Press, 2006). Herbert Hill, *Racism within Organized Labor: A Report of Five Years of the AFL-CIO, 1955–1960* (New York: NAACP, 1961). Lichtenstein, *Walter Reuther,* 378–79; Parmet, *Master of Seventh Avenue,* 299–310.
38. Ibid., 305–9. Richards, *Maida Springer,* 69–71; the quotation from Springer's letter to Edward Welsh of 13 September 1962 is on 270. The committee did not call Springer to testify. Dubinsky to ER, 24 September; and ER to Dubinsky, 9 October 1962, file Dubinsky (Dru-Dub), General Correspondence 1953–1962, AERP.
39. Black, *Casting Her Own Shadow,* 127–29, 194. ER to Reuther, 27 March 1962, folder 18, box 193, WPRC. ER, *Tomorrow Is Now,* 52.
40. Reuther to ER, 30 November 1961, folder 17; ER to Reuther, 28 September 1960; Reuther to ER, 5 October 1960; and Reuther to ER, 14 March 1961, folder 16, box 193, WPRC. "My Day," 19 June 1961.
41. For the level of the Reuther-Meany rivalry, see Lichtenstein, *Walter Reuther,* 366–67. Reuther to ER, 14 March 1961, folder 16; Reuther to ER, 30 November 1961, folder 17; and Reuther to ER, 18 April 1961, folder 16, all in box 193, WPRC.
42. "My Day," 13, 16 April 1962.
43. "My Day," 11, 25 August 1961, 22 June 1962.
44. "My Day," 9 May 1962.
45. Cobble, *Other Women's Movement,* 153–54; Peterson and Conkling, *Restless,* 103. For an earlier analysis of women's situation after World War II, including the President's Commission

on the Status of Women, see Cynthia Ellen Harrison, *On Account of Sex: The Politics of Women's Issues, 1945–1968* (Berkeley: University of California Press, 1988).

46. Ira Henry Freeman, "Bill Delaying Sprinklers Hit at Triangle Fire Memorial," *New York Times,* 26 March 1961; Kornbluh and O'Farrell, "You Can't Giddyup by Saying Whoa," 80–81. "My Day," 26 June 1961.

47. Cobble, *Other Women's Movement,* 155–59; Pastorello, *Power among Them,* 160–62.

48. *New York Times,* 14 March 1961. Scharf, "ER and Feminism," in Hoff and Lightman, *Without Precedent,* 245; Lash, *Years Alone,* 317. Cynthia Ellen Harrison highlights the importance of the commission's founding by executive order rather than congressional strategy in *On Account of Sex,* 109–11. The role of union women on the commission is detailed in Cobble, *Other Women's Movement,* 159–60; Peterson and Conkling, *Restless,* 106.

49. Cobble, *Other Women's Movement,* 160.

50. For a full discussion of the commission, its importance, and the compromises involved, see Cobble, *Other Women's Movement,* 159–68; Harrison, *On Account of Sex,* chap. 7, 109–37. For more on Murray's views, her relationship with ER, and her relationship with Maida Springer, see Pauli Murray, *Song in a Weary Throat: An American Pilgrimage* (New York: Harper & Row, 1987); for her views on the President's Commission on the Status of Women, see 347–51.

51. Esther Peterson interview, 61–63, Oral History Project, John F. Kennedy Library, and Peterson interview, 310–11, COHC. Katherine Ellickson, "Mrs. Roosevelt's Contribution to the Status of Women, 1962"; and Richard Lester to Ellisckson, 20 June 1976, both in folder 31, box 93, Katherine Ellickson Papers, ALUA. For an example, on committee members, see ER to Ellickson, 4 March 1962, folder 855, box 44, Esther Peterson Papers, Schlesinger Library, Harvard University; ER to Reuther, 18 December 1961, folder 17, box 193, WPRC. Historians have suggested that ER was a figurehead. For example, Cobble mentions only that she was the chairman (*Other Women's Movement,* 160–61). Harrison suggests that ER had a limited role advising, publicizing, and signing letters (*On Account of Sex,* 112). Peterson's account and related documents, by contrast, suggest more active involvement.

52. "My Day," 16 February 1962. Minutes of First Meeting, PCSW Document 18, 2; and Response of Mrs. Eleanor Roosevelt to Labor Secretary Goldberg, 12 February 1962, file 3, PCSW, ER General Correspondence 1953–1962, AERP.

53. Minutes of the First Meeting, 3–5.

54. Ibid., 5–8. For Ellickson on the ERA, see Katherine P. Ellickson, "Eleanor Roosevelt and the Commission on the Status of Women," in *Eleanor Roosevelt: An American Journey,* ed. Jess Flemion and Colleen M. O'Connor (San Diego: San Diego State University Press, 1987), 95. For differences among union representatives, see Cobble, *Other Women's Movement,* 170–72; and O'Farrell and Kornbluh, *Rocking the Boat,* 176–77. For the compromise, see Harrison, *On Account of Sex,* 126–30.

55. Minutes of Second Meeting, folder 3, PCSW, General Correspondence 1953–1962, AERP. Scharf, "ER and Feminism," 247–49, discusses public events but misstates ER's role as limited to one commission meeting.

56. "My Day," 30 April 1962. Schneiderman to ER, 21 May 1962, File Schneiderman (Schr–Schn) 1957–1962, General Correspondence 1953–1962, AERP.

57. Schneiderman to ER, 10 August 1962, file Schneiderman (Schr–Schn) 1957–1962, General Correspondence 1953–1962, AERP. Roosevelt, *Tomorrow Is Now,* 123–24.

58. Lash, *Years Alone,* 327–28; partial transcript, W. P. Reuther, 21 February 1968, Frank Cormier and William Eaton Collection, ALUA; Roosevelt, *Tomorrow Is Now,* 31–49.

59. ER to May Reuther, 14 September 1962; May Reuther to ER, September 1962, file Mr. & Mrs. Reuther 1960–1962, General Correspondence 1953–1962, AERP. ER to Peterson,

19 September; Peterson to ER, 1 October 1962, file Esther Peterson 1958–1962, General Correspondence 1953–1962, AERP. Harrison, *On Account of Sex,* 112.

60. President Kennedy's Commission on the Status of Women, *American Women* (New York: Charles Scribner's Sons, 1965), 59.

Epilogue

1. *News* (AFL-CIO), 10 November 1962. *News* (IUE-CIO), 22 November 1962. ILGWU, *Justice,* 15 November 1962. Telegram from the Family of Mrs. Franklin D. Roosevelt to Mr. and Mrs. Walter Reuther, 8 November 1962, folder 18, box 193, WPRC.

2. For their outstanding achievements both Peterson and Dubrow were awarded the Presidential Medal of Freedom, Peterson by President Jimmy Carter and Dubrow by President Bill Clinton. Peterson is quoted in Peterson and Conkling, *Restless,* 188. Evelyn Dubrow, interview by author, 19 July 2002, 9, ERPP.

3. Tom Kelly, "Ranking of America's First Ladies," 18 December 2008, Loudenville, NY: Siena Research Institute, www.siena.edu. Black, *Eleanor Roosevelt Papers,* vol. 1. For Glendon's conclusions, see *A World Made New,* 228, 236–37.

4. For a critique of today's labor relations system according to the human rights framework, see James A. Gross and Lance A. Compa, eds., *Human Rights in Labor and Employment Relations: International and Domestic Perspectives* (Champaign, IL: Labor and Employment Relations Association, 2009). U.S. Department of Labor, Bureau of Labor Statistics, Union Members Summary, 22 January, 2010, www.bls.gov (accessed 3 February 2010).

5. ER, remarks at the United Nations, 27 March 1953, in Black, *Courage in a Dangerous World,* 190.

Note on Sources and Bibliography

The idea for this book first emerged from the stories told by union women in more than eighty oral history interviews from the Trade Union Woman Oral History Project that Joyce Kornbluh and I reviewed for the book *Rocking the Boat: Union Women's Voices, 1915–1975.* They shared fascinating anecdotes about meeting with Eleanor Roosevelt at the White House, visiting her Val-Kill home at Hyde Park, and joining her on campaigns and at meetings. Yet a search of labor history and women's history found little to document or explain the union women's tales. Earlier books, such as Irving Bernstein's acclaimed volumes on American workers and the New Deal, as well as more recent works such as David M. Kennedy's Pulitzer Prize–winning *Freedom from Fear* or Nelson Lichtenstein's biography of Walter Reuther, *The Most Dangerous Man in Detroit,* addressed Eleanor Roosevelt in a few sentences, if they mentioned her at all. I have drawn on these volumes for much of the historical background in this book, but not for ER's contributions.

The growing literature in women's labor history, such as Annelise Orleck's *Common Sense and a Little Fire* or Dorothy Sue Cobble's *The Other Women's Movement,* as well as early volumes such as Nancy Schrom Dye's work on the Women's Trade Union League, *As Equals and as Sisters,* and the critical writings of Alice Kessler Harris on working women in general, *Out to Work,* and Rose Schneiderman in particular in *Gendering Labor History,* offered rich background and insight about union women and began to shed light on their relationships with ER. Esther Peterson's autobiography, *Restless,* and Yevette

Richards's biography *Maida Springer* provided more depth and complexity. I conducted several new interviews and soon discovered the autobiographies and biographies of Rose Schneiderman and Lucy Randolph Mason and the poems of Hilda W. Smith.

I owe a great debt to many authors who have produced fine work on Eleanor Roosevelt, and they are included in the bibliography. Especially important, however, are Blanche Wiesen Cook's biographies, *Eleanor Roosevelt,* volumes 1 and 2; Allida Black's three volumes of ER's writings and her political analysis of the postwar years, *Casting Her Own Shadow;* Susan Ware's study of women in the New Deal, *Beyond Suffrage;* and Joyce Kornbluh's account, *A New Deal for Labor Education.* These books reinforced the importance of ER's commitment to workers and her relationships with labor unions, and the authors encouraged me to pursue the story. Much has been written about the Universal Declaration of Human Rights, particularly Mary Ann Glendon's volume *A World Made New;* these sources provided important detail and perspective on the declaration, the process, and ER's role in it, but not on the role of the unions together with ER. All these works led me to others, providing the context of ER's full and complicated life, and offering a solid foundation from which to explore material in the archives.

There is an enormous amount of scholarly work on Franklin D. Roosevelt and the events shaping the Roosevelts' lives—the Progressive Era, World War I, the Great Depression, the New Deal, World War II, and the cold war—as well as research on the labor movement, women's rights, civil rights, and human rights. This book is by no means a comprehensive history. The bibliography reflects a selected number of volumes I used to provide the basic historical background necessary to illuminate ER's work with the labor movement.

Eleanor Roosevelt championed many causes during her long life, and she spoke and wrote prolifically. (See the documentary record in Allida Black's edition of *The Eleanor Roosevelt Papers,* volume 1.) Her output is daunting: 27 books, approximately 580 articles, over 8,000 columns, and an average of 75 speeches a year. She received on average 175,000 letters each year while she was in the White House and 50,000 annually in the years that followed. Her syndicated columns and radio and television shows reached millions of people. Her "My Day" columns provide the most comprehensive record of the American worker and labor issues as ER saw them. I read them all, and those that mention unions, on average two per month, guide this narrative beginning in 1936. Eleven speeches, published in the proceedings of union conventions, combined with the coverage of the events in labor newspapers and correspondence, provide a depth of insight into the occasions, the issues, and her friendships with union leaders and members.

This book builds on the historical record in several different substantive areas and incorporates existing research with new evidence—letters, speeches, articles, photographs, and the voices of union members. There are gaps in the historical record. Many of the participants in this story did not write journals or letters, and many ideas were relayed in meetings and private conversations with no records kept. Union offices moved, files were lost. I have drawn on the work of many historians to provide the context and refer the reader to sources where much more can be found on the historical events covered here, the labor leaders and unions introduced, and the massive literature on the Roosevelts. To the extent possible, I have let the people involved speak for themselves. When the pieces of the puzzle are brought together, a strong new picture emerges of Eleanor Roosevelt's vision of social and economic justice, how it developed and changed over time, and how she contributed to and was affected by the labor movement. Rich materials from many different sources are assembled here, in one place, to tell the story.

Selected Writings of Eleanor Roosevelt

A complete bibliography of Eleanor Roosevelt's writings and media presentations is available at the Eleanor Roosevelt Papers Project, www.gwu.edu/~erpapers, and includes a link to her FBI file.

Columns

"My Day." 31 December 1935–26 September 1962.

"My Day" columns used in this volume are from the Anna Eleanor Roosevelt Papers (AERP), Franklin D. Roosevelt Presidential Library and Museum (FDRL). All columns are now available online from the Eleanor Roosevelt Papers Project. The dates may vary slightly. See www.gwu.edu/~erpapers.

"If You Ask Me." *Ladies Home Journal,* June 1941–May 1949, and McCalls, June 1949–November 1962.

Columns used in this book are found in the volumes of selected columns: *If You Ask Me,* 1946, and *The Wisdom of Eleanor Roosevelt,* 1963.

Union Convention Speeches by ER

ACWA. *Report of the General Executive Board and Proceedings of the Fourteenth Biennial Convention.* Chicago, IL, 15–19 May 1944.
——. *Twentieth Biennial Convention: GEB Report and Proceedings.* Washington, DC, 21–25 May 1956.
AFL-CIO. *Proceedings from the First Constitutional Convention.* New York, 1–5 December 1955.
——. *Proceedings of the Fourth Constitutional Convention.* Miami, 1–6 December 1961.
CIO. *Proceedings of the Sixth Constitutional Convention.* Philadelphia, 1–5 November 1943.

——. *Final Proceedings of the Seventh Constitutional Convention.* Chicago, 20–24 November 1944.

——. *Proceedings of the Sixteenth Constitutional Convention.* Los Angeles, 6–10 December 1954.

ILGWU. *Report and Proceedings: Twenty-fourth International Convention.* New York, 27 May–8 June 1940.

IUE. *Proceedings of the Third Annual Convention.* Buffalo, 17–21 September 1951.

TWUA. *Proceedings of the Third Biennial Convention.* New York, 10–14 May 1943.

UAW. *Proceedings of the Sixteenth Constitutional Convention.* Atlantic City, 9 April 1957.

Articles by ER

"How to Interest Women in Voting." *Women's Democratic Campaign Manual* (Washington, DC, 1924): 102–3.

"The State's Responsibility for Fair Working Conditions." *Scribner's Magazine* 93 (March 1933): 140.

"Why I Went to Bloody Run." McNaught Syndicate, 3 December 1933.

"They Keep Their Power to Dream." McNaught Syndicate, 3 December 1933.

"Mrs. Roosevelt Writes for Miners' Wives." *United Mine Workers Journal* (March 1936): 24.

"In Defense of Curiosity." *Saturday Evening Post,* 24 August 1935.

"Every Worker Should Belong to a Trade Union Says Mrs. Roosevelt." *American Federationist* 48 (1941): 14–15.

"Women Must Use Their Power." *Advance,* 27 October 1944.

"Why I Am Opposed to Right-to-Work Laws." *AFL-CIO Federationist* 66 (1959): 5–7.

Books by ER

It's Up to the Women. New York: Frederick A. Stokes, 1933.

This Is My Story. New York: Harper and Bros., 1937.

If You Ask Me. New York: D. Appleton–Century Company, 1946.

This I Remember. New York: Harper, 1949.

India and the Awakening East. New York: Harper, 1953.

UN: Today and Tomorrow. With William A. De Witt. New York: Harper, 1953.

You Learn by Living. New York: Harper, 1960.

Autobiography. New York: Harper, 1961.

Tomorrow Is Now. New York: Harper and Row, 1963.

The Wisdom of Eleanor Roosevelt. McCall Publication, 1963.

Edited Volumes of ER's Writings, Correspondence, and Press Conferences

Asbell, Bernard, ed. *Mother and Daughter: The Letters of Eleanor and Anna Roosevelt.* New York: Fromm International, 1988.

Beasley, Maurine Hoffman, ed. *The White House Press Conferences of Eleanor Roosevelt.* New York: Garland Publishing, 1983.

Black, Allida M., ed. *What I Hope to Leave Behind: The Essential Essays of Eleanor Roosevelt.* Brooklyn: Carlson, 1995.

——. *Courage in a Dangerous World: The Political Writings of Eleanor Roosevelt.* New York: Columbia University Press, 1999.

——. *The Eleanor Roosevelt Papers.* Volume 1. *1945–1958.* New York: Charles Scribner's Sons, 2007.

Lash, Joseph P., ed. *Love, Eleanor: Eleanor Roosevelt and Her Friends.* Garden City, NY: Doubleday, 1982.

——. *A World of Love: Eleanor Roosevelt and Her Friends, 1943–1962.* Garden City, NY: Doubleday, 1984.

Neal, Steve, ed. *Eleanor and Harry: The Correspondence of Eleanor Roosevelt and Harry S. Truman.* New York: Scribner, 2002.

Archives

Anna Eleanor Roosevelt Papers (AERP), Franklin D. Roosevelt Library (FDRL), Hyde Park, NY.

Archives and Records Management Section (ARMS), United Nations (UN), New York.

Brotherhood of Sleeping Car Porters Records (BSCPR), A. Philip Randolph Papers (APRP), Manuscript Division, Library of Congress (LOC), Washington, DC.

CIO Secretary-Treasurer Collection, James B. Carey Files (CIO Carey), Archives of Labor and Urban Affairs (ALUA), Wayne State University, Detroit.

Eleanor Roosevelt Papers Project (ERPP), George Washington University, Washington, DC.

Esther Peterson Papers, Schlesinger Library on the History of Women in America, Radcliffe Institute, Harvard University, Cambridge.

Frances Perkins Papers, Rare Books and Manuscript Library, Columbia University, New York.

Frank Cormier and William Eaton Collection, Archives of Labor and Urban Affairs (ALUA), Wayne State University, Detroit.

Highlander Research and Education Center Records, 1917–1978, Wisconsin Historical Society (WHS), Madison.

Hilda Worthington Smith Papers (HWSP), Schlesinger Library on the History of Women in America, Radcliffe Institute, Harvard University, Cambridge.

International Ladies' Garment Workers' Union (ILGWU), David Dubinsky, President's Records, 1932–1966 (DDPR), #5780/002, Kheel Center for Labor-Management Documentation and Archives, Martin P. Catherwood Library, Cornell University, Ithaca, NY.

James [Westbrook] Pegler Papers, Herbert Hoover Presidential Library, West Branch, IA.

Katherine Ellickson Papers, Archives of Labor and Urban Affairs (ALUA), Wayne State University, Detroit.

Martin Luther King Jr. Papers Project (MLKP), Stanford University, Palo Alto.

National Sharecroppers Fund Collection (NSFC), Papers, 1942–1969, Archives of Labor and Urban Affairs (ALUA), Wayne State University, Detroit.

New York Newspaper Guild (NYNG) Records, Series 1 General Files, 1934–1950, Tamiment Library/Robert F. Wagner Labor Archives, New York University, New York.

New York Women's Trade Union League Papers (NYWTULP), Women's Trade Union League Papers (WTULP), Microfilm Edition, 1981, Cecil H. Green Library, Stanford University, Palo Alto.

Office of the President, George Meany (OPGM), George Meany Memorial Archives (GMMA), National Labor College, Silver Spring, MD.

Oral History Collection of Columbia University (COHC), New York.

Oral History Project, John F. Kennedy Library, Boston.

Philip Murray Papers, American Catholic History Research Center and University Archives, Catholic University, Washington, DC.

Records of the President's Office of the IUE, 1938–1965 (IUE Carey), International Union of Electronic, Electrical, Salaried, Machine & Furniture Workers Collection, Special Collections and University Archives (SCUA), Rutgers University, New Brunswick, NJ.

Roosevelt Family Papers Donated by Children (RFPDC), Franklin D. Roosevelt Library (FDRL), Hyde Park, NY.

Rose Schneiderman Papers (RSP), TAM 018, Tamiment Library/Robert F. Wagner Labor Archives (TL), New York University, New York.

Rose Schneiderman Papers, Women's Trade Union League Papers (RSP, WTULP), Microfilm Edition, 1981, Cecil H. Green Library, Stanford University, Palo Alto.

Sidney Hillman Papers 1930–1946 (SHP), Amalgamated Clothing Workers of America Records (ACWAR), 1914–1980, #5619, Kheel Center for Labor-Management Documentation and Archives, Martin P. Catherwood Library, Cornell University, Ithaca, NY.

Toni Sender Papers, 1934–1964 (TSP), Wisconsin Historical Society (WHS), Madison.

Twentieth Century Trade Union Woman Oral History Project: Vehicle for Social Change (TUWOHP), Institute of Industrial Relations, Bentley Historical Library, University of Michigan, Ann Arbor.

UAW President's Office, Walter P. Reuther Collection (WPRC), Archives of Labor and Urban Affairs (ALUA), Wayne State University, Detroit.

Women's Trade Union League (WTUL) Publications, Women's Trade Union League Papers (WTULP), Microfilm Edition, 1981, Cecil H. Green Library, Stanford University, Palo Alto.

Union Papers and Journals

ACWA, *The Advance,* Kheel Center
AF of L, *American Federationist,* GMMA
AFL-CIO, *Federationist,* GMMA
AFL-CIO News, GMMA
BSCP, *The Black Worker,* WHS
CIO, *News,* Kheel Center
IBEW, *Electrical Workers' Journal.* The IBEW has a small archive at their headquarters in Washington, DC.
IBEW, *Journal of Electrical Workers and Operators,* Washington, DC.
ICWU, *Chemical Worker,* University of Akron
ILGWU, *Justice,* Kheel Center
IUE-CIO, *IUE-CIO News,* SCUA
TNG (ANG), *Guild Reporter,* Stanford University
UAW, *Ammunition,* ALUA
UMW, *UMW Journal,* Pennsylvania State University
WTUL, *Life and Labor Bulletin,* WTULP

Interviews by Author

Labor Leaders

Dubrow, Evelyn, ILGWU, 19 July 2002, Washington, DC.
Fraser, Douglas, UAW, 30 May 2003, Detroit.

McGill, Eula, ACWA, 8 October 2002, telephone.
Olsen, Tillie, CIO Auxiliary, 22 May 2003, Berkeley.
Reuther, Victor, UAW, 18 July 2002, Washington, DC.
Springer, Maida, ILGWU, 28 October 2002, Pittsburgh.

New Deal Economists

Dunlop, John, Harvard University, 21 November 2002, Cambridge.
Galbraith, John K. (with Allida Black), Harvard University, 19 November 2002, Cambridge.

Other Oral History Interviews

Carey, James B., COHC, 1956–58.
Gardner, Jackson (Pat), COHC, 1955.
McGill, Eula, TUWOHP, 1978.
Newman, Pauline, TUWOHP, 1978.
Perkins, Frances, COHC, 1955.
Peterson, Esther, COHC, 1976–83.
Peterson, Esther, John F. Kennedy Library, 1966, 1970.
Randolph, A. Philip, Lydon B. Johnson Library, 1968.

Other Sources

Anderson, Jervis. *A. Philip Randolph: A Biographical Portrait.* New York: Harcourt Brace Jovanovich, 1973.
Anderson, Totton J. "The 1958 Election in California." *Western Political Quarterly* 12, no. 1, pt. 2 (1959): 276–300.
Barnard, John. *American Vanguard: The United Autoworkers during the Reuther Years, 1935–1970.* Detroit: Wayne State University Press, 2004.
Beasley, Maurine Hoffman. *Eleanor Roosevelt and the Media: A Public Quest for Self-Fulfillment.* Urbana: University of Illinois Press, 1987.
Beasley, Maurine Hoffman, Holly Cowan Shulman, and Henry R. Beasley, eds. *The Eleanor Roosevelt Encyclopedia.* Westport, CT: Greenwood Press, 2001.
Bernstein, Irving. *The Lean Years: A History of the American Worker, 1920–1933.* Boston: Houghton Mifflin, 1960.
——. *Turbulent Years: A History of the American Worker, 1933–1941.* Boston: Houghton Mifflin, 1970.
——. *A Caring Society: The New Deal, the Worker, and the Great Depression: A History of the American Worker, 1933–1941.* Boston: Houghton Mifflin, 1985.
Black, Allida M. *Casting Her Own Shadow: Eleanor Roosevelt and the Shaping of Postwar Liberalism.* New York: Columbia University Press, 1996.
Black, Ruby A. *Eleanor Roosevelt: A Biography.* New York: Duell, Sloan and Pearce, 1940.
Boris, Eileen. "The Quest for Labor Standards in the Era of Eleanor Roosevelt: The Case of Industrial Homework." *Wisconsin Women's Law Journal* 2 (1986): 53–74.
Burns, James MacGregor. *Roosevelt: The Lion and the Fox.* New York: Harcourt Brace Jovanovich, 1984.
Burns, James MacGregor, and Susan Dunn. *The Three Roosevelts: Patrician Leaders Who Transformed America.* New York: Atlantic Monthly Press, 2001.

Carson, Clayborne, Stewart Burns, Susan Carson, Peter Holloran, and Dana L. H. Powell., eds. *The Papers of Martin Luther King, Jr.* Vol. 3. *Birth of a New Age, December 1955–December 1956.* Berkeley: University of California Press, 1997.

Caruthers, Osgood. "4 in Soviet Label Reuther Traitor." *New York Times,* 30 October 1959.

———. "Soviet Continues Reuther Attack." *New York Times,* 31 October 1959.

Chateauvert, Melinda. *Marching Together: Women of the Brotherhood of Sleeping Car Porters.* Urbana: University of Illinois Press, 1998.

Cherny, Robert W., William Issel, and Kieran Walsh Taylor, eds. *American Labor and the Cold War: Grassroots Politics and Postwar Political Culture.* New Brunswick: Rutgers University Press, 2004.

Cobble, Dorothy Sue. *The Other Women's Movement: Workplace Justice and Social Rights in Modern America.* Princeton: Princeton University Press, 2003.

Cook, Blanche Wiesen. *Eleanor Roosevelt.* Vol. 1. *1884–1933.* New York: Viking, 1992.

———. *Eleanor Roosevelt.* Vol. 2. *1933–1938.* New York: Viking, 1999.

Critchfield, Richard. "Toni Sender: Feminist, Socialist, Internationalist." *History of European Ideas* 15, no. 4–6 (1992): 701–5.

Davis, Kenneth Sydney. *FDR: The Beckoning of Destiny, 1882–1928; A History.* New York: Putnam, 1972.

Dickmeyer, Elisabeth Reuther. *Putting the World Together.* Lake Orion, MI: Living Force Publishing, 2004.

Downey, Kirstin. *The Woman behind the New Deal: The Life of Frances Perkins, FDR's Secretary of Labor and His Moral Conscience.* New York: Doubleday, 2009.

Dubinsky, David. "Instead of the McCarthy Method." *New York Times,* 26 July 1953.

Dubinsky, David, and A. H. Raskin. *David Dubinsky: A Life with Labor.* New York: Simon and Schuster, 1977.

Dubofsky, Melvyn, and Warren R. Van Tine, eds. *Labor Leaders in America.* Urbana: University of Illinois Press, 1987.

Dye, Nancy Schrom. *As Equals and as Sisters: Feminism, the Labor Movement, and the Women's Trade Union League of New York.* Columbia: University of Missouri Press, 1980.

Endelman, Gary Edward. *Solidarity Forever: Rose Schneiderman and the Women's Trade Union League.* New York: Arno Press, 1982.

Flemion, Jess, and Colleen M. O'Connor. *Eleanor Roosevelt: An American Journey.* San Diego: San Diego State University Press, 1987.

Foner, Philip Sheldon. *Women and the American Labor Movement.* Vol. 1. *From Colonial Times to the Eve of World War I.* New York: Free Press, 1979.

———. *Women and the American Labor Movement.* Vol. 2. *From World War I to the Present.* New York: Free Press, 1980.

Fraser, Steve. *Labor Will Rule: Sidney Hillman and the Rise of American Labor.* New York: Free Press, 1991.

Freeman, Ira Henry. "Bill Delaying Sprinklers Hit at Triangle Fire Memorial." *New York Times,* 26 March 1961.

Freidel, Frank Burt. *Franklin D. Roosevelt.* Boston: Little, Brown, 1952.

Fried, Albert. *FDR and His Enemies.* New York: St. Martin's Press, 1999.

Ganett, Lewis. "Another View of Mrs. Roosevelt as a Guildsman." *Guild Reporter* 29, no. 23 (1962).

Glen, John M. *Highlander: No Ordinary School.* 2nd ed. Knoxville: University of Tennessee Press, 1996.

Glendon, Mary Ann. *A World Made New: Eleanor Roosevelt and the Universal Declaration of Human Rights*. New York: Random House, 2001.

Goldin, Claudia D. "The Role of World War II in the Rise of Women's Employment." *American Economic Review* 81, no. 4 (1991): 741–56.

Goldman, Harry. "Pins and Needles: When Social Significance Comes to Broadway." Ithaca, NY: Kheel Center, Cornell University, 1977.

——. "When Social Significance Came to Broadway: 'Pins and Needles' in Production." *Theatre Quarterly* 7, no. 28 (1977–78): 25–40.

Goodwin, Doris Kearns. *No Ordinary Time: Franklin and Eleanor Roosevelt: The Home Front in World War II*. New York: Simon and Schuster, 1994.

Gross, James A., and Lance Compa. *Human Rights in Labor and Employment Relations: International and Domestic Perspectives*. Champaign, IL: Labor and Employment Relations Association, 2009.

Grutzner, Charles. "New Laws Asked on Migrant Labor." *New York Times*, 8 December 1959.

Harrison, Cynthia Ellen. *On Account of Sex: The Politics of Women's Issues, 1945–1968*. Berkeley: University of California Press, 1988.

Hickok, Lorena A. *Reluctant First Lady*. New York: Dodd, Mead, 1962.

Hickok, Lorena A., Richard Lowitt, and Maurine Hoffman Beasley. *One Third of a Nation: Lorena Hickok Reports on the Great Depression*. Urbana: University of Illinois Press, 1983.

Hill, Herbert. *Racism within Organized Labor: A Report of Five Years of the AFL-CIO, 1955–1960*. New York: NAACP, 1961.

Hoff, Joan, and Marjorie Lightman, eds. *Without Precedent: The Life and Career of Eleanor Roosevelt*. Bloomington: Indiana University Press, 1984.

Hoffman, Nancy. *Eleanor Roosevelt and the Arthurdale Experiment*. North Haven, CT: Linnet Books, 2001.

ILGWU. *Moving On*. Nation Picture Bureau, 1934.

Jensen, Joan M., and Sue Davidson, eds. *A Needle, a Bobbin, a Strike*. Philadelphia: Temple University Press, 1984.

Katz, Ralph. "AFL-CIO Chiefs Attacked for Censuring Randolph." *New York Times*, 14 October 1961.

Kennedy, David M. *Freedom from Fear: The American People in Depression and War, 1929–1945*. New York: Oxford University Press, 1999.

Kessler-Harris, Alice. *Out to Work: A History of Wage-Earning Women in the United States*. New York: Oxford University Press, 1982.

——. *Gendering Labor History*. Urbana: University of Illinois Press, 2007.

Korey, William. *NGOs and the Universal Declaration of Human Rights: A Curious Grapevine*. New York: St. Martin's Press, 1998.

Kornbluh, Joyce L. *A New Deal for Workers' Education: The Workers' Service Program, 1933–1942*. Urbana: University of Illinois Press, 1987.

Kornbluh, Joyce L., and Mary Frederickson, eds. *Sisterhood and Solidarity: Workers' Education for Women, 1914–1984*. Philadelphia: Temple University Press, 1984.

Kornbluh, Joyce L., and Brigid O'Farrell. "You Can't Giddyup by Saying Whoa: Esther Peterson Remembers Her Organized Labor Years, 1930–1960." *Labor's Heritage* 5, no. 4 (Spring 1994): 38–59.

Lash, Joseph P. *Eleanor and Franklin: The Story of Their Relationship, Based on Eleanor Roosevelt's Private Papers*. New York: Norton, 1971.

——. *Eleanor: The Years Alone*. New York: Norton, 1972.

Lee, Alton R. *Eisenhower and Landrum-Griffin: A Study in Labor-Management Politics.* Lexington: University Press of Kentucky, 1990.

Leeder, Elaine J. *The Gentle General: Rose Pesotta, Anarchist and Labor Organizer.* Albany: State University of New York Press, 1993.

Lichtenstein, Nelson. *Walter Reuther: The Most Dangerous Man in Detroit.* Urbana: University of Illinois Press, 1997.

——. *Labor's War at Home: The CIO in World War II.* 1987. Reprint, New York: Cambridge University Press, 2003.

——. *State of the Union: A Century of American Labor.* Princeton: Princeton University Press, 2003.

MacLean, Nancy. *Freedom Is Not Enough: The Opening of the American Workplace.* Cambridge: Harvard University Press, 2006.

Malkiel, Theresa Serber, and Françoise Basch. *The Diary of a Shirtwaist Striker.* Ithaca, NY: Cornell University Press, 1990.

Martin, George Whitney. *Madam Secretary, Frances Perkins.* Boston: Houghton Mifflin, 1976.

Mason, Lucy Randolph. *To Win These Rights: A Personal Story of the CIO in the South.* New York: Harper, 1952.

May, Elaine T. *Homeward Bound: American Families in the Cold War Era.* New York: Basic Books, 2008.

Milkman, Ruth, ed. *Women, Work, and Protest: A Century of U.S. Women's Labor History.* Boston: Routledge and Kegan Paul, 1985.

——. *Gender at Work: The Dynamics of Job Segregation by Sex during World War II.* Urbana: University of Illinois Press, 1987.

Miller, Kristie. *Isabella Greenway: An Enterprising Woman.* Tucson: University of Arizona Press, 2004.

Morgan, Ted. *A Covert Life: Jay Lovestone, Communist, Anti-communist, and Spymaster.* New York: Random House, 1999.

——. *Reds: McCarthyism in Twentieth-Century America.* New York: Random House, 2003.

Morsink, Johannes. *The Universal Declaration of Human Rights: Origins, Drafting, and Intent.* Philadelphia: University of Pennsylvania Press, 1999.

Murray, Pauli. *Song in a Weary Throat: An American Pilgrimage.* New York: Harper and Row, 1987.

O'Farrell, Brigid. "A Stitch in Time: The New Deal, the International Ladies' Garment Workers' Union, and Mrs. Roosevelt." *Transatlantica* 1, Beyond the New Deal (2006), http://transatlantica.org.

O'Farrell, Brigid, and Joyce L. Kornbluh. *Rocking the Boat: Union Women's Voices, 1915–1975.* New Brunswick: Rutgers University Press, 1996.

Olsen, Tillie. *Yonnondio.* New York: Delacorte Press/Seymour Lawrence, 1974.

——. *Silences.* New York: Delacorte Press/Seymour Lawrence, 1978.

Orleck, Annelise. *Common Sense and a Little Fire: Women and Working-Class Politics in the United States, 1900–1965.* Chapel Hill: University of North Carolina Press, 1995.

Parmet, Robert D. *The Master of Seventh Avenue: David Dubinsky and the American Labor Movement.* New York: New York University Press, 2005.

Pastorello, Karen. *A Power among Them: Bessie Abramowitz Hillman and the Making of the Amalgamated Clothing Workers of America.* Urbana: University of Illinois Press, 2008.

Payne, Elizabeth Anne. *Reform, Labor, and Feminism: Margaret Dreier Robins and the Women's Trade Union League.* Urbana: University of Illinois Press, 1988.

Perkins, Frances. *The Roosevelt I Knew.* New York: Viking Press, 1946.

Pesotta, Rose, and John Nicholas Beffel. *Bread upon the Waters.* Ithaca, NY: ILR Press, 1987.

Peterson, Esther, and Winifred Conkling. *Restless: The Memoirs of Labor and Consumer Activist Esther Peterson.* Washington, DC: Care Publishing, 1995.

Powers, Richard Gid. *Not without Honor: The History of American Anticommunism.* New Haven: Yale University Press, 1998.

President Kennedy's Commission on the Status of Women. *American Women.* New York: Charles Scribner's Sons, 1965.

Randolph, A. Philip. "First Lady and Mayor LaGuardia Join Citizens' Committee." *The Black Worker,* September 1941.

Raskin, A. H. "Meany Says Nehru and Tito Aid Reds." *New York Times,* 14 December 1955.

——. "Right-to-Work Laws at Issue in Six States." *New York Times,* 26 October 1958.

——. "Steel Strike Fought over Basic Concepts." *New York Times,* 16 August 1959.

——. "A Loss for Jim Crow." *New York Times,* 21 January 1960.

Reuther, Victor G. *The Brothers Reuther and the Story of the UAW: A Memoir.* Boston: Houghton Mifflin, 1976.

Richards, Yevette. *Maida Springer: Pan-Africanist and International Labor Leader.* Pittsburgh: University of Pittsburgh Press, 2000.

Robinson, Archie, and George Meany. *George Meany and His Times: A Biography.* New York: Simon and Schuster, 1981.

Rollins, Alfred B., and Hendrien Kaal. *Roosevelt and Howe.* New York: Knopf, 1962. Reprint, Alfred B. Rollins, introduction. New Brunswick: Transaction Publishers, 2001.

Salmond, John A. *Miss Lucy of the CIO: The Life and Times of Lucy Randolph Mason, 1882–1959.* Athens: University of Georgia Press, 1988.

Schatz, Ronald W. *The Electrical Workers: A History of Labor at General Electric and Westinghouse, 1923–1960.* Urbana: University of Illinois Press, 1983.

Scheuer, Jeffrey. "Legacy of Light: University Settlement's First Century." New York: University Settlement House, 1985.

Schlesinger, Arthur M., Jr. *A Thousand Days: John F. Kennedy in the White House.* 1965. Reprint, Boston: Houghton Mifflin, 2002.

Schneiderman, Rose, and Lucy Goldthwaite. *All for One.* New York: P. S. Eriksson, 1967.

Schrecker, Ellen. "Comments on John Earl Haynes', 'The Cold War Debate Continues,'" www.fas.harvard.edu/~hpcws/comment15.htm.

Shaddox, Abagail M. "From Back Bench to Oval Office: The Letters of Lucy Randolph Mason and Eleanor Roosevelt." *Southern Studies: An Interdisciplinary Journal of the South* 14, no. 1 (2007): 13–31.

Smith, Hilda Worthington. *Selected Poems by Hilda Worthington Smith.* Ithaca, NY: Institute for Education and Research on Women and Work, School of Industrial and Labor Relations, Cornell University, 1977.

Smith, Thomas G. "Negotiating with Fidel Castro: The Bay of Pigs Prisoners and a Lost Opportunity." *Diplomatic History* 19, no. 1 (Winter 1995): 59–86.

Stark, Louis. "WLB Kept in Power," *New York Times,* 4 June 1943."

Steinberg, Alfred. *Mrs. R: The Life of Eleanor Roosevelt.* New York: Putnam, 1958.

Sugrue, Thomas J. *The Origins of the Urban Crisis: Race and Inequality in Postwar Detroit.* 1996. Reprint, Princeton: Princeton University Press, 2005.

——. *Sweet Land of Liberty: The Forgotten Struggle for Civil Rights in the North.* New York: Random House, 2008.

Tyler, Gus. *Look for the Union Label: A History of the International Ladies' Garment Workers' Union.* Armonk, NY: M. E. Sharpe, 1995.

U.S. Department of Labor, Bureau of Labor Statistics, "Union Members Summary," 22 January 2010, www.bls.gov.

Von Drehle, David. *Triangle: The Fire That Changed America.* New York: Atlantic Monthly Press, 2003.

Ware, Susan. *Beyond Suffrage: Women in the New Deal.* Cambridge: Harvard University Press, 1981.

——. *Partner and I: Molly Dewson, Feminism, and New Deal Politics.* New Haven: Yale University Press, 1987.

Weiler, Peter. "The United States, International Labor, and the Cold War: The Breakup of the International Federation of Trade Unions." *Diplomatic History* 5, no. 1 (2007): 1–22.

West Virginia Archives, "Scotts Run," *West Virginia History* 53 (1994): 1–19.

Whitman, Alden. "Free-Swinging Critic," *New York Times*, 25 June 1969.

Wiebe, Robert H. *The Search for Order, 1877–1920.* New York: Hill and Wang, 1967.

Witwer, David. *Corruption and Reform in the Teamsters' Union.* Urbana: University of Illinois Press, 2003.

——. "Westbrook Pegler and the Anti-union Movement." *Journal of American History* 92, no. 2 (2005): 527–52.

Zieger, Robert H. *The CIO, 1935–1955.* Chapel Hill: University of North Carolina Press, 1995.

ACKNOWLEDGMENTS

Eleanor Roosevelt insisted that everyone, in his or her own way, must accept personal responsibility and then act collectively to resolve problems if we are ever to reach the goal of a just and fair society. With this book I have tried to follow her example. It has been an individual responsibility and often a very solitary enterprise. Yet it also reflects a wonderful collective effort, and it is my pleasure to thank all of those who so generously and graciously gave their time, ideas, and support. Now that it is finished, I hope it will inspire action.

My heartfelt thanks to Joyce L. Kornbluh and the dedicated union women whose voices were captured for posterity by the Twentieth Century Trade Union Woman Oral History Project. Especially inspirational and informative were Evelyn Dubrow, Eula McGill, Esther Peterson, and Maida Springer, all of whom I had the privilege of interviewing after reading their oral histories. Their stories about Eleanor Roosevelt first led me to explore the connections between the First Lady and the labor movement.

I took my questions to one of the preeminent Eleanor Roosevelt scholars in the country, Allida M. Black, editor of the Eleanor Roosevelt Papers Project at George Washington University. Allida's knowledge, energy, and passion for ER and her dedication to excellence in scholarly endeavors, robust political action, and sound public policy set a tremendously high standard that I have tried my best to meet. My debt to Allida is incalculable for her enthusiastic encouragement, thoughtful questioning, skilled fund raising, and tireless review of unwieldy drafts. My gratitude extends to the entire staff of the ER

Papers Project for always taking time to answer my questions and making me feel at home as I pursued documents and photographs and helped create the labor Web pages, especially: Christopher Alhambra, Mary Jo Binker, Chris Brick, Eleanor Greene, Kristen Gwinn, June Hopkins, Christy Regenhardt, John Sears, Michael Weeks, and the many students who fill the offices with the youthful energy, humor, and hard work that ER so valued.

The book would not have been possible without the stimulating conversations and exchange of ideas with Mary Frederickson; one simply could not have a better colleague and friend. Her work on women's labor education continues to inspire me. Sue Cobble provided early encouragement and much-needed critical insights as the work developed. Her writing on union women set a high standard and has informed and enriched the story. Appreciation is due to Grey Osterud, whose substantive contributions and fine editing skills made the narrative stronger, clearer, and more compelling. Chris Owens has been a wonderful colleague from beginning to end. A special thank you to Mary Jo Larson, Anne Stone, and Herb Stone for thoughtful suggestions and good common sense.

My early efforts benefited enormously from participation in the visiting scholars program at the Institute for Research on Women and Gender (now the Clayman Institute for Gender Research) at Stanford University. The seminar presentations and lively exchanges with a group of thoughtful interdisciplinary scholars expanded my vision and focused my thoughts. The Senior Scholars were nurturing yet rigorous: Susan Groag Bell, Edith Gelles, Phyliss Koestenbaum, Karen Offen, Elizabeth Roden, and Marilyn Yalom. Especially generous with their time and ideas were fellows Shelley Fisher Fishkin, Michele Pridmore-Brown, and Alice Silverberg. Joanne Martin and Myra Strober, colleagues and friends, provided sustained interest, assistance, and good cheer. Also at Stanford, Sue Englander at the Martin Luther King Jr. Papers Project, Maggie Kimball of the University Archives, and the staff at the Hoover Library all offered welcoming places to work and led me to new material.

It was a great pleasure to work with Catherine Collomp on the New Deal era, and Bill Issel's continued interest and his review of the cold war period were greatly appreciated. Discussions with Sheldon Freidman and Mary Beth Maxwell contributed to my understanding of labor rights as human rights. Presentations at meetings of the American Sociological Association, the American Studies Association, the Bay Area Labor History Workshop, the United Association for Labor Education, and a conference on the New Deal at the University of Paris, as well as meetings of the Coalition of Labor Union Women and the California Trades Women enabled me to benefit from both scholarly and activist points of view.

In any project about Eleanor Roosevelt, one must recognize the enormous contributions of the Franklin D. Roosevelt Presidential Library and Museum and give high praise to the excellent staff. A grant from the Franklin and Elea-nor Roosevelt Institute, under the direction of Verne Newton, made my first visit to the library possible. Director Cynthia Koch and the entire archival staff over a period of years made my return visits to Hyde Park both productive and a joy: Lynn Bassanese, Bob Clark, Ray Teichman, Karen Anson, Matt Hanson, Virginia Lewick, Bob Parks, Mark Renovitch, and Nancy Snedeker. My sincere appreciation to the Roosevelt family for continuing to share their family story, and to Nancy Roosevelt Ireland and the Eleanor Roosevelt Literary Estate for granting permission for my work to go forward.

To bring ER and labor together required searching many archives with labor resources. My immense gratitude is humbly offered to: Richard Strassberg, Patrizia Sione, and Barbara Morley, Kheel Center for Labor-Management Documentation and Archives, Cornell University; Mike Smith, William LeFevre, Carolyn Davis, Dan Golodner, Kathy Schneling, and Mary Wallace, Archives of Labor and Urban Affairs, Wayne State University; Lynda De Loach, Bob Reynolds, Sarah Springer, the George Meany Memorial Archives, National Labor College; Francis Blouin, the Bentley Historical Library, University of Michigan; Kathy Kraft and Marie-Helen Gold, Schlesinger Library, Harvard University; Tim Corlis and Bob Golon, Special Collections and University Archives, Rutgers University; John Russo, Center for Working-Class Studies, Youngstown State University; Susan Sherwood, Labor Archives and Research Center, San Francisco State University; Gail Malmgreen, Robert F. Wagner Labor Archives, New York University; and Harry Miller, Wisconsin Historical Society. Able assistance was also provided by the archivists at Akron University, Catholic University, Columbia University, Georgetown University, the Hoover Institute, the Library of Congress, Pennsylvania State University, and the United Nations. A special note of thanks to the photography archivists who were sometimes able to locate and place people who didn't leave a clear written trail.

Partial funding for this project was received from the Twenty-first Century ILGWU Heritage Fund. I also deeply appreciate support from Jay Mazur and Muzaffar Chishti. Outreach to identify union members with memories of Eleanor Roosevelt was greatly aided by Sandra Feldman and Rita Freedman, American Federation of Teachers; Linda Foley, the Newspaper Guild/CWA; and Susan Cowell, UNITE! A warm thank you to all of those who provided additional stories. Discussions on the use of materials for labor education was facilitated by Leyla Vural, May Chen, and the staff of UNITE! Local 23–25. The opportunity to participate in a UNITE! Convention brought to life the types of events that ER experienced.

My understanding of ER and the union leaders she knew was greatly enhanced by talks with people who knew them, and I genuinely regret that this book was not finished in time for several of them to see it. Many thanks to Dave

Davidson, John Dunlop, Doug Fraser, Philoine Fried, John K. Galbraith, Joe Glazer, Gloria Johnson, Doris Linder, Joyce Miller, Elaine Newman, Tillie Olsen, and Sol Stetin. A special debt of gratitude goes to the late Victor Reuther for sharing his memories of ER and his brother Walter. For their help on this project, I thank then students Anne Cortina, Lucy Nicholas, Tyler LeCao, and Jason Sotlar. Lynn Watts provided excellent interview transcriptions. The final production owes a great deal to the competence, hard work, and good humor of Lindy Cummings and Evan Joiner.

Fran Benson and the staff at Cornell University Press provided the framework without which this book could not have been completed. Fran's interest in the topic early on was a source of strength to keep me going when first the archives and then the footnotes seemed overwhelming. Her interest, gentle encouragement, and persistent questions about the overall meaning of the book enabled me to explore the issues but then cut the story to a size and shape that readers could learn from and enjoy. Always friendly and helpful, Emily Zoss, Susan Specter, and Amanda Heller have been a pleasure to work with.

Last but my no means least important has been the enduring love and support of my extended family, near and far, who gently asked after the book. Paul, Bobbi, Jeff, Naomi, Tad, Ali, Patrick, Angela, and Mike continue to shape my world in new and interesting ways. The children, Yuri, Tomás, Ben, Donovan, and Carly, provided special inspiration for working on a book about economic and social justice in a world free of corruption and discrimination for their futures. My greatest gratitude goes to my husband, T. J. Glauthier. He has been there for me, without fail, encouraging my travel, reading drafts, providing critical but always constructive comments, and asking insightful questions as I have struggled to bring order and meaning to the documents and data. His belief in this book, its importance to the historical record, and the fun of telling a good story have sustained me in every way.

Of course, the views and conclusions are my own, and any errors, however inadvertent, are my responsibility. As an activist scholar I have tried to tell this story accurately and fairly. I am not, however, without some bias as a member of UAW Local 1981 and a Democrat. Having assumed personal responsibility, I hope that this book will now lead to collective action. Thank you all.

INDEX